D1608106

ALSO BY MICHAEL MALICE

Dear Reader: The Unauthorized Autobiography of Kim Jong Il
The New Right: A Journey to the Fringe of American Politics
The Anarchist Handbook

the
White
Pill

the White Pill

a Tale of Good and Evil

by

Michael Malice

All I maintain is that on this earth
there are plagues and there are victims,
and it's up to us, so far as possible,
not to join forces with the plagues.

Albert Camus

ISBN: 9798366737548

CONTENTS

For my parents

who got me out

and on behalf

of all the children

who never did

Chapter 1

"DOESN'T ANYBODY SMILE IN RUSSIA ANYMORE?"

Ayn Rand was not laughing.

This was no laughing matter. In the fall of 1947, Rand had been summoned to Washington to appear as a friendly witness before the House Un-American Activities Committee (HUAC). She was in a unique position, being the only witness to have come from the Soviet Union. As such, Rand understood that she could offer insight and perspective that even the most informed American would be somewhat ignorant of.

It had been a very long road for Rand to get to Washington, D.C. She had been born in czarist Russia in 1905 as Alice Rosenbaum, a name unknown to everyone in America. Even her native-born husband would spend their fifty years of marriage without ever learning her birth name. To Americans this sort of thinking is so paranoid as to be downright alien: if you can't trust your husband, who can you trust? But that was precisely the point for Rand. Unlike the people in that congressional room, she had seen firsthand what happens when the country you live in becomes a country where no one can be fully trusted. If, say, a family member would never betray you as long as they had breath in their lungs…well, there were mechanisms to take that breath away, and there were powerful men who knew how to exploit those mechanisms extremely well.

When Alice had entered young adulthood she was increasingly moved by philosophy and the world of ideas. Strong-willed to the point of obstinacy—she was later notorious for arguing with her young protégés until dawn about whether a movie they liked was, in fact, a good one—Alice's outspoken personality would not serve her well in Lenin's newfound Soviet Union. Things started getting downright dangerous by the time she was attending Petrograd State University. She had seen herself what happened to outspoken classmates who felt comfortable getting up in class and denouncing what had been going on politically. As a freshman in 1921, Alice watched one student give an anti-Communist speech during student council elections:

> Alice never forgot the shock of the day she arrived at school to discover that the arrogant young man had been arrested in the night, and was to be sent to the slow, terrible death of Siberia. She never saw or heard of him again. [...] By the end of that school year, there were no more anti-Communist speeches on campus, and there were no more anti-Communists on the student council.[1]

By the spring of 1924 it got even worse, with students being purged all over the Soviet Union simply due to their family's economic class. "It was done under the slogan of 'We will not educate our class enemies,'" Rand later wrote. "Thousands of young people were expelled from schools all over the country and were denied an education, in payment for the 'sins' of their ancestors."[2] As the daughter of a pharmacist, Alice was clearly part of the despised bourgeois class. Between her background and her temperament, her family agreed that she had little future in Russia. She would either be vanished herself, or she would have to do the vanishing.

It was during her university years that Alice had strongly fallen in love with America and published her first two works. The first was a biographical sketch of the actress Pola Negri, while the second was entitled *Hollywood: American Movie City*. Alice was not alone. To Russians, the word "abroad" had come to take on a miraculous meaning. As she later explained it:

> The meaning of that word for a Soviet citizen is incommunicable to anyone who has not lived in that country. If you project what you would feel for a combination of Atlantis, the Promised Land and the most glorious civilization on another planet, as imagined by a most benevolent kind of science fiction, you will have a pale approximation. "Abroad," to a Soviet Russian, is as distant, shining and unattainable as these; yet to any Russian who lifts his head for a moment from the Soviet muck, the concept "abroad" is a psychological necessity, a lifeline and soul preserver.[3]

It took until 1926, when Alice was twenty years old, for her to gain permission to go abroad, during one of the brief thaws when Soviet citizens were still allowed to step foot outside of the Soviet Union. The pretense was that Alice was going to visit American relatives, but this was a brazen lie. Everyone understood that she would never return to Russia. At her going away party, one of the older guests pulled Alice aside and asked her to make him a promise. "Tell them that Russia is a huge cemetery and we are all dying slowly," he said. And so she left her homeland, not with wistful remorse, but with "complete loathing for the whole country, including the czarist period."[4]

Her grasp of English being somewhat spotty, the rechristened Ayn Rand made her way to Hollywood, American movie city, to try and make it as a screenwriter. A lack of skill in language would be somewhat mitigated since this was still the era of silent movies, where concept could make up for a lack of dialogue. In September 1926 she bumped into superstar director Cecil B. DeMille as she left his studio after being told there were no job openings. DeMille gave her a ride in his roadster and then gave her a part in *The King of Kings*, his epic film about Jesus.[5]

Sure she was just an extra, but Ayn Rand had officially made it into the movies. It was the first of many odd jobs she would hold in Hollywood.

While shooting the film Rand spotted a young actor with a minor role named Frank O'Connor. For Rand it was love at first sight, but there was one small problem: she was part of the crowd, so there was really no way for him to see her back. Rand carefully watched the steps he took as the scene went on—and then "accidentally" tripped him. "I met a very interesting and funny Russian girl on the set," he told his brothers that night. "I couldn't understand a word she said."[6] O'Connor soon married that very interesting and funny Russian girl.

By the mid-1930s Rand began shopping around her first full-length novel. Originally called *Airtight*, the book she retitled *We the Living* "is as near to an autobiography as I will ever write."[7] Mindful of how to market a book—especially at the heights of the Great Depression—Rand's angle was a clever one. The novel was:

> the *first* story written by a Russian who knows the living conditions of the new Russia and who has actually lived under the Soviets in the period described. My plot and characters are fiction, but the living conditions, the atmosphere, the circumstances which make the incidents of the plot possible, are all true, to the smallest detail. There have been any number of novels dealing with modern Russia, but they have been written either by émigrés who left Russia right after the revolution and had no way of knowing the new conditions, or by Soviet authors who were under the strictest censorship and had no right and no way of telling the whole truth. My book is, as far as I know, the first one by a person who *knows* the facts and also *can tell* them.[8]

For the rest of her life, Rand tried to tell everyone—especially Americans—just how bad a totalitarian government could be. Yet it was very much an uphill battle. American intellectuals were either uninterested in hearing what she had to say or flat out dismissed her. The intelligentsia knew better, even the ones who had never been to Russia—*especially* the ones who had never been to Russia. At Macmillan, for example, a young man named Granville Hicks had the job of recommending whether given titles should be published. As a proud member of the Communist Party and editor of the Marxist periodical *New Masses*, for him publishing *We the Living* would be downright heretical.

"I was a good boy,"[9] would be the opening line of Hicks' autobiography. And since he was good it wasn't much of a stretch that he was right, which logically meant that those who disagreed with him were not just wrong but downright evil. Born in New Hampshire and trained by Harvard, only ever getting as far away as Ohio, Hicks believed he understood what was happening in the Soviet Union better than the woman whose accent was so thick that DeMille had nicknamed her "Caviar."

Despite employing Hicks, Macmillan ended up publishing *We the Living* in 1936. Ironically enough, Hicks shortly thereafter turned his back on the Soviet Union and, like many others, drifted from communism to democratic socialism to liberalism. He too would testify in front of the House Un-American Activities Committee, not once but twice. "I insisted that there could be no compromise with Communism,"[10] he would eventually (and unambiguously) write.[11]

We the Living was not particularly successful. Though it sold out of its first printing run, Macmillan had destroyed the publishing plates, precluding the possibility of a second printing. When Rand tried to place her follow-up novella *Anthem* there the following year, it was rejected. "The author does not understand socialism,"[12] read the rejection letter. It would be her 1943 novel *The Fountainhead* that finally put Rand on the map. The theme, as she put it, was "individualism versus collectivism, not in politics, but in man's soul."[13]

The Fountainhead's plot stressed the central importance of integrity for the creative mind, this being Rand's definition of "selfishness" as embodied in the book's creator-hero Howard Roark. Counter to this was the selfishness of Peter Keating, the conventional social climber who had no real "self" to speak of, and that of Gail Wynand, Rand's condemnation of the Nietzschean superman who sought to rule over his fellow, lesser men ("A leash is only a rope with a noose at both ends."[14]).

The novel became a smash hit almost entirely through word of mouth. Rand would often be criticized for her tendency to have her characters spontaneously deliver long, extemporaneous speeches. The climax of her 1957 epic *Atlas Shrugged* has one hero go on for what would be three hours if read aloud. Yet Rand can perhaps be given some leeway because despite her didactic, explicit prose, virtually none of the reviewers of *The Fountainhead* even so much as acknowledged its theme of the individual against the collective. The one major exception was Lorine Pruette from the *New York Times*, to whom Rand sent an awkward letter of gratitude: "If it is not considered unethical for an author to want to meet a reviewer, I would very much like to meet you."[15]

The success of *The Fountainhead* led to Hollywood banging on Rand's door for the movie rights. She held the line at an astronomical fifty thousand dollars—and got it. When it came time for her to buy a new coat for the winter, Frank put his foot down. "You can buy any kind of coat you want—provided it's fur," he told her. "And any kind of fur you want—provided it's mink."[16] Having accomplished her goal of being a best selling author, Rand turned her sights back to the movie industry and what she saw as anti-American propaganda being spread—unknowingly—by Hollywood.

Under the auspices of the Motion Picture Alliance for the Preservation of American Ideals (MPA), Rand authored *Screen Guide for Americans* in 1947. If every film had women presented exclusively as clumsy dimwits, for example, eventually a large segment of the population would get a certain impression even if the filmmakers had not set out to spread misogyny. Similarly, Rand understood that many films could be informed by communist principles even if no one on the crew could find Petrograd on the map. As she saw with the reviews of *The Fountainhead*, American intellectuals could be oblivious to ideas even if they were spelled out explicitly in interminable speeches.

As Rand laid it out:

> The purpose of the Communists in Hollywood is not the production of political movies openly advocating Communism. Their purpose is to corrupt our moral premises by corrupting non-political movies—by introducing small, casual bits of propaganda into innocent stories—and to make people absorb the basic principles of Collectivism **by indirection and implication**.[17]

Rand had a simple list of Don'ts that she thought would discourage such a thing from happening. Don't smear the free enterprise system, industrialists, wealth, American political institutions, independent men, the profit motive or success. Don't glorify failure, depravity or the collective, or deify "the common man." Finally, don't take politics lightly. "Freedom of speech does not imply that it is our duty to provide a knife for the murderer who wants to cut our throat," Rand insisted. Therefore,

> when you make pictures with political themes and implications — *DON'T* hire Communists to write, direct or produce them. You cannot expect Communists to remain "neutral" and not to insert their own ideas into their work. Take them at *their* word, not ours. *They* have declared openly and repeatedly that their first obligation is to the Communist Party, that their first duty is to spread Party propaganda, and that their work in pictures is only a means to an end, the end being the Dictatorship of the Proletariat. You had better believe them about their own stated intentions. Remember that Hitler, too, had stated openly that his aim was world conquest, but nobody believed him or took it seriously until it was too late.

It was the MPA that supplied friendly witnesses to the HUAC committee, and Rand was more than a little squirmy about being asked to testify. In typical Ayn Rand fashion, she sat down and wrote out her thoughts in order to come to what she would regard as a rational conclusion. To begin with, did the committee have any business to investigate the matter at all? Americans have a right to join any political party that they want, and they have a right to privacy as well. Take a look at the Know Nothing Party. The nativist 19th century party had gotten its nickname because when its members were asked about membership they replied, "I know nothing."

Yet for Rand, being a member of the Communist Party wasn't some mere First Amendment issue, akin to being a Republican or Democrat. This was because "membership in the Republican or Democratic Party is an open, public matter. It involves no initiation, no acceptance of an applicant by the party, and no card-bearing. […] It is a membership which cannot be refused to him and which he is free to abandon any time he chooses." On the other hand, "[m]embership in the Communist Party is a formal act of joining a formal organization whose aims, by its own admission, include acts of criminal violence."[18]

Yet Rand went even further in her thinking:

> Membership in the Communist Party does not consist merely of sharing the ideas of that Party. That Party is a formal, closed, and secret organization. Joining it involves more than a matter of ideas. It involves an agreement to take orders to commit actions—criminal and treasonable actions.
>
> These rights are based on and pertain to the peaceful activity of spreading or preaching ideas, of dealing with men by intellectual persuasion. Therefore, one cannot invoke these rights to protect an organization such as the Communist Party, which not merely preaches, but actually engages in acts of violence, murder, sabotage, and spying in the interests of a foreign government. This takes the Communist Party out of the realm of civil law and puts it into the realm of criminal law. And the fact that

> Communists are directed and financed by a foreign power puts them into the realm of treason and military law.[19]

It is theoretically possible to make the case that "free speech" includes the right to reveal American secrets, whatever they may be, to hostile foreign powers. It is far harder to make the case that this is analogous to, say, joining the Democratic Party or even the Socialist Party. A better analogy would be joining the Ku Klux Klan, another conspiracy dedicated to using force up to and including terrorism against American citizens in order to further one's desire for control of a population. One might perhaps have the legal right to join the Klan as a "peaceful" member, but to claim that there are no moral issues to be had is a hard pill to swallow.

Rand had been asked to testify specifically about a minor film called *Song of Russia*, among a couple of others. She thought this was missing the point entirely. "If I testify only about *Song of Russia*, which was a bad-plot movie, and years old, and of no importance—if this is the worst Hollywood has done—it amounts to almost a whitewash," she wrote. "What was much more important was to show the really serious propaganda going on right now and about America—not some musical about Soviet Russia that wouldn't fool anybody, and that failed very badly at the box office anyways."[20] In other words, because the movie flopped, it couldn't *really* be considered propaganda because it didn't even work. Insisting to the contrary would seem paranoid and silly. Smearing wealth is "communist propaganda"? Oh please! Leftist playwright Lillian Hellman spoke for many when she insisted "there has never been a single line or word of Communism in any American picture at any time. There has never or seldom been ideas of any kind."[21]

Yet even Rand was oblivious to the machinations that went into making the film. Under FDR's war effort, Hollywood worked closely with Washington to ensure that films met with governmental approval in order not to hinder the fight against the Axis. As such, the assigned government apparatchik had more than a few concerns about the *Song of Russia* script. It simply wouldn't do to tell the American people that Stalin could not be trusted. *Song of Russia*'s viewers might get the wrong idea, and the "dangerous conclusion that such audiences may reach is that no treaty with Russia is worth more than the paper on which it is written." In fact, as a later government operative opined, "A study of Russia's diplomatic history since the last war shows that she perhaps more than any other nation has stood by her diplomatic agreements."[22]

The government's advice to the filmmakers was to have the film's Russian heroine make this point explicitly to the American hero—and, thereby, not just to the American audience but to audiences around the globe: "If Nadya can clear this up in John Meredith's mind, she will clear it up in the minds of millions of other peoples in the world." After all, the New Dealer insisted, Stalin wanted peace and had no choice but to make a treaty with Hitler: "Russia embraced the Nazi-Soviet pact only after all her previous efforts at world collective peace had failed."[23]

In later years the Soviet Union became notorious for its use of "Potemkin villages," entirely false communities made for the purpose of deceiving foreign visitors. Here were Potemkin villages on the screen—made not by the Russian government, but by Hollywood creators at the prodding of the American government. *Song of Russia* screenwriter Richard Collins explained his thinking at the time: "We have the right to lie because we are the future—we're the good guys."[24]

Reassured that she would be able to speak about ideas and not merely about some minor B-movie, Rand agreed to testify before the committee. Throughout her career, she stressed the primary importance of ideas when it came to what moved nations. She began her testimony by insisting that the committee define exactly what it was that it was supposedly investigating:

> Nobody has stated just what they mean by propaganda. Now, I use the term to mean that communist propaganda is anything which gives a good impression of communism as a way of life. Anything that sells people the idea that life in Russia is good and that people are free and happy would be communist propaganda. Am I not correct? I mean, would that be a fair statement to make, that that would be communist propaganda?

> Visualize a picture in your own mind as laid in Nazi Germany. If anybody laid a plot just based on a pleasant little romance in Germany and played Wagner music and said that people are just happy there, would you say that that was propaganda or not, when you know what life in Germany was and what kind of concentration camps they had there? You would not dare to put just a happy love story into Germany, and for every one of the same reasons you should not do it about Russia.

But Rand was talking to politicians, and politicians tend to like ideas even less than they tend to like honesty. Congressman John S. Wood (D-Ga.) was Chairman of the Committee, and he was a bit taken aback after listening to the rest of Rand's testimony: "I gather, then, from your analysis of this picture your personal criticism of it is that it overplayed the conditions that existed in Russia at the time the picture was made, is that correct?" he began. "Do you think, then, that it was to our advantage or to our disadvantage to keep Russia in this war, at the time this picture was made?"

"I ask you," Rand said, "what relation could a lie about Russia have with the war effort?"

"You don't think it would have been of benefit to the American people to have kept them in?"

"I don't believe the American people should ever be told any lies, publicly or privately," Rand insisted. "I don't believe that lies are practical."

Congressman John McDowell (R-Pa.) was also baffled by her testimony. "You paint a very dismal picture of Russia," he pointed out. "Doesn't anybody smile in Russia anymore?"

"Well, if you ask me literally," she replied, "pretty much no."

McDowell was incredulous. "That is a great change from the Russians I have always known, and I have known a lot of them. Don't they do things at all like Americans? Don't they walk across town to visit their mother-in-law or somebody?" In a sense, it was a perfectly natural question. How could her perspective be so different from everything he had seen and heard himself? This wasn't just some man off the street. McDowell was a sitting Congressman, well-read and well-informed, who had an entire staff to keep him abreast of the latest political news. Obviously the newspapers might have been a bit skewed—especially about such a secretive country as the USSR—but surely they couldn't *all* be wrong.

For a woman notorious for long-winded ideological speeches in her novels, Rand's reply to Congressman McDowell might be the most powerful statement she ever produced:

> Look, it is very hard to explain. It's almost impossible to convey to a free people what it's like to live in a totalitarian dictatorship. I can tell you a lot of details. I can never completely convince you because you are free, and it's in a way good that you can't even conceive of what it's like. Certainly they have friends and mother-in-laws. They try to live a human life, but you understand that it is totally inhuman. Now try to imagine what it's like if you are in constant terror from morning to night and at night you are waiting for a doorbell to ring, if you are afraid of everything and everybody, if you live in a country where human life is nothing, less than nothing, and you know it. You don't know who when is going to do what to you because you may offend someone, where there is no law and no rights of any kind.[25]

The next Representative—freshman Congressman Richard Nixon of California—had no further questions.

Though Rand was told she'd be allowed to return to discuss broader issues, that never ended up happening. In fact the hearings wrapped up faster than expected, and little came of them at all. As for Rand herself, her testimony had virtually no impact. Despite her unique biography, she was just one person, and one person's perspective is little more than an anecdote. Perhaps she was lying, or exaggerating. Or forgetful? Memory is a tricky thing, after all. Perhaps Rand just had a very bad experience in her Russian days—or perhaps she was simply a straight-up crackpot. Perhaps it was some combination of all those things. Nevertheless, the question remained: was she wrong?

Chapter 2

ALMOST IMPOSSIBLE TO CONVEY

The year was 1875, and in America there was a call in the air: the call of revolution.

The War of Independence had overthrown the forces of monarchy and aristocracy in the United States. Four score and seven years later, the Civil War brought an end to the peculiar institution of slavery. It was now time for the trilogy to come to its moral and logical conclusion, with the overthrow of the exploitative capitalist class and the installation of a socialist system based upon liberty, equality, and brotherhood.

The end of the 19th century had brought a tide of wretched refuse from Europe, huddled masses eager to find a better life for themselves and their families. These marginalized people, the lowest of the low even where they had come from, brought their fringe ideologies with them. It stood to reason that those who had been completely diminished by the systems of the day would regard those systems as not just bad but as downright malevolent.

At the time, the terms "socialist," "communist," and "anarchist" were used somewhat loosely and interchangeably because the prophesied Marxist society was one in which the state had famously "withered away." There was great disagreement about what a socialist system would look like in practice, but two things were clear. First, that socialism was both inevitable and scientific, the way of the future. Second, that the capitalist ruling class was not going down without a fight.

The Second Amendment states that the right to bear arms shall not be infringed, and ties this right to a well regulated Militia being necessary to the security of a free State. The immigrant socialist groups took such rights seriously, for the poverty-stricken masses had little else to their name. In Chicago, a group of German-Americans incorporated themselves as the Lehr und Wehr Verein ("Educational and Defense Society"), and began training as a militia. They had the guns, and they had the will. They practiced in order to be prepared for when the proletarian revolution finally began. They were Americans. Revolution was their heritage.

The Illinois state legislature thus passed a law in 1879 that decreed that militias had to have a license ("shall not be infringed"?). The Lehr und Wehr Verein sued on Second Amendment grounds, and were defeated all the way up to the highest court. Their hope was that the Supreme Court would affirm the Second Amendment right to allow private citizens to form militias. After all, was not America herself the product of the common man forming militias and revolting against the British? Just as the poor "sans-culottes" of the later French Revolution, Washington's army was so hard up for materiel that they were often shoeless.

The Supreme Court did not agree. The 1886 *Presser v. Illinois* Supreme Court case established that "state legislatures may enact statutes to control and regulate all organizations, drilling, and parading of military bodies and associations except those which are authorized by the militia laws of the United States." It further stated that the Second Amendment to the United States Constitution limited only the power of Congress and the national government to control firearms, not the states. In a bizarre twist of history, one of the earliest restrictions of the Second Amendment was against the militant left.

The Supreme Court decision may have seemed, on its face, to be a decision in favor of law and order, and against political violence. But if anything, it simply changed the form of revolutionary fervor among the socialists. Militias? That was so 18th century. The Industrial Revolution was underway, and that entailed a new, modern form of violence to bring about the socialist future.

Decades before Ayn Rand was born, a man named Alfred Nobel had also spent his youth in her native St. Petersburg. As a teenager he was sent by his father to France to apprentice with a chemist. There, he befriended one Ascanio Sobrero, who had discovered a substance that he called pyroglycerine. Like many other revolutionary discoveries, pyroglycerine was found largely due to a combination of an accident and a quality mind that deduced what the hell had just happened.

Swiss chemistry professor Christian Friedrich Schonbein had been experimenting with nitric and sulfuric acid. Spilling some by mistake, he wiped the liquid away with his wife's cotton apron. Yet when he went to dry the apron by the fire, it vanished in a flash in a virtual spontaneous combustion. Adding the cotton's cellulose to the acid mixture had somehow created a new substance with highly unusual properties. It was Sobrero's idea to try and substitute glycerine for the cellulose due to chemical similarities between the two compounds. What he found is that this new substance not only burned but was downright explosive. It was as nitroglycerine that Sobrero's discovery would come to be known worldwide, but nitroglycerine was not particularly stable or safe by itself.

Nobel personally knew how dangerous nitroglycerine can be. In 1864 his younger brother Emil had died at the age of twenty from an explosion that came about from experimenting with the substance.[26] It fell upon Nobel to invent a mercury fulminate blasting cap to ensure that the nitroglycerine would only detonate when desired. He also mixed nitroglycerine with diatomaceous earth in order to give it some stability and make it safe for transport. Nobel envisioned dynamite being used for mining, saving laborers an enormous amount of time from digging through solid rock. Yet for many, the deadliness of Nobel's dynamite was not a hazard but a selling point. To his unmitigated horror, dynamite was quickly adopted as a weapon of war. If dynamite could blow up a boulder in a mine, imagine what it could do to an enemy platoon. It was to this that many in the anarchist wing of socialism put their hopes.

It was a German anarchist named Johann Most who made that connection in the context of the revolutionary class struggle, realizing that dynamite was an invention that would irrevocably alter the calculus of political violence. Born in Germany, Most had developed untreatable frostbite on his face as a boy. This somehow turned into cancer, and a chunk of his jawbone had to be removed to save his life. No matter; beards were fashionable at the time, and Most covered his disfigurement accordingly.

It was Most who took the politics of violence into new directions. He advocated what he called "the propaganda of the deed," the idea that murder could be a useful technique to ensure given ends. Rather than being ashamed of such violence, the revolutionary should boast about his actions. As Most wrote in 1885:

> The great thing about anarchist vengeance is that it proclaims loud and clear for everyone to hear, that: this man or that man must die for this and this reason; and that at the first opportunity which presents itself for the realization of such a threat, the rascal in question is really and truly dispatched to the other world. [...] In order to achieve the desired success in the fullest measure, immediately after the action has been carried out, especially in the town where it took place, posters should be put up setting out the reasons for the action in such a way as to draw from them the best possible benefit.[27]

For Most, enthusiasm and revolutionary fervor were all well and good—but "what is to be done?" Rhetorical bombthrowing was dangerous enough. Literal bombthrowing was something else altogether. Most published a pamphlet called *Revolutionäre Kriegswissenschaft*, translated into English as *The Science of Revolutionary Warfare*. The subtitle made no bones about the purpose of the work: *A Little Handbook of Instruction in the Use and Preparation of Nitroglycerine, Dynamite, Gun-Cotton, Fulminating Mercury, Bombs, Fuses, Poisons, Etc., Etc.* Thanks to Most, anyone could now make weapons of mass destruction from the comfort (if not exactly the "safety") of their own home.

Terror had become democratized, and dynamite called to young socialist extremists like a siren song. As one anarchist writer later put it:

> When Free Speech is suppressed, when men are jailed for asking food, clubbed for assembling to discuss their grievances, and stoned for expressing their opinions, there is but one recourse—violence. The ruling class has guns, bullets, bayonets, police, jails, militia, armies and navies. To oppose all this the worker has only—dynamite.[28]

"Once we are in an era when things are really happening," Most prophesied, "it would be stupid to consider amateur dynamite production. Dynamite factories and explosives warehouses can be seized just like anything else." Violent revolution—and the subsequent ultimate workers' victory—would soon follow as night followed day.

It was a few months after the 1886 *Presser* decision that matters came to a head. In 1867 Illinois had passed a law mandating an eight-hour workday, but the law proved largely toothless. The same pattern was repeated in state after state, as laws were subverted or ignored. The democratic process seemed to be entirely stacked against the workers.

A national strike was held on May 1, 1886, with around 350,000 workers protesting to demand shorter hours. From that year forward, May 1 would be commemorated worldwide as a way to celebrate the accomplishments of the working class and to advocate for better conditions for laborers. Change was clearly on the horizon, but it was unclear what form it would entail. The tension between labor and capital seemed to be escalating out of everyone's control, just twenty years after what had already been the bloodiest conflict that America had ever seen. The corporate press did its part to add fuel to the fire. As the *New York Times* opined on April 25, 1886:

> The strike question is, of course, the dominant one and is disagreeable in a variety of ways. A short and easy way to

> settle it is urged in some quarters, which, is to indict for conspiracy every man who strikes, and summarily lock him up. This method would undoubtedly strike a wholesome terror into the hearts of the working classes.
>
> Another way suggested is to pick out the labor leaders, and make such examples of them as to scare the others into submission.[29]

On May 4, 1886, a rally was called for Chicago's Haymarket Square. Estimates about the number of attendees vary from several hundred to a few thousand. What isn't in dispute is that—much to the relief of all concerned—the rally was peaceful. None of the speakers who took to the podium urged the workers to violence. Mayor Carter Harrison came by to personally observe the situation, leaving when he was satisfied that nothing out of order would occur. At around 10:30 p.m., a police inspector ordered the crowd to disperse "in the name of the law." It was somewhat easy to understand why the workers had been denied their Second Amendment rights, but now they were also being denied their First Amendment "right of the people peaceably to assemble."

That's when someone threw a bomb.

The anarchists later regarded it as the act of an agent provocateur. The police regarded it as the act of an anarchist eager to light the powder keg that would begin the workers' revolution. If it had been an anarchist, they did not take heed of Johann Most's admonition to proclaim the propaganda of the deed. As a result, to this day no one knows who threw the explosive or why. What is known is that one police officer was killed immediately, and several others received mortal wounds. Gunfire was thereupon exchanged between the police and the workers, with several more people being killed.

Eight men were arrested as a consequence of the events, though their connections to the killings varied from thin to nonexistent. Only two had even been present when the bomb had gone off, with two others having previously left after giving their respective speeches. Despite all this, the men were tried as a group for accessory to the murder of officer Mathias

Degan. For many Americans it was clear that a foreign ideology dedicated to the violent overthrow of lawful authority was bearing fruit. Someone had to pay. These individual men had preached violent terrorism; they had gotten their wish; hang them for it.

All eight men were found guilty, seven of them sentenced to hang while one received a fifteen-year sentence. It was a conviction without precedent. They were being tarred with the radicalism of the most extreme anarchists even though most of them spoke out against violence. They appealed all the way up to the Supreme Court, but were denied. Two of the men pled with Governor Oglesby for clemency, bending the knee in order to save their lives. Their petition was granted, and they would be spared the gallows.

Four of the remaining five men refused to beg. They had done nothing wrong, and found it obscene to have to renounce their philosophy of equality and brotherhood. They refused to recognize the trial as legitimate, and they pointed out that there had been no evidence presented whatsoever to connect them to the bombthrower. Instead of hanging separately, they each decided, they would all hang together—and hang they would.

Of the eight, the one who would perhaps have the greatest impact on the socialist movement was a young bombmaker named Louis Lingg. If Che Guevara can be regarded as a symbol of youthful rebellion to oblivious hipsters, Louis Lingg far better fulfills that role for those who know their history. Almost a century and a half after his death, his most famous photograph stares at the viewer with the sizzling smolder of a contemporary male model. Even the police captain who guarded him couldn't help but muse about what a stud the young anarchist was. "Many callers came to sympathize with Lingg as well as to admire his handsome physique," wrote Captain Schaack, "and, as he would not allow his hair to be cut after his incarceration, his flowing, curly locks added to his picturesque appearance."[30]

Police officers had found bombs when they searched Lingg's room after the Haymarket massacre. To address the issue as to why, his attorney weakly explained that his client "had a right to have his house full of dynamite." He couldn't have thrown the bomb, because he was at home making bombs.

In court Lingg raged at the judge, doubling down on his ideology:

> I tell you frankly and openly, I am for force. I have already told Captain Schaack, "if they use cannons against us, we shall use dynamite against them." I repeat that I am the enemy of the "order" of today, and I repeat that, with all my powers, so long as breath remains in me, I shall combat it. I declare again, frankly and openly, that I am in favor of using force.
>
> Perhaps you think, "you'll throw no more bombs"; but let me assure you I die happy on the gallows, so confident am I that the hundreds and thousands to whom I have spoken will remember my words; and when you shall have hanged us, then—mark my words—they will do the bombthrowing! In this hope do I say to you: I despise you. I despise your order, your laws, your force-propped authority. Hang me for it!

They would never get the opportunity to hang Lingg.

At one point during the men's imprisonment, a box had fallen open in a common area where they congregated—and out of it had fallen a bomb. Upon investigating the box the officers discovered it had a false bottom containing three other bombs ready to be detonated at a moment's notice. Lingg had said "we shall use dynamite against them," and mere days away from the gallows he seemed ready to make good on his promise. Much like what the officers had found in Lingg's home, it seemed as if this box "had been made according to Lingg's instructions by some handy carpenter who was a close friend". [31]

Captain Schaack described Lingg's reaction at being found out:

> It was evident from his actions that the discovery greatly troubled him. His face became almost livid with rage, his

> eyes fairly snapped fire, and he fumed in his cage like an imprisoned beast of prey. He was speechless with anger, and every motion betrayed an energy of passion that was fearful to behold. [...] Thereafter, as might have been expected, Lingg was more carefully watched than ever.[32]

The increased surveillance was of little use. Four days later, one day before the men were sentenced to hang, an explosion rocked the prison from Lingg's cage:

> Officials were soon in the cell and found Lingg lying on his side on the couch, with one arm thrown over his head and the other resting on a little table. A stream of blood was coursing down the pillow, and pools of it had gathered upon the bedding. The deputies raised him up gently. A ghastly sight met their gaze. The lower jaw had been almost entirely blown away, the upper lip was completely torn to shreds, the greater part of his nose was in tatters, only a fragment of his tongue remained, and every vestige of front teeth had disappeared. What remained of his cheeks looked like flesh torn by vultures, and every jagged part bled profusely. The inside of his upper jaw was horribly lacerated. It looked as though no man could survive such a wound for a moment after its infliction. And yet the bomb-maker was alive and breathing regularly.[33]

It's unclear how the bomb got smuggled in. Schaack speculated that Lingg had a confidante among those who visited him. Perhaps it was the mysterious girlfriend who had visited him every day for the previous four months. In any event, Lingg took his death sentence out of the hands of the state. It took him hours to die—plenty of time for him to use his blood to write his parting words "Hoch die Anarchie!" ("Hurrah for anarchy!") on the walls of his cell.

The other men would have to wait a day to meet their maker. On November 11, 1887, Adolph Fischer, George Engel, August Spies and Albert Parsons were hanged. Parsons had been a journalist. He went on the lam when the news hit, but was eventually coaxed to return to Illinois to face trial so long as his comrades were up for the same charges. The thought of the death penalty had then seemed like a complete absurdity. Parsons faced animosity his entire life, working for the Confederacy as a teenager, then turning Republican before turning anarchist. His wife Lucy was a former slave, an interracial relationship at a time where the idea of one was as radical as anarchism.

"This is the happiest moment of my life!" Fischer announced from the platform. Parsons stepped forward, asking the sheriff for permission to say a few words. "Let the voice of the people be heard!" he pleaded—and was then hanged before he could say anything else. The authorities had refused to let Lucy or her children see Albert as he was being killed by the state, and she was of course inconsolable.

There are several versions of August Spies' last words. The exact phrasing of what he said is lost to history, but the underlying message was consistent across all accounts. "The day will come," he predicted, "when our silence will be more powerful than the voices you are strangling today." In this Spies was correct. A statue to the Haymarket martyrs would be erected near Chicago six years later, and the men would be posthumously pardoned by the governor. For them it was far too little, too late. But while this battle might have been lost, the war against the capitalist class would go on. An entire generation of young socialists were inspired and galvanized by the socialists' courage and convictions—and none more prominent than the diminutive woman known as Emma Goldman.

Born in the Russian Empire in 1869, Emma Goldman had moved with her sister from St. Petersburg to Rochester, New York in 1885. By age seventeen she was married to a fellow worker, and by age eighteen divorced from him. The feisty young woman grew radicalized by the travails of the Haymarket martyrs. "I devoured every line on anarchism I could get, every word about the men, their lives, their work," she recalled. "I read about their heroic stand while on trial and their marvellous defence. I saw a new world opening before me."[34] Her heart was especially moved by Louis Lingg, "you young giant who preferred to take your own life rather than allow the hangman to desecrate you with his filthy touch."[35]

Soon Goldman made her way to New York City. On her very first day there, she ran into another young anarchist from Eastern Europe named Alexander Berkman. The word "soulmate" is used in different contexts, but it is rare to encounter two people whose lives were so intertwined as Berkman's and Goldman's would become. They were literal and figurative partners in crime, lovers and friends, and—perhaps most importantly—lifetime comrades in the cause of liberating the workers from the forces of oppression.

The night they met, Berkman took Goldman to hear a talk from the man whose legend had already grown across the continents: Johann Most himself. Most became something of a mentor to the two young revolutionaries, their heads full of visions of overthrowing the state by any means necessary. Though impassioned and determined, they still remained destitute. As the anniversary of the Haymarket executions approached, Emma, "Sasha" and their friends wanted to commemorate the event. But there was one small problem: they could only afford one wreath.

> At first we wanted to buy eight wreaths, but we were too poor, since only Sasha and I were working. At last we decided in favour of Lingg: in our eyes he stood out as the sublime hero among the eight. His unbending spirit, his utter contempt for his accusers and judges, his will-power, which made him rob his enemies of their prey and die by his own hand—everything about that boy of twenty-two lent romance and beauty to his personality. He became the beacon of our lives.[36]

That shining beacon soon inspired the pair to direct action. The summer of 1892 was one of the most pivotal moments in the history of American labor. Eight miles to the east of Pittsburgh stood the

Homestead Steel Works. They were owned by the Carnegie Steel Company, a powerhouse in the increasingly important steel industry. The workers at the plant were unionized under the auspices of the Amalgamated Association of Iron and Steel Workers, one of—if not the—strongest unions in the country.

The three-year contract that had been negotiated by the union was set to expire. The negotiations that had begun in February had quickly turned sour and intense. The workers weren't even striking for a raise; rather—and despite increasing profits for Andrew Carnegie—they were refusing to accept a pay *cut*. Henry Clay Frick, chairman of Carnegie Steel, unveiled an unprecedented weapon of capital: the lockout. Strikes had been deployed by labor before, with varying degrees of efficacy. In an early parallel to "you can't fire me, I quit," it was Frick who temporarily shut down his own plant and fired everyone employed therein. The union would not be recognized, he proclaimed. Going forward negotiations would be welcome, but only between Carnegie Steel and workers on an individual basis.

Tensions increased when Frick began to hire replacement employees to maintain production in the heavily fortified plant. Technically they would not even be considered scabs, since the union members were no longer Carnegie employees of any kind and therefore not really on strike. Both sides clearly saw the conflict as a proxy for the broader issue of capital versus labor in the United States. This was brinkmanship, with important ramifications for the entire country. All over America, people were eagerly following the latest happenings from Homestead—including a pair of young anarchists from New York City.

Then matters got deadly. As Goldman later recounted:

> Frick had fortified the Homestead mills, built a high fence around them. Then, in the dead of night, a barge packed with strike-breakers, under protection of heavily armed Pinkerton thugs, quietly stole up the Monongahela River. The steel-men had learned of Frick's move. They stationed themselves along the shore, determined to drive back Frick's hirelings. When the barge got within range, the

> Pinkertons had opened fire, without warning, killing a number of Homestead men on the shore, among them a little boy, and wounding scores of others.[37]

To this day it remains a matter of historical dispute as to who opened fire upon whom. Most sources evade the issue entirely: "Inevitably, shots were fired," recounts Britannica.[38] "The two groups exchanged gunfire," recounts History.com.[39] "No one knows which side shot first," admits PBS's *American Experience*.[40] What isn't in dispute is that several Pinkerton men and workers were killed and many more were injured. Things had clearly gotten out of hand—but no one wanted to blink. If anything, both sides wanted to dig in their heels even more now that people had died.

The state militia was called in, and on July 18th the town of Homestead was placed under martial law. Politicians reached out to Frick on behalf of the union, not even pleading to compromise but merely to reopen negotiations. Frick refused. Andrew Carnegie, conveniently vacationing in Scotland, had also been hardened by the events. Though previously not a particularly anti-union figure, this was now far too much. "Never employ one of these rioters," he telegrammed Frick. "Let grass grow over the works."

Berkman and Goldman hadn't taken Louis Lingg's appreciation for the use of force lightly. Blood had been spilled and men—men who were fathers that were simply trying to feed their children—had been killed. In their eyes, Frick was the embodiment of the inhuman capitalist oppressor—and the two of them were going to do something about it. How many more laborers had to die, whether at the hands of the state or of the Pinkertons, before the workers stood up for themselves? Berkman's thoughts turned to murder. Revolution was imminent, obviously so, and assassinating Frick would be the spark that finally set it off. Berkman would be considered a hero, and everybody would clap.

First Berkman tried experimenting with dynamite. But despite Lingg's inspiration and Johann Most's guidebook, he couldn't quite figure out how to make a working bomb. So be it. Frick was a man, and they would simply have to commit the "propaganda of the deed" the old-fashioned way: Berkman would track Frick down and shoot the bastard. He made his way to Pittsburgh while Goldman stayed behind. Five days after martial law had been declared, Berkman walked past Frick's secretary into the capitalist's office and drew a revolver. The first bullet hit Frick in the ear. John Leishman, vice-chairman of Carnegie Steel, was in the office and immediately tackled Berkman from behind. Berkman fired again, hitting Frick in the neck. The three men wrestled, and a third bullet went nowhere. That's when Berkman pulled out his knife, and stabbed Frick repeatedly.

This being an office building, there were plenty of men around to hear the noise. It took several of them to subdue Berkman. As he was taken away, doctors quickly removed the bullets from Frick's body and bandaged the wounds. Frick never lost consciousness and even refused anesthesia. Nor did Frick lose his will in the slightest. Before he even left for the hospital, he issued a statement:

> This incident will not change the attitude of the Carnegie Steel Company towards the Amalgamated Association. I do not think I shall die, but whether I do or not, the Company will pursue the same policy, and it will win.

In this Frick was absolutely correct. Not only did the assassination attempt fail completely, it only served to humanize Frick and gain him sympathy. That the capitalist newspapers would condemn Berkman was no surprise: "There are no worse enemies of the workingmen of this country than these same ignorant and reckless Socialists and Anarchists of foreign origin, who make so much noise about the rights and wrongs of society of which they have no intelligent comprehension," said the *New York Times*.[41]

But it didn't stop there. The condemnation of Berkman's assassination attempt was unambiguous and virtually universal. During his lifetime Marx had reportedly been disappointed when the workers he tried to agitate toward violent revolution were utterly uninterested in anything of the kind. They were happy to settle for better wages and reasonable working hours, not full-scale bloody war. This should have prepared Goldman and Berkman for the reactions to their strike on Frick.

Hugh O'Donnell had been elected chief of the strikers' advisory committee by members of the Amalgamated Association. His judgment of Berkman's attack was as damning as that of the *Times*: "Thus it would seem that the bullet from Berkman's pistol, failing in its foul attempt went straight through the heart of the Homestead strike." Even Berkman's mentor Johann Most denounced the assassination attempt: "Berkman is my enemy. He is no good. I hate him as much as I hate Frick, and Frick is the Czar of America."[42] The popularizer of the euphemism "the propaganda of the deed" found that the deed served far more to propagandize the side of the capitalists.

Alexander Berkman was only twenty-one years old, and it looked as if his life was already over—and his biggest accomplishment was to make a sympathetic figure out of Henry Clay Frick. Berkman wouldn't even have the option of martyring himself in prison as Louis Lingg had. Though he hid an explosive capsule in his cheek, it was uncovered by the police before he even had the chance to detonate it. Instead Berkman was sentenced to the maximum term under the law: twenty-one years in prison.

The Homestead unrest proved to be a total victory for the capitalists. On November 20, 1892 the workers voted to return to work on Frick's terms. The union was found to be powerless and collapsed, not just as a local but as a national force. In 1891 the AA could count on 24,000 members. By 1895 that number was down to 8,000, a drop of two-thirds. Henry Clay Frick went on to live a long ripe life, dying in New York City in 1919 at the age of sixty-nine. His art collection and home would thereupon be turned into a museum, colloquially known as the Frick.

Emma Goldman, on the other hand, was left alone. Berkman's imprisonment and what she saw as Most's betrayal did little to stifle her passion for agitating on behalf of the workers and pushing toward a society liberated from the forces of capitalism and the state. Strongly marginalized, she decided to take the fight to her former mentor. At first she wrote an article criticizing his repudiation of Berkman. When Most ignored that Goldman took action—and bought a horsewhip:

> At Most's next lecture I sat in the first row, close to the low platform. My hand was on the whip under my long, grey cloak. When he got up and faced the audience, I rose and declared in a loud voice: "I came to demand proof of your insinuations against Alexander Berkman."
>
> There was instant silence. Most mumbled something about "hysterical woman," but he said nothing else. I then pulled out my whip and leaped towards him. Repeatedly I lashed him across the face and neck, then broke the whip over my knee and threw the pieces at him. It was all done so quickly that no one had time to interfere.[43]

Disgusted with Most and those who sought change through the electoral process, Goldman continued to write and give speeches every chance she could. She paid her way by working at various jobs such as nursing, often under a pseudonym. Of all the people who would hear her speak, one man in particular would have a profound effect on history: Leon Czolgosz.

Czolgosz (pronounced *Chowl*-gosh) was merely one of the eight million visitors to 1901's Pan-American Exposition, held in Buffalo, New York. The most famous of those visitors was William McKinley, president of the United States. McKinley visited the grounds on September 5th, and then returned again the next day. Unbeknownst to the president—and unbeknownst to Emma Goldman, who was in St. Louis—Czolgosz had been stalking McKinley all day. Czolgosz had a gun with him and was prepared to cast his bullet for a Teddy Roosevelt presidency. Patiently the radical waited in a long line for his chance to meet the president. When the president finally extended his hand in greeting, Czolgosz shot him twice.

It took McKinley a week to die, and for a period it seemed as if he would pull through. For his part, Czolgosz spoke freely and downright proudly about his crime:

> [W]hat started the craze to kill was a lecture I heard some little time ago by Emma Goldman. She was in Cleveland and I and other Anarchists went to hear her. She set me on fire. Her doctrine that all rulers should be exterminated was what set me to thinking so that my head nearly split with the pain. Miss Goldman's words went right through me and when I left the lecture I had made up my mind that I would have to do something heroic for the cause I loved.

Just as the killing of several police officers at Haymarket Square prompted the view that this surely had to be the result of some anarchist conspiracy, it seemed absurd that Czolgosz was a lone gunman in the vein of President Garfield's assassin Charles Guiteau. It wasn't that long ago that Mary Surratt had broken the glass ceiling by becoming the first woman to be hanged by the Federal government for her alleged part in the John Wilkes Booth conspiracy. Goldman looked set to repeat that dubious honor.

Czolgosz had indeed met Goldman before. He did hear her speak just as he claimed, four months prior. Later he began to hang around anarchist circles and his behavior was so odd—odd by anarchist standards, mind you—that there had been wide concern that he was some sort of undercover spy. The anarchists would have been lucky if that had been the extent of what he had been hiding.

Unsure of what to do, Goldman fled to Chicago. She was staying at a friend's house when she heard the sound of breaking glass, and then saw a man holding a gun come through the window. Though Goldman would remain a militant atheist all her life, she surely must have appreciated the cosmic coincidence that the officer who nabbed her was none other than Captain Herman Schuettler—the very same man who had arrested Louis Lingg fourteen years prior. Goldman could have made it a point to disavow Czolgosz, to utter some vapid platitude about the senselessness of political violence, to claim that McKinley's family was in her thoughts and prayers—or at least thoughts, in this case. All these things she refused to do.

While claiming "I never advocated violence," Goldman simultaneously refused to denounce Czolgosz's actions. "I am not in a position to say who ought to be killed," she said. "The monopolists and the wealthy of this country are responsible for the existence of a Czolgosz."[44] Absolving the shooter of his guilt, Goldman went on to make clear where her sympathies lie:

> I feel that the man is one of those unfortunates who have been driven by despair and misery to commit the deed. I feel deeply with him as an individual, as I would feel with anybody who suffers. If I had means, I would help him as much as I could; I would see that he had counsel and that justice was done him.[45]

William McKinley had been the first president elected in something approaching a contemporary political campaign, with Ohio senator Mark Hanna doubling campaign fundraising from four years prior and outspending the Democratic candidate several times over. Goldman made sure to remind Americans of that fact as McKinley lay dying. "Mark Hanna has been the ruler of this country," she insisted, "not McKinley. McKinley has been the most insignificant ruler this country has ever had. He has neither wit nor intelligence, but has been a tool in the hands of Mark Hanna. Other Presidents have had heart or something, but this poor fellow—God forgive him, since he knows nothing—is a tool in the hands of the wealthy."[46]

Goldman could barely even bring herself to wish McKinley a safe recovery: "What I don't see is why they would make more fuss about a president than anybody else. All men are born equal."[47] If all that weren't enough, Goldman made sure to denounce the arresting officers as well. "I feel sure that the police are helping us," she said, adding that they "are making more anarchists than the most prominent people connected with the anarchists' cause could make in ten years. If they will only continue I shall be very grateful: they will save me lots of work."[48]

Despite headlines that had explicitly said "President Will Soon Recover," William McKinley succumbed of his wounds eight days after being shot, on September 14, 1901. Two days later, Goldman was released from prison. There was nothing the police could do. It is hard to imagine the level of hatred that Goldman then inspired in America. This advocate of what seemed to be a deranged foreign ideology was utterly unapologetic (though, being innocent of any crime, there was little for her to really apologize for), and upon being arrested in conjunction with the president being shot had basically replied, "I sympathize with the gunman and McKinley is a boring idiot. P.S. Fuck the police."

Even Berkman couldn't paint the vapid William McKinley as some monster intent on crushing the workers. Hearing the news from his prison cell, he took a more nuanced, peaceful view than Goldman did, insisting that though "McKinley was the chief representative of our modern slavery, he could not be considered in the light of a direct and immediate enemy of the people." He further explained what he saw as the distinction between his act and Csolgosz's:

> In modern capitalism, exploitation rather than oppression is the real enemy of the people. Oppression is but its handmaid. Hence the battle is to be waged in the economic rather than the political field. It is therefore that I regard my own act as far more significant and educational than Leon's. It was directed against a tangible, real oppressor, visualized as such by the people.[49]

Minstrels would later joke, "Can you tell me the difference between the dew that falls on the grass and the late President McKinley? Well, sir, one is mist from the heavens and the other is missed from the earth." But the time for humor was still some ways away. The fact that "Red Emma" was free to walk the streets was regarded as a moral obscenity, and something would need to be done about it.

The anarchists had taken it as their mission to destroy government. It was a fight that the government had no problem enjoining, and a fight that the political class had no problem exploiting in order to further its power. If the anarchists wanted war, then the commander-in-chief stood ready to give it to them. Less than three months after McKinley succumbed, his successor addressed Congress. Doubling down on the ideology behind the hanging of the Haymarket martyrs, the first President Roosevelt said:

> The anarchist, and especially the anarchist in the United States, is merely one type of criminal, more dangerous than any other because he represents the same depravity in a greater degree. The man who advocates anarchy directly or indirectly, in any shape or fashion, or the man who apologizes for anarchists and their deeds, makes himself morally accessory to murder before the fact. The anarchist is a criminal whose perverted instincts lead him to prefer confusion and chaos to the most beneficent form of social order. His protest of concern for workingmen is outrageous in its impudent falsity; for if the political institutions of this country do not afford opportunity to every honest and intelligent son of toil, then the door of hope is forever closed against him. The anarchist is everywhere not merely the enemy of system and of progress, but the deadly foe of liberty. If ever anarchy is triumphant, its triumph will last for but one red moment, to be succeeded for ages by the gloomy night of despotism.[50]

In 1901 there were still many former slaves living in America. Yet for Roosevelt, "Anarchy is a crime against the whole human race; and all mankind should band against the anarchist. His crime should be made an offense against the law of nations, like piracy and that form of manstealing known as the slave trade; for it is of far blacker infamy than either." As bad as slavery was, to Roosevelt anarchy was worse.

President Roosevelt intended to stop this anarchist menace which he believed had claimed the life of his presidential predecessor. In 1903 Roosevelt signed into law the Anarchist Exclusion Act, banning people from immigrating to the United States if they were anarchists, beggars, or epileptics. "I earnestly recommend to the Congress that in the exercise of its wise discretion it should take into consideration the coming to this country of anarchists or persons professing principles hostile to all government and justifying the murder of those placed in authority," Roosevelt declared. "They and those like them should be kept out of this country; and if found here they should be promptly deported to the country whence they came[.]"

If this be treason, Goldman and Berkman intended to make the most of it.

Chapter 3

YOU CAN'T EVEN CONCEIVE OF WHAT IT'S LIKE

Prison had been rough on Alexander Berkman. Fourteen years in wretched conditions were very deleterious to his health, let alone his state of mind. But in 1906 Berkman finally found himself a free man. In some sense he quite literally did not know what to do with himself, having spent virtually his entire adult life locked away. Transitioning to anything resembling normalcy would have been difficult for anyone, let alone a notorious political extremist and attempted assassin.

Goldman had been publishing a journal entitled *Mother Earth* to spread their ideology, and Berkman joined her there and on speaking tours. But the youthful fire was certainly dulled as he realized how much more productive he could have been with his time, if he only hadn't failed in his assassination attempt (or, perhaps, if only he had succeeded).

In 1908 the enormously popular President Roosevelt anointed his Secretary of War William Howard Taft to succeed him as president. Taft handily defeated William Jennings Bryan in the latter's third and final attempt to win the White House as the Democratic Party nominee. By 1912 Roosevelt reversed course, insisting he had only promised to serve two *consecutive* terms, not two total terms. He expected Taft to step aside, but the president of the United States refused. "Even a cornered rat will fight," Taft insisted.

It would be a tough fight, even for the elephantine president. Roosevelt's 1904 election victory over historical footnote Judge Alton B. Parker had yielded him the biggest landslide since the days of James Madison nearly a century prior. (To put matters in further perspective: Roosevelt did better in his reelection bid than Abraham Lincoln did during his.) The 1912 presidential election looked to be one for the record books, and it certainly was. The former President Roosevelt tried to grab the Republican nomination from the current President Taft, and almost succeeding in doing so. When that failed, Roosevelt made good on his threat and ran as a third-party candidate. Not to be outdone, Socialist candidate Eugene V. Debs also made a strong showing, eventually nabbing 6% of the popular vote.

Even though he received both a smaller percentage of the popular vote and fewer votes in total than William Jennings Bryan had received four years prior, when all was said and done it was Democrat Woodrow Wilson who was elected president of the United States. He was only the second Democrat to win the White House since the Civil War. Wilson's 1916 bid for reelection would be a much more difficult task. The last sitting Democrat to be reelected president had been Andrew Jackson, in 1828. Further, in the intervening four years, the GOP had done a good job of mending old wounds and rallied around former New York state governor—and current Supreme Court justice—Charles Evans Hughes as their candidate.

The outbreak of the Great War in Europe threatened the peace in the United States. President Wilson and the Democrats ran on Wilson's record, reminding the voters that "He kept us out of war." It was factual but not truthful. Yes, Wilson "kept us out of war"—but not for much longer. The 1916 election was a squeaker, with fewer than four thousand votes separating the candidates in California. In taking the Golden State Wilson took his reelection victory (much to the chagrin of Teddy Roosevelt, who absolutely despised him).

In March 1917, Woodrow Wilson was sworn in for his second term as president. On April 2, 1917 he asked for—and received—a declaration of war from Congress, officially entering the United States into the Great War. Yet Wilson was hardly the only politician given to brazen chicanery. General Erich Ludendorff of Germany knew that there were several ways to win a war. The most obvious of course was on the battlefield. But getting the enemy to withdraw—or even lose his nerve—was also an effective mechanism. The crafty Ludendorff accordingly sought "to improve peace possibilities through the internal weakening of Russia,"[51] one of Germany's foes at the time.

This was an opportunity for Communist agitator Vladimir Lenin, who was widely regarded as a lunatic. Lenin's Bolshevik worldview was based on the Marxist "scientific socialist" idea of the violent overthrow of governments in the name of imposing a "dictatorship of the proletariat" to usher in communism all over the globe. In 1905 Lenin had taken part in a very failed attempt to overthrow the czar, which resulted in his exile from Russia.

As extreme as Lenin's ideology was his rhetoric; two mechanisms by which it was easy to dismiss him as being utterly unpersuasive to most people. As Lenin biographer Victor Sebestyen pointed out, "Those who disagreed with him were 'scoundrels,' 'philistines,' 'cretins,' 'filthy scum,' 'whores,' 'class traitors,' 'silly old maids,' 'windbags' (one of his favourite epithets, found frequently in his writings) and 'blockheads.'" He often went obscene, and then "his opponents were invariably 'shits' or 'cunts.'"[52] By 1917 Lenin was thus both a has-been and a joke—but still a possible troublemaker. As historian Edward Crankshaw put it, "the German government…saw in this obscure fanatic one more bacillus to let loose in tottering and exhausted Russia to spread infection".[53]

A provisional parliamentary government was put in charge of Russia after the czar had been forced from the throne in early 1917. Seeking to distance itself from the czar's autocratic methods, the parliamentary government did not prevent Lenin from returning. Financed by Kaiser Wilhelm, Lenin was put on a sealed train with a group of comrades from his exile in Zurich, Switzerland—one can't let the pathogen spread throughout Europe, mind you—and taken on a circuitous route back to Russia. The group traversed Germany before taking a ferry to Sweden, traveling the entirety of the country. From there it was a quick exchange to Finland, then part of the Russian empire, and finally dismounting to great fanfare in St. Petersburg on April 16, 1917, after a journey of eight days.[54]

Two months later, on June 15, 1917, President Wilson signed the Espionage Act of 1917 into law. In brazen defiance of the First Amendment, the Act made it a felony to interfere with the draft. In 1916, keeping us out of war was a winning slogan. By 1917, working to keep us out of war was a crime. The very same day that the Espionage Act became law, Goldman and Berkman were arrested. Their office was searched, and the authorities were delighted to seize a list with the contact information of every anarchist and sympathizer.

Bail was set for the pair at $25,000 each. They were on thin ice, and they knew it. Berkman was not a citizen. Further, in 1908 the government had revoked the citizenship of Goldman's teenage husband as a means of revoking her subsequent claims to citizenship as well. The trial was an open-and-shut case, with the pair sentenced to two years in prison. Nor were the two alone. Many others who opposed the draft were incarcerated, including the aforementioned Socialist presidential candidate Eugene V. Debs. For Wilson, liberty was a luxury not to be permitted at the present stage of development. When America was out of danger, only then might free speech be indulged in.

Then the impossible happened. General Ludendorff was no fool, and the bacillus he had sent to Russia had not only infected the armed forces but had somehow metastasized. Lenin had many Red Guards under his control. Further, his Bolsheviks had persuaded enough of the population to their perspective that they controlled a majority of the Petrograd Soviet, one of the workers' councils that framed Russia's halting steps toward democracy.

Key to this growing Bolshevik influence was Leon Trotsky, well-known for his philosophical bent, unparalleled speaking skills, and historic ego. Trotsky was brilliant and, like so many other brilliant men, never forgot it for a moment. Though Trotsky had come on board to the Bolshevik cause quite recently, he quickly became second only to Lenin in terms of both influence and of articulating the Bolshevik philosophy.

Bolsheviks had refused to take part in the provisional government from the beginning, and their control of the Petrograd Soviet was a sticking point for the government's ability to do much of anything. On October 24th things came to a head. Lenin and Trotsky's forces seized control of Petrograd, proclaiming themselves as the new government. It was, as journalist John Reed famously labeled it, ten days that shook the world. "Without exaggeration," Berkman wrote, "I may say that the happiest day of my existence was passed in a prison cell—the day when the first news of the October Revolution and the victory of the Bolsheviki reached me in the Atlanta Federal Penitentiary."[55] The Russian Civil War had begun.

Just like the United States, what would become the Soviet Union was a country founded on a conscious philosophy. While America was based on the classical liberal principles of a propertied society largely free from state interference, Lenin's Russia was to be a nation where virtually all of society was to be managed by the government in the name of equality and for the total benefit of all.

In those early days, everything was on the table. It was a perfect inversion of G. K. Chesterton's fence. Chesterton had argued that if one came upon a fence crossing the road, it must have been put there for some reason at some point. It is perfectly possible that the reason no longer existed. But until one knew what that reason had been, one should err on the side of maintaining structures which had once served some purpose. They might still be performing some function not entirely apparent. In the same way that modern art experimented with abolishing perspective and realism in color and form, the new Russia was intended to entirely remake society—and even the nature of man himself.

By 1918, the Bolsheviks' Code on Marriage, the Family and Guardianship envisioned a "withering away" of the family itself at some point in the future.[56] Preferring one's children over others smacked of bourgeois values and inequality, both between families and within the family itself. No parent could do as good of a job educating their children as the government could. Indeed, it made perfect sense: the same government was going to educate—if not reeducate—the entire adult population as well. Love for one's children was "narrow and irrational," which state educators were not.[57]

Why not speculate about a world where women gave birth, returned to the workforce, and had their children raised in a colony by caretakers far better trained in childrearing than their birth mothers ever were? This would immediately solve the unfair situation of some children having bad parents. Assurances were made that in this more equal future the mother would, of course, be able to see her child if and when she wanted: "She only has to say the word."[58]

The newfound Bolshevik approach was encapsulated in arguing, as the dean of the department of law at Moscow State University later did, that "[w]e should not aspire to a highly stable family and look at marriage from that angle. Strengthening marriage and the family—making divorce more difficult—is not new, it is old: It is the same as bourgeois law." It wouldn't be much of a "revolution" if everyone simply did things the way grandma did. If things were old, they were therefore inherently in need of being undone in this new society of the future.[59]

Not only was the biology of the family open to discussion, but so was the biology of man himself. One communist writer mused that "We do not know whether, during Communism, emotions will disappear, whether the human being will change to such an extent that he will become a luminous globe consisting of the head and brain only, or whether new and transformed emotions will come into being."[60]

All this was of course some time away (and they would eventually experiment with a new calendar too, with a five-day week). The first Bolshevik reforms were far more modest than turning people into globes, but still entirely radical in their approach, eventually decreeing that:

> All private property was nationalized by the government.
> All Russian banks were nationalized.
> Private bank accounts were expropriated.
> The properties of the Russian Orthodox Church (including bank accounts) were expropriated.
> All foreign debts were repudiated.
> Control of the factories was given to the soviets.
> An increase in wages and an eight-hour working day.

Yet proclaiming a new government and actually governing were two entirely separate situations. Extraordinary times called for extraordinary measures. Lenin had explicitly asked how a revolution could be made without executions.[61] In this he might have been technically correct. It had given George Washington no pleasure to preside over the hanging of turncoat John André, for example. But Lenin envisioned his dictatorship of the proletariat as one "maintained through violence" and "a power unbound by laws."[62]

On December 19, 1917, mere weeks after seizing power in the October Revolution, Lenin issued a decree to form an Extraordinary Commission ("Tchrezvychainaia Komissiia" in Russian, or Tcheka/Cheka for short) for Combating Counter-Revolution and Sabotage. What made the Tcheka so extraordinary was that it was, just as Lenin said, a secret police with power unbound by laws and superior to them. It was tasked with the power to "persecute and break up all acts of counter-revolution and sabotage all over Russia." And since the revolution was defined as being embodied by the Bolshevik government itself, any opposition to it could thereby quite logically be claimed to be an act of counter-revolution and/or sabotage.[63]

The Tcheka took their work quite seriously, working in some ways independently of Lenin but not shying away from shedding blood in achieving its goals. "The Tcheka is not a court," the head of the Tcheka publicly stated in 1918. "We stand for organized terror. This should be frankly admitted. The Tcheka is obligated to defend the revolution and conquer the enemy even if its sword does by chance sometimes fall upon the heads of the innocent."[64, 65] Nor was this new secret police particularly secret about its activities. If anything, its brazen superiority to the legal system was a testament to its power and a reminder of the relative powerlessness of the Russian people.

The Bolsheviks' other major priority, however, was to get Russia out of the Great War. Communism was meant to be a worldwide class revolution, not simply a Russian experiment, and warring with Germany was certainly antithetical to that goal—and to the goal of Lenin gaining greater power. At first the Bolsheviks had teamed up with several other leftist movements in order to implement and stabilize the newfound socialist structure. Their primary rivals were the Mensheviks, "Bolshe" being Russian for "greater" and "Menshe" meaning "fewer" meant a supposed reflection on the relative popularity of the two groups.

Whereas the Bolsheviks favored one-party rule and rapid social change, the Mensheviks leaned more toward political pluralism and an incremental approach. In addition there were the Social-Revolutionists (AKA "Left SRs"), a party with an agrarian base who believed in democratic socialism. Finally—and in no small number—there were Alexander Berkman and Emma Goldman's comrades, the Anarchists. The factions were united against the remaining White army, those forces still loyal to the czar who were endangering the success of the Revolution.

In December 1917, Trotsky as Foreign Minister sent Bolshevik agents to the Belarussian town of Brest-Litovsk to negotiate with the Germans. Thinking that the October Revolution would soon cause the workers of the world to unite and lose their chains, Lenin's instructions were simple: "String out the talks until there is a revolution in Germany—or as long as possible."[66] Trotsky did his best to run out the clock, but the German offer was simple too: Germany would get to keep the lands it was in occupation of, namely, Poland, Lithuania, Courland, and most of western Ukraine.

The terms were humiliating, and Lenin's comrades in government were having none of it. Lenin was unsure of what to do, or rather unsure of what he could get away with. Finally, on February 9, 1918, German General Hoffman offered an ultimatum: the Russians had one day to sign the treaty, or else Germany would invade. Trotsky had an unprecedented response. He said that Russia was leaving the war, but he also refused to sign a treaty to that effect. The Germans did not quite know what to make of this—or of the Russians in general, one might add.

The Russians dawdled again. The Germans threatened again. Finally, their patience ran out. In late February they invaded, and in doing so captured more territory in three days than they had in the previous three years combined. Capturing Petrograd was no longer an impossibility, and if the Germans captured Petrograd it really would be the end of the Russian Revolution (if not Russia herself).

Lenin managed to convince his comrades that they needed to sign the treaty. But General Hoffman was no fool either. As Sebestyen put it:

> Apart from the territory they had already lost they were forced to give up the Baltic states, Finland and nearly all Ukraine to the Central Powers and the ports of Kars, Andalan and Batum to the Turks—1.8 million square kilometres, sixty-two million people, around 32 per cent of its best agricultural land, 54 per cent of its industry and 89 per cent of its coalmines.[67]

This was in addition to an indemnity of 120 million gold rubles. It was devastating and it was humiliating. Lenin was denounced as a German spy and a traitor. Karl Radek had traveled with Lenin on his sealed train, but now snarled that if "we had five hundred courageous men in Petrograd we would put you in prison."

"Some people may indeed go to prison after this," Lenin replied, chillingly and prophetically, "but if you will calculate the probabilities you will see that it is much more likely that I will send you rather than you send me." Though the cost was extraordinary, it bought Lenin more time to let the Revolution develop. Further, it established him (and, to a lesser extent, Trotsky) as the person who was in a position to speak for Russia.

Lenin had seized power in 1917 under the slogan of "All power to the soviets!", meaning the workers' councils who would supposedly be making decisions nationwide. But soon Lenin was saying that "All this sentimentality and prattle about democracy has to be cast overboard."[68] By 1918 rival political parties who had supported Lenin's Bolsheviks in their seizure of power began to be made illegal. "All power to the soviets" quickly became "all power to the Bolsheviks."

Lenin apparently never did say the quote that is often ascribed to him: "The capitalists will sell us the rope with which we will hang them." What he actually said was far less pithy and far worse. In his view, Bolshevism was "a social system based on blood-letting,"[69] and the blood flowed from the beginning. "This is the hour of truth," Lenin wrote to a comrade in July of 1918. "It is of supreme importance that we encourage and make use of the energy of mass terror directed against the counterrevolutionaries".[70] It was mere weeks after Lenin's letter when his own blood would be spilled, for there was an attempt on his life on August 30, 1918. A young woman from a rival political party managed to shoot him three times, causing injuries from which he would never fully recover.

Yet the biggest victim of Lenin's shooting was the Russian population, for this gave the Bolsheviks a pretext to unleash the Red Terror. On September 1, 1918, one newspaper urged vengeance:

> We will turn our hearts into steel, which we will temper in the fire of suffering and the blood of fighters for freedom. We will make our hearts cruel, hard, and immovable, so that no mercy will enter them, and so that they will not quiver at the sight of a sea of enemy blood. We will let loose the floodgates of that sea. Without mercy, without sparing, we will kill our enemies in scores of hundreds. Let them be thousands; let them drown themselves in their own blood.[71]

As one prominent Tcheka operative advised, "Don't seek for incriminating evidence as to whether the prisoners took part, by deed or word, in a rebellion against the Soviet government. You have to ask him what class he belongs to, what is his origin, his education and profession. It is those questions that should decide the fate of the defendant—and therein lies the meaning of the red terror."[72] Even Lenin thought that was going too far, but such concerns did little to stem the flow of blood.

Less than a week after the assassination attempt came a declaration in Moscow from the War Commissar:

> The working class of Soviet Russia arose, threateningly declaring that for every drop of proletarian blood it will shed torrents of blood of those who go against the revolution, against the Soviets and proletarian leaders. For every proletarian life it will seek to destroy the scions of

> bourgeois families and white guardists. From now on the working class declares to its enemies that every single act of white terror will be answered with a ruthless, proletarian, mass terror.[73]

Terror and class warfare became official state policy. "Enough of this long, sterile and vain talk about red terror," opined the *Weekly Tcheka* in September 1918. "It is time, while it is not late yet, to carry out, by deed and not in word, a ruthless and strictly organized mass terror."[74] "Bourgeois" concepts like privacy and individualism were anathema, and the population itself was recruited to become an extension of the surveillance state. A 1918 commissar's order spelled out what this meant in practice when he sought to flush out targets from the citizenry: "In case the guilty ones are not turned over to the authorities, one person out of ten will be shot, irrespective whether he is guilty or not".[75]

Lenin was not unique in using the police to impose his will on the citizenry. Woodrow Wilson's idea of sending Americans to fight European battles was an inversion of the well-established Monroe Doctrine. It took until Teddy Roosevelt for a president to leave the United States while in office, and even then it was only to check in on progress in the Panama Canal and to tour America's new protectorate of Puerto Rico.

Socialists in America were strongly opposed to entering the Great War. For Goldman and Berkman, the entire situation was absolute madness, government at its lowest and most evil. The various heads of state at war included the King of Italy, the Czar of Russia, the German Kaiser, the Sultan of the Ottoman Empire and Franz Joseph, who was both an emperor *and* a king. This is who the working classes should give their lives for? Men without a pot to piss in should die so that sultans and kings maintained their hold on power? At least Carnegie had been producing something of value in his mills.

The Socialist Party in Philadelphia printed and mailed fliers to young men who were about to be drafted into war. Under the heading of "Long Live the Constitution of the United States," the subhead included the text of the Thirteenth Amendment which forever made involuntarily servitude illegal in America. "When you conscript a man and compel him to go abroad to fight against his will," the flier asserted, "you violate the most sacred right of personal liberty, and substitute for it what Daniel Webster called 'despotism in its worst form.'...*If you do not assert and support your rights, you are helping to 'deny or disparage rights' which it is the solemn duty of all citizens and residents of the United States to retain...*"[76]

As far as anti-military pamphleteering went, this was as mild as it got. But even such a pamphlet was considered too dangerous to be allowed circulation. The Party's General Secretary Charles Schenck was sentenced to prison, with the case going all the way up to the Supreme Court. If anything was to be protected by the First Amendment, then surely it would be political speech such as this—except that it wasn't.

The membership of the Court at the time consisted of three Taft appointees, two from Roosevelt, one from McKinley and three from Wilson. The Court recognized that "in many places and in ordinary times, the defendants, in saying all that was said in the circular, would have been within their constitutional rights. But the character of every act depends upon the circumstances in which it is done." Congress shall make no law abridging the freedom of speech, *but.*

In a unanimous decision, the Court upheld the Espionage Act and its blatant assault on principles of free speech. In the sort of mental gymnastics only a legal mind could present with a straight face, Justice Oliver Wendell Holmes, Jr. compared the pamphleteering to causing a riot: "The most stringent protection of free speech would not protect a man in falsely shouting fire in a theatre and causing a panic." To begin with, theatres are private property, and therefore there is no right to yell anything in any theatre at any time, any more than a person could wander into a radio station and start broadcasting from its microphones. But even presuming Holmes' point that yelling fire would cause people to get trampled, the consequences of such yelling would be immediate and direct. Nothing in Schenck's pamphlet would cause people to get worked up and riot. If anything, it called for them to calmly and methodically think through their rights as free men, and to act accordingly in the name of minimizing death. It would have been no surprise to anarchists that in the Supreme Court there was a bipartisan, unanimous consensus in favor of the powers of the government and against the rights of the individual citizen.

Tensions began to escalate. In 1918 fifty-five radicals were deported from the United States—but the United States government deported the wrong ones. April of 1919 saw over thirty letter-bombs being mailed to various government officials and other powerful people, with the apparent intention that they would be delivered and opened on May 1, May Day. The bombs were all packaged similarly, and after one exploded (blowing off the hands of a senator's housekeeper as well as his wife's teeth) the others were thereupon intercepted.

The violence then increased. Nine bombs were detonated across eight cities on June 2nd, but only managed to kill one night watchman. Most concerning was the bomb meant for Attorney General A. Mitchell Palmer, which detonated prematurely in front of his Washington D.C. townhouse. The explosive took out its young anarchist carrier, as Assistant Secretary of the Navy Franklin Delano Roosevelt and his wife Eleanor witnessed the aftermath from their home across the street—an aftermath that included a piece of the bomber's body landing on their doorstep.

Attorney General Palmer naturally took action against these threats against the state and private citizens. Though only twenty-four years old, Palmer put Justice Department lawyer J. Edgar Hoover in charge of a series of raids designed to investigate and infiltrate the nests of radicalism that pervaded throughout the United States. Berkman and Goldman were of course natural and obvious targets for the Hoover dragnet, and were arrested and imprisoned.

So it was that on December 21, 1919, 250 radicals were deported to Russia aboard the USAT *Buford*—with Berkman and Goldman among them. Hoover personally came to New York City to see the pair off. "Haven't I given you a square deal, Miss Goldman?" he asked. Goldman was fifty years old, Berkman forty-nine. They had lived their entire adult lives in the United States, and were departing to a country they wouldn't recognize. It was a country that no one could recognize, for there was no other country like it anywhere on earth.

The two were optimistic. Landing in Russia was "the most sublime day of my life," Berkman wrote. "Thus my pious old forefathers must have felt on first entering the Holy of Holies. A strong desire was upon me to kneel down and kiss the ground".[77] Times were hard, desperately so, but the nation was still at war and restrictions on liberties were somewhat to be expected. Lenin assured his comrades that things would liberalize and improve once the civil war ended and the era of "war communism" drew to a close.

Nevertheless there remained widespread squalor and hunger. The White Army forces of the czar were not yet defeated, and an allied blockade against the Bolsheviks made matters even more difficult. One couldn't expect to liberate the workers of the world without an enormous counterreaction, both domestically and abroad. Yet that didn't explain the brutal oppression Goldman and Berkman were both personally witness to, outdoing the worst oppressions of the czar by far. As bad as things were in the United States, people weren't being imprisoned in large numbers due to their political ideology. In Lenin's Russia, that was swiftly becoming the norm.

Berkman did his best to square his anarchist views with what would become known as Marxism-Leninism, writing:

> Since my early youth, revolution—social revolution—was the great hope and aim of my life. It signified to me the Messiah who was to deliver the world from brutality, injustice, and evil, and pave the way for a regenerated humanity of brotherhood, living in peace, liberty, and beauty.
>
> I knew that the Bolsheviki were Marxists, believers in a centralized State which I, an Anarchist, deny in principle. But I placed the Revolution above theories, and it seemed to me that the Bolsheviki did the same. [...] They resolutely applied Anarchist methods and tactics when the exigency of the situation demanded them. [...] Had not Lenin himself frequently asserted that he and his followers were ultimately Anarchists—that political power was to them but a temporary means of accomplishing the Revolution? The

> State was gradually to die off, to disappear, as Engels had taught, because its functions would become unnecessary and obsolete.[78]

An anarchist had bombed the Bolsheviks' Moscow Committee building on September 25, 1919, a few months before Berkman and Goldman had arrived in Russia. The assault was denounced by anarchist leaders throughout the Soviet Union, but to little matter. Lenin unleashed the power of the Tcheka, and hundreds were arrested and tried. Lenin personally assured Berkman that "We do not persecute Anarchists of ideas, but we will not tolerate armed resistance or agitation of that character." But as historian Paul Avrich pointed out, "Unfortunately for the 'ideological' anarchists, the Cheka did not bother to run its prisoners through a catechism of anarchist doctrine before meting out retribution."[79]

The Haymarket martyrs had been regarded by socialists of all stripes as victims of an evil oppressive regime, innocents who had been killed simply for having unpopular anarchist ideas. Now the Tcheka was doing the same thing on a scale one hundred times over, and supposedly doing so in the name of a working-class revolution.

"Liberty," Lenin told Berkman, "is a luxury not to be permitted at the present stage of development. When the Revolution is out of danger, external and domestic, then free speech might be indulged in." Insisting that "enemies must be crushed, and all power centralized in the Communist State," Lenin admitted that in "this process the Government is often compelled to resort to unpleasant means; but that is the imperative of the situation, from which there can be no shrinking. In the course of time these methods will be abolished, when they have become unnecessary."[80]

Goldman's stature was prominent enough within revolutionary circles that she too managed to arrange a meeting with Lenin. "Since my arrival I found scores of Anarchists in prison and their Press suppressed," she said to him. "I explained that I could not think of working with the Soviet Government so long as my comrades were in prison for opinion's sake."

To his credit, perhaps, Lenin spoke frankly with the revolutionary anarchist. He bluntly told Goldman that free speech "is, of course, a bourgeois notion. There can be no free speech in a revolutionary period. We have the peasantry against us because we can give them nothing in return for their bread. We will have them on our side when we have something to exchange. Then you can have all the free speech you want—but not now."[81]

Fine, in times of siege there needed to be limits set on political discourse. But that didn't explain or justify the barbarism of Lenin's secret police. As Goldman recounted:

> Corruption was rampant; it put in the shade the worst crimes of the Jacobins. [...] The depravity of the Tcheka was a matter of common knowledge. People were shot for slight offences, while those who could afford to give bribes were freed even after they had been sentenced to death. It repeatedly happened that the rich relatives of an arrested man would be notified by the Tcheka of his execution. A few weeks later, after they had somewhat recovered from their shock and grief, they would be informed that the report of the man's death was erroneous, that he was alive and could be liberated by paying a fine, usually a very high one. Of course, the relatives would strain every effort to raise the money. Then they would suddenly be arrested for attempted bribery, their money confiscated and the prisoner shot.[82]

It wasn't merely the corruption but the brutality. One of the refrains against the czar—and not just from leftists—was against the brutality of his reign, unique among European countries. The czar too had a secret police force called the Okhrana, and it had served as a badge of honor among the first Bolsheviks to have been imprisoned by them or even targeted by them. But the Okhrana's scope and methods didn't come close to what Lenin had in mind. He understood perfectly well that it would be impossible to entirely remake a society easily. There would always be an enormous percentage of any population driven by what would be described as a "petty bourgeois" mentality, a sort of vague conservatism not in the sense of being right-wing but in the sense of being inarticulately opposed in principle to change.

As Goldman herself witnessed:

> early in the morning mounted Tchekists would dash by, shooting into the air—a warning that all windows must be closed. Then came motor trucks loaded with the doomed. They lay in rows, faces downward, their hands tied, soldiers standing over them with rifles. They were being carried to execution outside the city. A few hours later the trucks would return empty save for a few soldiers. Blood dripped from the wagons, leaving a crimson streak on the pavement all the way to the Tcheka headquarters.[83]

Maybe it was irony, maybe naivete. There seems to be little question that, because Berkman and Goldman shared a common enemy with the Bolsheviks who proclaimed solidarity with the workers, they hoped that Lenin and Trotsky could have been partners when it came to the social revolution. Yet Lenin had never made a secret of his bloodlust, and in this he took after Marx and his visions of end-of-times social revolution.

The reasons for which a human life could be exterminated multiplied rapidly after the October Revolution. Not only was the population itself under threat of execution, but so too were the soldiers caught up in the military. On June 16, 1920, Trotsky accordingly issued the following order in his role as military leader:

> 1) Scoundrels who exhort soldiers to retreat, deserters who do not carry out military orders, will be shot.
> 2) Any soldier who unwarrantedly abandons his military post will be shot.

> 3) Anyone who throws away his rifle or sells even part of his equipment, will be shot.[84]

A gun was officially worth more than a soldier's life. But the terror did not merely consist of the threat—and practice—of executions. For Lenin, it had to be applied to the entire population as necessary. "We have not learned to wage the class struggle in the newspapers as skillfully as the bourgeoisie did," Lenin pointed out. "Remember the skill with which it hounded its class enemies in the press, ridiculed them, disgraced them, and tried to sweep them away." He demanded that class enemies, whether entire factories or mere individuals, be publicly denounced and denigrated in the newspapers. Public humiliation would ensure that everyone would do as they were supposed to. "How many of them have we found, how many have we exposed and how many have we pilloried?"[85] he demanded. No matter how many it had been, clearly it had not been enough for Lenin's taste. Very quickly the idea of a "class enemy" grew to become someone who defied Lenin.

After traveling with Lenin on the sealed train, Karl Radek had become a major figure in the Comintern, the Communist International organization dedicated to spreading communist ideas throughout the world. In May of 1920 Radek personally asked Berkman to translate Lenin's newest essay into English. Berkman asked for a week; Radek said it needed to be done in three days.

Berkman skimmed "The Infantile Sickness of Leftism" and saw that it was an attack on anarchism and other Left revolutionary ideologies. Anarchism was specifically and nonsensically described as a "petty bourgeois ideology" at a time when the term referred to middlebrow shopkeepers and their mindless conservatism, which was as antithetical to anarchist revolutionary fervor as possible. By this point, however, "petty bourgeois" was the Bolsheviks' slur of the moment, more an expression of derision than anything else. In his essay Lenin went on to denigrate "the ultrarevolutionists suffocating in the fervor of their childish enthusiasm."[86] Berkman must have taken little comfort in the fact that Lenin didn't call the anarchists "shits" and "cunts."

At that very moment, Berkman knew that a group of anarchist political prisoners were undergoing a hunger strike to demand better treatment. Torture in the passive sense was the norm for prisoners of the Bolshevik state. They were sometimes put into "hot cellars," windowless, subterranean cells that measured three feet by 1.5 feet. Eighteen people would be crammed into this space, such that some could not even reach the floor and had to lean on the shoulders of the others. The lack of circulating air made it impossible to keep a lamp alight or even to strike a match to begin with. The prisoners could not leave for a breath of fresh air or even to relieve themselves. (This was in contrast to the more aggressive "cold cellar," where naked prisoners were lowered down and then had water poured onto them in the freezing Russian winter.)

It was the anarchist prisoners who Berkman thought of as he read Lenin's words. "I saw their burning eyes peering accusingly at me through the iron bars," Berkman recalled. "'Have you forsaken us?' I heard them whisper." He insisted on being allowed to write a preface to Lenin's essay. He could not in good conscience translate an attack on his ideals without adding some defense of them.

Berkman was not, of course, allowed to defend himself or his ideals. After his refusal to submit to Lenin's wishes, Berkman was very much persona non grata in "the hearth of the Revolution," one which the anarchist had previously regarded as "the torch whose light is visible throughout the world, and proletarian hearts in every land are warmed by his glow."[87] Word went around very quickly, and comrades who had previously greeted Berkman warmly now dismissed him with the curtness with which one dismisses an unwanted stranger.

Berkman was hardly alone in all this. Lenin's new society was based on class warfare, wherein a person's previous social class (and that of his family and ancestors) determined his value as a human being. "The Bolsheviki have turned the intelligentsia into a class of hunted animals," one of his comrades told him. "We are looked upon as even worse than the bourgeoisie. As a matter of fact, we are much worse off than the latter, for they usually have 'connections' in influential places, and most of them still possess some of the wealth they had hidden. They can speculate; yes, even grow rich, while we of the professional class have nothing. We are doomed to slow starvation."[88]

Berkman and Goldman had held out every possible hope that the workers' revolution could be salvaged. "For eighteen months, months of anguish and heartrending experience," Berkman wrote, "I clung to that hope." The two were idealists and they were ideologues, but they were not completely blind. As he put it:

> Every day the damning evidence was accumulating. I saw the Bolsheviki reflect the Revolution as a monstrous grotesque; I saw tragic revolutionary necessity institutionalized into irresponsible terror, the blood of thousands shed without reason or measure. I saw the class struggle, long terminated, become a war of vengeance and extermination. I saw the ideals of yesterday betrayed, the meaning of the Revolution perverted, its essence caricatured into reaction. I saw the workers subdued, the whole country silenced by the Party dictatorship and its organised brutality. I saw entire villages laid waste by Bolshevik artillery. I saw the prisons filled—not with counter-revolutionists, but with workers and peasants, with proletarian intellectuals, with starving women and children.[89]

Then came Kronstadt.

Kronstadt was a naval base located on an island just outside St. Petersburg. During 1919 a naval detachment of communist sailors had defended the city against the counter-revolutionary White forces. It was a pivotal time, when it was not at all clear that the Reds would be able to carry the workers' revolution through to the end. These heroes of the Revolution would later be immortalized in the 1936 Soviet film *We Are From Kronstadt*, screened as an example of Russian excellence at the 1937 Paris World's Fair.[90]

By 1920 the impossible seemed to have become reality. The Bolsheviks had had to face opposition at home and abroad while the rest of the world was itself involved in the Great War. Yet the White armies were finally defeated by the Reds, and "war communism" would finally be able to be on its way out. Now that the Russian Civil War was over, the men of Kronstadt demanded that the Bolsheviks keep their word and lessen the authoritarianism which had supposedly been crucial during wartime. In March of 1921 they rebelled against Lenin's forces, protesting in the streets and insisting upon their rights under socialism. The insurrectionists issued a fifteen-point manifesto, asking what had been promised for years by the ideology of socialism generally and by the Bolsheviks specifically:

> In view of the fact that the present Soviets do not express the will of the workers and peasants, immediately to hold new elections by secret ballot [...] Freedom of speech and the press for workers and peasants, for Anarchists and Left-Socialist parties. [...] Freedom of assembly for labor unions and peasant organizations. [...] To liberate all political prisoners of socialist parties [...] A commission to review the cases of those held in prisons and concentration camps. [...] To equalize the rations of all who work [...] To permit free individual production, on a small scale, by one's own efforts.[91]

In response, the insurgents who Trotsky himself had called "the pride and glory of the revolution" were now freely—and baselessly—accused of taking orders from foreign powers or being agents of the czar, if not both. A leaflet was issued from the Bolsheviks' defense committee, invoking Pyotr Wrangel's recently defeated White Army. The sailors had twenty-four hours to surrender. If they didn't then they would suffer just like Wrangel's forces were suffering, dying like flies of hunger and disease. If they surrendered they would be pardoned. But if they chose to continue with their rebellion, "you will be shot like partridges."[92] Trotsky personally approved a plan to gas the insurgents if necessary.[93]

Berkman and Goldman were beside themselves. To threaten the men who had been so crucial in overthrowing the White Army was unconscionable, especially when all they were demanding was what had been promised to them all along. The sacrifices of today would lead to the rewards of tomorrow; such was the mindset that had kept revolutionaries going despite years of hunger and penury.

Desperate to avoid further killing, the two anarchists wrote to the Petrograd Soviet of Labor and Defense, offering their services in an attempt to resolve the dispute peacefully and amicably. The sailors too wanted peace, wiring to the authorities that "We want no bloodshed. Not a single Communist has been harmed by us."[94] Goldman and Berkman urged the Bolsheviks to allow a commission of five people to go and negotiate. "In the given situation this is the most radical method," they wrote. "It will be of international revolutionary significance."[95]

Berkman heard the sound of the Bolsheviks' decision himself, on March 7, 1921. "Distant rumbling reaches my ears as I cross the Nevsky," he recalled. "It sounds again, stronger and nearer, as if rolling toward me. All at once I realize that artillery is being fired. It is 6 P. M. Kronstadt has been attacked!" The Bolsheviks had never meant what they said, and now the brave men of Kronstadt were paying the price with their lives. As Trotsky later put it: "'lying and worse' are an inseparable part of the class struggle."[96]

"Days of anguish and cannonading," Berkman continued. "My heart is numb with despair; something has died within me. The people on the streets look bowed with grief, bewildered. No one trusts himself to speak. The thunder of heavy guns rends the air." Ten days later, it was all over. Kronstadt had fallen, and hundreds of sailors and workers were scattered dead in its streets.[97]

Two thousand rebels were taken prisoner after the rebellion, with many of them executed on the spot. The remainder were taken to various Russian prisons. The Petrograd jails were overcrowded even by the inhuman standards of the Bolsheviks. This situation was resolved by having them shot in batches over a few months.[98] Others were sent to labor camps, where instead of the mercy of a bullet they faced death from starvation and exhaustion. Amnesty was promised to those rebels who had managed to escape to Finland. The ones who returned, believing the Bolsheviks' promises, were immediately sent to labor camps.

With the defeat of the Kronstadt rebellion, the Bolshevik victory was now complete and total. "The time has come," Lenin decreed, "to put an end to opposition, to put the lid on it; we have had enough opposition."[99] A mere nine days after Kronstadt fell, Lenin publicly declared war on those former allies who had been useful in putting over Bolshevism to the Russian people: "An open proof of one's Menshevism should be sufficient ground for our revolutionary courts to confer the highest punishment, that is, shooting."[100] Over one thousand Mensheviks were arrested in Ukraine alone.[101]

As Avrich recounted:

> During the Civil War, the Bolsheviks, menaced by Whites on every side, had allowed the pro-Soviet parties of the Left a precarious existence under continuous harassment and surveillance. After Kronstadt even this was no longer tolerated. All pretense of a legal opposition was abandoned in May 1921, when Lenin declared that the place for rival socialists was behind bars or in exile, side by side with the White Guards. A new wave of repressions descended on the Mensheviks, SR's, and anarchists, whom the authorities had charged with complicity in the revolt. The more fortunate were permitted to emigrate, but thousands were swept up in the Cheka dragnet and banished to the far north, Siberia, and Central Asia. By the end of the year the active remnants of political opposition had been silenced or driven underground, and the consolidation of one-party rule was all but complete.[102]

This is why Berkman and Goldman left the Soviet Union in 1921 with complete loathing. Her memoir of her time there was split by her publisher into two books, given the titles of *My Disillusionment in Russia* (1923) and *My Further Disillusionment in Russia* (1924). Berkman's *The Bolshevik Myth* came out the following year. The two never stopped speaking about what they had seen firsthand in Russia, warning the rest of the world of the horrors that the Russian citizenry were enduring.

The Bolsheviks often invoked mercilessness and ruthlessness in furthering their aims, and Goldman did not at all hold back when it came to spelling out exactly what she saw and exactly why she so condemned it:

> As an Anarchist […] I would naturally insist on the importance of the individual and of personal liberty, but in the revolutionary period both must be subordinated to the good of the whole. Other friends point out that destruction, violence, and terrorism are inevitable factors in a revolution. As a revolutionist, they say, I cannot consistently object to the violence practised by the Bolsheviki.[103] […] The argument that destruction and terror are part of revolution I do not dispute. I know that in the past every great political and social change necessitated violence.[104]
>
> Yet it is one thing to employ violence in combat, as a means of defence. It is quite another thing to make a principle of terrorism, to institutionalize it, to assign it the most vital place in the social struggle.[105] […] The sense of justice and equality, the love of liberty and of human brotherhood—these fundamentals of the real regeneration of society—the Communist State suppressed to the point of extermination. Man's instinctive sense of equity was branded as weak sentimentality; human dignity and liberty became a bourgeois superstition; the sanctity of life, which is the very essence of social reconstruction, was condemned as unrevolutionary, almost counter-revolutionary.

> I should have been content if the Russian workers and peasants as a whole had derived essential social betterment as a result of the Bolshevik régime.[106] [...] Two years of earnest study, investigation, and research convinced me that the great benefits brought to the Russian people by Bolshevism exist only on paper, painted in glowing colours to the masses of Europe and America by efficient Bolshevik propaganda. As advertising wizards the Bolsheviki excel anything the world had ever known before. But in reality the Russian people have gained nothing from the Bolshevik experiment.[107]

"Those familiar with the real situation in Russia," Goldman also wrote, "and who are not under the mesmeric influence of the Bolshevik superstition or in the employ of the Communists will bear me out that I have given a true picture. The rest of the world will learn in due time."[108]

But the rest of the world didn't want to learn it. They often didn't even want to hear it. Nor could the Russian people know that there were still people abroad advocating for their liberties. Censorship increasingly became the norm in Russia. Books "that have become obsolete, or are of little value, and to an even greater extent, harmful and counter-revolutionary books" were forbidden—and of course it was the Bolshevik state that determined whether a book was "obsolete" or "of little value." The Russian Revolution had brought about a new, unprecedented form of government on earth. It therefore followed that books from before 1917 could all accordingly be regarded as "obsolete."[109]

Many books were burned, including the works of Descartes, Plato, Schopenhauer and virtually every other philosopher. Marx's rival Bakunin and the anarchist Kropotkin were prohibited. Leo Tolstoy's world-famous novels escaped censure, but his non-fiction works advocating Christian anarchism did not. Important books were not entirely destroyed. Kant, for example, could still be found in academic libraries, but could only be given out "under the strictest responsibility of the chief librarians."[110]

In 1924 Goldman was invited to give a dinner talk in London. A slew of left-wing influencers were there, eager to hear "Red Emma" speak. Among the varied luminaries that evening was Harold Laski, who would later become the inspiration for the villain of Ayn Rand's *The Fountainhead*. Goldman opened her speech to wild applause. "I have rarely had a more attentive audience until I mentioned Russia," she recounted. "Shifting of chairs, turning of necks, and disapproval on the faces before me were the first indications that all was not going to be so harmonious as it seemed at first."[111] Goldman did not mince words in the slightest: "To call the present Soviet Government a workers' experiment is the most preposterous lie ever told. The time has come when silence on the Russian situation makes you a party to the crimes which are being committed there."[112]

The more she went on, the worse it got. "Some diners jumped to their feet and demanded the floor," Goldman recalled. "They never would have believed, they said, that the arch-rebel Emma Goldman would ally herself with the Tories against the Workers' Republic. They would not have broken bread with me had they known that I had gone back on my revolutionary past." When she finally finished what she came to say a person could have heard a pin drop.

Until the day she died, Emma Goldman never stopped advocating for the workers of Russia, and for the workers all around the world. She never stopped fighting for the common man who dared stand up against the state. "The fact is that the Communists are the forerunners of fascism," she wrote in 1933. "Neither Mussolini nor Hitler have made a single original step. All they had to do is follow and copy faithfully the steps taken by Lenin and Stalin."

For many at the time, this was regarded as an absurdity. The fascists and the communists despised each other, fighting in the streets on sight. Their respective strategies were strongly based on the need to defeat that opposing worldview. What could the two possibly have in common?

Chapter 4

UNDERSTAND IT IS TOTALLY INHUMAN

Vladimir Lenin is fairly characterized as a fanatic and an ideologue. But Lenin indisputably had a pragmatic side as well, and consistently adjusted strategy to obtain results that he wanted. It might be cruel to point out that the sailors of Kronstadt died for nothing. Yet simultaneously with their massacre and complete defeat came an utter U-turn in Bolshevik planning. It was time for what Lenin called a "New Economic Policy," or NEP for short.

Gone were the utopian attempts to move toward a money-free society, where everything would be rationed equally by the state. Instead of grain being requisitioned by the government, producers would now pay a tax in kind. Peasants were once again permitted to dispose of their surplus as they wished, reintroducing an element of production for profit. Public services were no longer free, and attempts were made to encourage foreign investment. Big business, just like banking, remained strictly under government control. But small businesses were allowed to develop—and not only did they develop, but they quickly thrived. The biggest surprise was the relegalization of hiring labor, a direct contradiction of communist principles of equality and a reintroduction of elements of class warfare. As a result of this a whole new population of "nepmen" developed, men who quickly gained wealth as small-scale producers.

To communist ears all this sounded suspiciously like a return to capitalism, and Lenin admitted as much by referring to this strategic retreat as "State capitalism." To the true believers this was both utter madness and a complete betrayal. They had fought—and won—a civil war against the forces of the czar and the united opposition of nations abroad. Many had starved and everyone had suffered in an effort to recreate society and bring about a new form of country, if not a new form of humanity.

In a sense Lenin defeated the forces of Menshevism by adopting their ideas and practicing them. The Mensheviks had argued for years that the road to socialism had to be built slowly and cautiously, otherwise the inevitable errors in central planning would cost many people their lives. Now, acknowledging this indisputable realization bore the strictest penalty: death. Refusing to acknowledge that his rivals had been right all along, Lenin threatened them with the harshest of penalties if they tried to point out that they had been correct in their perspective, telling them that "if you don't refrain from openly enunciating such views, you will be put against the wall, for if you insist upon airing your political views under the present circumstances when we are finding ourselves in an even more difficult situation then at the time of the white-guardist invasion, we shall have to treat you as the worst and most harmful white-guardist elements."[113]

As he further put it:

> When certain people, who may even be guided by the best possible motives, begin to sow panic just at the time when we are carrying out a retreat beset with vast difficulties, at a time when it is vitally important to retain good order in retreating, it is necessary to punish severely, ruthlessly, the slightest violation of discipline.[114]

Rather than spreading the workers' revolution abroad and throughout the world, in 1921 Lenin now turned to the Western liberal democracies for help. And through a quirk of history, the man who Lenin turned to to save his fledging nation from mass starvation and poverty was none other than the American named Herbert Hoover.

In an 1893 speech in New York's Union Square, Emma Goldman had urged the hungry poor to "demonstrate before the palaces of the rich; demand work. If they do not give you work, demand bread. If they deny you both, take bread." Without the capitalists growing rich on the backs of the workers, the argument went, there would be plenty of food for everyone. Yet the capitalists were crushed in Russia, and there remained plenty of hunger for everyone.

In 1914, Herbert Hoover had been a businessman living in London who he had gotten involved with a very peculiar crisis. Belgium was under German occupation, with the food produced there being largely requisitioned for the German army. Great Britain, on the other hand, had imposed an economic blockade on German territory to make sure no aid reached her opponents. Hoover, via his Commission for Relief in Belgium, managed to negotiate with both warring sides in order to keep the Belgian population from starving.

Hoover's monumental achievement caught the attention of people the world over. In 1917 the Federal government set up the United States Food Administration to manage the supply and distribution of food throughout the United States, both to make sure everyone (especially everyone in the armed forces) would have access to food, but also to make sure that wartime hoarding and profiteering would be eliminated or, at the very least, kept to a minimum. Given his success in feeding Belgium, President Wilson naturally tasked Herbert Hoover with running the organization.

Though his name later became synonymous with Republican apathy, it was Hoover who was utterly apathetic about publicly joining the GOP in 1920. "The Great Engineer" did so only because he saw the Republicans' electoral prospects were brighter that year than the Democrats' were. Even a fool could see that 1920 would be a watershed year for the Republicans, and though Hoover was many things a fool was not one of them. After recapturing the Senate in 1918 the Republicans picked up an additional ten seats in 1920, winning every single contest outside of the Solid South. The House results were even more lopsided, with the GOP solidifying control of the chamber 303 to 131. The crown jewel was the White House, and the electoral result was a complete bloodbath.

The year 1920 had started with Assistant Secretary of the Navy Franklin Roosevelt writing to a colleague that, "I have had some nice talks with Herbert Hoover before he went west for Christmas. He is certainly a wonder and I wish we could make him President of the United States. There could not be a better one."[115] Months later—and despite some feelers from the stroked-out incumbent sitting in the Oval Office—the Democrats nominated Ohio Governor James M. Cox on the 44th ballot, with FDR as his running mate. Opposing him was sitting United States Ohio Senator Warren G. Harding. It was then quite unusual for a senator to be nominated for the presidency, and no one had ever been elected to the White House directly from the Senate before. Harding ended up winning the election 60%-34%, a bigger popular vote landslide than Teddy Roosevelt's in 1904 and the biggest since James Monroe ran basically unopposed for reelection in 1820.

Harding appointed Hoover as Secretary of Commerce but allowed him to maintain his role as program director of the American Relief Administration, the successor to his United States Food Administration. Now, however, the organization was tasked with feeding the starving nations of wartorn Europe. Hoover had previously attempted to help feed Russia in 1919, but Lenin knew that foreign aid invariably came with a price and refused what he regarded as foreign meddling in Russia's affairs.

As a young man Lenin had witnessed the effects of famine firsthand. In 1891 a combination of a dry autumn and a brutally cold winter caused the death of many seedlings in Russia. Those that remained were blown away by an unusually windy spring in 1892.[116] Hundreds of thousands of people starved to death, and the hated czar was held to blame. Now history was repeating itself, in the exact same areas, only this time it was Lenin who reigned over a Mother Russia unable to feed her children.

At first Lenin refused to acknowledge that there was a problem, and he even forbade the media from using the words "famine" and "starvation."[117] But banning the discussion of starvation did nothing to alleviate hunger, and despite unofficial scattered relief efforts the problem only increased. Russians headed to their train stations in hopes of receiving food—or being able to go to where some food was—but the gatherings turned to scenes of utter inhumanity. Starvation is a very curious thing, for before starvation consumes an individual they often engage in ways completely incomprehensible in better times.

Lenin's hometown was Simbirsk, and that is where one aid worker saw the unimaginable:

> Nursing babies have lost their voices and are no longer able to cry. Every day more than twenty dead are carried away, but it is not possible to remove all of them. Sometimes corpses remain among the living for more than five days…A woman tries to soothe a small child lying in her lap. The child cries…For some time the mother goes on rocking it in her arms. Then suddenly she strikes it. The child screams anew. This seems to drive the woman mad. She begins to beat it furiously, her face distorted with rage. She rains blows with her fist on its little face, on its head, and at last she throws it upon the floor and kicks it with her foot. A murmur of horror rises around her. The child is lifted from the ground, curses are hurled at the mother, who, after her furious excitement has subsided, has again become herself, utterly indifferent to everything around her. Her eyes are fixed, but are apparently sightless.[118]

By 1921 Lenin's political position was far more secure than in 1919. Yes, accepting aid from the United States would be humiliating, and yes, it would be thrown in his face as evidence of the failure of communism to feed the people. Yet it was precisely Lenin's fanatical ideology that permitted him to engage in public acts of great humility. It was the Revolution and the people that mattered far more than him. While at first insisting that "one must punish Hoover, one must publicly slap his face so the whole world sees" (how dare he try to keep millions from starving!), by the summer of 1921 Lenin was persuaded to accept help from abroad. He would only do so with a major caveat, left unstated publicly. For Lenin, "the main thing is to identify and mobilize the maximum number of Communists who know English to introduce them into the Hoover Commission and for other forms of surveillance."[119] If the Americans were up to something, Lenin would know.

If anyone should have been suspicious, it was Herbert Hoover and his team. Eventually they had to pull out of their relief efforts after discovering the Bolsheviks were simply taking the grain and selling it for export. The rebellions in towns rife with starvation throughout the country were put down with complete mercilessness, with more than one village being razed and all its inhabitants slaughtered. At least one million people died, and almost certainly far more. But all this terror and suffering was a mere practice run for what was to come in the following decade.

On the morning of May 26, 1922, Lenin got out of bed in a very ill state. His doctor was summoned and immediately knew what had happened: although he was only fifty-two years of age, Vladimir Lenin had had a stroke. Though not in particular danger physically, the mental consequences were far more worrying to the Bolshevik leader. Lenin now had trouble walking and moving his arm. He also found himself unable to write, and even basic multiplication became too much for Lenin to handle.[120] Recalling the suicide pact that Karl Marx's son-in-law had made—and fulfilled—with his wife in 1911, Lenin asked his own wife to deliver him cyanide. Unable to go through with it, the couple instead decided to send for one man who they felt certain was cold-blooded enough to go through with helping Lenin kill himself: Joseph Stalin.

The man who became known as Joseph Stalin was born as Iosif Dzhugashvili in what is now the country of Georgia in 1870. For various legal and cultural reasons, many of the revolutionary Bolsheviks had to operate under pseudonyms at the time. Fake names allowed them to write articles without fear of getting caught, and to travel internationally without detection. Lenin himself was born as Vladimir Ilyich Ulyanov, for example. Leon Trotsky was Lev Bronstein, which allowed him to marginally obscure his Jewish roots—a major issue in violently anti-Semitic Russia. So did the name Stalin serve to make Dzhugashvili seem more Russian. Not only that but he sounded downright heroic, as Stalin translated to "Man of Steel."

Yet despite the heroic moniker, Stalin's actions in joining the early Bolshevik party were unambiguously villainous. As Soviet historian Roy Medvedev recounted Stalin's early revolutionary activities:

> To Stalin belongs the dubious honor not only of participating in but organizing several major terrorist acts—or as they were then called, "expropriations" ("exes" for short). These consisted mainly of armed robberies of banks, mail coaches, and steamships. The Bolsheviks considered such actions permissible at the time as a means of replenishing the party treasury, buying weapons, and making an impact on the tsarist administration. Especially famous was the [1907] robbery of the Tiflis State Bank, which brought more than three hundred thousand rubles into the Bolshevik coffers. This "ex" was carried out by a group of fighters including Kamo ([the alias of] S.A. Ter-Petrosyan), but Stalin and Leonid Krasin organized and planned the operation. [...] The organization of such actions required of Stalin not only cold-bloodedness, craftiness, and ruthlessness but also links with the criminal world of Georgia. Many acts of expropriation were accompanied by human losses, but these were killings "in the interest of the cause."[121]

By 1920 Stalin managed to hold a good amount of power within the Bolshevik Party, having had various roles over the years including editing the prominent journal *Pravda* (Russian for "Truth.") But Stalin was nowhere as influential as, say, Trotsky had been when it came to the development of Marxist ideology, especially as applied to the Russian

Revolution. Trotsky knew very well how brilliant and important he was, and this had the inevitable consequence of rubbing many Party members the wrong way. Stalin kept somewhat to the background and worked Party members in order to build personal support.

Per his wishes, Stalin did come visit the stroke-ridden Lenin, and he apparently promised to put Lenin out of his misery if things ever reached that point. But Stalin also managed to convince Lenin that suicide would be premature. No one doubted that Lenin was a fighter, and now he fought hard to regain his faculties. Yet even the great Vladimir Lenin could only do so much, and that December saw Lenin fall victim to two minor strokes followed by another major one. Lenin would never write another word until the day that he died.

Lenin again sent word to Stalin pleading to be put out of his misery—one can only imagine how awkward taking the dying Lenin's dictation must have been—but Stalin again refused. Soviet Russia had been Lenin's vision, and he had been the driving force of remaking the country in line with the edicts of Marxist dialectical materialism. But now that he was incapacitated, there arose the question of who should replace the man who even his enemies admitted was entirely unique and irreplaceable.

Lenin's incapacitation led to a major change in Soviet history. He had subscribed to the idea of a worldwide workers' revolution, country by country. Stalin, on the other hand, envisioned a Union of Soviet Socialist Republics—a country where formerly independent states would be subsumed under one new nation, heavily centralized in Moscow. For Lenin and many others—especially the Ukrainians and Stalin's native Georgians—this was unconscionable and hearkened back to Russian nationalism of the worst kind. In a sense both men got their way. The USSR was proclaimed on December 28, 1922, including delegates from Ukraine, Belorussia and Transcaucasia in addition to Russia herself. On paper the various republics still had a great deal of autonomy. But this would quickly fall away, and control increasingly took place within Moscow.

As Lenin recuperated, the Soviet Union was run by a troika consisting of Stalin, Lev Kamanev and Grigory Zinoviev. Stalin took control of Lenin's living arrangements when his health reached a point of no return. The man he trusted with his death Lenin now had no choice but to trust with his life. Stalin strictly controlled who could visit and what sort of correspondence would go in—or out. He wouldn't have been able to do these things to Lenin if Lenin weren't stuck in a wheelchair. But Lenin was. He was in that chair, and he was effectively Stalin's prisoner with no recourse or means of reaching the outside world. It was on January 21, 1924, that Vladimir Lenin took his last breath without needing Stalin's assistance at all. His faculties at the end were a mere shadow of those which had completely rewritten world history less than a decade prior.

This left the Soviet Union at a crossroads. Would it continue the vision as a beacon of hope around the earth, inspiring revolution within one nation after another? Or would the focus become more internal? Stalin strongly favored the latter view, campaigning on a vision of "socialism in one country." On the other side—far more in line with the ideas of Marx and Lenin—remained Leon Trotsky and his followers.

As is so often the case, an argument over philosophy served as a convenient pretext to obscure a raw power struggle. Kamanev and Zinoviev continued to side with Stalin against Trotsky, and slowly but surely the Bolshevik visionary was driven from his seats of power without Lenin to protect him. Nor did Trotsky have an enormous amount of support within the Communist Party itself: the man who understood Marxist politics perhaps better than anyone alive had a fairly poor appreciation for party politics. Niceties and schmoozing were not his forte, to put it mildly, and it cost him dearly (though if he were more of a raw politician and less of an ideologue he would not have been Trotsky to begin with).

By 1927 Stalin succeeded in expelling Trotsky from the Communist Party, and by early 1928 he was expelled from the Soviet Union itself. Trotsky was no longer welcome in the very country he had been instrumental in creating. He settled at first in Turkey, as Stalin further consolidated power and plotted to eliminate his one-time rival from the face of the earth. For his part, the loquacious Trotsky had no shortage of thoughts about how the Revolution was betrayed, and why things in the Soviet Union seemed to have gone so horribly wrong.

Life remained difficult in the USSR for years after the Russian Civil War had been won by the Bolsheviks. Housing became even more of a concern as rural citizens flocked to the rapidly industrializing cities in search of work and food. Families became crammed into apartments that had already been occupied by other families, and both eviction and trying to find a new place to live effectively became impossible. Some of this was by design in keeping with communist ideology: The ultimate vision was to have homes without kitchens so that everyone would eat communally in government-run cafeterias. True-believer communist architects designed buildings where everyone would have to share bathrooms as well, as part of an assault on bourgeois concepts such as shame, privacy and individualism.[122]

This created an enormous incentive for families to turn in those living with them to the authorities for the most specious of reasons, if not downright lies. One phone call and the living quarters for one's family instantly doubled. What's the harm? If they weren't guilty of one thing then surely they were guilty of another. And if they hadn't done anything, then they would have nothing to fear from the Tcheka, right? This became such a commonplace occurrence that it was even joked about in popular magazines of the time: "Just think, Masha, how unpleasant. I wrote a denunciation on Galkin and it turns out that Balkin has the bigger room."[123]

As bad as housing was, the food issue was even worse. In part this was due to the difficulties of production and distribution. But in part this was also by design, and Stalin's war on Ukraine remains one of the most horrific episodes in twentieth-century history. It all began with the first Five-Year Plan in 1928, a reversal of Lenin's NEP policies and a return to a socialist, planned approach to the economy. Part of this plan was an increased focus on collectivization of the farmland. Instead of farmers being allowed to work their own land and hand over some of what they produced to the state, the goal was to combine plots into giant enterprises under government control.

The theory was that collectivized farms would be more efficient and productive. This would allow for more grain to be exported, which in turn could be used to finance greater industrialization in the rest of the Soviet Union. The main opponents to this plan were the larger and wealthier farmers known as the kulaks. The "liquidation of the kulaks" was the plan to shatter their place in society—and the primary target of this "liquidation" was the Ukraine, invariably described as "the breadbasket of Europe" due to its fertile lands.

The kulaks themselves were treated in one of several ways. Those most dangerous to the state received prison sentences or were even executed. Some were deported deep into the Soviet Union, with almost two million people being moved in the years 1930-1 alone.[124] Others were simply kicked off their land and out of their native villages. Anyone opposing such moves was invariably regarded as either a kulak themselves or a kulak sympathizer, which was little better.

Yet being reduced to serfs of the state was a bridge too far, not just for the kulaks but for much of the peasantry. It was too reminiscent of those worst aspects of czarism that they had bitterly fought against for decades. As the amount of grain demanded by the Bolsheviks increased, so did the defiance of the farmers. Land was abandoned. Farm animals were slaughtered for meat and hides rather than being handed over to the government with nothing to show for it. Some state officials were met with violence, and riots occurred several times as peasants were forced to hand over the fruits of their labor.

The concept was that under socialism, without either the kulaks to exploit the peasants or the capitalist class to seize unearned value in the form of profits, every year would see increases in production. This might perhaps make some sense in a factory setting, as workers better learned the necessities of their roles and figured out ways to produce more efficiently. When it came to agriculture this was virtually impossible, since so much of production was dependent on the changing weather.

The year 1930 had been a very favorable one for crops, while the year 1931 had far worse conditions. Nevertheless the government quotas remained the same. This was close to an impossibility but the dekulakization only made it worse. By eliminating so many who had managed the larger farms, the Bolsheviks had thereby also eliminated a great deal of technical farming expertise. Collectivized farm animals had no one personally responsible for them, and little to feed them with besides. The newfound state serfdom resulted in work slowdowns and stoppages as an ongoing form of protest. Not only was no one working, but the Communist Party of Ukraine had to admit that many of the workers weren't even getting paid.

Official Soviet figures admitted that the harvest requisitions had fallen from 7.7 million tons from the total 1930 harvest of 23.9 million tons, to 7.2 million tons from the 1931 harvest of 18.3 million tons.[125] Hungry peasants had no choice but to consume the grain they would have otherwise saved for the following year, which already guaranteed that the 1932 harvest would be a disaster. To make matters worse, much of the grain that was requisitioned was being exported instead of being used to feed the Soviet citizenry.

In the summer of 1932 an edict came from on high. Reaffirming that public property is "the basis of the Soviet system," it therefore somewhat logically followed that "those attempting to steal public property must be considered enemies of the people." It concluded by legally equating stored grain as state property—and proclaiming that those who stole this newfound "state property" receive as a punitive measure "the highest measure of social defense: execution."[126] The law left some leeway, allowing for a prison sentence of "no fewer than ten years." In capitalist America, Emma Goldman had urged the hungry workers to take food. In Soviet Russia, hunger now became grounds for the death penalty.

December 1932 saw the reintroduction of another despised law. One of the frequent criticisms of socialists against the czar was the internal passport system, used to keep track of who went where in Russia. Starvation was now causing even more people to flee from the countryside to the cities, leaving fewer behind to work the land and further perpetuating the problem. Stalin revived internal passports, which allowed for more efficient deportation of both individuals and populations—as well as de facto trapping people in the villages where they were. Travel within the Soviet Union became a matter of permission, not a right—but it also became a punishment.[127]

As historian S. J. Taylor wrote:

> Victims about to be deported were stripped of their shoes, and their clothes were taken and given to lower peasants as

> a bribe to ensure their cooperation. Kulak children were left as beggars on the street. [...] Those transported to Siberia faced insuperable hardship. If a village existed, they were squeezed into it. Otherwise, they were simply abandoned without shelter in extreme cold and ordered to build dwellings. Many managed to do so by working almost around the clock, without sleep, in order that they and the others would not freeze to death. Those employed as forced labor in mining regions faced starvation rations of one bowl of thin gruel a day and eight to ten ounces of bread. They died in waves, their numbers replenished by the arrival of new deportees.[128]

The passport system was reintroduced alongside a program of urban registration. The passports included name, age, sex, nationality—and social position. Only approved persons were allowed to reside within cities. When the secret police registered everyone, they made it a point to expel any kulaks or those who were otherwise disenfranchised. This created an enormous incentive for people to renounce their class origins or other affiliations, though often to little avail.

Like something out of Exodus, government-approved activists descended onto the Ukraine's villages like a biblical plague in the winter of 1932-33. Everything that was edible they were to take, and they were given special tools to make sure that every nook in every home could be searched for the slightest crust of bread or grain of wheat. Even a corncob being dried out in order to harvest the seeds for planting in the spring was fair game.

As historian Anne Applebaum recounts:

> The activists also had instructions to return, to surprise people in order to catch them unaware and with their food unguarded. In many places the brigades came more than once. Families were searched, and then searched again to make sure that nothing remained. "They came three times,"

> one woman remembered, "until there was nothing left. Then they stopped coming." Brigades sometimes arrived at different times of day or night, determined to catch whoever had food red-handed. If it happened that a family was eating a meagre dinner, the activists sometimes took bread off the table. If it happened that soup was cooking, they pulled it off the stove and tossed out the contents. Then they demanded to know how it was possible the family still had something to put in the soup.[129]

Not only was there no place to hide food, but there was little possibility to hide having *had* any food. Anything other than increasing gauntness was an indication that a person was, somehow, providing for themselves. One glance at a face told the activists everything they needed to know. If a person somehow managed to find and conceal food, that only forestalled the inevitable. Their own body would betray them. Starvation was not simply a consequence: it was the goal, and it was the law. Stalin intended to break the Ukrainians once and for all.

It thus became common for villagers to spy and inform on one another. Turning in a neighbor for having a sack of grain might be the easiest and safest way to procure food for one's family. Not only was there a guarantee of a meal, but there was also now a guarantee that said meal wouldn't be seized by the requisitioners. Further, those who could not produce a quota of grain were subject to a fine of five times the value of what the grain would have been—yet another reason to seize property and savings. Not having the food to fulfill one's quota was taken as evidence—if not downright proof—that one must have been hiding it. And if the food was being hidden, then why wasn't it being handed over?

Many of the tactics could only be explained by pure sadism. In some villages the requisitioners went from house to house killing all the dogs—and taking their bodies with them for good measure. Fingers would be slammed in doorways, or needles jammed under fingernails. Those found concealing food "were robbed of their remaining possessions, evicted from their homes, and thrown into the snow without any clothes."[130] To ensure that the starving peasants did not somehow steal the food that they so desperately needed, fields and barns were kept under armed guard. The activists even came for the tools used for making food, breaking millstones necessary to process grain. If they took soup from a hungry family, they made sure to take the pot as well.

The Soviet media accordingly began a campaign portraying the kulaks as illiterate, selfish, subhuman hicks. If you were hungry—and everyone was hungry—it's because the greedy kulaks were hoarding food. After all, everyone knew that the Ukraine was the breadbasket of Europe. It is little surprise that those few who managed to make their way to the cities, destitute and barely clothed, were therefore often treated with unmitigated contempt and as worse than animals. As one Soviet citizen later recalled:

> One day, as I waited in a queue in front of the store to buy bread, I saw a farm girl of about 15 years of age, in rags, and with starvation looking out of her eyes. She stretched her hand out to everyone who bought bread, asking for a few crumbs. At last she reached the storekeeper. This man must have been some newly arrived stranger who either could not, or would not, speak Ukrainian. He began to berate her, said she was too lazy to work on the farm, and hit her outstretched hand with the blunt edge of a knife blade. The girl fell down and lost a crumb of bread she was holding in the other hand. Then the storekeeper stepped closer, kicked the girl and roared: "Get up! Go home and get to work!" The girl groaned, stretched out and died. Some in the queue began to weep.[131]

Even basic human sympathy was grounds for suspicion, which was then grounds for arrest and the most serious legal consequences. "Some are getting too sentimental here," the storekeeper announced to the crowd. "It is easy to spot enemies of the people." Everyone on that line would have known what he meant by those words, and what danger they would have put themselves in if they had fed the starving teen. As one 1934 Soviet novel later put it regarding the kulaks, "Not one of them was guilty of anything; but they belonged to a class that was guilty of everything."[132]

Pregnant women trying to steal food were beaten to death, with their remaining children invariably starving. Children who tried to feed themselves were shot as well. Digging mass graves became grueling work, and barely-living kids and the elderly were tossed alongside the dead in order to save the extra trips. Their last hours on earth would be spent slowly dying, surrounded by the corpses of their countrymen.[133]

While a kulak had originally meant a small-time farmer, such kulaks had only accounted for no more than five percent of the population. Simply having three cows and twenty-five acres was enough to brand one as a kulak. But the system in place to identify the kulaks created the most malevolent of incentives. "It was so easy to do a man in," recalled one Ukrainian writer. "You wrote a denunciation, you did not even have to sign it. All you had to say was that he had paid people to work for him as hired hands, or that he had owned three cows."[134] Worse, the poorest could do little to defend themselves, while the wealthier residents could afford to bribe their way out of baseless accusations.

The interconnectedness of economics led to a ripple effect throughout the economy. The mass slaughter of farm animals led to an acute leather shortage. As a result, making shoes on an individual level became a felony in order to force everyone to have to get their shoes from the government—which often fell apart immediately.[135]

It is easy to see why the Russian population at large was oblivious to what was being done to the rural Ukrainians, and how they could be led to regard them as the villains instead of the victims—especially after centuries of rivalry or outright animosity between the two peoples. The dishonesty of the Soviet press can be seen through a typical *anekdot*, which was the Russian method of using humorous stories to state otherwise-unspeakable truths:

> One day Soviet President Mikhail Kalinin was in Moscow making a speech about how much the country had

> improved. He got particularly excited discussing the new twenty-story skyscrapers on Karl Marx Street in Kharkov.
>
> A worker in the audience quietly stood up to protest. "Comrade Kalinin, I live in Kharkov. Almost every day I take a long walk on Karl Marx Street. I haven't seen any skyscrapers."
>
> "That's the trouble with you!" barked Kalinin. "You waste your time promenading, instead of reading the newspapers and learning what is going on in the country!"

As for the rest of the world, their mechanism for learning about what was happening abroad was a function of what they read in their own newspapers. They had little other choice but to trust the media to uncover the truth and to keep them informed. This the media did not do. As Hitler prepared to seize power in Germany for the first time, the Western papers did pretty much all they could to deny and obscure Stalin's starvation of millions.

Journalists working in the Soviet Union were in a very tricky position. The entire state edifice was organized against them being able to report honestly and fairly on the situation within the socialist country. Their housing and accommodations were a function of the state, which could be revoked overnight without explanation at any time. Their internal communications would be monitored—and they themselves were often followed around as well. Worse, any story that they filed had to make its way past the Russian censors, whose job it was to make sure that the Soviet position was represented abroad in the best possible light.

The tricks the censors could use were infinite. A reporter on deadline might as well bang his head against the wall when up against a faceless gigantic bureaucracy. A censor could easily claim (sometimes even honestly) that he needed approval from his supervisors before allowing a story to be released—supervisors who did not feel the slightest bit of pressure or inclination to approve a story, and whose names and contact information would not be available to the frantic journalist. The pressure on the censors from their supervisors was similarly quite intense. One negative story in the Western media, and it would quickly become clear who it was that let such an article out of the country for publication.

The mechanics of bureaucracy meant that what could easily pass muster one week would be regarded as completely beyond the pale the next. Sometimes this would be a function of the Party line changing; today's Hero of the Revolution would be tomorrow's enemy of the people. But other times it would come down to simple mindgames. Any given reporter was constantly aware that he was there at the discretion of the Soviet Union and that it would do well for him to err on the side of caution when it came time to report on what he saw and heard.

There was thus an enormous incentive for Western journalists to write stories sympathetic to the Soviet point of view. In addition, there were very many Western journalists who genuinely *were* sympathetic to the Soviet point of view. A country built on equality, where everyone is provided for, where hunger and poverty were abolished, certainly sounded like a noble goal irrespective of what was transpiring all around.

One Russian correspondent described the mindset of his colleagues, pointing out that

> every nation has its contingent of professional interpreters of Russia who have made it their life's career to maintain appearances for the U.S.S.R. as Utopia-in-construction. With few exceptions they are a high-minded crew, coloring and concealing things with the noblest motives. Devotees of the theory of multiple truths, they speak more candidly than they write, and they think more candidly than they speak. They would as soon give the undiluted truth to their politically backward countrymen, whether readers of *The Nation* or the comic strips, as they would administer poison to children. Theirs is the logic of old-fashioned mothers who lie about sex to pubescent daughters—the American public, in their view, is simply too young, politically speaking, for the facts of Russian life. A few of them, I know, have inner qualms; the rest, on the contrary, feel

> positively heroic, strong in their ability to dispense with petty bourgeois prejudices about truth and mass brutality.[136]

When it came to coverage of the Soviet Union, first and foremost was the paper of record: the *New York Times*. The *Times'* man in Moscow was a reporter named Walter Duranty. There is something to be said for the fact that as a young man he was close friends with satanist Aleister Crowley, whose shaved head and declaration that "Do what thou wilt shall be the whole of the law" so shocked Victorian sensibilities. In addition to smoking opium with Crowley, Duranty began an intimate relationship with Crowley's mistress before marrying her himself.

In 1929 Duranty managed to secure an interview with the world's most sought-after subject: Stalin. His reporting from within the USSR earned him the 1932 Pulitzer Prize, journalism's highest honor. It was Duranty who in 1921 had insisted that "In a country rotten with corruption the communists are honest."[137] In 1923, after Lenin's famine that also killed millions, Duranty wrote that "Lenin has often been called the 'Red dictator.' This designation is wrong; Lenin never had the right to dictate, although in practice his opinion generally carried the day."[138] Lenin earned his position because of his greatness, insisted Duranty: "The secret of Lenin's authority, which did in fact amount to dictatorship, was that long experience had proved him right far oftener than his colleagues."[139]

Duranty also downplayed the mass terror unleashed by Lenin's secret police:

> In point of fact, it is doubtful whether the total number of Cheka executions throughout the whole period up to 1922 surpasses 50,000. I once asked a group of bitterly anti-Bolshevik Englishmen, most of whom were in Russia when the revolution occurred, in which all lost dear friends or property, what they estimated the total Cheka executions at. No one put the figure higher than a hundred thousand for the whole country. The majority placed it much lower. One,

> quoting as an analogy the French revolution, whose victims the great historian Michelet estimates at 4000—put it as low as 20,000.
>
> Though lives were cheap in Russia and the Cheka leaders pitiless in defending the revolution when in danger, they would have defeated their own object by the wholesale slaughter of workers and peasants on the scale reported abroad.[140]

In 1922 the Tcheka was briefly reorganized as the GPU. In terms Americans could understand, Duranty explained that meant that "in exceptional cases exceptional rights will be given to the detectives of search, arrest, and so forth. But beyond that, a measure of civil rights and freedom not greatly different from those enjoyed in America, France, or England is promised to Russians and foreigners alike, and I venture to say that no one who behaves himself has any more to fear from the 'Gay Pay Oo' than the average American citizen has from the Department of Justice."[141] After all, "Stalin is anything but remote or autocratic in method."[142]

In 1932 and 1933, the *New York Times* was denying that the Soviet government was targeting the Ukrainian rural population with terror and genocide, just as less than a decade later it would obscure the news that Hitler was targeting German Jews.[143] Duranty covered it up from the very beginning, explicitly telling readers in November of 1932 "[t]here is no famine or actual starvation, nor is there likely to be."[144]

Sometimes his choice of words was quite telling. "It is a mistake to exaggerate the gravity of the situation," he continued. "The Russians have tightened their belts before to a far greater extent than is likely to be needed this winter." But Russians, just as with any other group of humans, only have to "tighten their belts" when they are losing weight. In the West this is sometimes due to a change of diet or exercise. In Soviet Russia in 1932 it most certainly was not.

Over the following days Duranty went on to report that "the food shortage is insignificant as compared with conditions in 1920"[145] and that the Bolsheviks "are simply trying to introduce a new form of farming which they believe to be better and more efficient, not only for the peasants but for the nation as a whole."[146] As people went insane from hunger and were driven to, in some cases, eat their own children, *New York Times* readers could rest assured this was simply a new form of farming.

Of course, it was possible that Duranty was simply naïve. Maybe he was being played by Stalin's forces to repeat what they wanted, right? Well no, the *New York Times* reporter went out of his way to reassure American audiences that this was not the case. He let them know that "I have just completed a 200-mile auto trip through the heart of the Ukraine and can say positively that the harvest is splendid and all talk of famine now is ridiculous." Indeed, "[t]he populace, from the babies to the old folks, looks healthy and well nourished."[147] As for why so many of the peasants were traveling so far looking for food, he had an explanation: "Today the labor turnover runs to 100 percent or more per year, due partly no doubt to hard conditions and the hope of finding something better elsewhere, but even more to an ancient habit of wandering and the desire for change."[148] Duranty's readers could thereupon be happy to explain that, for Russians, searching for food was just a custom and not at all an urgent necessity in the face of death.

Duranty's message worked. There was a systemic consensus among Western journalists covering the USSR to minimize the nature and causes of the Ukrainian catastrophe. There were only a few exceptions. When the *London Times* published an unsigned article about what was going on, Duranty swiftly went on the attack:

> To the *London Times* correspondent collectivization is one of the blackest spots in his gloomy picture. He writes: "During the last two years 70,000,000 peasants have been driven from 14,000,000 holdings onto 200,000 collective farms. Those who have proved themselves successful farmers (i.e., kulaks) are hunted down, exiled to labor and timber camps in the north, massacred, and destroyed." For anyone who knows the situation here as well as the writer

> in question clearly does, this is a deliberate and ingenious perversion of fact.[149]

Not content to claim that there was no mass hunger—let alone millions more starved to death—Duranty did what he could to dissuade others from trying to uncover the truth of the matter independently. Not only did the West know everything going on, why the Russians and Ukrainians themselves knew it too! "The Soviet press has made no secret of the food shortage and its effects," lied Duranty. "There is no need of a foreign observer to tour the villages, where it commonly happens that the disgruntled or disaffected elements talk loudest while others are busy working."[150] There is something uniquely craven about a journalist telling others, explicitly, that there was "no need" to investigate areas to which travel was forbidden, for obvious reasons.

Fortunately there was one reporter who did not agree that there was "no need" of an independent observer to tour the villages, and he did exactly that. A young Brit named Gareth Jones had worked as a private secretary to Prime Minister Lloyd George before becoming a journalist. It was on the strength of his connection to the former Prime Minister that he was allowed access to the Soviet Union, in hopes of strengthening ties between the USSR and the United Kingdom. On March 10, 1933, Jones took a train from Moscow toward the Ukrainian capital of Kharkiv. Though he was just twenty-seven years old, Jones had been around the halls of power enough to know when something wasn't adding up.

Rather than disembark the train at his destination, Jones got off forty miles early and proceeded to walk through the Ukrainian countryside and see for himself just what was going on. Unlike all his other fellow journalists, Jones knew better than to accept the words of the Soviets and to be content that, whatever was happening in these forbidden areas, it couldn't be all *that* bad. This was an era where cameras were nowhere near as ubiquitous as they would be several decades later. As such, there remains virtually no photographic evidence of what Jones saw with his own eyes, and of course taking photographs of the mass starvation (which officially wasn't even happening) was completely illegal. We only have Jones' notes of what he saw and heard. As he walked through village after village, the peasants all told him the same thing: *We haven't had bread for over two months. We are doomed.*[151]

After he left the Soviet Union Jones held a press conference announcing his findings, and his articles were syndicated in various publications. The pushback was enormous and immediate. The Soviet ambassador to London ripped into Lloyd George, and George disavowed any knowledge or connection to Jones' trip. The restrictions on reporters travelling outside Moscow were tightened.

Jones had not been entirely alone. Malcolm Muggeridge had as strong of a leftist pedigree as anyone else in Great Britain. His father had been one of the founders of the Fabian Society, dedicated to gradually transforming the United Kingdom into a socialist nation via incrementalism. The Fabians were strongly interconnected with the London School of Economics, and they were instrumental in the creation of the British Labour party. Yet he too had learned something of what was going on in the Ukraine. Cleverly, Muggeridge filed his three stories via a diplomatic bag as a way to get them out of the USSR while bypassing the eyes of the censors.

The worst reactions to Jones was perhaps that of the Moscow press corps, who colluded to announce to the rest of the world that Jones was a fabulist at best if not simply a brazen liar—and taking the lead in this once again was of course Pulitzer Prize winner Walter Duranty. His thirteen-page *New York Times* article was titled "Russians Hungry, But Not Starving".[152] There was no one to defend Jones, and that's where things stood. Even Muggeridge did not stick his neck out against all his colleagues on Jones' behalf. Hitler was rattling his sabers in Berlin, and one mustn't do too much to upset his archenemy Joseph Stalin.

It is difficult to calculate lives lost when the numbers are so high, and when there is a concentrated effort by the authorities to minimize or deny that atrocities had occurred. The current historical consensus of what has become known as the Holodomor is that almost four million people starved in Ukraine alone, with over one million others in the broader Soviet Union. The media in the USSR had been boasting for several years about the booming economy, naturally leading to increased population growth. Statistically, the predicted population was expected to be 170 million in 1937. Yet when the census came in, the number came in at a far lower 162 million.[153]

Those results were never published. Publicly it was claimed that the census had been "disrupted by contemptible enemies of the people." Then came the repercussions for gathering truthful information that reflected poorly on both Stalin and the Soviet Union. The head of the census bureau was executed along with his colleagues. In Ukraine itself, the Kyiv-based editor of *Soviet Statistics* was killed, as was the head of the economics department at the Ukrainian Academy of Sciences. The replacements to all these men understood what their job was, and when they redid the census they dutifully reported a population of 170 million.[154]

Malcolm Muggeridge was asked decades later what the consequences were for him letting the world know that "[t]he famine was an organized one."[155] "Me? What happened to me?" he mused. "Oh yes. I couldn't get work."[156] Gareth Jones, on the other hand, was murdered while on location in northern China in 1935, with both his family and British Prime Minister Lloyd George believing that he had been personally targeted by his assailants for political reasons. His death came one day short of his thirtieth birthday.

In September 1957 a destitute Walter Duranty wrote to *New York Times* publisher Arthur Hays Sulzberger requesting a monthly pension for his past work. Though in the August 24, 1933 *New York Times* Duranty had claimed that "any report of a famine in Russia is today an exaggeration or malignant propaganda," by 1941 even Duranty had to admit that "I myself was lamentably wrong about the extent and gravity of the 'man-made famine' in Russia during the fight to collectivize the farms, in 1930-33. But every reporter who is worth his salt tries always to tell the truth." Whether this was a confession that Duranty was not worth his salt or another brazen lie in the service of denying the murder of millions of people is somewhat ambiguous.

Sulzberger chose not to give Duranty a pension. But despite the fact that the journalist hadn't worked at the *Times* for seventeen years—and despite the fact that Duranty had repeatedly lied about mass starvation in the "paper of record"—Sulzberger nevertheless cut Duranty a personal check for $2500[157], exactly half the average annual salary at the time.[158]

Chapter 5

THEY TRY TO LIVE A HUMAN LIFE

Despite Stalin's ability to keep the famine hidden from Western eyes, he was not able to persuade an increasingly hungry Russian citizenry that all was well. It is relatively easy to persuade a captive population that there were military victories overseas or that there was a bumper harvest domestically. It is impossible to persuade a starving citizenry that they are actually well-fed. Every week that went by, every hungry mouth, was a threat to Stalin's hold on power. Stalin understood perfectly well that he would make a great scapegoat when things went wrong. At the time, the idea that he would be considered the equal of the glorious Lenin was absurd; it in fact would be expected that Stalin would fall far short of the revolutionary genius.

Fortunately and quite naturally, Stalin found his own scapegoat in Leon Trotsky. Stalin promoted an extreme xenophobia throughout the Soviet Union, which made it easy for him to portray Trotsky as a nefarious foreign boogeyman eager to undermine the USSR despite Stalin's—and the people's—best efforts. The consequences of communicating abroad or reading foreign material became downright deadly, which heavily worked toward allowing the media to manufacture a false reality.

Decades later, there would be a Russian adage involving whomever the current Russian leader happened to be at the time. In the leader's desk were two letters from his predecessor. One day, when things got terribly bad, he took out one of the letters and read it. "Blame everything on me," his predecessor had advised. The advice worked. By claiming that the current crisis was due to his predecessor, the Russian leader once again persuaded the masses of his greatness. But it didn't last that long. A while later, crisis hit the Soviet Union again. Desperate, the leader opened up the second missive. It just said: "Sit down and write two letters."

The question of Stalin's successor was not a hypothetical one. The Bolsheviks had just experienced Lenin's passing at a mere fifty-three years of age. Stalin was a heavy smoker throughout his life, and enjoyed his liquor as much as any Russian did. By the 1930s he had already been experiencing arterial spasms and heart disturbances, enough to greatly concern his doctors.[159] January 26, 1934 saw the beginning of the two-week-long Seventeenth Communist Party Congress, and with it came talk about Stalin's successor. Stalin's health gave members cover to discuss what to do if he had to go.

The general consensus at the Congress was that his successor would be Sergei Kirov. Kirov not only received greater applause than Stalin at the event—an occurrence that would not only be impossible a few years later but perhaps literally unthinkable—but he was popular across the Party and with the Russian population at large. Even the Communist revolutionaries of the Politburo seemed not to have realized that in moving toward having a quasi-official replacement for Stalin, what they had done was to place a target directly on said replacement's back—and their own.

On the afternoon of December 1, 1934, a young man named Leonid Nikolayev entered Communist Party headquarters and waited outside Kirov's office on the third floor for him to arrive. When Kirov finally came—without his bodyguard for some reason—Nikolayev shot him in the back and killed him. The idea that such a brazen assassination could have been the work of a lone gunman was implausible, to put it mildly. The rumors within the NKVD (the current iteration of the Tcheka) immediately began to point the finger to Stalin himself, as did much of the subsequent evidence. Whether Stalin had orchestrated Kirov's murder or not, there is no question that he took advantage of the assassination to launch a terror upon the Soviet Union the likes of which the world had never seen.

Kamanev and Zinoviev had sided with Stalin against Trotsky in the triumvirate that had governed Russia during Lenin's last year. Yet the summer of 1936 saw a trial in which they and several other Old Bolsheviks confessed to conspiring with Trotsky and contributing to conditions that would lead to the killing of Stalin and the overthrow of the Revolution. Other such trials quickly followed. Men who had fought alongside Lenin when Bolshevism was still widely regarded as a utopian fantasy now publicly proclaimed that they had been working with Nazi Germany and imperialist Japan to restore capitalism to Russia. Not only was their testimony unconvincing, but so too was their affect. The fervor with which they stood up to proclaim their guilt contrasted strongly with their zombie-like demeanor.

The trials raised more questions than they answered. What made them switch sides, if they did indeed switched sides? Conversely, what could possibly be done to such hardened revolutionaries to get them to admit their betrayals? "Certainly one expects false testimony in a trial involving capital crimes," observed one American reporter. "But one expects it in the direction of self-defense."[160]

The Society of Old Bolsheviks was among the many groups targeted with mass arrest. Their collective memoirs had discussed their fellow comrades during the days of anti-czarist struggle—and Stalin's name was conspicuously absent more often than not. He had not been a major player, and they were all living eyewitnesses to that very simple fact. One by one, they began to disappear. Many were transferred to new jobs in other cities—but they never arrived.

Not content to destroy the Old Bolsheviks, Stalin took things one step further: the Association of the Former Political Exiles and Katorga Prisoners. Far before the heady days of 1917, these were the men who took the struggle to the hated czar and ended up paying the price with imprisonment. The katorga system had been a series of labor camps throughout Siberia and the Russian Far East that served the dual purpose of physically isolating prisoners from the population-at-large, while also breaking their spirits due to forced manual labor. Worse, since the environment was so inhospitable, there wouldn't be much need to enforce discipline. Not only was food barely forthcoming, but the prisoners had to work hard merely to stay alive from one day to the next. Many of these men, who had been regarded by the czar as the biggest threats to his domination, were now regarded by Stalin in the exact same way. But in this case, there would be no release of them from their imprisonment. Many were now deported to the Far East, but others simply vanished.

There is no parallel to these sorts of events in American history. Not even the consequences for the leaders of the Confederacy came close—and the case against them could easily have been made on facts which were not in dispute. It would take something like President John Adams arresting, one by one, all of the members of the Constitutional Convention. And not just arresting them, but watching Thomas Jefferson stand up and declare that he had been a closet Loyalist the entire time, and was actively working to restore King George to power over these United States.

As one journalist put it:

> Imagine, if you can, the three million Americans holding the most strategic posts of power and influence in our country being suddenly subjected to a pitiless public inquiry into their past history even unto their great-grandparents, into their political faith, private conduct, and more intimate personal foibles. Imagine this inquiry conducted under conditions which made it the duty of every neighbor and charwoman and office boy to question and accuse these upper three million. Imagine that, and you have some inkling of what took place in Russia.[161]

Key to these trials was getting the men to confess. The use of confessions served several important functions. Most obviously, confessions allowed the Soviet Union to maintain the façade of a country run honestly and objectively, not subject to the whims of whoever was the ruler at the time. Second, it allowed for plausible deniability for both those internally and abroad who were advocates of the Soviet Union. All they had to say was, "The situation was complicated, but they confessed. What else was the government supposed to do? Let them free?" Finally—and most perniciously—is that the confession of one person was extremely effective leverage against the next one. If one's close comrade confessed that both of you were plotting to assassinate Stalin, suddenly one's legal position became murky even under the best of circumstances. Better to play ball, perhaps, and cut a deal in hopes of getting off easy.

Not only did the confessions serve to implicate the defendants of their alleged crimes, they also served a further purpose: scapegoating for the ongoing and enormous economic hardships. The greater the number of men who confessed to plotting with Trotsky for every crime imaginable—and several that were objectively unimaginable—the greater Stalin looked in comparison, and the more justified the purge of society became.

As early as 1928 Stalin had famously insisted that "as we move forward, the resistance of the capitalist elements will increase [and] the class struggle will intensify". Meaning, repression and state authoritarianism in some contexts should be expected to increase, not lessen, as communism remade society. After all, "we are ousting and ruining, perhaps without noticing it ourselves, by our progress towards socialism, thousands upon thousands of small and medium capitalist industrialists. Is it possible to think that these ruined people will sit in silence, not trying to organize resistance? Of course not."[162]

The trouble for Stalin was that Trotsky hadn't been in the USSR since 1929. If he had somehow been conspiring to undermine the Soviet Union, with its tight control of foreign communications, then he had to have done so by meeting with the accused while they were out of the country. And that was precisely what the accused began to say. During his trial in August 1936, Old Bolshevik Eduard Holtzman testified as he had been instructed: "I arranged with [Trotsky's son] Sedov to be in Copenhagen within two or three days, to put up at the Hotel Bristol and meet him there."[163]

The problem with any totalitarian dictatorship is that, even if it managed to utterly control all communication within its borders (itself not a forgone conclusion), it had very little ability to control communications abroad. Rather than merely deny Holtzman's accusations, the exiled Trotsky asked the worldwide media a very simple question: under what passport name and type, if not his own, did Holtzman travel to Denmark? The Danish authorities would have had a record of his travels.

It was immensely crucial for the trial that Holtzman's testimony pass muster, because Holzman supposedly received instructions from Trotsky that he then distributed as orders to his co-defendants. But Holtzman would never be asked the question that Trotsky demanded. He and all his co-defendants were quickly sentenced to death and executed the day after. Six days later, a Danish paper broke the news that there was no way for Holtzman or anyone else to have met Trotsky at the Hotel Bristol. The hotel didn't even exist, having been demolished in 1917.

As time went on and as more and more innocent people were drawn into Stalin's Great Terror, the stories used to retroactively establish their crimes became increasingly implausible and even literally impossible. As Trotsky pointed out, "If one believes the indictment, the leadership of the economy was not in the hands of the 'genial, infallible leader,' but in the hands of an isolated man, already nine years in banishment and exile" (i.e., Trotsky himself).[164] Indeed, how could the deported Trotsky have more control over goings-on in Russia than Stalin, especially given the nature of the centrally-planned Soviet system? Trotsky seemed to almost take on a supernatural character, wherein everything that went wrong in the USSR was due not just to his views but to his direct orders from abroad.

In that vein Bolshevik leader Georgy Pyatakov went from being a fierce rival of Lenin's, to a member of the Supreme Economic Council under Stalin, to being his prisoner. Stalin's prosecutors learned their lesson from the Holtzman testimony. Pyatakov had spent time in Berlin in December 1935, and had daily conferences with various firms there. He was made to sign a confession that while abroad he had also corresponded with Trotsky, who was known to have been in Norway at the time. This was regarded as not damning enough; the idea came that he had to have met with Trotsky as well. Now came the issue as to where and when this could have happened.

The problem was that Trotsky had been staying in the Norwegian town of Veksal. For Pyatakov to get from Berlin to Oslo, drive to Veksal, have a meeting, and then return, would have taken two days at a minimum due to the trains. Further, there were enough eyewitnesses to show that Pyatakov had in fact been in Germany pretty much every day. Well, this was the 20th century. If Pyatakov couldn't have taken an imaginary, nonexistent train, then he certainly could have taken an imaginary, nonexistent plane. This Pyatakov dutifully stood up in court and testified to, that he had taken a plane near Oslo, and then drove to meet Trotsky to talk about overthrowing the Soviet government.

Just two days later, the Norwegian press exposed this too as impossible.

There was only one airfield near Oslo where Pyatakov's plane could have landed, Kjeller Aerodrome. Norway's *Afterposten* newspaper pointed out that no civil aeroplane had landed there during December 1935. Shortly thereafter came more news: no foreign plane had landed there from September 1935 through May 1, 1936 either. Weakly, the Russians issued a statement pointing out the utter non-sequitur that Kjeller Aerodrome receives planes all year round, and that "the arrival and departure of aeroplanes is possible also in winter months."[165] There was nothing else that they could say. Once again, they were caught in a blatant lie, and worse: one forced into the mouth of yet another defendant. What had been done to Pyatakov, to all these men, to get them to confess to things they didn't do and couldn't have done?

Trotsky saw an opportunity. He publicly challenged Stalin to have him extradited to the Soviet Union from Norway to face accountability as Pyatakov's accomplice. "I can prove that the story of the visit is false from beginning to end," Trotsky said, "The entire system of 'voluntary confessions' would be thoroughly discredited." He also demanded that Pyatakov's "testimony must be verified *immediately, before he is shot.*"[166] Stalin didn't take the bait. One week after Pyatakov's confession and five days after the newspaper demonstrated its impossibility, the man who had made his mark in communist history as the original First Secretary of the Communist Party of Ukraine was shot alongside twelve of his fellow defendants.

But there were more ghosts from the past that were a threat to Stalin's rule, including Lenin himself. After having had two strokes and aware that his time on earth was limited, Lenin had written what became known as his testament. The document laid out what he hoped would happen after he was gone, while warning of problems that were already brewing at the time. Lenin critiqued both Trotsky and Stalin, correctly predicting that their rivalry and opposite personalities might lead to a split within the Party. Despite Stalin's efforts to rewrite history as being Lenin's chosen heir and spiritual twin, Lenin in fact had grave misgivings about the thug known as Joseph Stalin:

> Stalin is too coarse and this defect, although quite tolerable in our midst and in dealing among us Communists, becomes intolerable in a Secretary-General. That is why I suggest that the comrades think about a way of removing Stalin from that post and appointing another man in his stead who in all other respects differs from Comrade Stalin in having only one advantage, namely, that of being more tolerant, more loyal, more polite and more considerate to the comrades, less capricious, etc.

The document was immediately suppressed in Russia when Lenin's widow released it, but the entire testament was published in Western papers in 1926. Trotsky, still hopeful of leadership at the time, publicly claimed that the testament was an untrue forgery. But it was not, and Stalin knew this perfectly well—and not only did Stalin know it, but so did Bolshevik leader Ivan Smirnov. Smirnov had demanded that the testament be put into force, and had also sided with Trotsky as part of the so-called "Left Opposition" to Stalin.

It's of course no surprise that Stalin also wanted Smirnov taken out as part of his trials. Never one to bite his tongue, Smirnov had already been imprisoned for several years by the time that the trials had come around. Of all the alibis available to a prisoner accused of conspiring against the state, Smirnov had an exceptionally good one.

The prosecutor did his best with what he had, even acknowledging the apparent—and actual—absurdity of his accusations. He claimed that "we know that while in prison Smirnov organized contacts with his Trotskyites, for a code was discovered by means of which Smirnov, while in prison, communicated with his companions outside." (As one refugee later put it: "What could he write to them: 'Aim at Stalin's head, not at his belly'?")

To westerners this might sound plausible. Our relatively liberal penal system allows for all sorts of materials to be smuggled in and out of prison, up to and including narcotics and weaponry. Communicating with the outside world is a given; even people in solitary confinement can send and receive letters. But to Russians the claims against Smirnov were a complete farce of a story. Political prisoners were often vanished without a trace, with no word to their families as to where they were sent and why. Asking too many questions was asking for trouble as well. Spouses knew perfectly well that they just as easily could have joined their partners in being condemned for decades for no real reason whatsoever. Letters to and from prisoners, when allowed, were highly scrutinized by the authorities as well. To plot from behind bars and not leave any evidence behind was simply an absurdity.

The case against Smirnov did not hold up to the thinnest scrutiny, and there wasn't even much of an attempt at making it plausible. No code was ever produced, and the prosecutor didn't even bother showing a letter that had ostensibly been encoded. Further, he didn't mention even one name of someone with whom Smirnov was allegedly conspiring—and this was at a time where there was no shortage of people being coerced into admitting that they had been in a conspiracy. To no surprise, Smirnov was convicted and executed in May of 1937.[167]

As reporter Eugene Lyons pointed out:

> For every important Bolshevik "confessing" and prostrating himself before Stalin, hundreds were disposed of in the dark, dozens took their own lives, refusing to give

> themselves to Stalin's show trials. Presumably they died defiant. The impression was manufactured that all those accused admitted guilt and saluted the master of the Kremlin. The terrifying truth is that only those willing to go through the mummery were brought to trial. Whatever the pressures employed in months and years of solitary confinement, whatever transpired in the torture chambers of the G.P.U., only those who succumbed totally were exhibited to the world. The pre-condition for exhibition was their consent to play an assigned and rehearsed role.[168]

In field after field, an official Communist Party line became a new orthodoxy from which deviation was regarded as nothing more than heresy. Even as he was on his way out of power in 1924, Trotsky was still claiming that "The party is always right" and "One cannot be right against the party."[169] On this Stalin agreed with his rival. "An Enemy of the People," he once said, "is not only one who does sabotage but one who doubts the rightness of the Party line. And there are a lot of them and we must liquidate them."[170] It was not only impermissible to be a critic but one could not even be an agnostic, let alone a skeptic. The freedom of speech and expression that had long been a promise of socialism had given way to a system where even freedom of thought was intolerable, and grounds for execution.

In the 1920s, for example, the linguist Nikolai Marr's speculative theories about language became effectively regarded as fact. His "proletarian" science (which was good linguistics, as opposed to the bad "bourgeois" linguistics) held that all the languages of the earth not only derived from one original language but from just four sounds, specifically *rosh*, *sal*, *ber*, and *yon*. Professors opposed to this nonsense were exiled, their books withdrawn from circulation, and finally arrested.[171] Meteorologists were imprisoned for failing to predict weather that would harm crops. An epidemic one year resulted in many horses losing their lives, and the vaccines offered did not work to stem the plague. Several bacteriologists were accordingly arrested.[172] Astronomers were rounded up, since some of their theories of sunspot development were decreed to be decidedly un-Marxist.[173]

The most famous example of the assault on reason was that of biologist Trofim Lysenko, who rejected Gregor Mendel's genetic theories. Marxism being strongly in favor of the nurture side of the nature/nurture debate, Lysenko thought Mendel's ideas that genes exist and that they can transmit characteristics were decidedly reactionary and, therefore, clearly must have been wrong. As a result of Lysenko's influence Soviet biology became regarded worldwide as an ideologically-driven joke, including Lysenko's claim that he managed to cross a tomato with a potato.[174] A creative mind cannot function in an environment where just thinking outside the box can have literally deadly consequences.

Under these conditions, anyone with technical expertise inevitably became a suspect when something invariably went wrong. The problem with communism is that eventually you run out of possible scapegoats for failure—at which point acknowledging or even noticing that something was wrong itself becomes a form of treason. In 1937, for example, an elderly photographer was executed after one of his apprentices turned him in for pointing out that the quality of photographic paper had been better before the Revolution (Served him right for lying!).[175]

As the kulaks were to blame for issues with food and agriculture, so too emerged a class of invisible foes responsible for problems in industry: the wreckers. Because the Soviet system was a perfect one and the ideology not just correct but *scientifically* correct, it logically followed that all industrial mistakes must be the result of sabotage by invisible, omnipresent wreckers.[176] One American engineer pointed out the obvious problem with this perspective:

> When you are over-mechanized, if you have too much machinery in a plant, especially with inexperienced people, you will have a larger percentage of breakdowns and a larger percentage of repair-costs…There were continuous minor breakdowns, mostly at the beginning, and due to poor

> material and workmanship, and later on, due to the habit which they have of forcing production too fast, inexperienced men, machinery that has not been properly tuned up to put it rapidly into operation. And even after they get started, after the machinery is tuned up, by overloading. That is characteristic of plants all over the Soviet Union and the cause of very much trouble, very many breakdowns.[177]

Such logic did not matter. Someone had to be responsible, and that "someone" was found time and time again. In 1937 the Railway Minister said that "I cannot name a single line, a single road, where there is no Trotskyite-Japanese wrecking. What is more, there's not a single branch of railway transport where such wreckers have not turned up."[178] He ordered the arrests of thousands of railway administrators and managers, an enormously costly assault on technical skill. The more communism failed to deliver on its promises of abundance and happiness, the greater the evidence that imaginary wreckers were undermining the workers' utopia.

Eventually showing up twenty minutes late to work was not just grounds for mandatory dismissal but a felony. "Losing your job was interpreted as a soft sort of treason against society," explained historian Sheila Fitzpatrick, "since everyone was supposed to be working as hard as they could on behalf of everyone else. Termination would not lead to unemployment or another position." By decree, such people "should be sent to timber camps, peat works, shoveling snow and other jobs and moreover only in places that are experiencing an acute shortage of labor."[179] In other words, given Russia's demographic distribution, only to those places that were barely inhabited.

Domestically, the Russian papers could point to trials where alleged wreckers admitted to their crimes, such as placing bombs in order to cause mines to collapse even though the charges were, in every sense of the term, incredible. As one member of the French National Federation of Miners pointed out:

> I defy any technician, however competent, to organize the systematic placing of a mine in an explosive state without the inspectors, even if they were complete idiots, perceiving it within an hour. If the service of inspection for the security of the mines at Kemerovo did not perceive this thing, it is either incompetent or non-existent. If it exists, it is even more culpable than the other accused, and since it is the mode in Moscow to shoot, its members should be the first to be shot. If it did not exist, then we were lied to about the protection of the workers' safety.[180]

The arts themselves fared even worse. Art by its nature is open to interpretation, which would itself be a crime in a system where vacillating from the officially decreed truth could be derided as counter-revolutionary or petit-bourgeois or whatever the slur of the moment happened to be. Dmitri Shostakovich was and remains one of the great composers of all time, an innovator in an era where innovation was dying in a country where innovation was suspect. On January 26, 1936, Stalin stormed out of the premiere of Shostakovich's new opera *Lady Macbeth of Mtsensk*. Two days later Shostakovich was in the far-north town of Archangel to attend some performances. There he saw the headline in *Pravda*: "Muddle Instead of Music," reviewing his newest work as "a grotesquery suited to the perverted tastes of the bourgeois." Ten days after that came a newspaper attack on one of Shostakovich's ballets, accusing him of "formalism" (a term that basically meant "heretical") and he himself "a slick and high-handed fraud." The message was clear and clearly understood by his colleagues, who took it upon themselves to denounce him publicly.

Some in the artistic community still stood up for the brilliant composer. The writer A. Lezhnev said that "I view the incident with Shostakovich as the advent of the same 'order' that burns books in Germany." Lezhnev would be the first to be tortured and shot. Theater director Vsevolod Meyerhold denounced the "angry, cruel headlines" and complained that his friend "is now in very bad shape." As for Meyerhold, Shostakovich had often stayed in his Moscow apartment. It was there that the director's wife, the actress Zinaida Raikh, was stabbed to death in the eyes, and their apartment given to an NKVD chauffeur. Mikhail Tukhachevsky, a Marshal of the Soviet Union, wrote to Stalin to defend Shostakovich. He, too, was tortured and shot, and his body dumped in a landfill. Shostakovich's librettist, Adrian Piotrovsky, was arrested and shot. A former lover of Shostakovich, the writer Galina Serebryakova, was vanished. The composer's brother-in-law, a brilliant physicist known for his research into liquid crystals; his sister Mariya; his mother-in-law; his uncle—all were arrested.[181]

Even if the man on the street felt something wasn't quite adding up, it was very difficult for him to get the full picture—especially in a culture where questioning authority could have deadly consequences for oneself and one's entire family. The newspapers were filled of boasts about enormous achievements of production and the success of heroic "Stakhanovite" workers, yet there were no clothes in the stores and no food on the shelves. Clearly there was some disconnect. Sure the papers might make mistakes or have a bias, but they couldn't realistically be filled with lies, week after week year after year. That would be a conspiracy theory of the highest order, which is obviously absurd. Only crazy people would think there was a conspiracy to control the news and what information reached the public. The only possible logical alternative was that someone must have been keeping the productive socialist bounty from reaching the people. It had to be the wreckers.

It is not that hard to convince a person that a given article is deceptive or that all the newspapers were, to some extent, fudging the truth. The papers were written by human beings, and human beings make mistakes or are blinded by their worldview. As Upton Sinclair famously said, "It is difficult to get a man to understand something, when his salary depends upon his not understanding it." Yet as fallible as humans are, one could at least count on the camera to tell the truth. A photograph was, ostensibly, an objective capture of a moment in time.

Yet even here the Soviet authorities put their hands to work with the practice of *unpersoning*. Trotsky was airbrushed out of a famous picture of him alongside Lenin in Red Square, for example. A viewer seeing the photo would logically conclude that he had misremembered things, for there was Lenin delivering his speech, by himself, in black and white. As various Communists lost favor they would be vanished from imagery and thereby from history. Pictures of groups of men that included Stalin and Lenin would be reduced to just the two of them to illustrate an alleged closeness. One notorious picture of Stalin and three of his comrades was edited to display two of them and then one and then a final iteration of Stalin standing alone. By rewriting the past—even the past in recent memory—Stalin began to rewrite the present.

Thus, as time went on, in one very specific way the communist system started to "work." As one Soviet escapee later wrote:

> The search for truth, the urge to understand the meaning of life, is wholly alien to the younger generation which has passed through the school of the Communist Youth Organization. For them, all problems have been solved; there is a standard answer to every question. The language of these intellectually impoverished young people is larded with ready-made phrases. They quote Stalin instead of thinking for themselves; they derive their opinion from *Pravda* editorials. They are arrogant and complacent, and everything that pertains to them is the greatest thing there is: their country, their power, their leader. Theirs is also the greatest misery and oppression, but they are unaware of this, for they have never known anything but Soviet life. The members of this younger generation have neither sympathy nor understanding for their elders; there is no bond between them. If anyone puts forth a thought which does not fit into the pattern laid down by Stalin, they do not argue against it, but they react with such suspicion of the other's true intentions and hidden thoughts that he quickly learns to keep his ideas to himself.[182]

Yet a regime in complete control of the media and official communications is still unable to have complete control over critical thinking. Further, all it takes is that one mind—one out of tens of millions—to ask uncomfortable questions, and from there even some trusting people start to seek responses simply due to curiosity alone. Eventually all the lies can turn the simplest person into an accountant, simply because things didn't add up. One day a Communist could be posited as the greatest hero of the Soviets—and the next he was one of the villains of all time. If he had been a villain the entire time (which was certainly possible), then at best the information being presented had been mistaken and should have been taken with a grain of salt. At worst, the media and history books were grossly unreliable—in which case mass persuasion becomes infinitely more difficult.

The Soviet Union was the biggest nation in the world, and had a large population. Within that population were enough savvy people who saw the show trials for what they were, a farce in a country where things to laugh about were increasingly becoming the exception. Graffiti started to appear on factory walls: "Down with the murderer of the leaders of the October Revolution!" This was an enormous problem for Stalin. As long as there could be conceivable alternatives to his reign, someone might choose to do something about it.

There was one group of men who knew with absolute certainty and proof what he had been up to with the show trials and what his level of involvement was. He solved it like he solved so many other of his problems: through killing. In the fall of 1936 Stalin turned his guns on the interrogators themselves. He started at the top, switching out Genrikh Yagoda with Nikolai Yezhov as People's Commissar for the Interior (i.e., head of the NKVD, the newest iteration of the secret police). Stalin could claim innocence of the entire terror, for now he had Yagoda as a convenient scapegoat to blame—just as there had been scapegoats for all of the USSR's economic and social failures. Yagoda's downfall was an interesting case of "careful what you wish for."

Yezhov brought three hundred officials with him. They were the understudies in Stalin's play of terror, and the entire main cast was about to be replaced.[183] In March 1937 Yezhov dispersed many of the main NKVD personnel, ostensibly to have them check on various regions of the Soviet Union. Separated and isolated, the men would never reach their supposed destinations. Their assistants met with the same fates. Yezhov also took control of the passport group so the agents couldn't travel abroad, and took control of the NKVD aviation squadrons so they couldn't commandeer a plane.

Then began the mass arrests of Stalin's secret police.

Some of the interrogators turned to suicide, knowing full well the privations they would certainly face under arrest—for they themselves had been the perpetrators. A few jumped to their deaths from the NKVD's office windows, in plain view, during the day, in central Moscow. There was not even the pretense of a trial for many of the others. Three thousand were executed in 1937 alone. Yagoda's judges—men who rubber-stamped the sentences of hundreds of thousands of innocent people—were also arrested en masse. "Many prisoners found considerable satisfaction in meeting their own examining judges, who had bawled the accusation of counterrevolutionary and spy at them, in prison on the same charges," wrote one survivor.[184]

For good measure Yezhov arrested Yagoda's family, exiling the man's wife, parents, sisters, nieces and nephews.[185] Yagoda himself would finally be executed at the start of 1938. The biggest crime in the Soviet Union was knowing Stalin's secrets, and the inevitable penalty for even the suspicion of such a thing was death.

In 1937 Stalin's purge reached the highest levels of the military as well, men who theoretically could have deposed Stalin in a coup. Eight leading Red Army generals were arrested, with the newspapers full of claims that they had been working for "a foreign state" (namely Nazi Germany). Within one day they were all tried and executed, with no evidence of their crimes—or even clarity as to their nature—presented either publicly or abroad. The fact that three of them were Jewish was of little relevance to the already-demented accusation. Stalin was more concerned about a hypothetical threat to him personally from his own generals than about the threat to the Soviet Union already being posed by Hitler. Losing some of the USSR's greatest elite military minds would cost many lives down the road during World War II, both in the Soviet Union itself and in Europe as a whole.[186]

Those who had owed their appointments to the eight executed generals thereby fell under suspicion. Three of the five marshals of the Red Army were arrested, as well as thirteen out of fifteen army commanders, eight out of nine admirals, fifty of fifty-seven army corps commanders, 154 out of 186 division commanders, twenty-five of twenty-eight army corps commissars, and all sixteen army commissars.[187] Positions that were filled were just as quickly removed from office as well. It took months for the mania to die down, until the top military brass was entirely staffed by men who owed their positions to Stalin.

Voicing disapproval of any of this was itself grounds for arrest. Mikhail Tukhachevsky was Marshal of the Soviet Union, the highest position in the military, when he was executed for being a German spy in 1937. When one Russian woman heard the news she commented about what a handsome man he had been. She was turned in and sentenced to ten years for "extolling an enemy of the people"—an "enemy of the people" who had been the pride and joy of the USSR mere days prior.[188]

What Stalin unleashed with his Great Terror was an assault on civil society itself. The bourgeois model is very much predicated on private individuals looking after one another to some extent, whether as neighbors or as members of a church. Yet for Stalin, any connection that was private was a threat to the common good that was the basis of socialism. The private interconnections that make up civil society were transformed from being the basis of a nation's flourishing and stability into something to fear.

Entire ethnicities within the USSR were rounded up and deported, in an effort to sever the relations between the peoples and their ancestral lands to better remake the men and women in line with communist principles. The Kuban Cossacks had been deported to Siberia in the early 1930s, with parents and children automatically separated from one another in the process. Later too were deported eight various nationalities such as the Chechens, the Ingushi and the Crimean Tartars in numbers totaling roughly 1.75 million people. The Kalmyks, a population of Mongols who practiced Buddhism, were sent to the Far East where most of them perished. Kurds, Gypsies, Koreans, Finns, and Estonians were also uprooted en masse. The Greeks were accused of conspiring to hand over part of the Ukraine to Greece; two hundred thousand of them would be deported as a consequence of this nonsensical claim.[189] Half of Kazakhstan's entire population eventually consisted of peoples exiled from other lands.[190]

One 1937 NKVD order demanded ethnic cleansing via the arrest of "all remaining Polish war prisoners from the 1920-21 Polish-Bolshevik war; all Polish refugees and emigrants to the Soviet Union; anyone who had been a member of a Polish political party; and all 'anti-Soviet activists' from Polish-speaking regions of the Soviet Union." The broad nature of the order led to the arrest of those who merely had a Polish-sounding last name.[191] The guards were instructed to "beat the Poles for all you are worth," which resulted in plenty of confessions as well as incriminations regarding other innocent people. As a result of this one NKVD order alone over one hundred thousand people were executed without trial.[192]

Jewish socialists who escaped Hitler to the Soviet Union were accused of being not just "filthy refugees" but also "Nazi spies."[193] Over half a million Jews were executed, while many others sent to prison camps. "At last the dreams of our beloved Czar Nicholas, which he was too soft to carry out, are being fulfilled," quipped one captive. "The prisons are full of Jews and Bolsheviks."[194] German, Austrian, Yugoslav, Italian, Bulgarian, Finnish, Baltic, English, and French Communists who emigrated to the USSR were all shot or imprisoned. Thousands of Polish Communists fleeing Hitler were executed just in 1937.[195] Historian Robert Conquest wrote how:

> After the defeat of the Socialist rising in Vienna in 1934, several hundred members of the Socialist defense organization Schutzbund took refuge in Russia. They were welcomed as heroes, and marched past in a body in the Red Square to applause and congratulations. By mid-1937, they had been arrested and sent to camps "almost without exception."[196]

Collecting stamps, speaking the internationalist language of Esperanto or simply having a pen pal were grounds for arrest. A veterinarian was even arrested for treating dogs that belonged to foreigners.[197] The writer Isaak Babel was arrested and shot for having met French author Andre Malraux, which meant that Babel must have been a spy. His books remain with us—as does his mugshot, taken before he was executed at the age of 45. *Pravda* and *Izvestia* were the two major periodicals in the Soviet Union; virtually their entire staffs were disappeared at one point.[198]

Not only was contact with the outside world considered virtually synonymous with spying, being a foreigner was in and of itself a mortal sin. The American Communist Party saw African-Americans as a target group to further their cause, promising them a society based on full racial equality. Despite being a hero to leftists everywhere, FDR used very little political capital to further civil rights for African-Americans. The 1935 pamphlet *The Negroes in a Soviet America* claimed that "Roosevelt's policies have had the effect of increasing the slavery of millions of Negro toilers in the South"[199] while the "methods of the N.A.A.C.P. have proved to be treacherous".[200] The argument was that "[a]mong the most important allies of the working class is the Negro people in the United States"[201] and that the "Communists fight for the right of the Black Belt territory to self-determination" (meaning the creation of a Negro Republic in "approximately the present area in which the Negroes constitute a majority of the population").

Langston Hughes, one of America's most beloved poets, fell in with the Soviets for a time, and NAACP cofounder W.E.B. DuBois ended his days as a Communist. More than a few Black Americans went to live in the Soviet Union as part of Stalin's outreach. Jamaican engineer Robert Robinson immigrated to the USSR in 1930. Years later he admitted that "Every single black I knew in the early 1930s who became a Soviet citizen disappeared from Moscow within seven years."[202]

During 1937-8, the arrests turned to members of the government itself. The People's Commissars for Heavy Industry, Finance, Agriculture, Interior Trade, Education, Military Industry, Justice (!), State Farms, Communications, and Sea and River Transport were all arrested. The Chairman of the State Bank was rounded up, as was the Secretary of the Central Executive Committee. The president of the Ukrainian Republic vanished, while Panas Lubchenko (who held a position akin to Ukrainian prime minister) was arrested and killed himself in jail. All of his deputies and virtually all the other members of the party's Central

Committee were shot, a total of 99 of the 102 members. The president of the Belorussian Republic also killed himself. Stalin had introduced a new constitution in 1936—and everyone who had worked on it were later executed as traitors.

The purges had also consisted of expelling a large percentage of lower-ranking members from the Communist Party. It had become all too apparent that even Soviet man responds to economic incentives, and that many people identified as Bolsheviks simply to further their position. By 1937 there was a concern that there were more ex-Communists than there were current members of the Party—and surely those kicked out of the Party would hardly be expected to be loyal to it now.[203]

But those were the lucky ones. That Seventeenth Congress where Kirov had been discussed as Stalin's probable successor ended in massacre. Specifically, "of the 139 members and candidates of the Central Committee who were elected at the Seventeenth Congress, 98 persons, i.e., 70 per cent, were arrested and shot (mostly in 1937-1938)." In addition, "of 1,966 delegates with either voting or advisory rights, 1,108 persons were arrested on charges of anti-revolutionary crimes, i.e., decidedly more than a majority."[204]

The fewer people one knew and interacted with, the better. Not content with turning colleagues against one another in their given fields, Stalin's campaign took on a systemic attempt to create a society where no one could trust anyone else, including husbands and wives, and parents and children—to say nothing of neighbors or coworkers or the like.

The suspicion was akin to a web, as anyone who associated with an ex-Communist (or who had previously been known to associate with them once they had been Party members) became suspect. If two untrustworthy men grabbed lunch together, who's to say that they hadn't sat there conspiring against the people? Better to be safe than sorry when dealing with disgruntled potential saboteurs.

The end result was the creation of guilt by association, but even the concept of guilt took on a radically different meaning. A person was inherently guilty if he opposed—or was opposed by—the state. That in and of itself was a crime—and not just a crime, but one for which death was often the necessary penalty. The government had no choice, because millions of lives and the entire future of mankind were supposedly at stake. Being friends with an enemy of the state was a crime for not turning them in—but being ignorant that they were an enemy of the state was a crime for not being cautious enough.

Author-philosopher Hannah Arendt explained the perverse incentives that the Great Terror unleashed into Russian society:

> Mass atomization in Soviet society was achieved by the skillful use of repeated purges which invariably precede actual group liquidation. In order to destroy all social and family ties, the purges are conducted in such a way as to threaten with the same fate the defendant and all his ordinary relations, from mere acquaintances up to his closest friends and relatives. The consequence of the simple and ingenious device of "guilt by association" is that as soon as a man is accused, his former friends are transformed immediately into his bitterest enemies; in order to save their own skins, they volunteer information and rush in with denunciations to corroborate the nonexistent evidence against him; this obviously is the only way to prove their own trustworthiness. Retrospectively, they will try to prove that their acquaintance or friendship with the accused was only a pretext for spying on him and revealing him as a saboteur, a Trotskyite, a foreign spy, or a Fascist. Merit being "gauged by the number of your denunciations of close comrades," it is obvious that the most elementary caution demands that one avoid all intimate contacts, if possible—not in order to prevent discovery of one's secret thoughts, but rather to eliminate, in the almost certain case of future trouble, all persons who might have not only an ordinary cheap interest in your denunciation but an irresistible need to bring about your ruin simply because they are in danger of their own lives. In the last analysis, it has been through the development of this device to its farthest and most

> fantastic extremes that Bolshevik rulers have succeeded in creating an atomized and individualized society the like of which we have never seen before and which events or catastrophes alone would hardly have brought about.[205]

By design, the Soviet worldview was a complete inversion of Western bourgeois individualism. "There will be some innocent victims in this fight against Fascist agents," the head of the NKVD told his officers at one point. "We are launching a major attack on the Enemy; let there be no resentment if we bump someone with an elbow. Better that ten innocent people should suffer than one spy get away. When you chop wood, chips fly."[206]

Indeed, not having anyone to inform on might itself be taken as a form of guilt. If one's neighbors were all arrested for being spies or wreckers, why did the vigilant Soviet citizen not notice? A generalized sense of paranoia was heavily inculcated by the media and current events. "A radio listener heard Chopin's Funeral March played the day Zinoviev and Kamenev were executed and wrote in to share his suspicions that it was a signal from Trotskyite conspirators," recounted Fitzpatrick.[207] Illiterate peasants were accused of being Trotskyists and went to prison asking what being a Tractorist meant.[208]

Mere "suspicion of espionage" was itself made a felony, carrying with it a sentence of eight years. What this meant in practice was explained by one prisoner:

> Every Soviet citizen is suspected of espionage if he has ever been abroad or ever associated with a foreigner. Naturally every foreigner is suspect.
>
> Association means any correspondence with relatives, friends, acquaintances or professional colleagues abroad. People who were earlier sent abroad by the state itself for study or training are suspected of espionage because of these very journeys. So are the employees of diplomatic and

> trade missions abroad. Similarly, any encounter with a foreigner inside the Soviet Union can be dangerous.[209]

The manner in which the arrests were made was not exactly conducive to calming down the population. It was always in the middle of the night when a car could be heard stopping on a street, in an era where there were very few motorists. Then would come the sound of men walking up the stairs and pounding on a door when everyone in the building was asleep. A search of the location, some evidence seized, and the suspect would be taken away. Russians joked about the relief they felt when someone knocked on their door in the middle of the night to tell them that the house was on fire.[210]

Some of the fortunate ones thought ahead to pack a bag and were allowed to bring it with them. Others were lied to about only being brought in for a "brief chat." Parents innocently vanished without saying goodbye to their children, expecting to be back momentarily. One of those arrested later described the typical experience:

> From the moment he is arrested the prisoner is kept in constant suspense. No matter what is done to him or where he is taken, he is given no explanation. This permanent uncertainty and complete helplessness in the grip of a silent, uncanny power, produces in every prisoner exactly what it is expected to produce: fear. He begins to fear every change in his condition. Perhaps it may be a change for the better—but he is afraid anyhow. And the NKVD plays with virtuoso skill upon this fear. Even when the prisoner is not called for interrogation, he is never allowed to settle down.[211]

The examinations of the accused were often invasive and humiliating. As Aleksandr Solzhenitsyn wrote, "The destructive intent of the first hours of prison is to isolate the new prisoner from his fellows, so that there is no one to offer him any encouragement, so that the weight of the whole elaborate apparatus bears down on him alone."[212] Women would be taken into an unheated staircase, stripped naked, and then ordered to lift their hands up. Then every crevice was examined in view of other people. Men were treated no better, being forced to spread their buttocks and demonstrate there was nothing under their genitals. Anything that could be used to harm others—or oneself—was confiscated. One prisoner recalled how her cellmate's "glasses had been taken away, of course, for anyone who had glass might use it to cut open her veins."[213]

It is unclear which situation was worse: the cells where the prisoners were packed shoulder to shoulder, with the room filling with the hot air of people desperate to breathe, or the cells where the prisoners were kept in complete isolation for months or even years at a time. The methods that the latter type of prisoners used to keep themselves from going insane varied from working out math problems over and over to reciting all the poetry they had ever heard to closing their eyes while walking in small circles and recalling past trips that they had taken. Some were kept in solitary confinement for so long that they lost the ability to speak, the muscles in their mouth having become atrophied due to lack of use.[214]

As for the former, their humanity was stripped from them as well as they were reduced to animals in cages:

> The whole process of the disintegration of personality took place before the eyes of everyone in the cell. A man could not hide himself here for an instant; even his bowels had to be moved on the open toilet, situated right in the room. He who wanted to weep, wept before everyone, and the feeling of shame increased his torment. He who wanted to kill himself—in the night, beneath the blanket, trying to cut the veins in his arm with his teeth—would be quickly discovered by one of the cell's insomniacs, and prevented from finishing the job.[215]

Because any private relationship was a threat to the public order, the authorities took care to make sure that the prisoners themselves didn't form bonds in their captivity. Applebaum describes one NKVD order from 1935 which explicitly forbade prisoners "to talk, shout, sing, write on the walls of the cell, leave marks or signs anywhere in the prison, stand at the windows of the cell, or attempt to communicate with those in other cells in any way."[216] Worse, the other prisoners would themselves be at risk if they noticed something but kept quiet about it. This is not even to mention the many informers throughout the prison system, who relished the opportunity to have something to report to the authorities in exchange for bettering their own personal situation.

Napping was also forbidden, so that even sleep was denied to the accused as a means of escaping their horrific reality. Strong electric lights throughout the prisons never turned off. What might seem like a waste of precious electricity made sleeping at night difficult, especially when combined with the cramped sleeping conditions and rules forbidding prisoners from covering their faces or obscuring their hands under the blankets.

Yet the interrogators themselves were also under enormous personal duress. "If some of you entertain doubts and vacillations," Yezhov told his men, "if some of you, for this or that reason, do not feel strong enough to cope with the Trotskyite-Zinovievite bandits, then let them say so and we shall release them from the investigation."[217] It was a beautiful piece of totalitarian doublespeak. The only reason someone might feel the need to show mercy to those who were plotting against the people would be some sort of sympathy with them, or some sort of squeamishness about the Party's process. Both were themselves clear grounds for arrest, and the interrogators more than anyone else knew exactly what that would entail. Getting confessions out of the accused thereby became a matter of life and death for the captors themselves. Evolutionary pressures encouraged the most evil and ruthless to succeed, since what was rewarded was not serving justice but rather getting the prisoners to confess.

Not every interrogator was driven by sadism or mindless obedience. Tales abound of those who were frustrated to the highest degree by a prisoner's intransigence. They knew perfectly well that the prisoner was telling the truth about their innocence, but they resented having to work so hard in order to get them to sign their confession. As one Communist explained it:

> The Russian Communists are absolutely impregnated, more exactly infected, with this theory of two truths: one, the real truth, for the initiates, for a small governing circle; the other, the lie truth, for the non-initiates, the great mass of the people. In its ultimate development this philosophy of two truths has led to the lie which permeates the whole social life to the point of hypocritical and lying declarations and testimony and the monstrous trials of the "penitents."[218]

People arrested for absurd reasons had little room for recourse. Conquest described how one Czech citizen "is reported as having had to confess that he became a German agent early in the First World War, at a time when neither Czechoslovakia nor the Soviet Union existed."[219] Ostensibly they could write to the authorities to set the record straight, and many wrote letter after letter to anyone and everyone, including Stalin himself. The ones who were most loyal to the Party or to Stalin personally were usually the ones who took the longest to get the picture, and it was often years before they realized that no one would be coming to their aid. The guards understood this situation, with one admitting to his captive that "we never arrest anyone who is not guilty. And even if you weren't guilty, we can't release you, because then people would say that we are picking up innocent people."[220]

Stalin was perfectly aware that many of those arrested were entirely innocent. Far from the fist-pounding dictator from Hollywood films, he loved to have a good drink and tell jokes with his comrades. And just as the average man in the Soviet Union spoke forbidden truths using humor, Stalin too loved to tell a good *anekdot*. As he himself put it:

> One day a boy was arrested by the NKVD and accused of writing *Eugene Onegin*. "That was written by Pushkin," insisted the boy. Well a few days later the interrogator ran into his parents on the street. "Congratulations!" he said. "What for?" they asked. "Your son confessed to writing *Eugene Onegin*!" he told them.[221]

As the show trials and purges continued, one massive unanswered question remained. If there were, in fact, dozens of "Trotsky-fascist" conspirators operating in the highest levels of the government of the Soviet Union, how is it that the authorities could point to one and only one person killed by all these plotters, namely Kirov? Many thousands of men and women were vanished if not slaughtered by the secret police. How could the class enemy, which was supposed to be pernicious, pervasive and powerful, not claim even *one* other victim?

John Dewey and several other prominent American intellectuals sought to answer that question. Under the leadership of the seminal American progressive, the Dewey Commission investigated the evidence against Trotsky and others in order to come to an objective conclusion about what was going on in the Soviet Union. They were led to some obvious questions about the information provided by Stalin's prosecutors:

> It is evident even from this incomplete list of alleged terrorist groups that the alleged conspiracy ramified widely—into Caucasia, Transcaucasia, the Ukraine, Siberia—and involved a large number of people. It is therefore astonishing, assuming that the evidence represents the truth, that it was discovered only after five years (according to several accused it began in 1931), and that during those five years, in spite of "intense activity," it resulted, according to the records themselves, in precisely one assassination: that of Commissar S. M. Kirov, on December 1, 1934.

> [The accused include] Smirnov, leader of the famous Fifth Army during the Civil War and conqueror of Kolchak; Muralov, a leader of the October Revolution in Moscow and former Commander of the Moscow Military area; Mrachkovsky, one of the heroes of the Civil War in the Urals and former head of the Urals Military District; Drobnis, a soldier of the Civil War, twice condemned to death by the Whites and once shot by them and left for dead. These men had records of courage, resolution, and action in the service of the Communist revolution and the Soviet state. It is hardly credible that if they had decided to overthrow the Soviet government through terrorism they would have gone about it in such dilatory and amateurish ways[.][222]

Naturally, Stalin thus turned to creating more victims (perhaps the first imaginary victims in Soviet history). Maxim Gorky was one of the greatest and most renowned authors of all time, not just in Soviet Russia but throughout the world. As such, it was widely known that he had passed away in 1936 at the age of sixty-eight. Valerian Kuybyshev had been a member of the Politburo that governed the USSR and one of Stalin's closest economic advisers; he was only forty-six when he died in 1935. Finally, Vyacheslav Menzhinsky had been chairman of the secret police for eight years before dying in 1934 at the age of fifty-nine.

All that was left to do was to demonstrate that these three men had actually been murdered, and the existence of the anti-Soviet, anti-Stalin conspiracies would be established. Anger over learning that one of Russia's most beloved authors had been killed would surely drive the public into fits of rage against the perpetrators. Having found some victims and invented the crimes, it now simply became a matter of getting confessions. But who was there to blame? As economic calamity could be blamed on wreckers, so could health issues naturally be blamed on the doctors.

Yet their doctors needed to confess to crimes that not only hadn't they committed, but to crimes that have never even occurred to begin with. Gorky, Kuybyshev, and Menzhinsky had all died of natural causes. Yezhov set to work. He realized that he wouldn't need to break all three doctors. All he had to do was to break one and then have him turn on his two colleagues. He thus set his sights on Professor Dimitri Pletnev, who had a reputation as the most outstanding heart specialist in the USSR.

One of Yezhov's female NKVD operatives accused Pletnev of having bitten her breast in the course of examining her three years prior. It was completely false and utterly absurd, but the newspapers ran with it all the same. After decades of hard work the doctor's reputation was reduced to the newspapers' new epithet for him: "the sadist Pletnev." The respected medical professional was then publicly denounced by former friends and students (not that they had much choice in the matter). Over the years of his career Pletnev had treated some of the most prominent citizens of the Soviet Union—all of whom now ignored his desperate letters beseeching them to help clear his name.[223]

The second target, Dr. Levin, had treated both Stalin and his daughter—though such connections did him little good. Dr. Kazakov was the final target of the accusations. One at a time, the men were sat down and told what they had done: Yezhov's predecessor Yagoda had summoned each of them individually and demanded that they murder their patients. The court heard testimony that the "doctor-poisoners" took Gorky from an overheated room and into freezing cold over and over until he died.[224] The men had supposedly been too afraid to defy Yagoda and either warn their patients or turn him in (despite personally having direct access to the highest officials, including Stalin himself).[225] Pletnev was spared death, but Kazakov and Levin were executed. In any event, Kirov was legally no longer the sole victim of those plotting against Stalin and his men.[226]

Chapter 6

TRY TO IMAGINE WHAT IT'S LIKE

The NKVD had no shortage of ways to get their victims to confess to crimes. There was no shortage of simple brutality to effect a confession, though a very few resisted. The Polish-born Konstantin Rokossovsky was a brilliant military man and great innovator when it came to the art of modern warfare. He was forty years old when he was arrested, and Yezhov's men began to work him over for claims of being a spy and a foreign agent.

They broke his ribs and smashed his toes with a hammer. The NKVD men pulled out his fingernails, and nine of his teeth as well. When that was not enough they told him that he was going to be executed, taking him in front of firing squads but never actually shooting him. But Rokossovsky never broke, and when he was later freed and worked alongside Joseph "Man of Steel" Stalin against the forces of Hitler he did so with a smile full of new steel teeth.[227]

The physical brutality committed against the accused was invariably loud enough for other prisoners to hear, and this was by design. It was the NKVD's way of letting those in its power know that it would be their turn sooner rather than later. One prisoner recalled the effect such inhuman sounds had on her: "I thought about the fact that the man had gone on calling his torturers 'comrade' when they were already beating him; he could think of no other word for them and called them 'comrade' when they fell upon him like beasts." At a certain point the accused "understood and in his agony cried out to the only loyal name left to him: 'Mom.'" "Mom, my head!" she and all the others heard him scream, over and over.[228]

Sometimes the pressures weren't so brutal in their application. The tale of the pseudonymous Comrade Ivanov was one such example. An Old Bolshevik with an impeccable pedigree, he had repeatedly been arrested by the czar. After the Revolution, he and his equally beyond-reproach wife had made the mistake of siding with Trotsky. They were deported to Siberia before being brought back and imprisoned in Moscow in 1936. It took four months of trying to break Ivanov, but Old Bolsheviks don't break easy. What was four months in a Moscow prison to a man who had done ten years doing hard labor in some godforsaken corner of Russia?

Eventually Yezhov himself attempted to discover what was taking so bloody long. After seeing Ivanov refusing to break, Yezhov simply phoned Ivanov's mother-in-law in the man's presence. "This is the NKVD. Comrade Ivanov wants to know how his children are." It was the middle of the night, she told him, and the younger boy was sound asleep. "Do you want me to give her a message?" Yezhov asked Ivanov.

"Tell her to take good care of the boy," Ivanov replied.

The Bolsheviks did in months what the hated czar couldn't do in a decade: they broke Paul Ivanov. He cried when they hung up the phone, and signed whatever confession they put in front of him.[229]

Historian Orlando Figes points out that

> In 1935, the Soviet government had lowered the age of criminal responsibility to just twelve—partly with the aim of threatening those in prison with the arrest of their children if they refused to confess to their crimes (a second decree that year allowed the arrest and imprisonment of relatives of anyone who was in prison for crimes against the state). In effect a hostage system was declared.[230]

By that point the execution of children had been standard though unofficial practice for quite some time. It was one of the ways that the *bezprizorniye*, the orphans of war and famine, had been culled in previous years, but that was done under the cover of darkness. Making teenagers liable for the death penalty caused an enormous backlash in even communist-friendly Western circles. Yet by making it official certain other actions were now not only possible but in a sense unremarkable. It was Yezhov's policy for his interrogators to have a copy of the decree on their desks. "We are also told," recounted Conquest, "that fear of reprisals was made more dramatic and emotionally effective by the display on the interrogator's desk of private belongings of members of the family."[231]

It's amazing what human beings will do when their families are threatened, and when they're aware of how little they can do to save them. Eventually "every inquisitor of the NKVD was obliged to have on his desk during the interrogation of the arrested Bolsheviks the law which decreed the application of the death penalty to children."[232]

But even this wasn't the worst of what was done to get confessions out of various men and women. Stanislav Kosior had been instrumental in implementing Stalin's assault on the Ukrainian peasantry. One of the surviving photos of Kosior has him seated in a row directly below Stalin. Stalin has his hand atop Kosior's bald head, and the two men both have big goofy smiles on their faces. It was a bit out of character for Bolsheviks, who were meant to look tough and ruthless.[233]

As General Secretary of the Ukrainian SSR Communist Party it was Kosior who issued several decrees imposing the confiscation of grain, as well as deporting thousands of families. He was also complicit in covering up the causes of the mass famine, using the Ukrainians themselves as scapegoats for the millions that died. In December 1933, Kosior addressed the All-Union Central Executive Committee of the Soviets. There he offered up an alternative history wherein Stalin was saving the Ukrainians instead of decimating them:

> Throughout the two-year period, much as we tried to revive the agricultural economy, we failed to do it. You, comrades, all know that considerable aid in the form of food and seeds was given, not only to Ukraine but also to other districts and regions of the Soviet Union. This must be credited to the exceptional persistence on the part of Comrade Stalin, who succeeded in accumulating, even under such circumstances, certain reserves that were afterwards used to aid a number of provinces. These reserves helped considerably to plug the gaps that were a result of our errors in many localities.

Stalin's purge made its way through the Soviet power structure to silence virtually anyone who knew too much about his atrocities. Kosior had insisted that the causes of the Holodomor "lay not in objective conditions, but mainly in the low quality of our local work, the calibre of our local leadership."[234] But Kosior knew perfectly well what had caused the famine, and that forbidden knowledge was itself largely enough to sign his (literal) death warrant. In January 1938 Stalin recalled Kosior to Moscow and made him deputy prime minister of the USSR. He was arrested four months later.

There are few of us who know what it means to experience torture. The closest analogue is an action movie. The hero is tied to a chair, with his hair carefully tousled and his lip split open. Though exhausted he is defiant against his captors. His refusal to back down is both a source of frustration to his foes and a testament to his strength. It is a powerful image—but also a Hollywood fabrication. Historian William O'Neill pointed out that tortures weren't simply used by Stalin's men to get a confession, but also to effect "the complete disintegration of his individual personality."

As O'Neill explained:

> A man woken up in the middle of the night, unable to satisfy his most elementary physical needs during the hearing, sitting for hours at a time on a small hard stool, blinded by

> the light of a powerful bulb directed straight at his eyes, surprised by sudden, cunning questions and by an overwhelming crescendo of fictitious accusations, sadistically taunted with the sight of cigarettes and hot coffee on the other side of the table, and all this going on for months, sometimes even years—under these circumstances he is ready to sign anything. That, however, is not the essential point. A prisoner is considered to have been sufficiently prepared for the final achievement of the signature only when his personality has been thoroughly dismantled into its component parts. Gaps appear in the logical association of ideas; thoughts and emotions become loosened in their original positions and rattle against each other like the parts of a broken-down machine; the driving-belts connecting the past with the present slip off their wheels and fall sloppily to the bottom of the mind; all the weights and levers of mind and will-power become jammed and refuse to function; the indicators of the pressure gauges jump as if possessed from zero to maximum and back again. The machine still runs on larger revolutions, but it does not work as it did—all that had a moment before appeared absurd now becomes probable even though still not true, emotions lose their colour, will-power its capacity. The prisoner is now willing to admit that he had betrayed the interests of the proletariat by writing to his relatives abroad, that his slackness at work was sabotage of socialist industry.[235]

It is unclear what torture methods were attempted on Kosior to get a confession. The most frequently used was known as the Conveyor, where the prisoner is not allowed to sleep and is questioned endlessly. Every four hours his interrogator would be replaced by a new, fresh man just like a conveyor belt—and so the questioning would resume again, as he stood against a wall without sleep for over a week if necessary.[236] "The NKVD investigators tortured prisoners for many hours at a stretch, and repeatedly," recounted Medvedev. "Brutalized interrogators disfigured prisoners. They not only beat them and kept them from sleep, food, and water; they gouged out eyes and perforated eardrums, pulled out fingernails and toenails, broke arms and legs, burned their victims with redhot irons, and mutilated sex organs."[237]

Others were beaten until their eyes popped out of their heads, a level of violence so inhuman as to seem like something out of a cartoon. Prisoners who were beaten to death were legally registered as having had heart attacks.[238] In some cases the murder was more extreme, such as when the "head of the cross-examined prisoner is tightly bound with cord into which a small stick, a nail or a pencil is inserted; by rotating this inserted stick the cord wound around the skull tightens to such an extent that finally the skull is scalped, the skin with the hair of the head coming clean off the skull."[239]

Did Kosior stare down his captors with anger? Did he taunt them through the blood and pain, one eye half-closed? Did he beg? Ask to speak with Stalin—or demand it? Did he insist on his innocence until his voice went hoarse—or did he save his energy and breath, knowing there was no point? If Kosior had to stand in water for days on end he did not break. If the NKVD subjected him to the Swallow—where he was hoisted up by his arms and legs tied behind him—he did not break.

It is unknown whether Kosior's refusal to break earned him the grudging respect of his captors or simply angered them even more. It remains unclear whether they had their eventual ace in the hole the entire time and were toying with him, or if their idea only came when nothing else seemed to work—or perhaps there was a line even the NKVD wanted to avoid crossing if there remained any possibility of avoiding it. What we do know is that the interrogators brought in Kosior's sixteen-year-old daughter Tamara, and raped her in front of him.[240]

That did it. That finally broke Stanislav Kosior.

Kosior duly signed the confession that he, an ethnic Pole, had been a Polish spy. His execution was not immediate; he managed to outlive Tamara, who committed suicide by throwing herself in front of a train. Whether Tamara's death should technically be counted as one of the NKVD's victims is an academic question. It is unlikely it was she who the *New York Times* had in mind when they published a 2017 opinion piece explaining "Why Women Had Better Sex Under Socialism."[241] But history has at least recorded her name, unlike those of so many thousands of others whose very existence has been entirely wiped away.

The trials as a whole left viewers worldwide with a logical dilemma. It was Granville Hicks himself who pointed out that there were only two real conclusions one could draw from the events. "If these men were innocent," he wrote years later, "the administration of the Soviet Union was a vicious, ruthless tyranny. But if, on the other hand, they were guilty, then the leadership of the Communist movement had been desperately corrupt from the very beginning."[242]

Yet the show trials worked, even on (or rather, *especially* on) those men and women who were Western media influencers of their time. As George Orwell put it, "What was frightening about these trials was not the fact that they happened—for obviously such things are necessary in a totalitarian society—but the eagerness of Western intellectuals to justify them."[243] Take the case of Dorothy Parker. She was the Samantha Bee of her day, and her comrade James Thurber the Stephen Colbert. The two were part of the famous Algonquin Round Table, which spent the 1920s meeting for lunch every day—and exchanging bon mots—in New York City's Algonquin Hotel. The group was strongly associated with the *New Yorker* magazine and its sensibilities. As Parker herself later described it:

> They came there to be heard by one another. "Did you hear what I said last night?" [...] People look at it rosily now, and it wasn't. I promise you it was not good. It was the terrible day of the wisecrack, so there didn't have to be any truth. There's nothing memorable about them, about any of them.[244]

A century later Parker remains synonymous with American wit, and was probably the first woman in the United States to be known for her sharp tongue. Her life story was made into an inexecrable 1994 film entitled *Mrs. Parker and the Vicious Circle*, wherein Jennifer Jason Leigh drunkenly stands up and spontaneously delivers Parker's sayings in front of various audiences over the course of ninety minutes.

Though Parker never did write that "if you don't have anything nice to say about someone, come sit next to me," it certainly does read in her voice. As a theater reviewer she quipped that "I know who wrote those lyrics and I know the names of the people in the cast, but I'm not going to tell on them." When an editor pressured her for overdue work she replied that she was "too fucking busy, and vice versa." "Men seldom make passes at girls who wear glasses" was originally a couplet of hers entitled "News Item." And there was that wholesale libel on the Yale prom: "If all the girls attending it were laid end to end," Mrs. Parker said, "she wouldn't be at all surprised."

Parker was also a strong advocate of social justice, and threw aside her trademark sarcasm and irony when it came to the issues that mattered to her. In 1927 it was the Sacco and Vanzetti case that gripped America. The two self-described anarchists were accused of murdering a bank guard during an armed robbery and accordingly sentenced to death. Progressives around the nation were taken with the cause of the immigrant men, and the case dragged on for years. In 1927 Parker was arrested and fined a paltry $5 for "loitering and sauntering" after taking part in a rally for their defense. It would be to no avail; the pair would be electrocuted in August of that year. Yet when it came to Stalin's trials of innocent men, Parker and her comrades had an entirely different approach.

As literary critic Lionel Trilling wrote in his 1966 essay "Young in the Thirties":

> In any view of the American cultural situation, the importance of the radical movement of the Thirties cannot be overestimated. It may be said to have created the American intellectual class as we now know it in its great size and influence. It fixed the character of this class as being, through all mutations of opinion, predominantly of the Left. And quite apart from opinion, the political tendency of the Thirties defined the style of the class—from

> that radicalism came the moral urgency, the sense of crisis, and the concern with personal salvation that mark the existence of American intellectuals.[245]

Indeed, a large cross-section of the American intelligentsia tripped over themselves to defend Stalin's purges and the executions that followed as a result of them. A letter to that effect was published in *The Daily Worker* on April 28, 1938, and then repeated for good measure in *New Masses* on May 3—the same exact day that Stanislav Kosior was arrested. Parker's name was easy to miss among the many signatories; it was below that of Granville Hicks. None of the people who added their names to the letter had a gun to their head. It was their free choice to go out of their way to make known their support of Stalin's actions and to take a public stand on his behalf, to use their elevated status to let average Americans know how important it was for the Soviet government to have the right (if not the duty) to execute its own citizens.

"We, the undersigned, are fully aware of the confusion that exists with regard to the Moscow trials and the real facts about the situation in the Soviet Union," it began. Simply put, the reports of the trials "have by sheer weight of evidence established a clear presumption of the guilt of the defendants." The basic American liberal concept of a presumption of innocence until proven guilty, a basic element of human rights designed to protect the powerless against the accusatory state, was gladly flipped on its head.

"In fact," the influencers claimed, "most newspapers have discarded the earlier charges of 'frame-up' and now admit the validity of the trials." This might have been, perhaps, less of a commentary on the validity of the trials than on the decency of most newspapers. The alleged point of the "confusion" was in part to "obscure the truth about the achievements of the Soviet Union as recorded by honest progressive opinion." (These achievements supposedly included "magnificent gains in industry and agriculture.")

The letter went on to repeat Stalin's claims that the defendants "resorted to duplicity and conspiracy and allied themselves with long-standing enemies of the Soviet Union. Degeneration may therefore be charged to the defendants, and not to the Soviet Union, which gains strength internally and externally by the prevention of treason and the eradication of spies and wreckers." "Eradication" of course being a euphemism for the death penalty, with "wreckers" in practice being anyone who is disobedient or even skeptical—or who has simply been accused of it. But again: any setbacks in the Soviet Union weren't the fault of communism or the USSR or Stalin. It was the fault of those men who had been captured and imprisoned.

By this point in time there had already been concern in Hollywood and in Washington over those Americans who preferred the USSR to the United States and were secretly plotting with the Soviet government. Members of the Communist Party in the United States were complaining about the personal costs of joining the Party, when their beloved Communist country made membership in any other political party—even in the past—grounds for imprisonment, labor camps, and certain death.

In an amazing bit of projection, the celebrities claimed that the Soviet Union's "growing vitality and self-defense measures" restrained its foes from open attack so that the "opponents of the Soviet Union have therefore been forced to resort to covert means." Supposedly these enemies "have disseminated reactionary propaganda and financial patronage" within the USSR. It was not that Soviet agents had been placed throughout the West, but the other way around. If anything, it was Hitler who was pulling the strings in US circles, not Stalin: "No one denies the penetration of the American continent by fascist propaganda".

The letter ended by asking American liberals to "support the efforts of the Soviet Union to free itself from insidious internal dangers". In other words, not only were the purges and the hundreds of thousands sent to camps something to tolerate or explain away. No, Stalin should have the backing of every good American leftist with a conscience. As the motto went, "Communism is 20th century Americanism."

"The same editors and writers who once spoke up [...] for Sacco and Vanzetti," Lyons later wrote, "who presumably cherished the memory of the world response to a Dreyfus or Mendel Baylis case, now gave every benefit of the doubt to an omnipotent state and its firing squads, rather than to its victims.[246] [...] There were no intellectual acrobatics which the fellow-travelers would not undertake to save their lovely faith in Russia. Year after year they had accepted and explained away horror and super-horror: falsifications of history, corruption, terror, man-made famine, the death penalty for minor thefts, the punishment of relatives for alleged crimes committed by members of their family thousands of miles away, capital punishment for young children, concentration camps with a population running into millions."[247]

In some ways the love affair with Stalin was even stronger in the United Kingdom than in the United States. The Englishman H.G. Wells was a major pioneer in the field of science fiction, with books like *The Time Machine*, *War of the Worlds*, and *The Invisible Man* still widely read today. Wells' genre of science fiction is not to be confused with Russia's "scientific socialism," which is the fiction that, among other things, a planned economy would have no shortages or surpluses. The experts would know exactly how much and what needed to be produced, and they would make that and only that.

In 1934 Wells had become one of the lucky few, either from the USSR or abroad, who managed to interview the surprisingly reclusive Stalin. At one point, regarding the imminent collapse of capitalism as a functioning system, Wells chided Stalin, stating that "It seems to me that I am more to the Left than you." While Wells had a strong reputation of being a socialist in the United Kingdom, he also had a strong reputation in general. If Stalin was more to the center than Wells, then clearly the leader's ideology couldn't be all that bad. By definition, it wasn't that extreme if the mainstream Wells was further to the fringe than Stalin was. "I have never met a man more candid, fair and honest," Wells wrote of Stalin, "and it is to these qualities, and to nothing occult and sinister, that he owes his tremendous undisputed ascendancy in Russia."[248]

George Orwell was a hardcore leftist throughout his life, and like some many others around the world made the journey to Spain to take part in the Spanish Civil War. The battle between a broad coalition of leftists, from Stalinists to anarchists, against the ultra-nationalist forces of Francisco Franco was in many ways perceived to be a proxy for the growing European conflict between fascism and its opponents. What Orwell saw permanently turned him against authoritarian communism, becoming one of its fiercest and most perceptive critics with his masterpieces *1984* and *Animal Farm*. As he later put it, "Every line of serious work that I have written since 1936 has been written, directly or indirectly, *against* totalitarianism and *for* democratic socialism, as I understand it."

Yet in 1938 Orwell's British publisher Victor Gollancz refused to publish *Homage to Catalonia*, Orwell's memoir about his Spanish experience and what he saw as Communist duplicity against their supposed allies. Gollancz had co-founded the Left Book Club, a list that catered to socialists and published several exclusive titles. To paraphrase Orwell's famous quote, some leftists were more equal to others, and criticism of Stalinist communism was not to be done. "The upshot is that," Orwell wrote, "if from time to time you express a mild distaste for slave-labour camps or one-candidate elections, you are either insane or actuated by the worst motives."[249]

Another prominent British intellectual was the aforementioned Harold Laski, whose political career would culminate in becoming the UK's Labour Party chairman. He went even further than most, making a point to praise Stalin's prosecutor as "doing what an ideal Minister of Justice would do if we had such a person in Great Britain."[250] Laski would eventually get in trouble for announcing that "If Labour did not obtain what it needed by general consent, we shall have to use violence even if it means revolution." It is understandable why Laski was the inspiration for the villain in Ayn Rand's *The Fountainhead*. In Laski Rand saw "'the man who couldn't be, and knows it," someone who hated the good *because* it was the good. As she recalled:

> After seeing Laski, I just had to remember how he lectured—his mannerisms, the pseudo-intellectual snideness, the whole manner of speaking on important subjects with inappropriate sarcasm as his only weapon, acting as if he were a charming scholar in a drawing room, but you could sense the bared teeth behind the smile, you could feel something evil[.][251]

Pat Sloan was a British Communist who spent some time in the USSR. He freely told his fellow citizens that:

> Compared with the significance of that term in Britain, Soviet imprisonment stands out as an almost enjoyable experience. For the essence of Soviet imprisonment is isolation from the rest of the community, together with other persons similarly isolated, with the possibility to do useful work at the place of isolation, to earn a wage for this work, and to participate in running the isolation settlement or 'prison' in the same way as the children participate in running their school, or the workers their factory.

"The Soviet labour camp provides a freedom for its inmates not usual in our own prisons in this country," he went on to say.[252]

Yet it was not merely the left-wing fringe of the intellectual class that came to such conclusions. *The Nation* and *The New Republic* were and remain highly respected outlets that Americans turn to to learn about the issues of the day and how they should feel about them. As Lyons commemorated:

> What was *The Nation*'s first reaction to the announcement of the initial "Trotskyist" trial? Not even decent astonishment. "It was to be expected that under the velvet glove of the New Soviet constitution," it wrote, "there would still be the firm outlines of the iron hand. There can be no doubt the dictatorship in Russia is dying and that a new democracy is slowly being born." The impending death of thousands of communists was thus another confirmation that the dictatorship is dying![253]
>
> The gallant *New Republic* in its first reaction blandly assumed that the fantastic charges compounded by the

> G.P.U. were true. "Perhaps the deepest lesson to be learned from the Russian trial," it declared, "is the profound, unchangeable stubbornness of human nature. From the standpoint of practical expediency, these men had little to gain and much to lose by their effort to bring down the Soviet state in ruins."[254]

Perhaps the deepest lesson here might not be about "the profound, unchangeable stubbornness of human nature." Rather, it might have something to do with the profound, unchangeable stubbornness of *The Nation*, *The New Republic* and other such journals—the very same outlets that still presume to hector Americans on a daily basis about ethics and decency, without shame or even irony.

As horrific as it was for Stalin and his men to turn family members into hostages, they weren't always used to leverage confessions or the like. Loyalty to family was a quintessentially bourgeois worldview, the private interest over the public good, and any hint of that was anathema to good Communists. Husbands and wives turned against one another with ease. Just being married to an enemy of the people was in and of itself illegal, a crime that a husband or—far more frequently—a wife could do very little to deny. Things were even stricter for those in the military. Starting in 1934, a military man who fled when abroad would subject not merely his spouse but his entire family to get sent to a prison camp.

Mikhail Kalinin was chair of the Presidium of the Supreme Soviet, the Soviet Union's head of state, but even that could not protect his wife from being arrested, tortured and sentenced in 1938 to fifteen years for supposedly being aligned with Trotsky. Kalinin knew better than to protest, and dutifully carried on with his work. Paulina Zhemchuzhina was Vyacheslav Molotov's wife. His name remains with us in part due to the Molotov cocktail, invented by the Finns to fight the Russians. Molotov was second only to Stalin, and Zhemchuzhina served as Moscow's de facto first lady after Stalin's second wife killed herself (or was she murdered?) in 1932. When Stalin announced the arrest of yet another espionage ring, Molotov suspected that his wife would be included in the group. "What will become of Paulina Semionovna?" he asked.

"What a question!" Stalin barked. "Vyacheslav Mikhailovich still doesn't know how the Soviet government deals with imperialist spies!" Molotov's wife was soon arrested and sentenced to five years in a labor camp.[255] Nor was Stalin's own family safe. He personally approved the execution of his first widow's brother (his very own brother-in-law) which was carried out with all good haste.[256] Her mother was arrested and imprisoned as well. Stalin's second widow's brother-in-law was likewise shot.

As marriage itself thereby became fraught with danger, so too did the Soviet system attempt to use children against their own parents in other ways. Just as George Washington was mythologized as having admitted in his boyhood to chopping down a cherry tree because "I cannot tell a lie," the Soviet authorities developed folk heroes of a sort in order to spread moral messages on desirable behavior among the population. Most notorious of these was the story of Pavlik Morozov, a young boy who turned in his kulak father to the authorities for hoarding grain. Pavlik was then allegedly killed by his dad. In doing so he became a martyr throughout the USSR, with statues built in his honor. The message was so unambiguous that even a child could understand it (because, of course, the story was targeted precisely toward children): if your parents break the law, there is no higher moral response than to turn them in—even it cost you your own life.

The youngest themselves were not free from being arrested and put on trial, and getting them to confess was child's play. It only took a single night of interrogation to get one ten-year-old detainee to admit that he had joined a fascist organization at the age of seven. Other kids who were not suspects themselves were forced to publicly approve of the arrests and executions of their parents for having been spies.[257] Their entire class or school would assemble and the student would be berated until they denounced their mother and/or father in front of their fellow classmates.[258]

Children had been Bolshevik targets from the beginning. Russian author Sergei Masloff recounts the May 1920 arrest of a band of Moscow pickpockets all between the ages of 11 and 15:

> The children were confined in a cellar and isolated from the other prisoners. Threats and promises of reward were alternately used to make the children point out their accomplices. After some fruitless attempts to make them speak, several employees of the Che-ka entered the cellar, pounded the children with their fists, and, having knocked them down, kicked them with their heavy boots[…], they were dragged daily about the town on trams, in motor-cars and taken to railway stations to point out their accomplices. At first the children tried to pretend they knew no one. They were still more barbarously beaten that night, and they began to betray their associates. This torture went on for a fortnight: if a child had the bad luck not to meet or point out a comrade, he would be cruelly thrashed; to escape the savage punishment, the children finally pointed out innocent boys whom they did not know.

After three weeks of this the young thieves "were like small, hunted animals expecting an imminent death. They sobbed, trembled and shrieked in their sleep." The adult inmates, hardened prisoners themselves, "had never heard such heartrending cries as those of the children when they understood that they were going back to the cellar."[259]

There was a brief moment where children in several large cities organized in an attempt to fight back. Calling themselves Revenge for Our Parents, the students knew perfectly well that their families were innocent. Their youthful naivete is understandable but no less tragic. They issued a leaflet arguing against the mass arrest of so many loyal citizens—and then they were, of course, virtually all arrested themselves. Naturally so were their siblings and any remaining parents, in this case for having failed to denounce the pamphleteers for their counter-revolutionary activities.[260]

The number of cases of families being destroyed overnight was endless. A man could be arrested for whatever reason and then his wife for the crime of being married to him, leaving their children effectively orphaned. To compound the suffering there was an enormous disincentive for other families (and their own children) to take an interest in what was happening, lest they now appear to have been conspiring with enemies of the people.

Simply calling attention to the needs of such a child could easily be taken as criticism of the government ("Surely you're not implying we would let young people suffer, comrade?"), if not Stalin personally. One day there would be a family, and the next the child was not only alone but completely socially isolated and shunned by everyone around them. The epidemic of hopeless children who understandably started taking their own lives caused handwringing at the Kremlin.[261]

Some families did their best to help such cases, but it was understood very well that housing a child of an "enemy of the people" was done at great risk. After the assistant chief of Red Army Intelligence and his wife were executed, their apartment had been seized by the government. Their thirteen-year-old daughter had nowhere to go, and was taken in by a family whose daughter was a close friend of hers. Concerned, the foster father went to the head of the NKVD's secretary for advice as to how to best handle the situation. After agreeing that the "the matter is a very delicate one," the secretary gave his thoughts. "At any rate," he said, "it isn't proper for you to keep her. My advice to you is: try to get rid of her." The father of course did as he was advised.[262] The fate of such young girls put out into the street can be imagined but perhaps shouldn't be.

Those children who were a little older joined gangs and were often thereby arrested for genuine—if perhaps unavoidable—criminal behavior. Soviet prison survivor Gustaw Herling-Grudziński discussed their lifestyle in his memoir:

> Juvenile delinquents, like the boys in the cell, are the plague of the Soviet prisons[…]. Unnaturally excited, always ferreting in other men's bunks and inside their own trousers, they give themselves up passionately to the only two occupations of their lives, theft and self-abuse. Almost all

> of them either have no parents or else know nothing of their whereabouts. Throughout the vast expanse of the Russian Police State they manage to lead with astounding ease the typical life of "bzeprizomye" ("the homeless"), jumping goods-trains, constantly on the move from town to town, from settlement to settlement. They make a living by stealing and selling goods from government stores, and frequently they steal back what they have just sold, blackmailing unsuspecting purchasers with the threat of laying information against them. They sleep in railway stations, in municipal parks, in tram terminuses; often all their belongings can be wrapped in a small bundle tied with a leather strap.[263]

The easiest situations, perhaps, were those of the young people called upon to distance themselves from their ancestors and thereby the social class into which they had been born. "In order to cast off the circumstances of their birth," explained one Western reporter, "it became commonplace for young people to publicly denounce their families and thereby repudiate their bourgeois origins. This was often done with said parents' consent or even at their recommendation. To see these sorts of notices in the press was jarring to the outside world, and with good reason."[264] But even betraying one's own was not enough. In the perverted Soviet system, people who turned in family members were still in a sense connected in perpetuity to those "undesirable elements." Fitzpatrick recounts the incident of one Communist who informed on his mother-in-law before himself being accused of being related to her.[265]

The more antithetical to communist ideology one's ostensible status was, the greater the coup it became to get them to publicly turn against their own. As powerful of a statement as it might be to turn on one's parents, it was that much more impactful to turn on one's God. It was Karl Marx himself who famously wrote that "Religion is the sigh of the oppressed creature, the heart of a heartless world, and the soul of soulless conditions. It is the *opium* of the people."[266] Soviet newspapers printed letters to the editor from priests renouncing—and denouncing—religion. Even more intense were such moments as when worshippers sat in horror while their priest told them that "religion was a deceit and that he no longer wished to be a weapon in the hands of counter-revolutionaries." He then ripped off his vestments and left the church.[267]

This was a new society of the future. Instead of God there was only man—and that man was Joseph Stalin.

Chapter 7

AFRAID OF EVERYTHING AND EVERYBODY

The year 1933 saw Adolf Hitler come to power in an economically devastated Germany. By that point Benito Mussolini had been in office in Italy for a decade, and the following year would see Broadway singing his praises: "You're the top! / You're Harry Houdini / You're the top! / You're Mussolini." At the time, Mussolini was regarded as somewhat of a moderate, a fusionist who combined the best elements of socialist Russia and capitalist America to create the "third way" of fascism.

Talk of American revolution had been in the air since the days of Louis Lingg, and this buzz sharply escalated as newspapers dutifully reported that the Soviet Union was surviving its birthing pains. The Great Depression seemed to prove Marx's predictions of the internal self-contradictions of capitalism correct. It seemed only a matter of time before his other prediction—that of a revolution by the working class—would come true as well.

Early in 1932 over ten thousand veterans of the Great War had camped out in Washington, DC, living in shanties that they had assembled from random junk. Destitute, they demanded that the bonuses due to them in 1945 be made redeemable now. That July they were ordered to clear out by the police. They rioted instead, and two vets ending up getting killed. President Hoover now had ten thousand ex-military men on his front stoop. Things were escalating into a crisis, completely out of the president's control—seemingly par for the course for his administration. Hoover sent in troops to clear out the veterans that same day. Backed up by Majors George S. Patton and Dwight Eisenhower, General Douglas MacArthur led a military contingent and carried out Hoover's orders successfully—but the idea of literally sending in the tanks against hungry American veterans was a complete public relations disaster.

Throughout the 1932 presidential race, FDR successfully blamed President Hoover for indifference to the ongoing depression while also attacking him for his massive spending hikes (which he would manage to outdo several times over when he became president himself). The campaign against Hoover got so bad that the president received a telegram from some smart-aleck advising him to "Vote for Roosevelt and make it unanimous."[268]

Though the vote that November was not quite unanimous, the 1932 election was still as drastic a reversal of the previous vote as could be expected. In 1928 Hoover had taken forty states and now FDR snagged forty-two, dropping Hoover's percentage of the popular vote from a landslide 58% to a mere 40%. The Senate elections were a similar bloodbath, with FDR's Democrats winning twenty-eight out of thirty-four races and defeating Republican leader James Watson in the process. The Democrats picked up almost one hundred seats in the House of Representatives, giving them a lead of close to 3-to-1 and a record number of seats.

FDR's first hundred days in the White House were a massive leftward tilt in American governance, with the machinery of government moving at an unprecedented pace. Everything seemed to be on the table in terms of policy. It was very clear that this was a historic opportunity to remake the relationship between the private sphere and the public one. These were unprecedented times, and one lifelong leftist was inspired to try and do something about it.

Upton Sinclair remains the classic example of those journalist/activists then known as muckrakers (a more polite way of saying "shit-stirrers"). His novel *The Jungle* is still assigned in high school classes over a century after its publication. Decades before his book, the expression "Laws are like sausages: it's better not to see them being made" was an idiom based on the less-than-pleasant culinary process. It was Sinclair who showed Americans how the sausage literally got made. Ostensibly fiction, *The Jungle* claimed to portray, among other things, the unsanitary conditions in meat-packing factories. The apex of Sinclair's gruesome prose came with a worker falling into a vat and being rendered into lard for sale to the general public. They couldn't believe it's not butter.

After being serialized in a socialist newspaper the year prior, *The Jungle* was first published in book form in February 1906. President Teddy Roosevelt had been a harsh skeptic of the young Sinclair, but the novel worked its magic on the president as it did on so many others. By June 30 Roosevelt was signing into law the Federal Meat Inspection Act and the Pure Food and Drug Act, creating what would eventually become today's enormously influential Food and Drug Administration (FDA). Sinclair was only twenty-seven years old, and already his writing was changing the face of America. He was an influencer over a century before the term achieved its contemporary connotations.

Sinclair's stated purpose in writing *The Jungle* had been to spread the message of socialism to the American people. Instead, the Federal Government became a guarantor of the quality of products of private industry at public cost. Rather than the state operating the factories, the capitalists continued to produce their meat unabated. Despite the author's best efforts, his book did not whet the population's appetite for a socialist takeover of the meat industry. As Sinclair put it, "I aimed at the public's heart, and by accident I hit it in the stomach." To this day—largely due to Sinclair—it is regarded as an uncontroversial truth that the government is the best and only agency with the capacity to certify the safety of food. The alternative would "obviously" be mass death and illness.

Like virtually all other socialists at the time, Sinclair was somewhat critical of but not entirely opposed to communism. Hungry for political power and eager to spread his ideology, Sinclair ran for the House of Representatives in 1920 and for the United States Senate in 1922 under the banner of the Socialist Party. When both those failed, he tried to run for California governor in 1926 and again in 1930, earning roughly 4% of the vote each time.

But all that was before FDR's landslide. "Fifty per cent of the people are going to vote a certain ticket because their grandfathers voted that ticket," Sinclair realized. "In order to get anywhere, it is necessary to have a party which has grandfathers."[269] The author-activist accordingly tossed his hat into the ring as a Democrat for the 1934 California gubernatorial election. Despite having no political experience—and no affiliation with the Democratic Party for decades—Sinclair easily clinched the nomination. All that stood between him and the governor's office was hapless Republican governor Frank Merriam, who had only assumed office in June upon the death of his predecessor.

Sinclair's plan for California was bold and it was radical. His promise to End Poverty In California (EPIC) was based on a few principles, namely:

> Private ownership of tools, a basis of freedom when tools are simple becomes a basis of enslavement when tools are complex.
> Autocracy in industry cannot exist alongside democracy in government.
> The existence of luxury in the presence of poverty and destitution is contrary to good morals and sound public policy.
> The present depression is one of abundance, not scarcity.
> The cause of the trouble is that a small class has the wealth, while the rest have the debts.
> The remedy is to give the workers access to the means of production, and let them produce for themselves, not for others.

In short, the largest part of his EPIC plan was for the government to take over idle lands or factories and put the unemployed to work on them. Reporters had some very obvious questions for Sinclair, namely,

"Suppose your Plan goes into effect, won't it cause a great many unemployed to come to California from other States?" Sinclair's response did more harm than good. As he put it:

> I told Mr. Hopkins, the Federal Relief Administrator, that if I am elected, half the unemployed of the United States will come to California, and he will have to make plans to take care of them.
>
> I went on to discuss this subject. "Of course," I said, "I was making Mr. Hopkins a sales talk. But he recognizes the situation: the unemployed come to California every fall, because it is less easy to freeze to death here. The Federal Government is taking care of them where they are, and it will have to take care of them in California. Mr. Hopkins knows that."
>
> Someone asked if there was any way they could be kept out of California; and I said the only way was to keep the people of California so poor that those in other States would not envy their condition. In fact, they have to be kept a little poorer, because California is a pleasanter place to live in. Such was the program actually favored by our big business masters, I added.[270]

Now the question became whether FDR would endorse Sinclair and his leftist ideas, or if he would try and remain out of the fray. A Democrat hadn't been elected California governor in forty years, but FDR had carried the state by 58%-38% over Hoover four years after Hoover had won it 65%-34%. Clearly the possibility of a Governor Sinclair was very real.

After vacillating for a while, FDR finally agreed to meet with Sinclair. On September 4, 1934, Sinclair made his way to the president's upstate New York estate at Hyde Park for a conversation that, by all accounts, was highly amiable. In his typical reptilian fashion, FDR made sure that Sinclair left the meeting with the belief that the president agreed with him and would come out publicly against the very concept of profit. Roosevelt told Sinclair that he intended to give a speech on or around October 25th—right before the election—advocating Sinclair's preferred "production for use" as against production for profit. "If you will do that, Mr. President," Sinclair said, "it will elect me."[271]

FDR of course intended nothing of the kind. It only took him five days before he was throwing Sinclair under the bus, but doing so off-the-record to reporters so that the gubernatorial candidate was none the wiser. Not only calling the scale of Sinclair's EPIC plan "utterly impossible," FDR went on to paint Sinclair as a fanatic. "If Sinclair has any sense in him," the president said, "he will modify at least in practice this perfectly wild-eyed scheme of his and carry it on as a community experiment."[272]

It was on October 24th, not the 25th, Roosevelt did in fact give a speech. He told a group of bankers that America has "what we call—and accept—as a profit system." Rather than endorsing Sinclair's socialist vision, Roosevelt reiterated his view of free enterprise as the basis of the American economy.[273] On Election Day a couple of weeks later, Democrats won twenty-five out of thirty-four gubernatorial races. Two others were won by third-party candidates, and just seven won by Republicans—including California. The Progressive candidate in the election won 13% of the vote, in a race that Democratic nominee Upton Sinclair lost by 11%.

Sinclair did not take it well, and later claimed that his supporters were even more devastated: "Men and women broke down and wept when the certainty of our defeat became apparent. I know of women who cried the whole night through, and doubtless there were thousands. I know of one suicide, and at least one other attempt."[274] EPIC continued as a movement, and Roosevelt shamelessly adopted some of Sinclair's ideas as he further built up the New Deal in his attempts to battle America's ongoing Great Depression.

Four years later, Sinclair engaged in a public exchange of letters with the aforementioned journalist Eugene Lyons. Lyons had been a young communist sent to Russia under the auspices of the United Press in hopes that his ideological sympathy with the Bolsheviks would earn him greater access. The gamble paid off. At only thirty-two years of age—and three years before Walter Duranty—Lyons became the first Western journalist to interview Stalin. This increased access also meant increased information, and—just as with Emma Goldman and Alexander Berkman— Lyons became a harsh critic of the USSR after seeing with his own eyes what the Bolshevik experiment meant in practice. The debate between Sinclair and Lyons was a perfect stand-in for the broader cultural debate in the West as to what one's relationship to the Soviet Union should be, especially in the face of increasing German belligerence.

Yes, Sinclair was a socialist, but he was a *democratic* socialist. "I have been tireless in my insistence upon majority consent," he wrote, "and in my rejection of every suggestion of violence and dictatorship in bringing about social change." A champion of the working man, he resented being accused of things he did not identify as in the slightest: "Having been a Socialist for thirty-two years, and having set forth my ideas in a score of books and hundreds of magazine articles, I really thought I was safe from being called a Communist."[275] At the same time, he made clear that "when I criticize what Russia is doing, I criticize it as a friend who understands."[276]

The exchange of letters between Lyons and Sinclair was collected under the title *Terror in Russia?*. The question mark was no doubt Sinclair's, as Lyons knew for a fact what was happening in the Soviet Union. To his dubious credit, Sinclair did not shy away from acknowledging and justifying Stalin's brutality:

> I read not long ago of an American diplomat who had travelled over Europe, including Russia. He said, "It is a fact that the Russians have never learned to govern without killing." That was an unkind saying but if it is true, it is something we have to take account of. We do not kill our political opponents—at least not often—but in Russia it is a custom of long standing.[277]

There is something uniquely bizarre about hearing Upton Sinclair—one of the most popular and influential radicals in America history—rationalizing mass murder on the basis of tradition.

In words that would sound chilling within a decade, Sinclair's view of the mass Ukrainian starvation was that "I venture to doubt that five million were permitted to die." "Permitted" is one of those words that have different meanings. At the very least, Sinclair was claiming that the Soviet government wouldn't allow such a thing to happen without acting to prevent it. That Stalin was in fact responsible for those deaths didn't even enter Sinclair's thoughts as a consideration. "My guess," Sinclair continued, "is that it is nearer to one million, but that was enough." What basis Sinclair had for this admitted guess he never says. But what's a few million lives here or there?

The "system of socialized industry and collectivized agriculture," Sinclair summed up, is one which "has proved so disturbingly successful in the Soviet Union."[278] He was right: the elements of Stalin's collectivized agriculture which were most "successful"—the unremitting demand for grain which starved millions—were also the most disturbing. Again and again, Sinclair excused away any and all aspects of mass coercion. The Russians "did it by force because that is the only way that anything has ever been done in Russia." The principle of the Revolution was to create a new society, as Sinclair knew well. But once again, a tradition of violence was an explanation, if not a downright excuse. Then Sinclair made quite a bold prediction:

> Unless the Fascists succeed in defeating the Soviet Union in the war they are planning and taking away the Ukraine and other grain-producing land, no more people need die of hunger in the Soviet Union. At least that is my belief; the million or five million lives which were sacrificed will mean the saving of hundreds of millions of lives in future times.[279]

In this Sinclair was technically correct. Once Stalin's government ran out of people that he wanted to starve, he did in fact stop starving them. But what was even more disturbing was the handwaving away of millions of real, flesh-and-blood people for the sake of some imaginary future hypothetical. "There has never been in human history a great social change without killing," Sinclair dishonestly claimed. "Our civil war cost a million lives and five billion dollars. If anyone argues that Lincoln and Grant were mass murderers, the only way you can answer is to point out the gains in the preservation of the union and the ending of chattel slavery." The comparison between lives lost in warfare and lives lost due to oppression by the government seemed to be lost on Sinclair—as is the fact that the Civil War led to freeing the enslaved, while Stalin had done everything in his power to crush the Ukrainian population. At the very least there was the tacit admission that there had been a war waged against the farmers, who were supposedly the same people Sinclair had championed his entire life.

The man who saw firsthand how duplicitous politicians could be had no qualm about taking Stalin's propaganda at face value. For Sinclair and for many others of his stripe, the enormously lagging economy—no one was Ending Poverty In Russia anytime soon—was all the fault of wreckers who deserved whatever they got. Despite its decades-old secret police, the Soviet Union was somehow overrun with both Nazi and Japanese (!) agents. According to Sinclair, questioning Stalin's claims wasn't an exercise in prudence so much as one in absurdity. "That Germany and Poland, Roumania and Japan have been filling the Soviet Union with spies and *provocateurs* is something which no sensible person would doubt for a moment," he proclaimed. "If such persons were sent into this country, and committed wholesale wrecking of machinery and destruction of human life, we would shoot them; and no doubt other nations which were getting ready to make war on us would denounce it as a terrible and barbarous action." Those who questioned Stalin's executions were the ones acting in bad faith, and simply trying to weaken Soviet power. After all, Americans also shoot people who break machinery.[280]

Sinclair also regarded as absurd the concept that the Russian people faced heavy literary censorship. Replying to Lyons, he wrote "You doubt the benefits of [Soviet] education, saying that 'only words written by the ruling clique may be read.' Will you really defend such a statement, or is it merely a bit of rhetoric?" And how did Sinclair know that Russian citizens had access to whatever they would like to read? He knew because "more than three million of my books have been translated and published in Russia."[281]

Sinclair could not disprove that there was complete government control of political discourse within the USSR, so he instead just sort of denied it. In response to the accusation that "all these persons are entirely enslaved," he simply declared that "I am unable to believe this, and I think that if the ruling group in Russia has committed a 'betrayal of the basic principles of Socialism, workers' democracy,' the educated workers will find it out in the course of time, and will find a way to get that which has been so elaborately promised to them for the past twenty years." How they would find such things out—and how they would learn such things from a state which starved millions of its own citizens—Sinclair didn't even bother to hypothesize.[282]

Finally, Sinclair defended the mass executions of Stalin's political opponents—or rather, those who were alleged to have been his opponents: "As to the left-wing extremists who have been trying to hamper [Stalin] by sabotage and underground civil war, I have been shocked and cried by their fate; but". There was always a "but." Sinclair ignored that "sabotage and underground civil war" in the Soviet Union had come to be defined simply as disagreeing with Stalin, insisting that "when they started the war on Stalin they did so at their own risk, and perfectly well knowing it. If the medicine they had to swallow is bitter, the answer is that it is their own medicine, which they have been brewing and administering throughout their political careers."[283] Once again drawing parallels between Stalin and the Founding Fathers—both were revolutionaries, after all—Sinclair points out that "we hanged Major Andre, and you could hardly doubt that we should have hanged Benedict Arnold if we had been able to catch him."[284]

In regards to the "obviously phoney trials," Sinclair claimed to have taken a balanced view:

> Over and over again I ask myself: Is it conceivable that revolutionists, trained in a lifetime of war against the Czar, would go into open court and confess to actions which they had not committed? I ask: Is there any torture, any kind of terror, physical, mental, or moral, which would induce them to such a thing?[285]

Rhetorical questions are perhaps of use rhetorically, but they do not affect reality in the slightest. If an individual cannot conceive of an answer to a question, that does not mean or even imply that the answer is inconceivable. It could simply mean that his knowledge or imagination is limited. The man who wrote of greedy capitalists selling sausages made of human meat found it impossible that men, even men trained in a lifetime of war, could be tortured to such a degree that they would make false confessions—even if they were confessing to things which were demonstrably false and literally impossible.

The greater the atrocity, the more people would like to believe—or possibly even need to believe—that the reports were surely an exaggeration. It would clearly be preferable if none of Stalin's innocent victims had been tortured. If denial was not an option, then bargaining comes in: let's haggle and hope for half the number claimed, and that the tortures that were alleged were exaggerated in the manner of some trashy story in a forgotten pulp magazine.

"The Stalin epoch is replete with what appear as improbabilities to minds unfitted to deal with the phenomena," wrote Conquest. "Similarly with the argument that Stalin could not have killed millions of peasants, since that would have been 'economically counterproductive.'"[286] It was akin to the enormous skepticism in the West regarding early reports about Nazi atrocities. It was almost impossible to conceive of such extremes of evil, and to multiply it on the scale necessary to process the information put it past the capacity of decent people. It brings to mind Leonard Cohen's poem "All There is to Know About Adolph Eichmann." After listing the Holocaust engineer's eyes, weight and height as "normal," Cohen asked, "What did you expect? Talons? Oversize incisors? Green saliva?"

Writing in 1994, communist writer Eugene Genovese explained the thinking thus:

> About twenty years ago, picking up on some passages in Roy Medvedev's [1971 book] *Let History Judge*, I wondered if Comrade Stalin had not killed more communists than were killed by all the bourgeois, imperialist, Fascist, and Nazi regimes put together. "It can't be true," said I. "Has Comrade Medvedev taken up serious drinking?" So I sat down to do some rough arithmetic. (You do not have to be good at math to do that much arithmetic.) Alas, Comrade Medvedev had not taken up serious drinking.[287]

Contemptuous of the idea that "Stalin's government is no better than those of Mussolini or Hitler," Sinclair made clear the distinction:

> I have read Mussolini's speeches, and know that he is one of those imperialist conquerors who care so little about truth and consistency that they can argue that their growing population must have more land to expand to, and at the same time can adopt measures to turn the women of their country into brood-mares to raise more future soldiers in order that their country may be able to expand.

This was in contrast to Stalin, who cared a great deal about truth and consistency, and never dared dream of imperialistic conquest. "Having watched the international policy of the Soviet Union from day to day as it has developed," Sinclair went on, "I say that its record is pretty nearly perfect, and that upon that record it is entitled to the trust of every friend of democracy and peace."[288]

Sneering at the idea that Stalin and Hitler could ever work together, Sinclair chose to go with sarcasm. "I would have thought that the shooting of Tukhachevsky and other pro-German generals might be taken to have settled that question for a long time. But to admit that would be to attribute something good to Stalin,"[289] the author said, frustrated that Stalin wasn't getting credit for all the good that he had done. Though Tukhachevsky and the other generals had been tortured to confess to working with Hitler, by 1957 he and his executed colleagues would be acquitted by the Soviet Union of all charges and politically rehabilitated.

Sinclair's sign-off to the whole affair did not age well, to put it mildly:

> I give you one simple method, as certain as litmus paper in a test-tube, to determine whether the Soviet Union has now become counter-revolutionary…[W]hen Hitler learns that the Soviet Union has become counter-revolutionary, he will reduce the ardor of his crusade against it…When that happens I will admit that Stalin has sold out the workers.[290]

Sinclair was hardly alone or unique. On August 14, 1939, a group of self-described "400 leading Americans" penned an open letter "calling for greater unity of the anti-fascist forces and strengthening of the front against aggression through closer cooperation with the Soviet Union." It doesn't take much to make the argument that an alliance with Stalin was the right move for the United States to make after the 1941 Pearl Harbor attacks: the enemy of my enemy is my friend. Yet two years before the Japanese assault on Hawaii, there was already a great amount of agitation for the United States to work closely with Stalin. Not in the sense of holding one's breath, but in the sense that this would be an unmitigated good.

The traditional, strongest argument for Americans to ally with Stalin—that Hitler was a unique evil—wasn't invoked. Not only was there no reference to Hitler's crimes, there was no argument to be made that if Hitler wasn't stopped then millions would be killed (if that were even preventable to begin with). Indeed, Hitler's persecution of the Jewish people wasn't even mentioned by the "leading Americans" at all. Their only mention of anti-Semitism was to insist that the Soviet Union has made "the expression of anti-Semitism or any racial animosity a criminal offense." In other words, these self-described leaders were boasting about the criminalization of speech in the USSR.

"On the domestic scene the reactionaries [...] have encouraged the fantastic falsehood that the USSR and the totalitarian states are basically alike," they said. The signatories were troubled by a "recent manifesto issued by the so-called [*sic*] Committee for Cultural Freedom". This was the official name of the Dewey Committee which had investigated the charges against Trotsky and all the others put on trial by Stalin and his men. The Committee had concluded that "it is impossible for any honest person, on the basis of records so full of contradictions and deliberate falsifications as the records of both trials, to come to any conclusion concerning their guilt or innocence of other charges, or the nature of their crimes if any."[291] "While we prefer to dwell on facts rather than personalities," the leading Americans claimed, "we feel it is necessary to point out that among the signers of this manifesto are individuals who have for years had as their chief political objective the maligning of the Soviet people and their government, and it is precisely these people who are the initiators and controllers of the committee." We can't tell if Trotsky had meeting in hotels that no longer existed because the people asking questions had a history of "the maligning of the Soviet people."

The letter then offered ten points how "Soviet socialism" differed from fascism. First and foremost was the claim that the USSR "continues as always to be a consistent bulwark against war and aggression, and works unceasingly for the goal of a peaceful international order." "The Soviet Union has emancipated woman and the family," they insisted, "and has developed an advanced system of child care." The kids were "taken care of," that was for sure.

Brazenly, they went on to claim that "The best literature from Homer to Thomas Mann, the best thought from Aristotle to Lenin, is available to the masses of the Soviet people" in a country where reading the wrong book was grounds for imprisonment and extermination. The USSR had taken part in "extending scientific procedures to every field, from economics to public health," not mentioning that it was the Russian people who were being experimented upon.

The ninth point might be the most explicit in its adulation of Stalin's professed ideology. The American public was told by the great minds of the day that

> The Soviet Union considers political dictatorship a transitional form and has shown a steadily expanding democracy in every sphere. Its epoch-making new Constitution guarantees Soviet citizens universal suffrage, civil liberties, the right to employment, to leisure, to free education, to free medical care, to material security in sickness and old age, to equality of the sexes in all fields of activity, and to equality of all races and nationalities.

The cast of signatories might seem oddly contemporary, especially in terms of informing—or perhaps simply forming—American political opinion. There's a professor of medicine from Stanford and a professor of English from Smith, as well as English professors from Columbia, Harvard, Wellesley, Sarah Lawrence and NYU. Syracuse offered their Chairman of the Department of Geology and Geography, and Columbia also offered their Professors of Industrial Engineering, Sociology, and of Zoology (the latter certainly being in a position to advise on keeping beings in captivity). A professor of Christian ethics from Union Theological Seminary felt comfortable signing his name in good conscience, as did one from Yale University Divinity School. The poets William Carlos Williams and Langston Hughes appear alongside the head of Automotive Labs at MIT as well as one of its professors of mathematics. James Thurber, Dorothy Parker's partner-in-snide and staff writer from *The New Yorker*, makes an appearance. Williams College has two professors of Government, with Vassar offering a German professor, the University of California a professor of Slavic languages and a professor of Russian Language and Institutions, and economics professors from the University of Chicago and Bryn Mawr. Yale Medical

School, Harvard, Hunter, Columbia, NYU and Colgate round out the list. Finally there are editors from both *The Nation* and *The New Republic*, a ballet producer, several "artists," as well as Dashiell Hammett, Granville Hicks (again!) and Ernest Hemingway.

It was the role of these men and women to promote ideas to the American people. As creators of public opinion, they had the power to declare an ideology as being mainstream and desirable. Indeed, they were the ones who defined what mainstream, desirable discourse consisted of. The theory of "the marketplace of ideas" was often unable to compete with the reality of a monopoly of ideology—especially in an era where the flow of information was far more tightly controlled and technologically limited.

Arendt had thoughts on how those who were partial to Stalinism operated:

> The sympathizers, who are to all appearances still innocuous fellow-citizens in a nontotalitarian society, can hardly be called single-minded fanatics; through them, the movements make their fantastic lies more generally acceptable, can spread their propaganda in milder, more respectable forms, until the whole atmosphere is poisoned with totalitarian elements which are hardly recognizable as such but appear to be normal political reactions or opinions. The fellow-traveler organizations surround the totalitarian movements with a mist of normality and respectability that fools the membership about the true character of the outside world as much as it does the outside world about the true character of the movement.[292]

Days after the letter was published, Hitler not only reduced the ardor of his crusade against the Soviet Union but signed a non-aggression pact with Stalin. "One may accept or reject the ideology of Hitlerism as well as any other ideological system: that is a matter of taste," Soviet Foreign Minister Molotov decreed soon after.[293] News of the Molotov-

Ribbentrop Pact shook the world, and knowing he had nothing to fear from Stalin gave Hitler the freedom to invade Poland. Stalin likewise invaded from the east a little over two weeks later. American organizations that had advocated for involvement in Europe to fight fascism changed their names and slogans overnight—literally overnight—to advocating for "peace" and non-intervention. For many on the left, aligning with Hitler was a bridge too far and they permanently turned their backs on their infatuation with Stalin. As for Upton Sinclair, he never did end up admitting that Stalin had sold out the workers.

Chapter 8

IN CONSTANT TERROR FROM MORNING TO NIGHT

FDR was the first president to have his policy publicly guided by intellectuals, instead of mostly politicians or other prominent citizens. His "brain trust" was taken from the faculties of Harvard Law and Columbia, and the term ("trust" meant "monopoly") implied that all the great minds of the day were concentrated in his White House. As such, FDR was unusually attuned to what the creators of public opinion were saying at any given time—and he needed all the brain power he could get.

As the 1930s drew to a close, the Great Depression plodded on with no end in sight. Clearly capitalism wasn't working, and even the New Deal wasn't new enough for many leading thinkers of the day. Unemployment was at 19% in December of 1938, somewhat better than the 23.6% it had been when FDR was elected in 1932 but still nowhere near a palatable number. Worse, economic growth in 1938 had been negative for the first time in five years, shrinking at 3.3%.[294]

In many ways the year 1940 was an unprecedented one in American politics, largely because FDR intended to seek a third term. No president had been elected or even nominated to a third term before, despite several attempts by some to hold on to power. Even a stroke-ridden

Woodrow Wilson had to be told by his own party that his services would no longer be required in 1920.

Prior to 1940 it had basically been up to the party conventions to choose the vice presidential nominee. This resulted in some truly odd pairings, such as conservative President William McKinley being matched with vigorous upstart Teddy Roosevelt in 1900. In 1932 FDR had Speaker of the House John "Cactus Jack" Garner foisted upon him at the convention. The prickly Texan did not at all consider himself a subordinate to the president, being instrumental in helping engineer the defeat of FDR's 1937 court-packing scheme—the first major political defeat that the president had faced.

By 1940 Garner had enough, and declared himself a candidate for the presidency before FDR made any declaration about seeking a third term. When FDR decided that he himself was the only man for the job once again, having Garner on the 1940 ticket became a non-starter—as was the idea that choosing his running mate should be left up to the whims of the party.[295]

"This is no ordinary time," First Lady Eleanor Roosevelt told the convention. Her coded words did much to allow the attendees to cede their historic role and give FDR the man whom he had hand-picked as his running mate: Secretary of Agriculture Henry Agard Wallace, a former hardcore Republican turned strong New Deal advocate. Wallace was not an entirely easy person to put over, even by FDR to his own convention. A New Ager before the term existed, DNC Chairman Jim Farley worried that "people look on him as a mystic". What Farley was referring to was Wallace's fairly well-known interest in Eastern faiths like Buddhism and Zoroastrianism. More politically dangerous was what became known as the "Dear Guru" letters that Wallace had exchanged with Russian theosophist Nicholas Roerich, who was seen as a sort of neo-Rasputin with hypnotic sway.

FDR insisted Wallace was "not a mystic" but instead "a philosopher, a liberal philosopher."[296] And while there was some pushback among Democrats, President Roosevelt's hold over the party was enormous. "I won't deliver that acceptance speech until we see whom they nominate," he threatened to Party insiders. That was pretty much enough to put

Wallace over the top. He was nominated on the first ballot, despite the discomfort of many Democrats.

The 1940 GOP nominee was businessman Wendell Willkie, who had no previous political experience and who strongly shared FDR's vision of a firmly internationalist United States ensuring a fair and just world for peoples all over the globe. (It naturally followed that Willkie's first book would be entitled *One World.*) The Roosevelt/Wallace ticket was handily elected over Willkie, 449 electoral votes to 82. A year after the election came Pearl Harbor, the first foreign assault on US soil since 1812. America was now solidly and firmly involved in World War II.

The vice presidency is, historically, a thankless political position. Woodrow Wilson's Vice President Thomas Marshall was known for his wisecracks, and had quipped in 1912 that "Once there were two brothers. One ran away to sea, the other was elected Vice President, and nothing was ever heard of either of them again."[297] There is something to be said for the fact that Marshall's joke is far better known today than he himself is.

Henry Wallace's tenure as vice president was largely uneventful for the bulk of his term. It was still very much FDR's White House, and after Pearl Harbor the vice president's role became even more diminished than usual. It was only by 1944—the year Roosevelt would seek a fourth term—that Henry Wallace made major waves when he authored a pamphlet entitled *Our Job in the Pacific*. The contents would largely become a big deal due to one of the vilest people who had ever lived: Roald Dahl.

Dahl's name survives as one of the most widely-read and respected children's book authors of all time, with classic after classic to his credit like *James and the Giant Peach* and *Charlie and the Chocolate Factory*. A giant of a man, the 6'5" or 6'6" (accounts differ) Brit was quite vocal throughout his life about his racist and anti-Semitic views. Claims that "Hitler didn't just pick on them for no reason"[298] paled in comparison to his personal behavior. Dahl would eventually end up marrying actress Patricia Neal, who had played the romantic interest (and offscreen lover) to star Gary Cooper in the film adaptation of Ayn Rand's *The Fountainhead.* The movie's sexual tension had culminated in Neal's "rape by engraved invitation"[299] by Cooper. Dahl acted similarly after his wife suffered a serious of three strokes in rapid succession, temporarily putting her into a coma and causing newspapers to prematurely run her obituary. Her recovery process was nightmarish:

> We were sleeping together but sex hadn't entered my mind. So when his hand touched me I was stunned. [...] I did not tell him he couldn't do that, but I hoped he would hear my silent signal. Half my body was paralyzed and the other half rigid with tension. [...] I closed my eyes and did not move. I did not scream. I wanted to. It was agony. Agony.[300]

In 1944, however, Dahl's greatest claim to fame was having been shot down and badly burned during a Royal Air Force pilot mission over Greece. He was also a British secret service agent assigned to Washington, and it was in that capacity that he uncovered information that would help to torpedo Wallace's career. As Wallace biographer John C. Culver recounts:

> Dahl attended a social gathering at the Washington home of the Texas newspaper publisher Charles Marsh. There he saw Marsh and Wallace reviewing the manuscript of *Our Job in the Pacific*. After Wallace left, Marsh showed the manuscript to Dahl. The agent took the manuscript downstairs, where he said he could read it in privacy. Instead, he called a contact at British Security Coordination and told him to come quickly to Marsh's house. "I handed the draft through the car window and told him he must be back with it in fifteen minutes," Dahl recalled. "The man buzzed off to the BSC Washington offices and duly returned the manuscript to me on the dot."[301]

In the pamphlet Wallace advocated the decolonialization of East Asia, something entirely at odds with the British perspective at the time—especially the perspective of Prime Minister Winston Churchill. "You know Churchill is likely to ask the president to get a new vice president," Dahl correctly predicted. Churchill blew his top, and though the relationship between him and FDR was a complex and often difficult one, there is little doubt that the British animus toward Wallace affected the president's perspective.

The Brits were not alone. After four years in office Wallace had acquired a reputation of being too cozy with the radical left. Though clearly an ideological progressive, many Democrats also remembered that Wallace had been a loyal Republican not that long ago (in a period where men like the senators La Follette represented the vibrant left-wing tradition within the GOP). These concerns were especially important for White House insiders who could see firsthand that President Roosevelt was on his last legs, making the question of his possible successor one of utmost importance.

Three things happened on July 11, 1944. First, FDR officially announced that he would be seeking a fourth term as president. Second, FDR decided to dump Wallace from the ticket. Third, he met with Wallace to strategize about the forthcoming campaign. Just as with Upton Sinclair, Wallace left the meeting certain that FDR would shortly be endorsing him.

Ten days later—and with FDR's blessing—Democratic Party chairman Robert Hannegan and other party insiders used all the power at their disposal to make sure that Henry Wallace was removed from the ticket, and Senator Harry S. Truman nominated as the vice presidential candidate instead. The FDR/Truman ticket won another landslide, thirty-six out of the forty-eight states, while regaining twenty-two seats in the House after the 1942 midterms had reduced the Democrats' margin to a handful.

Five weeks after the inauguration FDR was posing for an artist when he either declared "I have a terrific pain in the back of my head" or "I have a terrific headache" before dying from a cerebral hemorrhage. Truman had been drinking with Speaker of the House Sam Rayburn when the call came for him to go to the White House immediately. There he met the First Lady and was told the news. Concerned, he asked Eleanor Roosevelt if there was anything that he could do for her. "Is there anything *we* can do for *you*?" she replied. "You are the one in trouble now."[302]

A year after he would have been inaugurated as president, Henry Wallace published a book entitled *Soviet Asia Mission* about his trip abroad as vice president. In it, Wallace discussed touring Siberia and the Far East, and his impressions of the people and places that he saw. While FDR was administrating concentration camps for Japanese-Americans at home, his vice president had been touring one in the Soviet Union—and offering his approval of the conditions that the prisoners faced.

There are very few loanwords that English speakers have borrowed from the Russian language. "Robot" is often considered to be one of these, even though the origin is Czech. "Bistro" is another, the allegation being that Russian customers would yell "Bistro, bistro!" ("Quickly, quickly!") at French waitstaff in attempts to get them to hurry—but this seems to be more of a good story than good etymology. But there is one word in English whose Russian origin is not in dispute: *Gulag*. The term's Russian origin is itself an acronym for *G*lavnoye *U*pravleniye *Lag*erey, which translates to Chief Administration of the Camps.

Lyons summed up the intellectuals' mindset regarding Russian oppression quite succinctly:

> To a good many onlookers the Russian revolution is a great experiment, in which sociological results to be attained justify a colossal human investment. The one hundred and sixty million inhabitants are the raw material of the experiment, and a formula for economic perfection is its objective. The application of pressure here and there, as required by the research experts, the exiling or physical extinction of a portion of the population—it's all part of the experimental process. Those who are squeamish are just white-livered sentimentalists in a class with vegetarians and anti-vivisectionists.

> It is the "guinea pig" theory of the revolution. [...] Of course the animals squeal. But why should superior people be bothered about the noise? When you peer down from above, watching "objectively," the Russians look quite small.[303]

French existentialist Jean-Paul Sartre was not unique though more explicit in his views, writing that "As we were not members of the Party it was not our duty to write about Soviet labor camps" and that "I find these camps intolerable, but I find *equally* intolerable the use made of them every day in the bourgeois press."[304] Theodore Dreiser was one of the great American novelists, still remembered for seminal works of naturalism such as *Sister Carrie* and *Jennie Gerhardt*. His sentiments in a 1933 missive mirrored Sartre's:

> I would answer your question about those Russian prisoners at once, except that I am so much interested in the present difficulties in Russia and in Russia's general fate, that I am not prepared, without very serious consideration, to throw a monkey-wrench such as this could prove to be, into their machinery. It seems to me, whether badly managed or well managed, that it is at least a set-up which should be preserved and fought for. If that means serious and, in some cases, seemingly cruel sacrifices, it is, as we say, just too bad. But, after all, if, by any process whatsoever, (this, or any other) Russia is seriously crippled or destroyed, what good would freeing those prisoners do?[305]

Yet unlike Sartre or Dreiser or virtually all of the "400 leading Americans," Vice President Wallace had visited the Soviet Union personally. And not only did he visit, he toured the Siberian Gulag town of Magadan himself. "Over 40,000,000 people have taken the place of the 7,000,000—mostly convicts—who miserably existed there under Imperial Russia," Wallace explained. He compared the Siberian growth in population to how "America after the Civil War developed her wild

West, pushing triumphantly to the Pacific and creating what Los Angeles, San Francisco, Portland, Seattle and Denver mean today."[306] One might think that perhaps the climate and therefore livability in Los Angeles would in and of itself make the comparison to Siberian development a reach, but that was hardly the worst of it.

Wallace credulously reported his Russian contact telling him that, "Twelve years ago the first settlers arrived and put up eight prefabricated houses. Today Magadan has 40,000 inhabitants and all are well housed."[307] Wallace helpfully explained that "urban growth in northern Siberia is a proof that the climate is not an insuperable obstacle to settlement in the Arctic," as if a bunch of adventurous families had all decided to pack up and try to make their claim in Siberia. He was just blown away by these plucky Russians: "The remarkable fact is that this Siberian urban growth is taking place in advance of rail and motor-road communications."[308] Wallace was oblivious to the reality that virtually all of these trips to Siberia were both one-way and permanent.

He made it a point to note that when it came to the NKVD everybody "treated them with great respect. […] I became very fond of their leader".[309] While boasting about how relatively well the shovel operators were paid (if the figures he repeats were even credible), Wallace neglected to mention that the nearby Karlag camp was a source of slave labor for the coal mines. Huge numbers of deportees were not even accused of any crimes, but were sent there simply due to their ethnicity—a constant issue in the heavily multiethnic Soviet Union. "The people of Siberia today are a hardy vigorous race," Wallace explained, "but not because they are whipped into submission. The only whip driving them is the necessity to master a vast new land."[310] Yet as of 2020, farmers were still uncovering dozens of bodies of people who had been executed by the NKVD.[311]

Wallace mused very enthusiastically about the literal song-and-dance performance that the Russians performed for him, gushing that "I don't think I have ever seen anything better put on by the talent of a single city." [312] It was actually not, as he characterized it, "a concert by a nonprofessional Red Army choir of service men stationed in the town" but one put on by prisoners. The conductor was a prisoner; the lead ballerina was a prisoner; and the choir was all prisoners. There were, in fact, almost no Red Army servicemen in Magadan.[313] The captives had rehearsed all night, and signed an oath to comport themselves as Soviet patriots. The two singers who had known English were shipped away, and when the vice president's show ended the prisoner-performers were loaded back into trucks and returned to the camp.[314] Whatever the dramatic content of the show, the circumstances surrounding it can only be described as a farce.

That "[t]he Soviets are definitely planning for a big increase of population in their eastern territory" was for Wallace not a premonition of vast human suffering but 20th century frontiersmanship because "Soviet Asia will see the rise of its own 'Pittsburghs, Clevelands and Detroits.'"[315] After all, "[t]here exist no other two countries more alike than the Soviet Union and the United States of America."[316] He took time to both praise "Marshal Stalin's wise leadership"[317] and to point out that "Roosevelt instantly felt at home with Stalin."[318] Wallace elsewhere asserted that the "people of the United States should have been taught the truth about the Russian Revolution from the very start,"[319] though what said truth is and who was lying about the Revolution he does not explain.

"This is nothing irreconcilable in our aims and purposes," Wallace concluded. "Those who so proclaim are wittingly or unwittingly looking for war—and that, in my opinion, is criminal."[320] How criticizing the Soviet system in general or, say, denouncing slave labor camps would be "looking for war" Wallace chooses not to make clear—not to mention who he imagines would be waging war on whom.

This claim of warmongering was a common tactic for the Henrys Wallace of the world. As Orwell himself pointed out, when "Henry Wallace is asked by a newspaper interviewer why he issued falsified versions of his speeches to the press, he replies: 'So you are one of those people who are clamouring for war with Russia.'"[321]

Wallace was happy to accuse his political opponents of wanting war. Wars weren't the result of power-hungry political leaders, no, they were the result of...*inequality*. "War in our generation began in 1914 and has, in the main, continued in one form or another for more than thirty years," he asserted. "When we dip deeply into the economic and scientific causes of these thirty years of terrible struggle we find the outstanding factor to be the unequal growth of industrialization and the consequent unequal growth of population and political power among nations."[322]

The worst part, perhaps, was how Wallace breezily dismissed the millions of people starved by Stalin in the Ukraine and elsewhere as merely a price to be paid for progress:

> Collective farming, to Stalin, was a method of making agriculture more productive, of getting the food surplus necessary to support urban workers. *We in the United States may regard the methods employed as too costly in human terms*, but there is no denying that it was a measure for integrating farm output with urban growth, and a necessary measure if the industrialization plan, out of which came Karaganda and the other new [Gulag] towns, was to succeed.[323] [Emphasis added.]

Part of Wallace's tour included information about a gold mine; he was not told that it had led to over sixteen thousand deaths in 1942 alone.[324] In fact few of the people Wallace encountered were what they appeared or claimed to be. Being a politician—and a politician with a great deal of knowledge about farming and agriculture—Wallace made it a point to chat with as many ordinary people as he could. The bureaucrats who were pretending that they worked at the pig farm were clueless about his questions regarding pig husbandry, but were saved by the quick work of the translators.

Decades after Wallace's visit, the hidden history of the Gulag system has become better understood. Technically speaking, its roots lay in the czar's katorga series of prisons which held so many of the Old Bolsheviks before the Revolution. That said, in 1916 there were fewer than 30,000 total prisoners, while the USSR's Gulag routinely held two million at a time.[325] Though the term Gulag came about under Stalin, by 1921 Lenin was already running eighty-four various camps for potential enemies and those deemed to be unreliable elements. That number became an archipelago of over 30,000 camps under Stalin, and it was under his reign that the camps began to be used for slave labor—especially in areas universally understood to be inhospitable to human life. Since many of the imprisoned were highly educated and technically skilled, it is no surprise that every Soviet industry from farming to military design was supported by the forced labor of prisoners.[326]

The first Gulag camp is widely regarded to be Solovetsky, for this was the first camp that had been established by the Tcheka independently of the larger Soviet justice system. It was there, in 1926, where the concept of using forced labor as a method of "reeducation" first began to be implemented.[327] A converted former monastery, Solovetsky was located on a series of islands northwest of the city of Archangel. Roughly the same latitude as Fairbanks, Alaska, temperatures average from 4.6°F in January to 61.7°F in July. In 1923 there were a few hundred prisoners there, mostly political foes (including former allies) of the Bolsheviks. By 1925 there were six thousand, including many of those who had fought in the Kronstadt rebellion.[328] That winter a quarter of them would die due to the terrible conditions they were living under, including the high workload, poor food, and an epidemic of typhus (a disease spread by lice).

It was at Solovetsky that the inhuman sadism we have come to associate with concentration camps reared its head. Gulag historian Anne Applebaum writes that

> Solovetsky guards had regularly left undressed prisoners in the old, unheated cathedral bell towers in the winter, their hands and feet tied behind their backs with a single piece of rope. They had also put prisoners "to the bench," meaning they were forced to sit on poles for up to eighteen hours without moving, sometimes with weights tied to their legs and their feet not touching the floor, a position guaranteed to leave them crippled. Sometimes, prisoners would be made to go naked to the baths, up to 2 kilometers away, in freezing weather. Or they were deliberately given rotten meat. Or they were refused medical help. At other times,

> prisoners would be given pointless, unnecessary tasks: to move huge quantities of snow from one place to another, for example, or to jump off bridges into rivers whenever a guard shouted "Dolphin!"[329]

Political prisoners under the czar—including Bolsheviks—had enjoyed certain a surprisingly high standard of living, with access to books, writing instruments, a fair amount of food and even decent clothing. At the early stage of what would become the Gulag system the prisoners still had the idea that they had rights. Their misconception was swiftly corrected. When one prisoner complained that someone had taken his parcel from home, he was stripped and tied to a post in the summer woods, helpless while swarms of mosquitos bled them dry. Others were executed at random, sometimes en masse. An accusation of plotting rebellion was enough of a pretense to kill as many people as the guards desired, with little possibility or time for the captives to disprove the accusation. The arbitrary nature of the murders created an atmosphere of constant terror, as it was intended to.

Solovetsky was just the beginning. It was in Siberia where the Gulag grew and grew as the Bolsheviks increased their power over the Soviet citizenry. Rounding up convicts often took a fair amount of time. Many would at first be loaded into trucks which on the outside were labeled "bread" or "fruits." They would sit organized in the shape of a chevron, with one person spreading his legs so the next could sit between them and so on with the next captive. In some cases waiting in the severe cold caused permanent physical damage for the adults and death for the child captives.[330]

Even without such extremes the train trip to the Far East was hardly idyllic. Lice—and the diseases they carried—were ubiquitous. The simple need to relieve oneself was used as a mechanism of control by some of the guards or even a simple exercise in cruelty by others. All it took was one prisoner losing bowel control or getting sick to turn the atmosphere in the carriage even more unbearable. It often took a month for the trip from Moscow to the Siberian Gulag region of Kolyma, a month in which the prisoner was literally removed from his former life and basic human civilization.

The traveling captives would often go days without any water, and when they were fortunate to receive their one full cup they would have to choose between drinking it all at once or rationing it out throughout the day.[331] Passengers sticking out their cups between the window bars to catch rainfall would be threatened with getting shot. Stops to discard the deceased were an inevitable occurrence. It goes without saying that many of the infants and children aboard the train cars never made it to the camps. Mothers often killed themselves, slitting their throats with glass, or sometimes grew mad in the conditions, forcing their infants to be taken care of by other women.[332]

Those who survived the train ride were still not done, for the Kolyma camps were only reachable by boat. Attempts were made to keep the nature and extent of the growing Gulag system secret from the population at large and from foreign countries. The NKVD need for complete secrecy caused them to force their human cargo below deck when close to Japan. In at least one instance a Russian ship hit a reef and the crew refused to ask for help lest the nature of their journey be exposed. There were of course no lifeboats for the prisoners, and though a few Japanese fisherman tried to assist over one thousand people died.[333]

The juvenile delinquents who so plagued the prison system were found here as well. They served a purpose in the sense of keeping the captive population in a state of huddled fear, as they reveled in hurling abuse at the adults such as by spitting on them or urinating on them. Actual criminals were part of the trip too, seizing control of the ship's plank. Literal murderers and the like, they far outnumbered the guards who themselves were often too afraid to intervene. They would have fun by tossing fish guts at the political captives who dared to stick out their heads, or by vomiting on those in the cargo when they got seasick.[334] These conditions made it harder and harder for the prisoners to think of themselves as civilized human beings with rights of any kind.

Indeed, the "counter-revolutionaries" sentenced for political purposes were legally and explicitly regarded as worse than mere murderers or rapists, who were at least still members of "the people." As one political prisoner explained:

> The criminals, however, were always told: You have broken the law and must pay the penalty for it, but you are not enemies of the people. The enemies of the people are the counterrevolutionaries [...] and they alone are responsible for everything that goes wrong in our country. They must be annihilated.[335]

Guards would be threatened or bribed by criminals to let men into the separate women's hold, gangs of whom had their way with the female captives one after another. One eyewitness described such a raid:

> Several men attacked each woman at once. I could see the victims' white bodies twisting, their legs kicking forcefully, their hands clawing the men's faces. The women bit, cried and wailed. The rapists smacked them back...when the rapists ran out of women, some of the bulkier men turned to the bed boards and hunted for young men. These adolescents were added to the carnage, lying still on their stomachs, bleeding and crying on the floor.[336]

The male captives, hundreds of them, sat there watching the whole thing. Any man who tried to assist would be crushed to death, as happened during another such raid.[337] After the guards blasted the hold with water to end the raid, they went down and dragged out both the women who had been injured and those who had been killed.

Much of the skepticism about conditions in the Soviet Union was based on the very rational premise that this sort of mistreatment made no sense, for a large number of the captives who finally reached the camps were useless in terms of labor due to the horrors they had suffered en route, horrors that in some cases could have been prevented by simply allowing them to have water. But that would have been extra work for the guards, who had little incentive to lift a finger to assist a group of people who had officially been declared to no longer be members of society or even the human race.

Arriving at the camps the captives were greeted by various signs, with one example being the claim that "With Just Work I Will Pay My Debt to the Fatherland," reminiscent of Auschwitz's notorious *Arbeit Macht Frei* sign.[338] Signage reminded the prisoners that he who does not work does not eat, but he who did work often didn't eat much either. Being too weak to fulfill one's work quota was often taken as evidence of the alleged counter-revolutionary behavior that got a person sent to the camps to begin with. Here at last were the wreckers made flesh, continuing their intransigence against the people's republic.

There was an idea in Kremlin circles that the camps should become economically self-sustaining. A caste system was introduced early on, with prisoners divided between heavy workers (who got the most food), light workers, and invalids who received half the food rations of the strong group. The critique that capitalism leads to the "rich getting richer" was here implemented as the organizing principle, with the strong getting stronger while the weakest grew weaker simply due to caloric intake alone.[339]

It was by 1937, during the Great Terror, where the nature of the camps took a turn. Stalin now sent regional quotas to the NKVD, telling them how many people he expected to be arrested, with the numbers broken down by each given region. It then became their role to find that amount of men and women to arrest and send away. If Stalin said to find ten thousand criminals in, say, the Turkmen Soviet Socialist Republic, the secret police would arrest ten thousand people regardless of whether that many criminals existed there or not.[340] Instead of merely being exploitative, with poor living conditions causing many to perish, the Gulag now became a place where the deaths of prisoners was regarded not as an accident or a cost or an afterthought but as an outright goal.

Outdoor work in the camps was compulsory all year around, only pausing if the temperature reached -50°C (-58°F). Working "inside" was not much better. Coal miners had to deal with water dripping on them, causing severe short-term and long-term consequences. In 1937 Stalin had also decided that the prisoners were being coddled. Thereafter it was forbidden for the prisoners to use fur to stay warm. They were forced to use wadding for protection and to walk in canvas shoes instead of felt boots—if they even had or were given shoes at all, which many did not.[341] Siberian blizzards are so notorious in their ferocity that even westerners know to fear them. All of this contributed to a near-total extermination rate in some locations, with Soviet sources themselves reporting a death rate of 97-98% of the inmates.[342]

When one free citizen tried to warn camp administrators that people in the camps might die, the response from the camp representative was clear: "What 'people'? These are enemies of the people." Other officials were as blunt: "We are not trying to bring down the mortality rate."[343] Captives were forbidden to refer to themselves as "comrades," which was the standard greeting in the rest of the egalitarian Soviet Union. And in a bizarre but logical twist, despite the increasing ubiquity of his image in the greater USSR at large, simply looking at Stalin's picture was also not allowed to them.[344]

Nevertheless, the captives were still often subject to workshops where the speakers blathered political ideology at them. One Polish Jew who got swept into the Gulag recalled how

> a professional agitator with the mentality of a six-year-old child would address the prisoners on the nobility of putting all their effort into work. He would tell them that noble people are patriots, that all patriots love Soviet Russia, the best country in the world for the working man, that Soviet citizens are proud to belong to such a country, etc. etc. for two solid hours—all this to an audience whose very skins bore witness to the absurdity and the hypocrisy of such statements.[345]

"For hours and hours the lecturer went on," recalled another camp survivor, "trying to prove that God did not exist, that He was nothing but some bourgeois invention. We should consider ourselves lucky to have found ourselves among the Soviets, the most perfect country in the world. Here in the camp we should learn how to work and at last become decent people."[346] "In our camps, you were expected not only to be a slave laborer, but to sing and smile while you worked as well," another former prisoner told Applebaum. "They didn't just want to oppress us: they wanted us to thank them for it."[347]

Prisoners often had to be beaten in order to get them to bathe in the freezing cold rooms that they would then have to stand around in naked afterward. In the Soviet Union the average person frequently had difficulty getting enough to eat, and in the Gulag food was disgusting even by prison conditions, often watery soups with fish heads or a piece of fat floating inside. Some prisoners were forced to eat outdoors, where the soup invariably froze.[348]

Antipathy toward organized religion was central to the communist state, and there was great pressure to break the spirits of prisoners who relied on their faith. One group of female prisoners refused to wear numbered clothing due to the dictates of their religion, so the numbers were stamped directly onto their skin. For added humiliation they were forced to attend camp roll calls in the nude.[349] In 1930 another religious group regarded Soviet passports, money and the like as symbols of the Anti-Christ and refused to have anything to do with it. They were shipped to an island in the White Sea and told they could have food only if they signed for it. When they repeatedly refused they were simply left there to starve to death, which they naturally all did.[350]

Diseases of malnutrition like pellagra were common in the camps, worsened by the theft of food by everyone from guards down to those prisoners working to prepare the meals. Peeling potatoes is viewed as a punishment in the American military, but in the Gulag it was a highly-coveted role that might have saved a given prisoner's life due to having access to nutrition. As with other prisons, cultural mores developed within the mini-societies that each camp became, with unspoken rules being enforced with, in some cases, extreme brutality. "If a prisoner stole clothes, tobacco, or almost anything else and was discovered, he could expect a beating from his fellow prisoners," recalled one survivor of the Gulag, "but the unwritten law of the camp [...] was that a prisoner caught stealing another's bread earned a death sentence."[351] Specifically, the thief would be tossed into the air over and over until he was seriously injured, and then would be thrown out of the barracks by his fellow prisoners to die.

The Kolyma basin is a huge Arctic region named for the river that cuts through it, though most of the rivers in the area are icebound for eight to nine months per year. At one point it held the distinction for recording the lowest temperatures on earth.[352] There was a song in Russia about the climate:

> Kolyma, wonderful land,
> Twelve months winter, the rest summer.
> For about two months in winter, there is no sunrise at all.

The brutal cold forced inmates to get creative in order to stay alive, and one of humanity's earliest mechanisms for maintaining warm bodies was practiced between prisoners or between female prisoners and guards. As a result of this, pregnancy in the Gulag was not an entirely uncommon phenomenon. Those children who managed to survive through to birth were fed by their mothers but housed separately from them (possibly for the best, given the conditions that prisoners lived under). After a year the babies were permanently taken from their mothers and handed over to the secret police. "You have broken the regulations," the women were told. "Connections with men are not permitted. Therefore the children are ours, not yours. They belong to the Security Organs, and we will bring them up." Estimates range as to whether it was 500,000 or a million such infants who were seized over the years.[353]

Those infants still fared better than the children who were imprisoned in the Gulag themselves, where even being seven years old was not enough to stave off beatings and humiliations (not to mention the omnipresent cold and hunger). Parentless boys and girls who were taken to associated "children's homes" had to deal with all of the above, as well as sexual assaults both from older children and administrators. Those who grew up in the inhuman conditions of the Gulag grew up to themselves become something inhuman, as recalled former prisoner Lez Razgon:

> They feared nothing and no one. The guards and camp bosses were scared to enter the separate barracks where the juveniles lived. It was there that the vilest, most cynical and cruel acts that took place in the camps occurred. If one of the prisoners' criminal leaders was gambling, lost everything and had staked his life as well, the boys would kill him for a day's bread ration or simply "for the fun of it." The girls boasted that they could satisfy an entire team of tree-fellers.[354]

One need not have grown up in the Gulag to become transformed by it. When World War II came strict new regulations came with it:

> A *ukase* was issued which provided that any worker who left his job in a war plant, no matter for what reasons, was subject to from six to eight years of imprisonment. Hundreds of young girls between the ages of eighteen and twenty were sent to Kolyma for running away to their villages because they could no longer endure the starvation in the cities where they had been forced to work. Some had only gone back home for a few days to visit a sick mother, but the factory manager would not give them any days off and when they returned they were arrested. They came as adolescents and were instantly transformed by Kolyma into full-fledged prostitutes.[355]

Much like being an NKVD head, running the Gulag was a powerful but personally very dangerous position. Gulag chief Fyodor Eichmans was shot in 1938, and his two successors both shot one after another in

1939.[356] All this fed into the mentality of "If only Stalin knew…!" True believers in the communist system explained away their own personal imprisonment as "a plot by the local NKVD," "the very cunning work of foreign intelligence services" or the ubiquitous invisible wreckers. Others better understood the consequences of a system built on destroying such bourgeois ideas as individualism, insisting that the "repressions are a historical necessity for the development of our society."[357]

Escape was impossible because there was simply nowhere to go in the Arctic wilderness. For a civilian to help an escapee would be a life-threatening risk in a region so unfitted to habitation to begin with. Herling-Grudziński discusses the story of one man who managed to get out of his Gulag, finally finding a nearby village after a week of wandering and then collapsing inside of the first hut that he found. The camp chief had reportedly never even bothered to send out a search team, knowing that the man "would either die in the forest or come back to the camp." Indeed, the "peasants drove him back to the camp and there the guards took him to the internal prison, where, still unconscious, he was beaten so cruelly that for three months he was near death, and even after his life had been saved he had to remain in the hospital for another two months."

The escapee survived only in order to serve as a living testament to the hopelessness of the prisoners' situations. "You can't escape from the camp, my friends," he repeatedly warned his fellows. "Freedom isn't for us. We're chained to this place for the rest of our lives, even though we aren't wearing chains. We can escape, we can wander about, but in the end we'll come back. That's our fate, our accursed fate."[358] Indeed, suicide wasn't even an option but not because it wasn't tempting. "The chief reason for the relatively low rate of suicide," explained one captive, "is the fact that prisoners are never alone."[359]

The workload was as varied as industry could be. The *Guide to the System of Corrective-Labor Camps in the USSR* recounts "the existence of camps organized around gold mines, coal mines, nickel mines; highway and railway construction; arms factories, chemical factories, metal-processing plants, electricity plants; the building of airports, apartment blocks, sewage systems; the digging of peat, the cutting of trees, and the canning of fish." Picture albums demonstrate the production of everything up to and including the proverbial kitchen sink, including "mines, missiles, and other army equipment; car parts, door locks, buttons; logs floating down rivers; wooden furniture, including chairs, cabinets, telephone boxes, and barrels; shoes, baskets, and textiles (with samples attached); rugs, leather, fur hats, sheepskin coats; glass cups, lamps, and jars; soap and candles; even toys—wooden tanks, tiny windmills, and mechanical rabbits playing drums."[360]

It is not an exaggeration to say that the economy of the Soviet Union was heavily predicated on—if not based entirely on—the forced labor of hundreds of thousands of innocent people being kept imprisoned in the camps of the Gulag. It only took a geological discovery in a remote region to launch a ship of thousands of prisoners in icy storms in the spring of 1940. When they landed they then had to build their new prisons while the guards stood by with bayonets. When a hurricane came the guards and prisoners were washed away alike, only leaving those who had managed to tie themselves to the posts that had been put up. Only a few hundred eventually managed to return to Magadan a year later, where the doctors proceeded to remove those body parts that had been taken by frostbite. As the prisoner-nurse later wrote, "not one failed to pay for his life with frozen hands or feet, frozen ears, nose or cheeks."[361]

Contact with the outside world was mixed at best. Some prisoners would be allowed visits with family members a couple of times a year, but even that was predicated on the family knowing where the captive had been taken. Worse, maintaining contact with someone convicted of being a counter-revolutionary or a kulak was very risky behavior. Some wives had the decency to visit in order to tell their spouses to their face that they had decided to divorce, and they could hardly be blamed for it. Letters and packages sent into and out of the camps were subject to inspection by guards in a country where even someone with impeccable class consciousness could expect to have their mail read by the authorities, and where the postal service hardly operated with any semblance of efficiency.

Food and gifts were prime for plunder by the guards, whereas letters piled up in stacks of thousands by guards who could not be bothered to distribute them. Families would assume the worst when their letters would be unreplied to, while prisoners would assume that they had been disowned when they had no contact from their loved ones. Even for the administrators themselves basic stationery and writing implements were hardly ubiquitous. A prisoner who possessed such items could easily be construed as sending secret missives against the authorities. For every captive whose life was saved by a parcel of food sent from home that somehow got past the guards—it took three years in one critical case[362]—there were many more whose starvation or malnutrition could have been prevented if they simply got what had been mailed to them.

The slave camps of the Nazis and President Truman's victory over them is widely remembered today, but the Gulag and Henry Wallace are largely forgotten. Though the level of appreciation for Truman has increased over the decades, during his 1948 reelection campaign he was popularly regarded as a bit of a screwup who lucked his way into the presidency. "We're just mild about Harry" was the slogan for the day, and it was a given that after four Democrat terms in the White House the next president would be another New York governor, Republican Thomas Dewey. Truman's 1948 upset election victory was captured by the famous photo of him holding up the mistaken *Chicago Daily Tribune* headline reading "DEWEY DEFEATS TRUMAN". What is less known is that Truman would later go on to win the record for the lowest-ever approval rating for a president as recorded by Gallup, hitting a shocking 22% (lower than even Nixon would ever get).

But there were two other major candidates running in 1948: Dixiecrat Strom Thurmond and—reviving the banner of the Progressive Party—Henry Wallace. A darling of the left, Wallace played to independents and Democrats who were disaffected by Truman. He scored some major endorsements, including architect Frank Lloyd Wright (inspiration for the protagonist of *The Fountainhead*), NAACP founder W.E.B. DuBois, and *Harold and the Purple Crayon* creator Crockett Johnson.[363] Albert Einstein was also a supporter of Wallace's[364], while on the other hand filmmaker Orson Welles refused to have anything to do with him. Welles regarded him as "a prisoner of the Communist Party" who "would never do anything to upset them." "I was very, very passionately against him," Welles said. "The left thought I was a real traitor."[365] As late as 1948, long after World War II had ended, Wallace's warmth toward Stalinism was not a dealbreaker for the influencers—but denouncing Wallace was.

The Wallace campaign did a fair amount of work to allow President Truman to position himself as the common-sense centrist he is widely remembered as today. Wallace finished fourth, with a little over one million votes and 2.4% of the vote total, a significantly smaller vote share than Socialist Eugene V. Debs had received when he had run for the presidency in 1920 while incarcerated.

As time went on, information came out from prisoners who had been there when Vice President Wallace had visited Magadan. One schoolboy at the time remembered Wallace's visit vividly because the "most unusual thing was that suddenly the windows of shops were full of Soviet foodstuffs. God knows where this stuff came from."[366] After Wallace left the products of course vanished as quickly as they had appeared.

In 1951 Wallace's reputation took another hit, when Regnery published Elinor Lipper's memoir of life in the Gulag, *Eleven Years in Soviet Prison Camps*. Lipper had been a Swiss national before being caught in the Gulag's web, and as a result was one of the very few people released from the camps who were later allowed to leave the Soviet Union. The book specifically discussed what conditions were like at Magadan where Lipper spent a total of eight years—including during Wallace's trip. It was yet another piece of evidence that Wallace had been utterly played for a fool by the Soviets.

"Every prisoner who was there at the time owes Mr. Wallace a debt of gratitude," she scoffed. "For it was owing to his visit that for the first and last time the prisoners had three successive holidays." In order to ensure that he never saw a single prisoner, none of them were allowed to leave the camp. And to make certain he couldn't accidentally see them in the yard, "movies were shown to the prisoners from morning until night for three days."[367]

Reading Wallace's friendly words about Ivan Nikishov, a key official in Magadan, Lipper wrote that

> It is too bad that Wallace never saw him "gamboling around" on one of his drunken rages around the prison

> camps, raining filthy, savage language upon the heads of the exhausted, starving prisoners, having them locked up in solitary confinement for no offense whatsoever, and sending them into the gold mines to work fourteen and sixteen hours a day, at no matter what human cost.

"Would these words bear repetition when the mounds of frozen corpses under the snow are one day disinterred to testify what the Soviet Union really is?"[368] she demanded of the rosy claims of Wallace and his fellow travelers.

It was in September 1952—in what would have been the last months of Wallace's second term as president—that Wallace finally admitted that he had been fooled by Stalin and his men. "I had not the slightest idea when I visited Magadan that this far-north Pacific port—center of a vast, sub-arctic gold field—was also the center for administering the labor of both criminals and those suspected of political disloyalty," Wallace wrote. "Nothing I saw at Magadan or anywhere else in Soviet Asia suggested slave labor. True, I had heard that many kulaks who had their farms taken from them in the early '30s had been sent to Siberia, but I had not the slightest idea that there were many slave-labor camps in Siberia in 1944 and that of these the most notorious was Magadan."

By 1952 there remained apologists for the USSR in the West, but far fewer flat-out advocates. As Wallace himself concluded: "More and more I am convinced that Russian Communism in its total disregard of truth, in its fanaticism, its intolerance and its resolute denial of God and religion is something utterly evil."[369]

By this point Robert Hannegan, the chairman of the Democratic National Committee who had been so instrumental in replacing FDR's running mate in 1944, had passed away at the very early age of forty-six. His St. Louis tombstone is simply inscribed: Robert Emmett Hannegan / June 30, 1903 / October 6, 1949. Unlike at the convention, his wishes were not honored. Hannegan had quipped that he wanted his tombstone to read: "Here lies the man who stopped Henry Wallace from becoming president of the United States."

Chapter 9

WAITING FOR A DOORBELL TO RING

Hitler and the Nazis were defeated in 1945. It was the Russians who had reached his bunker first, proudly raising the hammer-and-sickle flag of the Soviet Union over the Reichstag as well. Whereas the United States had lost a bit over 400,000 men in World War II, the USSR lost somewhere between eight and twelve million, in addition to a similar number of civilians. Further, Stalin sent many Russian ex-POWs to the Gulag upon their return to the USSR, both as punishment for having been captured and to isolate their knowledge about the outside world from the rest of the population.

After World War II was won, dominion over Eastern Europe was largely ceded to the Soviet Union by the Western powers. All the land that Lenin had surrendered to Germany under the Treaty of Brest-Litovsk had been regained by Stalin.[370] Bulgaria, Poland, Hungary, and Romania all had governments installed that answered to Moscow. The three Baltic states—Estonia, Latvia, and Lithuania—fared even worse, losing their status as nations and becoming incorporated into the USSR as new Soviet Socialist Republics. No one knew what to do with the Japanese colony of Korea, so they just drew a line down the middle in order to form a communist north and a capitalist south.

In Churchill's March 5, 1946 words, "an iron curtain has descended across the Continent. Behind that line lie all the capitals of the ancient states of Central and Eastern Europe. Warsaw, Berlin, Prague, Vienna, Budapest, Belgrade, Bucharest and Sofia, all these famous cities and the populations around them lie in what I must call the Soviet sphere, and all are subject in one form or another, not only to Soviet influence but to a very high and, in many cases, increasing measure of control from Moscow."[371] The Cold War had begun.

For a brief period the United States had been the world's only nuclear power, but a spy ring of Stalinists and fellow ideologues in various American classified agencies delivered the bomb to the Soviet Union by the end of the 1940s. By 1948 Czechoslovakia would also become taken over by a Soviet-led coup. The Cold War turned violent with each half of Korea declaring itself the rightful government of the entire country. This led to the Korean War where the United States and the newfound United Nations joined the forces of south Korea against the north Koreans with their Soviet allies—with now-communist China also lending a hand. The war effectively ended in a draw, and the Korean people paid the price with the utter decimation of their country.

Alongside Stalin through all this was the last and perhaps most malevolent of his many accomplices: Lavrentiy Beria. Beria is not as widely remembered as that of high-ranking Nazis like Joseph Goebbels, Heinrich Himmler or Rudolf Hess. The thing he is most remembered for is his infamous quote: "Show me the man and I'll show you the crime." This wasn't some throwaway line either. As the third and last of Stalin's NKVD leaders, Beria was in charge of the secret police and expanding the Gulag—with all that that entailed. "Let me have one night with him and I'll have him confessing he's the King of England," he bragged about one of his many captives.[372] As one *anekdot* put it:

> One nasty morning Comrade Stalin discovered that his favorite pipe was missing. Naturally, he called in his henchman, Lavrentiy Beria, and instructed him to find the pipe. A few hours later, Stalin found it in his desk and called

> off the search. "But Comrade Stalin," stammered Beria, "five suspects have already confessed to stealing it."[373]

While Beria knew what sort of stresses worked to get confessions out of the accused, he was also well aware of the limited efficacy of such methods. As he eventually admitted, "A person that's beaten will give the kind of confession that the interrogating agents want, will admit that he is an English or American spy or whatever we want. But it will never be possible to know the truth this way."[374] This of course did not deter Beria or his men in the slightest. "When we Bolsheviks want to get something done," he once said, "we close our eyes to everything else."[375] He was uniquely suited to run the secret police, a being of pure ruthlessness. "Beria is a man for whom it costs nothing to kill his best friend if that best friend said something bad about Beria," noted one of his subordinates.[376] It is clear why he got along so well with Stalin.

In some limited respects Beria was less of a butcher than his predecessors. When he took over from Yezhov in 1938 the worst of the Great Terror receded, and the number of victims caught began to decrease. Yet this mitigation of the wholesale assault on the populace was in contrast to the personal depravity that Beria himself visited on so many men, women and children who fell under his command. The vegetarian[377] had no qualms about inflicting enormous suffering on human beings and even relished the opportunity. His coup de grace might have been getting an agent past security and, after several failed attempts, having Trotsky successfully assassinated via an ice pick to the head in his Mexico City home in 1940.

If "show me the man" could be viewed as Beria's professional slogan, his personal one could be illustrated by his response to Tatiana Okunevskaya. Okunevskaya was a popular actress, and Beria invited her to perform for the Politburo. When she accepted the invitation he instead took her to a private home where he proceeded to try to get her drunk. Then, Beria undressed and began to seduce her. To further entice her he promised to free both her father and her grandfather from prison. "Scream or not, it doesn't matter," he told her. After he had his way with her and let her go he nevertheless had her arrested and sent to Siberia.

Nor did Beria keep his word about her family—because he couldn't. Both Okunevskaya's father and grandfather had already been executed.[378] The unfortunate actress was not alone, for Beria was one of the worst sexual predators of all time.

Beria had his men drive him around Moscow looking for women to pick up. Resistance from them would lead to extreme consequences, though compliance was not often a better option. Fifty years after Beria's death, they were still finding the remains of his victims on the grounds of his former home.[379] With a bureaucrat's obsessive attention to detail, both Beria and his bodyguard kept records of all the women that he engaged with. There does remain some dispute as to whether his sexual predations reached literal children, or if he contented himself with mere teenagers.

Stalin was quite aware of Beria's predilections. The man who had an entire country living in fear of him was still concerned about what Beria was capable of. When Stalin learned his daughter was at Beria's house, he called her in a panic and told her to leave right away.[380] Notably, Stalin was more than happy to look the other way so long as Beria was performing his job to Stalin's satisfaction. This fit in with Stalin's broader perspective on the utility of sexual assault. Stalin made this point explicitly when he was privately faced with criticism of the Red Army's transgressions as it made its way west toward Berlin:

> Do you see what a complicated thing is a man's soul, a man's psyche? Well then, imagine a man who has fought from Stalingrad to Belgrade, over thousands of kilometres of his own devastated land, across the dead bodies of his comrades and dearest ones. How can such a man react normally? And what is so awful in his having fun with a woman after such horrors?[381]

When Stalin wasn't looking the other way regarding the Red Army's rapes, he was actively engaging it to perform mass murder. After he had invaded Poland in 1939, Stalin was stuck with tens of thousands of

Polish prisoners of war that included many of the Polish intellectual elite. This had the potential to be a new anti-Soviet power center, which therefore had the potential to be a threat to Stalin's power. Beria, Stalin, and other top Soviet officials had a frank discussion about just what was to be done with the Polish captives. After much blunt talk came the decision: execution.

Matters looked very different two years later. Stalin was incredulous when Hitler broke their pact and invaded the Soviet Union under Operation Barbarossa. The Red Army desperately awaited instruction from the Kremlin for days as Stalin went missing, unable to believe what the reports were telling him from the front. The Nazis made massive advances, and preventable ones. Worse, Stalin's purges had wiped out most of Russia's best and brightest military leaders just a few years prior. "Everything's lost," a dejected Stalin said. "Lenin left us a great legacy, but we, his heirs, have shit it out our asses."[382]

As the Nazis worked their way east, they uncovered mass graves in Russia's Katyn forest. It was there where Beria's men had left the remains of all the massacred Polish prisoners of war. It was a major international embarrassment for Stalin, and Russian claims that the dead were victims of the Nazis were met with great skepticism. The Katyn massacre would be used for decades as evidence of the basic inhumanity underlying Stalin's regime.

Though Stalin's relationship with Hitler vacillated between rivals to non-aggressors to coconspirators against Poland to outright foes, there was one group that the two men both despised: Jews. Stalin's anti-Semitism was heavily informed by a couple of things. To begin with, Russia had historically been one of the most anti-Semitic countries on earth, both *de facto* and *de jure*. The promise of not only equality but mere safety in one's home drew a large percentage of Jews toward socialism both in Russia and abroad. This cultural tendency was compounded in Stalin by his personal hatred toward Trotsky. When Stalin met with Churchill and FDR at Yalta to plan against Hitler, he still found time to rant to the president about how Jews were parasites.[383] Stalin's comments were dutifully censored from the official published version of the conversation.

As historian Louis Rappoport pointed out:

> In the spirit of the Stalin-Hitler pact, all Soviet organs deliberately remained silent about the genocidal slaughtering of the Jews by the Nazi conquerors of Poland between September 1939 and June 1941, when the Nazis invaded the USSR. The silence continued even after Hitler invaded his former partner's empire. Stalin thus paved the way for the extermination of 1.5 million unsuspecting Jews in White Russia and the Ukraine.[384]

Any references to mass killings by the Third Reich were discussed in the Soviet press as simply targeting Poles or Ukrainians. The Nazis themselves were understandably baffled by Jewish obliviousness regarding Hitler's intentions in the western part of the Soviet Union. "The Jews are strikingly ill-informed about our attitude towards them and about the treatment Jews are receiving in Germany or Warsaw," said one Nazi report. "Although they do not expect to be granted equal rights with the Russians under the German administration, they do believe that we will let them alone if they apply themselves diligently to their work." When the Germans invaded the Ukrainian town of Kerostia the Jewish population accordingly greeted them with food as a welcome.[385]

No family—even his own—was safe from Stalin's modern pogrom. When Stalin's son Yasha was captured by Hitler's men, Stalin had Yasha's Jewish wife arrested as a plotter and thereby left his three-year-old granddaughter without parents. Abandoned by his father, Yasha killed himself a few months later. And when Stalin's daughter later fell in love with a Jewish screenwriter, Stalin had the man arrested as a British spy[386] before slapping the hell out of her for good measure.[387] "Such a war going on and she's busy the whole time fucking!" he screamed at her, despite the fact that she had only shared kisses with her crush.[388]

As the war proceeded any Jews in the Soviet Union who felt the need to organize came under great suspicion. Arrests of prominent Jewish writers and activists with international reputations could not simply be explained away easily. The Polish ambassador to the USSR demanded the release of leaders of the Bund, Poland's strongest and largest Jewish party, who had fallen in Russian hands. He was told that it "has been established that they were working on behalf of Germany." When he protested the absurdity of Jews from Poland working on behalf of Hitler, his protests were met with a shrug: "And yet Trotsky turned out to be a German agent."[389] Jews were arrested en masse and put on trial in the Soviet Union and Soviet-dominated countries—and then those same trials were used as proof of a Jewish conspiracy.[390]

In 1948 the Soviet Union became the first country to recognize the newly-declared state of Israel, expecting Israel to be a bulwark against the West due to violent conflict between the Israelis and the British rulers. Months later Stalin saw this would not be the case, and refused to allow Soviet Jews to emigrate. Future Israeli Prime Minister Golda Meir was Israel's first ambassador to the Soviet Union, visiting Moscow in September of 1948. When tens of thousands of Russian Jews came out to welcome her, Stalin ordered the arrest of any one of them who could be identified from photographs of the event.[391] During World War II a Soviet organization called the Jewish Anti-Fascist Committee was created to mobilize world opinion to help the USSR fight against Hitler. After the war, any Soviet Jew who wrote to them inquiring about Israel—a land where Jews would be safe from persecution—was arrested.[392]

Stalin's campaign against the USSR's Jewish population came with the same tortures and farcical accusations as had taken place in the Great Terror. Jewish intellectuals and writers began to be systematically driven from their jobs as traitors, and many of them were arrested too. Lena Shtern was the USSR's most prominent female scientist, a so-called "Einstein in skirts" whose discoveries regarding the blood-brain barrier still hold up decades later. That didn't save the seventy-one-year-old woman from arrest. Her interrogators called her an old whore and claimed that when she was at conferences abroad she had sold her body. "At my age I would be the one paying," she snapped. While many of her co-defendants were shot, she managed to receive the lighter sentence of deportation to Kazakhstan.[393] Shtern's Jewish gallows humor was one of the few mechanisms available to deal with the increasing newfound oppression, as another *anekdot* revealed:

The phone rings. "Please, may I speak with Abramovich?"
"He's not at home."
"Is he at work?"
"No."
"Is he out of town?"
"No."
"Did I understand you right?"
"Yes."[394]

Throughout his life Stalin liked to drink and he liked to smoke. Even as he entered his seventies, he would host drunken parties that lasted until five in the morning (fully expecting his subordinates to be available should he decide to ring them in the middle of the night).[395] As his health naturally deteriorated towards the end of his life, this was taken as proof that—obviously—the medical community was conspiring to kill him. Just as the wreckers had caused the health of the Soviet economy to falter, so it made perfect sense that Stalin's health was being wrecked by the top experts in the field. After all, he had finally quit smoking after fifty years. Stalin's doctor was obviously the best that the Kremlin had to offer, but when he advised total rest Stalin repeatedly screamed for the man to be put in irons. He took it not as informed medical opinion but as an attempt to remove him from power.[396] Stalin vividly remembered Lenin getting the same advice after his first stroke, and he knew better than anyone what had happened after that.

Stalin had reason to be suspicious. It is a certainty that members of the medical profession had acted, passively or tacitly, as his personal murderers on more than one occasion. The most notorious possibility was Lenin's widow Nadezhda Krupskaya, who as education leader in Russia had argued that "children must learn about factories and mines and farms, and how to increase production."[397] Stalin had never forgiven her for siding with Kamenev and Zinoviev after Lenin died, and as the years passed her relationship with Lenin had been publicly downgraded to "friend," "companion" and finally "assistant."[398] She died the day after her seventieth birthday celebration in 1939, at the height of the Great

Terror, and there was no shortage of suspicion that her death had not been due to natural causes.[399]

Dr. Miron Vovsi was designated as having been one of the central figures in a Jewish-guided "Doctors' plot" to murder Stalin and overthrow the USSR for the sake of some foreign nation, which shifted from the United States to Britain to Israel. A few years and a few miles from Auschwitz, the same wheels were turning again. As Vovsi's prison interrogator told him:

> We can't let our enemies misbehave. You will be punished. [...] We'll get rid of you and your filthy race. Hitler was our enemy, but he was right about the Jews, that they are vermin who must be destroyed. We'll bury you and your filthy race ten meters deep. We never let our corn grow too high. We cut it at the right time.[400]

A cadre of doctors was arrested, and Stalin explicitly demanded that they be tortured. He insisted that the interrogators "throw the doctors in chains, beat them to a pulp, and grind them into powder."[401] Once again, virtually all of them confessed to whatever was asked of them. The Soviet press began to increase references to "rootless cosmopolitans" and other universally-understood euphemisms for Jews that had been popularized by the Third Reich. Commissions were set up for the purposes of removing Jews from medical facilities.[402] Jewish medical school graduates began to be assigned to the Far East to practice.[403]

Open letters were written for publication in *Pravda*, cleverly demanding that Jews be sent to the Far East in order to "protect" them because "Soviet people are naturally outraged by the ever-widening circle of treason and treachery and the fact that, to our sorrow, many Jews have helped our enemies to form a fifth column in our midst. Simple, misguided citizens may be driven to striking back indiscriminately at Jews."[404] In Stalin's native Georgia, government agents brought dynamite to blow up synagogues. They chose to bide their time until the defiant Jews were deported rather than face resistance.[405]

The message was heard loud and clear throughout the communist nations. Mao's doctor in China was a Soviet Jew; agents were sent to arrest the man for supposedly trying to poison him. The president of Jewish advocacy organization B'nai B'rith met with US State Department officials and told them flatly that he believed that "the Soviets have decided on a campaign of extermination".[406] After all, the Soviet Union already had a functioning concentration camp system with an enormously high casualty rate. It seemed as if the Jews would need a miracle to stop the worst from happening again—and they got one.

It is not clear who precisely discovered Stalin on March 1, 1953. After neither his household staff nor his subordinates heard from him all day, a brave soul finally dared to enter his chambers to check in on him. Whoever it was found him on the floor, immobile but alive, in a pool of his own urine. Now the staff were in a dilemma about what to do. Nothing of import could be done in the Soviet Union without Stalin's approval, yet Stalin was clearly unable to grant it.

Beria was informed and then he got on the phone, but that only put the sword of Damocles over his head. He knew perfectly well what had happened to his predecessors, Yezhov and Yagoda. If it looked as if he were plotting against Stalin, he could be killed. If it looked as if he was conspiring with the doctors who had supposedly been plotting against Stalin, he could be killed. After much handwringing, the decision was made the following morning to ask the Minister of Health to get help.

There was one major problem. The best doctors in the country would have been the ones assigned to Stalin and other top Soviet officials—and those were the men who Stalin had accused of plotting against him. In what can be seen as either the height of irony or the epitome of farce—though probably both—the doctors who were being held in government torture chambers at that moment began to be questioned for medical advice. "Which specialist would you recommend for one of our most important people who has just had a stroke?" one was asked.[407] Unbeknownst to him, all eight of the specialists he recommended were also imprisoned. The captors had still more questions. Despite his confusion, the physician nevertheless did his best to explain to what a

"Cheyne-Stokes respiration" was. He was unaware that that had been the tentative diagnosis reached by the clueless doctors who had been sent to attend to the dying Stalin—men so incompetent they couldn't even figure out how to operate the artificial respirator.[408]

Stalin's daughter Svetlana was there to see the end. As her biographer Rosemary Sullivan described it:

> Stalin's death throes were agonizing. For several days he lay unconscious, choking on his own fluids as the cerebral hemorrhage spread throughout his brain. His face gradually darkened, his lips turned black. He was being slowly strangled.[409]

Stalin also began vomiting blood at one point. "At what seemed like the very last moment he suddenly opened his eyes and cast a glance over everyone in the room," Svetlana remembered. "Then something incomprehensible and awesome happened that to this day I can't forget and don't understand. He suddenly lifted his left hand as though he were pointing to something above and bringing down a curse on us all." And with that, Stalin perished.

It only took days after his death for the edifice that Stalin had built to start being undone, strongly suggesting that Soviet leaders really had been conspiring behind his back to plan a post-Stalin USSR. The Gulag system quietly began to be dissembled and a broad amnesty was declared, liberating minors, mothers with young children, and those serving terms of fewer than five years. Nearly a million total inmates were soon released, a mix of political prisoners and criminals in a nation where the line between the two was often blurred.[410]

Publicly the government began to acknowledge not just mistakes but brazen wrongdoing. The Internal Affairs Ministry released a statement acknowledging that the doctors that had been accused were arrested "without any legal basis" and admitting that they had been tortured into professing their guilt—a government confession without precedent in Soviet history.[411] *Pravda* referred to the newly-freed medical professionals as "honest and esteemed figures of our State" while also doing a complete reversal on one demonized Jewish writer, now rehabilitating him as that "People's Artist of the USSR who has been shamelessly slandered."[412]

But as one crisis ended another began, for it seemed apparent that Beria would be the one to take over for Stalin. Far less paranoid than Stalin had been, Beria nevertheless would have no issue dispatching those who got in his way. Worse, his sadism was well known throughout Kremlin circles. To have escaped Stalin's reign unscathed was no easy task. Now, Soviet leaders found themselves in a position where they might have to live in perpetual fear of what tortures Beria would visit upon them and their families.

It took fewer than four months after Stalin's death for Beria to be arrested. He was accused of a slew of crimes at a December 1953 trial and executed immediately thereafter. It was a conclusion he knew all too well, for it was a fate that he himself had doled out to many thousands upon thousands of innocents. In his place the comparatively unknown Nikita Khrushchev took on the role as the new leader of the Soviet Union.

Khrushchev was no saint. He too had a fair amount of blood on his hands from when he had been Party leader for Moscow, taking part in Stalin's purges. How much guilt can be ascribed to him personally is a matter of debate, for the circumstances very clearly had been "kill or be killed." Of all the people who Stalin had feared would betray him, it was Khrushchev who turned out to be the one that Stalin should have been most worried about.

After midnight on February 25, 1956, Khrushchev delivered a speech entitled "On the Cult of Personality and Its Consequences" to the 20th Congress of the Communist Party of the Soviet Union. It was a four-hour talk delivered behind closed doors, with no journalists or foreigners permitted to attend. Due to the unusual circumstances under which the talk was presented, it popularly became known as the Secret Speech. Three years after Stalin's death, Khrushchev turned his back not just on Stalin but on the very idea of Stalinism itself—and from the same rostrum that Stalin had recently occupied.

Khrushchev opened by pointing out that "it is impermissible and foreign to the spirit of Marxism-Leninism to elevate one person, to transform him into a superman possessing supernatural characteristics, akin to those of a god. Such a man supposedly knows everything, sees everything, thinks for everyone, can do anything, is infallible in his behavior." Khrushchev immediately went on to make clear that he was talking "specifically about Stalin" before denouncing his "absolutely insufferable character."

Khrushchev acknowledged that whoever opposed Stalin "was doomed to removal from the leading collective and to subsequent moral and physical annihilation" and that Stalin's confessions "were acquired through physical pressures against the accused." As a result, "honest Communists were slandered, accusations against them were fabricated, and revolutionary legality was gravely undermined…'enemies' were actually never enemies, spies, wreckers, etc., but were always honest Communists; they were only so stigmatized and, often, no longer able to bear barbaric tortures, they charged themselves […] with all kinds of grave and unlikely crimes."

As plain as day, the man who replaced Stalin condemned his murders and torture. "And how is it possible that a person confesses to crimes which he has not committed? Only in one way—because of application of physical methods of pressuring him, tortures, bringing him to a state of unconsciousness, deprivation of his judgment, taking away of his human dignity. In this manner were 'confessions' acquired."

Khrushchev did not even denounce bloodshed per se, but argued that it was only to be used in a specific context. It was a bit of historical revisionism that became known as the Good Lenin/Bad Stalin thesis:

> Lenin used such methods, however, only against actual class enemies and not against those who blunder, who err, and whom it was possible to lead through ideological influence and even retain in the leadership. Lenin used severe methods only in the most necessary cases, when the exploiting classes were still in existence and were vigorously opposing the Revolution, when the struggle for

> survival was decidedly assuming the sharpest forms, even including a civil war.

But as ex-communist James Burnham pointed out, the Good Lenin/Bad Stalin thesis was just more propaganda:

> It should not be supposed that the terror with which communism is linked is a transient phenomenon, a temporary device used and perhaps abused for some special "emergency of the revolution." Terror has always been an essential part of communism, from the pre-revolutionary days when Stalin, as "Koba," was directing the bombings whereby Bolshevik funds were assembled, through the years before 1917 when Lenin was approving the private tortures administered to political dissidents, into every stage of the development of the communist regime in power. Terror is proved by historical experience to be integral to communism, to be, in fact, the main instrument by which its power is increased and sustained. From the beginning of the communist regime in Russia, every major political and economic turn has been carried through by terror.[413]

Khrushchev then gave credence to the conspiracy theory that the murder of Kirov was neither the act of a lone gunman nor of those who ended up paying the price for the assassination, but of Stalin himself. He pointed how the agent assigned to protect Kirov "was killed in a car 'accident' in which no other occupants of the car were harmed" and how top NKVD officials were executed in 1937: "We can assume that they were shot in order to cover the traces of the organizers of Kirov's killing."

He went on to question the very basis of the Great Terror: "The mass repressions at this time were made under the slogan of a fight against the Trotskyites. Did the Trotskyites at this time actually constitute such a danger to our party and to the Soviet state?" Khrushchev went on to answer the question with a firm *no.* "Trotskyism was completely disarmed [...] Stalin put the party and the NKVD up to the use of mass terror when the exploiting classes had been liquidated in our country and when there were no serious reasons for the use of extraordinary mass terror."

Not content to condemn Stalin's crimes internally, he continued to savage him for what happened in the prelude to the Soviet Union entering World War II. "When we look at many of our novels, films and historical 'scientific studies,'" said Khrushchev, "the role of Stalin in the Patriotic War appears to be entirely improbable. Stalin had foreseen everything." In fact it was Churchill himself who "personally warned Stalin that the Germans had begun regrouping their armed units with the intent of attacking the Soviet Union." Khrushchev bluntly regarded the domestic Russian propaganda as nonsense:

> During the war and after the war, Stalin put forward the thesis that the tragedy which our nation experienced in the first part of the war was the result of the "unexpected" attack of the Germans against the Soviet Union. But, comrades, this is completely untrue. As soon as Hitler came to power in Germany he assigned to himself the task of liquidating Communism. The fascists were saying this openly; they did not hide their plans. [...] When the fascist armies had actually invaded Soviet territory and military operations began, Moscow issued the order that the German fire was not to he returned. Why? It was because Stalin, despite evident facts, thought that the war had not yet started, that this was only a provocative action on the part of several undisciplined sections of the German Army, and that our reaction might serve as a reason for the Germans to begin the war. [...] And what was the result of this? The worst that we had expected. The Germans surrounded our Army concentrations and consequently we lost hundreds of thousands of our soldiers. This is Stalin's military "genius";

> this is what it cost us. […] All the more shameful was the fact that, after our great victory over the enemy which cost us so much, Stalin began to downgrade many of the commanders who contributed so much to the victory over the enemy, because Stalin excluded every possibility that services rendered at the front should be credited to anyone but himself.

Khrushchev went on to confirm the mass deportations of entire peoples within the Soviet Union, grimly joking that the "Ukrainians avoided meeting this fate only because there were too many of them and there was no place to which to deport them. Otherwise, he would have deported them also." Claims which had been made with a straight face under Stalin were now met with laughter, for they were and always had been farcical: "Could it be possible that […] nationalist tendencies grew so much that there was a danger of Georgia's leaving the Soviet Union and joining Turkey?" Yet this was the accusation under which thousands of alleged Georgian separatists had been killed or exiled. As for the Doctors' plot, "we found it to be fabricated from beginning to end."

Trotsky was incorrect. The Party was not, in fact, "always right," as the Party's main spokesperson made clear over the course of four hours. The twist to the whole saga was that the ultimate wrecker was none other than Stalin himself. The way forward was clear. "It is necessary for this purpose," Khrushchev concluded, "to condemn and to eradicate the cult of the individual as alien to Marxism-Leninism and not consonant with the principles of party leadership and the norms of party life, and to fight inexorably all attempts at bringing back this practice in one form or another."

For many communists around the world, reading the transcript of Khrushchev's speech was the end of the line. They had been content for years to dismiss criticism of the Soviet Union in general and of Stalin in particular as capitalist propaganda. Though there were some vague attempts to pretend that reports of Khrushchev's speech were all a forgery or the like, few took such claims to heart. In America and other liberal democracies, Party members handed in their cards and quit. It turned out that the criticism had been true, all of it. The Soviet Union was no workers' paradise at all but a workers' slaughterhouse. The words of Mikhail Bakunin, Marx's foremost rival, came to mind: "When the people are being beaten with a stick, they are not much happier if it is called the People's Stick."

Throughout the Eastern Bloc a process of destalinization began. Two exceptions to this were China and north Korea, creating a rift between East and West that never fully healed. But in the other communist nations, Stalin's veneration began to be reversed. The Russian city of Stalingrad had been renamed in his honor in 1925; Khrushchev reverted it to Volgograd. In Prague there stood a gigantic fifty-foot-tall statue of Stalin leading a group of workers, one that took over five years to build. It was dynamited into nothing. Statue after statue, honor after honor, monument after monument—all began to fall. Yet the biggest, most famous communist monument was yet to come—and not in the Soviet Union, either. That honor would be visited upon the people of Germany: specifically, the citizens of Berlin.

Chapter 10

A COUNTRY WHERE HUMAN LIFE IS NOTHING

It would have been considered unthinkable, for the simple reason that no one would ever have a reason to think it: how do you divide a city in half? Though city life has many disadvantages, the advantages of cities are plentiful. Cities are centers of art and culture, breeding grounds for new ideas. Cities are centralized locations to do business, which means jobs. Cities are dense, with art and culture and business in somewhat close proximity to one another. The more urbanized a city tends to be, the more tightly packed it ends up being. It takes decades for cities to grow into an integrated whole, streets feeding into streets, neighborhoods developing their own character. Integration is both a natural and a manmade trend for cities.

After World War II, Germany was divided by the Allies into four occupation zones: Soviet, French, American, and British. The German capital of Berlin, located entirely within the eastern Soviet zone, was itself also split into four. Though Germany was still largely in ruins, local elections were still held in the Soviet Zone in the fall of 1946. Persisting in the narrative that Soviet totalitarianism was completely the opposite of Fascist totalitarianism by every important metric, the German Communists tried to win control through democratic processes. Despite Soviet efforts, the Social Democrats were the clear victors with 49% of the vote in a three-way race. Worse, the center-right Christian Democratic Union came in second. The Communist Party was a distant third, with 20% of the vote. In no district did they come in first, not even the ones where they had had majority support before Hitler's reign.

The Russians were in a bind and took appropriate measures. That winter they began mass arrests of supposed Nazis and subversives. In practice this simply meant anyone opposed to domination from Moscow, no matter where they happened to land on the political spectrum. Then came "the People's Police," a further hardening of authoritarianism under the USSR's control. Finally, the Soviets reopened the camps. Buchenwald—rechristened NKVD special camp Nr. 2—was near the city of Weimar, and Saschsenhausen—Nr. 7—a mere thirty-five kilometers from Berlin. Close to two hundred thousand people were rounded up and carted away when the world was still reeling from seeing the images of the Holocaust. Years later over ten thousand bodies would be uncovered at Saschsenhausen alone, the majority of whom were minors and the elderly.[414]

How to handle Germany was an enormously difficult question even just among the Western countries. The Western nations intended to reinvigorate Germany as a country partial to them. This, of course, had not sat well with Stalin, but the Russians were outnumbered three to one by the Americans, the British and the French in terms of control. Stalin withdrew from the Allied Control Council when he discovered that a plan was being drawn up by the Western powers to squeeze out Soviet influence. That June came the introduction of a new Deutschmark via the British and the Americans. Providing a stable effective currency would have enormous utility in a nation where hunger was rampant, the black market utterly out of control, and memories of Weimar-era hyperinflation still fresh.

On June 24, 1948, the Soviets did their best to seal off West Berlin from the rest of the country. They closed down the canals, they closed down the railways, and they closed down major roads. No one was getting in or out without them knowing about it and approving it. Food, coal, and medicine would soon become urgent problems. President Harry Truman was facing yet another crisis in his accidental presidency.

A conveyor belt of planes taking off from western Germany was organized as a response to the Soviet blockade, delivering what was needed to the beleaguered West Berliners. Soon there was a plane landing in West Berlin every minute, packed to the gills with necessary goods. Yes, an iron curtain had descended across the continent—but curtains can only reach so high.

The Berlin Blockade was a complete debacle for the USSR. Stalin had played hardball, hoping to extract confessions from his former Allies, and rather than negotiating with him the Western powers simply went their own way. In terms of reputation the blockade was even more of a disaster for the Soviets. Regardless of one's politics, preventing a civilian population from access to food and medication was widely regarded as not just wrong but downright unconscionable.

The Americans did not hesitate to rub their victory in Stalin's face. When it became apparent that the Russians were under orders to withhold fire, many of the Western planes intentionally flew in confrontational ways, all but daring the Soviet forces to do something about it. Discretion being the better form of valor, Stalin held himself back from launching what surely would have been World War III.

By 1949 West Germany (officially the Federal Republic of Germany) and East Germany (the German Democratic Republic, or GDR) became their own countries. The French, American and British occupation zones made up the former and would be a part of NATO, a multinational alliance dedicated to mutual defense. The Russian zone became the latter and in 1955 would cofound the Warsaw Pact, a counterweight to NATO that consisted of several communist nations dedicated to mutual military support and political ties. The Warsaw Pact nations—though nominally sovereign countries—very much became an interconnected group of nations heavily influenced (if not entirely controlled) by the Kremlin. The Cold War was hardening into two superpowers, with dueling spheres of influence.

This series of geopolitical conflicts meant that West Berlin was now effectively within a foreign country. A surprising number of Americans seem to think that Berlin is in the middle of Germany, and that when the country was split it was the border between the two Germanies that divided the city in half. In fact Berlin is entirely located within eastern

Germany, closer to Poland than to what became West Germany. West Berlin's isolation was not an entirely unique situation. The microstate of the Vatican is entirely within Rome, for example, and Lesotho is enclaved within South Africa. But in neither of these cases was there the international animosity and rivalry between various parties as there was between West and East Germany.

Despite East German propaganda and claims of being a workers' paradise, Germans began voting with their feet to immigrate to the West. They didn't even have to learn a new language or adapt to a new culture. It was the same precise population, so most of the typical barriers to immigration simply didn't exist. No amount of communist handwaving to the contrary could explain why, given the choice, citizens were choosing West Germany over East. Claims that the thousands of immigrants were somehow fascists or spies or provocateurs persuaded no one.

East Germany's leader Walter Ulbricht was thus left with a crisis on his hands and very few palatable options. His country was hemorrhaging citizens at an enormous rate. Worse, highly skilled, educated workers such as doctors and engineers were the first ones to flee in order to get far higher wages in the West. Over two thousand Germans were registered as refugees in the West on Sunday, August 13, 1961, alone. Ulbricht decided that the situation needed to stop. At 1 a.m. that day Operation Rose began. Tanks and personnel carriers surrounded West Berlin in case things got completely out of control. The street lights were turned dark to hide what the authorities were doing.

For perhaps the first time in history, Ulbricht was trying to disintegrate a city. There were 81 crossing points between West and East Berlin; 68 of them were shut down. All 193 of the streets on the border were closed. The railways, both above and below ground, were blocked. Even the shafts to the sewage system were inspected to make sure people weren't sneaking through. All this happened as barbed wire was beginning to be laid down alongside concrete bolsters and tank traps.[415]

One is tempted to think that "the reaction from the Western world was swift and furious," but that was simply untrue. It took a great deal of time for information about what was happening in Berlin to reach western Europe and the United States, and even then it wasn't all that clear exactly what the Communists were up to. The idea of enclosing an entire city—or even part of a city—was inconceivable and absurd, so it is little surprise that many people did not appreciate that yes, the East German authorities were laying the literal groundwork for what would later become the Berlin Wall. The official name was the *Antifaschistischer Schutzwall*, the "anti-fascist rampart." The Wall was so effective in keeping fascists out that not a single fascist even so much as tried crossing it into East Germany. The traffic was almost entirely in the other direction.

The West Berliners were up in arms. There had been, quite intentionally, no notice of what was about to happen. Many people were separated from their families, friends and colleagues. President Kennedy only found out that noon, and by then there was little that could be done about it. The East German authorities had made sure to construct their barriers strictly on GDR territory, and per the post-WWII agreements they continued to respect the rights of American troops and others to cross.

Though Western forces did not quite appreciate what was happening at first, some Germans understood the situation exactly. Conrad Schumann was one prime example. Though only nineteen years old, he was already an armed East German border guard. Thirty-six hours after the basis for the Wall started to be laid down, he stood face-to-face with the citizens of West Berlin, staring at one another across three-foot-tall barbed wire. Schumann listened to the West Berliners berating him in the harshest terms, comparing him—not unreasonably—to those who had guarded concentration camps not that long ago. He understood what staying in his position would necessitate. So at four in the afternoon, Conrad Schumann made the right decision: he chose peace.

Schumann paced back and forth, planning his next step in his mind. At that moment, photographer Peter Leiberg—himself only twenty years old—stood nearby and realized that the young border guard was up to something. Leiberg had experience photographing horses and knew when to take his shot. Yet his camera had no motor-drive. If something were to happen, Leiberg would have one and only one chance to get his picture.

On the far side of the barbed wire a West German police car pulled up, engine running, urging Schumann to defect. With one quick motion Schumann threw his cigarette aside, jumped the barbed-wire barrier, dropped his weapon to the ground, and ran into the car which took the young man away to safety. At the precise second that Schumann made his leap, Leiberg took his shot with his camera and got the photograph of the border guard hopping the fence to freedom. Less than two days after Operation Rose began, the world already had an iconic picture to represent those who chose to be free rather than to hurt their fellow man. Schumann's stated reasoning for his action was quite simple: he did not want to kill someone for crossing the street.

Close to where he jumped there now stands a statue of Schumann based on Leiberg's photo, complete with his gun over his shoulder and the barbed wire under his feet. Anyone can go look and ask themselves if they would have had the courage to leap for freedom when pressured to do evil. Schumann was not alone. Nine other border guards also defected within those first couple of days. Yet there remained—as there always remained—plenty of young men who were more than happy, for decades, to just follow orders and shoot their countrymen for leaving the workers' paradise. The darkness will always outnumber the stars.

In the very early morning of Friday, August 18, 1961, came the cranes. Behind Berlin's historic Brandenburg Gate, a beautiful landmark defined by five pathways, the GDR dropped concrete slabs to block the Gate in perpetuity. By the time the sun rose, a five-foot-tall barrier had risen like a middle finger to decency. In less than a week the emerging Berlin Wall had grown from an impossible hypothetical to drudging reality.

Ida Siekmann would be the first to die, only nine days after the Wall started getting built. Bernàuer Straße opened into the French sector, and the residents therein could easily pass to West Berlin. Five days after Operation Rose, the buildings' previous entrances were boarded up and new ones created. These new entrances ensured that the residents could only exit to spaces that were under Russian control.

Ida's sister, her only surviving relative, lived a few blocks away—but now she might as well have been on the other side of the world. Physical contact between them had became virtually impossible, and it was almost certain that other forms of communication would soon be banned as well. Contact with members of foreign nations was legally regarded as spying—something even Western countries do not exactly take lightly.

Siekmann had one opportunity to escape. People had been rappelling down from their windows into West Berlin. Others had jumped to escape, with firefighters waiting to catch them down below. On the morning of August 22, 1961, Siekmann threw a quilt and some other objects down to the street. The firefighters tried to get the rescue net open in time, time which was of the essence. If Siekmann did not manage to escape now she could be certain that she would never be allowed anywhere near the border again. She might be imprisoned or shot or who knows what else. Siekmann jumped before the net was ready, severely injuring herself in the process. A nurse by profession, she died en route to the hospital and became the first victim of the Berlin Wall. Her death came one day before her fifty-ninth birthday, one that she so desperately wanted to spend with her sister.

Siekmann's death shocked the world, but it had clearly been an accident. It was two days after she died that the shootings began. Like many Germans at the time, Günter Litfin lived in East Berlin but worked in West Berlin. He was prepared to move to a new apartment when the Wall came. Eager to flee, Litfin jumped into Humboldt Harbour and tried to swim across. The GDR guards yelled at him to swim back. One of them set his machine-pistol to automatic and unleashed a barrage of bullets. Sources disagree whether he was exiting the water or still swimming when the killshot hit the back of his neck. It took three hours for them to fish Litfin's body out of the water, and plenty of residents of West Berlin had been witness to the whole thing. He was only twenty-four-years old when he was killed.

Litfin worked for a fashion house so the East German authorities publicly disparaged him as being gay—with the nickname "Doll" to boot.[416] The press merely said that he died in a tragic accident. Indeed, Litfin's brother only learned about his death after he himself was arrested and interrogated all night. The funeral was held less than a week later under police supervision, and the Litfin family was advised not to cause any trouble.

Soon border guards were even shooting people who were turning around and returning to the GDR under threat of fire. Wilfried Tews was only fourteen years old when he tried to make a break for it. The border guards shot at him accordingly. Despite the admonition to make sure that an international incident not be provoked—not to mention the mandate forbidding the shooting of children—some of the gunfire reached West Berlin. The police there returned fire to the East, killing twenty-one-year-old guard Peter Göring with a ricocheting bullet. (Tews survived but sustained lifelong injuries.)

Now the East German authorities took the opportunity to create a martyr of their own. Göring's legend was spread in East Germany, the tale of a self-sacrificing man driven to protect his country at all costs from enemies abroad. It was claimed that he was murdered in connection with a French terrorist group. Göring was posthumously given a promotion, streets were named after him, and his gravesite became a holy site (or at least the communist equivalent of one). The GDR's attempt to valorize the border guard who tried to shoot a fleeing teenager was not entirely successful. The East German authorities were far better at creating martyrs the old-fashioned way: by killing innocents.

Peter Fechter became a household name about a year after the Wall was constructed. A bunch of East German kids planned to make a break for it one night, but when the agreed-upon time came around only Peter and his buddy Helmut Kulbeik had come up with the nerve. By this point, August 1962, the Berlin "Wall" was already a far more imposing edifice. There was a wire fence on the near side, which the two young men both managed to circumvent. Now they were in the death strip, the area between the wire fence and the further wall. Past the death strip was West Berlin. As the border guards opened fire, Kulbeik made it over. Fechter, however, was not quite so lucky. He was shot in the pelvis and slid down, lying there exposed.

A skirmish between the East and West German guards a few days earlier had left the East German guards too rattled to try and rescue Peter, while the West Germans could not reach him to help. As Fechter lay on the ground a crowd began to gather, chanting "Murder! Murder!" at the East Germans. They threw bandages down at the eighteen year old in an attempt to do something, anything, to save his life. He could hear West Berlin from where he lay, on the concrete and under the barbed wire.

An hour is an extraordinarily long time to die.

Did Fechter review his life, not in an instant, but in excruciating detail? Was he worried that he was causing a problem for his family? Maybe he was scared he hadn't told his mother enough times that he loved her. Maybe he regretted being too proud to thank his dad for how he had raised him—or maybe he didn't want to deal with thinking about them at all. For all we know his thoughts turned to some girl he had had a crush on at school, someone who he wrote excruciatingly bad poems for, a girl who thought him a nuisance but still liked having the attention. We don't know. We will never know. The only thing he had to keep that hard ground soft and warm was his blood.

As the minutes passed, Fechter's screams turned into pleas for help. There must have been some point where he wondered what was taking them some long to come get him, and then another point where he suspected help wasn't coming at all, and then a final one when he understood that this was the end. Nowadays there's a monument to him at the spot where he was killed. Anyone can go stand there and remember what it was like to be eighteen years old, to be a complete moron as all eighteen year olds are complete morons, and to think of all the things that happened in your life since being eighteen: that first date that was really the start of something special; that terrible stomachache; that argument where you said things you immediately knew you'd later regret. All those possibilities, both the great moments and the banal, that come with having one's entire life ahead of them. But Peter Fechter would have none of this, because some border guard just followed orders and shot the young bricklayer in cold blood.

This wasn't 1930s rural Ukraine or World War II era Dachau. This was Berlin in 1962, already heavily rebuilt from being bombed to oblivion and in the process of regaining its status as one of the great cities of the world. Photo cameras were common, and video increasingly accessible and affordable. Everyone all over the world could see the footage of Fechter's dying agony—it's still on YouTube—and they could watch his feet dangling as a guard eventually carried away the body, holding it in his arms exactly like a sleeping child. The East Germans later said he had been a fascist. But everyone understood what he was: another victim of the Berlin Wall.

The GDR never had a good reason as to explain why all these "fascists" were still to be found in East Germany, and why it would be a bad thing for them to leave the country. There was nothing to suggest that all or even many of the victims of the Berlin Wall were somehow special in any way. It didn't matter. True to the egalitarian principles of communism, the concrete monster consumed them all equally.

And so continued a cat-and-mouse game between the East German authorities and the East German population, as various parties tried different mechanisms to escape the GDR. As historian Frederick Taylor pointed out, the encased West Berlin was turned into "a bizarre prison in which paradoxically only those locked up inside were free."[417] In 1962 a defiant group of Germans (mostly students) struck a deal with America's NBC News to fund an escape tunnel in exchange for NBC being allowed to film it. The secret police tried to infiltrate the group—somewhat successfully, it turned out—but the two newcomers were misdirected by their suspicious comrades on the day when escape became a reality. The entire time, Peter Fechter's picture was attached to the growing tunnel's wall to remind the diggers exactly what they were working toward. By the time all was said and done, twenty-nine people would be able to make their way through to West Berlin. Eventually the tunnel sprung a leak that rendered it useless. But in the interim there were still escapees who arrived in West Berlin covered in water, mud, and no shortage of tears.

What worked for the young worked for the old. In May 1962, a dozen people escaped from the east by way of *Der Seniorentunnel*, "the Senior Citizens' Tunnel." Led by an 81-year-old man, a group of elderly people spent sixteen days digging a 160-foot-long, 6-foot-tall tunnel from within an East German chicken coop all the way to the other side of the Wall. According to one of the diggers, the tunnel was so tall because the old men wanted "to walk to freedom with our wives, comfortably and unbowed." Their wives were done crawling.

As the years went on, the buffoonish authoritarianism of the GDR often reached cartoonish proportions—as did the countermeasures to fight them. One group of East Germans simply dressed up as Soviet army officers and crossed freely.[418] But in an ironic bit of famed German engineering, it was twenty-year-old lathe worker Heinz Meixner who deduced an escape plan that no one else had thought of. A native Austrian who commuted from West Berlin to East for work, Meixner fell in love with a girl from the GDR named Margarete. He knew that he had to get her out, and his future mother-in-law for good measure.

Checkpoint Charlie was the most famous crossing point between the two Berlins. Meixner borrowed a scooter and went there to cross. Distracting the guard who was checking his passport, Meixner measured the height of the steel beam that lifted to allow cars to get through. It was approximately a yard off the ground, enough to prevent almost any car from getting past it—*almost* any car.

Meixner found an Austin-Healey Sprite sportscar for rent. Sans windshield, it stood 90 centimeters tall—room to spare. Meixner dutifully took off the vehicle's windshield, and let some of the air out of his tires for good measure. His fiancée fit into the space behind the driver, while the mother-in-law was stored in the trunk like the punchline to an old joke. Meixner surrounded her with thirty bricks in case the guards opened fire on the rear of the fleeing car.

On the morning of May 5, 1963, Meixner drove up to the guard from East Berlin and showed him his passport. This time Meixner floored it instead of going on to the customs inspection. He drove around the vertical bars, ducked his head, and easily drove under the steel beam before the guards could register what was going on. One is tempted to imagine them standing there shaking their fists at him as he made his successful getaway. In reality, however, Meixner was long out of their sight by the time the guards realized what that little red sportscar was up to. Heinz and Margarete were married in due course. Two months after Meixner's escape, a young man named Norbert Konrad attempted to do the identical thing with his East German girlfriend—renting the very same car that Meixner had. This time, however, Konrad left the windshield on so as not to arouse the border guards' suspicions. (It worked!)

But of course not every attempted escape to West Berlin ended in movie-like scenes of murder or freedom. Many people got cold feet. Others got warnings, or prison, or became targets of surveillance. Journalist Anna Funder interviewed a woman called Miriam who had attempted to scale the Wall in 1968 at the age of sixteen. By then the concrete obscenity had even more layers. Specifically:

> In its completed form the wall was 104 miles long, including 66 miles of reinforced concrete slabs. Built of the hardest concrete, to withstand ramming, each slab was six inches thick and weighed two and a half tons. The slabs were cemented together and topped with asbestos piping. Extra protection was provided by 302 observation towers, 65 miles of trenches, 259 dog runs, and 20 massive concrete bunkers. Next to the wall was a death strip of constantly raked sand, at least a hundred yards wide, equipped with hundreds of mines and automatic firing devices.[419]

Miriam got over the barbed-wire-topped fence just fine, though her hands remained "crazed with definite white scars" decades later.[420] She somehow traversed the brightly lit concrete strip and then pressed herself against a kink in the wall. Baffled as to how no one had spotted her, Miriam turned and locked eyes with the one guard who had: a German Shepherd dog who was chained to the wall. "I don't know why it didn't attack me," she later said. Maybe it was because she wasn't running or wasn't threatening it. Or maybe even a dog had the decency to know that it was wrong to attack a harmless teenage girl. Whatever the case, the German Shepherd walked away from Miriam.

Miriam then climbed the second barbed-wire fence. She could see the Western guards. She only had a little bit more to go—and then she triggered the tripwire. The sirens began immediately. The Western guards lit her up with a searchlight, to save her from being indiscriminately blasted by GDR weapons. As the Eastern border guards grabbed her they made it a point to call the teenage girl a piece of shit.

Miriam was taken and imprisoned in a 6.5' x 10' cell, without any contact with the outside world. For the next ten days, she was subject to interrogation combined with sleep deprivation. The schedule was always the same: bed at 8 p.m.; wake up two hours later at 10 p.m.; six hours of questioning and threats; and then bed again at 4 a.m. before being roused awake at 6 a.m. When she inevitably fell asleep, the guard would bang on the door or physically shake her. Eventually he took away her mattress too.

The questions for Miriam remained the same. Who put her up to it? Who conspired with her to make her foolish attempt to escape? A collective society needed collective punishment for crimes. Surely no sixteen-year-old girl would take it upon herself to defy the government of the German Democratic Republic. Eventually Miriam made up some ridiculous story about a man with little feet who frequented a bar that she knew of.

It was not uncommon for those under investigation to give the interrogators what they wanted. Nor did the questioners have to resort to the more brutal tactics of Stalin's era. Their typical strategy was a straightforward and effective one:

> The classic scenario was the "corner-to-corner" interrogation room. The room was on the second floor and overlooked the edge of the prison, allowing a tantalising glimpse of the outside world. The interrogator's chair and desk were situated at an angle to this window corner, facing into the room. When the prisoner was brought in, he was placed on an uncomfortable small stool in the far, interior corner of the room, so that he crouched there facing the interrogator, who was a good ten feet away. The psychological effect, which had been thoroughly researched, was to make the prisoner instantly uncomfortable and apprehensive, subject to an animal unease, which the interrogator could increase by simply staring at him, and saying things like "I have plenty of time. I have nothing but time." It was clear to the prisoner that, just out of his line of vision, a window revealed the world he had left weeks or months previously for a lonely, silent cell. Often the prisoner felt an overwhelming sense to talk,

> to make something happen that would get him off that stool and out of there.[421]

Miriam was sentenced to a year and a half in prison. The very first day the prison guards gave her her introduction. Naked, she was taken to a room with a deep bathtub. One guard held her legs and the other her hair, forcing her down into ice-cold water. Over and over they dunked her. When she was allowed to catch a breath the guards called the teenaged girl various names: *Filth. Bitch. Traitor.* She began to believe that they were killing her, which was precisely the point. Nor was what happened to Miriam unique. Mental torture was developed to its acme under the regime of the German secret police—for like so many others, Miriam had fallen into the hands of the Stasi.

Simon Wiesenthal made his name as a Nazi hunter, spending decades tracking down those members of the Third Reich who had managed to escape justice by fleeing abroad. His analysis of the East German secret police was a very blunt one: "The Stasi was much, much worse than the Gestapo, if you consider only the oppression of its own people. The Gestapo had 40,000 officials watching a country of 80 million, while the Stasi employed 102,000 to control only 17 million."[422] Roughly 2% of the East German population were informants, an enormously large percentage once one stops to think about it.

Most humans are surprisingly low in empathy, meaning they lack the ability to see things from other people's perspectives. Westerners tend to think that if we were to inform on our neighbors it would only be under duress or if they were doing something objectively wrong such as harming their children. In fact this is demonstrably not the case: there is rarely a shortage of people who will trip over themselves to inform on their countrymen without any pressure or even much tangible reward other than some sort of status or a sense of "I'm doing my part." Some quite literally just have nothing better to do. As one Stasi recruiter said, "Well, some of them were convinced of the cause. But I think it was mainly because informers got the feeling that, doing it, they were somebody. You know—someone was listening to them for a couple of hours a week, taking notes. They felt they had it over other people."[423] It was an easy way for low-status, obedient people to become more important than they otherwise would have been (in retrospect, an enormous incentive). Many—too many—of the Stasi's informers weren't drafted so much as they were volunteers. "It was pitiful, actually," the recruiter concluded. "They were hardly paid at all."[424]

After the Stasi files were eventually opened, Germans were allowed to learn who had informed on them and what they had said. This was a dilemma. "I think of the now famous case of Vera Wollenberger," wrote one journalist, "a political activist from my friend Werner Krätschell's parish in Pankow, who discovered from reading her file that her husband, Knud, had been informing on her ever since they met. They would go for a walk with the children on Sunday, and on Monday Knud would pour it all out to his Stasi case officer."[425]

A person can try and play out how they would feel if they learned that their spouse had been betraying them from day one, but this is purely hypothetical. Would it be akin to learning that they had had an affair on the side? Easier to deal with, since there wasn't any physical intimacy? Harder to deal with, since at least an affair can be rationalized as meaningless acts of pleasure? If they lied about this, what else did they lie about? Or is this such a specific type of lying that maybe that meant they were honest in other contexts? (Was it even lying if the things they said to the Stasi were the truth?)

As such, there are people in Germany whose job it is to prepare citizens for what they might find in these files:

> Frau Trümpelmann, who has a Church background, takes immense pains to help people through these shocks. She generally telephones beforehand to prepare them. She carefully explains about the nature of the files before settling them down in the reading room. She is at hand to comfort them as they read. But the strain on her is great. She has trouble with her eyes and her heart. How to work with poison every day and not yourself be poisoned?

> One of Frau Trümpelmann's recent readers had been imprisoned for five years under the communist regime, for attempting to escape to the West. Now she found out, by reading her file, that it was the man she was living with who had denounced her to the Stasi. They still lived together. Only that morning he had wished her a good day in the archive. The woman collapsed into Frau Trümpelmann's arms.[426]

Much of the Stasi's tactics seemed to come out of a spy thriller. Nowadays people are familiar with exploding ultraviolet ink packs used to mark and deter robbers. But decades earlier the Stasi had their own methods to secretly mark people: radiation. They had radioactive magnets for cars, put radioactive pins into clothes, and had radioactive pellets shot into tires. A radioactive spray could be surreptitiously used on anyone in a crowd, and if used on a floor it could make a target unknowingly leave radioactive footprints wherever they went. These techniques were only later put together because several prisoners all died from an unusual form of cancer, which led to investigators discovering a radiation machine.[427]

It was with the rise of Walter Ulbricht's successor Erich Honecker that the decision was made to lessen the Stasi's use of brute terror and focus on the infinitely more pernicious techniques of mental warfare. In the post-Stalin era, many dissidents in the Soviet Union and allied countries were sentenced to mental institutions for spurious reasons. You'd have to be insane to oppose the truth of communism, after all. Being a largely materialistic ideology, Marxism tends to be skeptical of psychiatry. But for those who challenged the government, Soviet authorities made an exception. Yet the Stasi did them one better with the concept of *zersetzung.*

Zersetzung is usually translated into English as "corrosion" or "disintegration." The word has similarities to the American concept of "gaslighting," after the film in which a husband surreptitiously convinces his wife that she is going insane and thereby trying to make it happen for real. The literal gaslighting in the film refers to his dimming lights in their home while insisting nothing had changed. What gives the German term an extra bit of sadism is that what was being corroded or disintegrated were the sane minds of those who the Stasi decided to target.

Zersetzung worked by, say, coming home and finding one's socks on the pillow for no reason. Did they leave their socks out, and simply forget? What about when it happened again the next day, and the day after that? If someone had in fact been there, why would the socks be misplaced and all the valuables present and accounted for? The mind would have infinite questions and no answers—and no one to ask for advice or explanation. Whether the mental state that inevitably followed should be referred to as "paranoia" is a pedantic question, as in the adage "Are you paranoid if they're really out to get you?"

But the Stasi often took things one step further. In a perfect inversion of Western police surveillance, they sometimes *wanted* a target to know they were being watched while simultaneously being completely unable to answer why. They would intentionally generate odd sounds on a target's telephone calls, or make it a point to be seen speaking with one's employers. The target would then be sent into a stage of justified fear, wracking their brain as to what they knew and who told what. The police would often stop the target repeatedly and search them every time. A target might find their bicycle's tires slashed—not just once but over and over. Clearly that wasn't a coincidence—but the police wouldn't slash bicycle tires, right? Or would they? But if not them, who else would be doing it—and for what possible reason? And why weren't *they* being arrested?

These were very effective techniques for breaking up social or political groups at any time. In a nation where so many of the population were informants, the natural reaction would be to suspect whomever one happened to be spending time with the most. It went both ways: a target's newfound paranoid behavior would be sure to arouse suspicion from others. If that didn't work, the Stasi could easily plant rumors to arouse suspicion anyway. Once a person had it in their head that someone else was behaving oddly, it virtually becomes a self-fulfilling prophecy. The mind would begin to notice perfectly innocuous things but perceive them through the lens of suspicion. The cost/benefit analysis as to whether to further interact with such a person was clear: better to distance oneself than possibly have one's entire life ruined.

The Stasi had another technique for breaking up groups, which by their nature tended to be regarded as conspiracies against the state. All it would take was one Stasi operative in an organization urging its members toward increasingly radical and aggressive actions. All the members could then be detained for associating with aggressive radicals or not turning them in. The Stasi could then also truthfully say that the group had been an audience to illegal conversations.

As insidious as the Stasi was to East Germans, it sometimes managed to extend its influence into West Germany as well. Any discontent in the GDR was routinely blamed on the relics of Hitler. An uprising of more than one million East Germans on June 16 and 17, 1953, was blithely defined as a "fascist coup attempt." Perhaps the most reprehensible of the Stasi's schemes was something codenamed "Aktion 'J'," as in Jew.[428] The Soviets had no problem finding subversive opponents in their midst—and where they could not be found, they were either invented out of thin air, or people were forced into confessing to crimes. The Stasi did the same thing, and they did it with quintessential German professionalism.

First, a Stasi operative was quietly sent to West Germany to find the names of people who had publicly made anti-Semitic statements. The plan was to send Jewish Holocaust survivors letters in the name of those anti-Semites. Some of these drafted letters survived in the Stasi files: "Haven't you had enough, you Jewish pigs? We forgot to gas you. Wake up, Germany!" To make matters worse, the Stasi also intended to send out (fake) letters *from* the Jewish targets of this fraudulent Nazism. "I don't dare give my name out of fear," one such draft included. Single-handedly, the Stasi could invent both Nazis and Jewish victims. As one senior Party official put it at the time, the destabilization in West Germany was necessary "even at the risk that some Jews would suffer from it."[429] Radicalism, even neo-Nazi radicalism, was viewed as a useful cudgel with which to denigrate the rival West Germany.

Indeed, in a masterpiece of propaganda and brazen bullshit, the GDR acted for decades as if Nazism had been largely or exclusively a West German phenomenon, and that the East Germans had been rescued from Nazism by the Russians. Immediately after WWII a monument was put up in eastern Dresden, in what was briefly called Red Army Square before being more subtly renamed Unity Square. The inscription read "Eternal glory to the fighters of the Red Army who fell in the battles against the German fascist conquerors for the freedom and independence of the Soviet homeland."

Yet the Stasi agents weren't free themselves either. Once you were in the Stasi, there was no exit. Funder tells a nightmarish story of one Stasi agent who tried to resign.[430] At one point he had assembled a few pamphlets for a friend's wedding. Unauthorized printing being a crime, the Stasi tracked him down from the typewriter that he used at work and arrested him for being a pornographer even though there was nothing risqué in the pamphlets.

Then, the Stasi went to the agent's wife and accused her of being in on her husband's "pornography career," both to her utter terror and very appropriate confusion. Pornography was a serious felony, and the two had a son. When she was questioned the district attorney merely asked her, "Is there anyone who could look after your little boy for the next five years or so?" The only way to save herself—and her custody of her son—was to distance herself from her husband by applying for a divorce. Helpfully, the DA had brought such an application with him, already filled out with all of her and her husband's information. All she had to do was sign—which she of course did.

The Stasi then went to see the agent in jail in order to tell him, truthfully, that his wife had signed a paper asking for divorce. Look, he could see for himself. There was her signature. So…did he want to reconsider the matter of his resignation? After all, he had "operational knowledge" and he couldn't simply be allowed to leave the organization. And now that he was rid of that bad influence wife…Why, if he remained, he would be eligible for promotion! He of course reconsidered.

After his release the agent refused to listen to his ex-wife's explanations, that woman who left him hanging when he had been at his lowest. It was only months later when their five-year-old son explained to his father what had happened that he put two and two together. The

Stasi had never even bothered to repair the family that they'd destroyed in order to get what they wanted.

Yet as sinister and feared as his Stasi were, East Germany's leader Erich Honecker was still not the most hated figure in the GDR. That honor would probably belong to the woman who became his third wife and longtime partner-in-crime: Margot Honecker. Just as it was Ilse Koch who was despised as "the Bitch of Buchenwald" over her camp commander husband Karl-Otto, Margot gained a reputation for cruelty and oppression all on her own.

Unusually in communist circles—and in democratic ones as well—Margot had become a prominent politician in her own right before hitching her wagon to Herr Honecker's. The communist countries had youth movements to prepare future party cadres, and East Germany's Free German Youth was co-founded by Erich in 1946. Three years later Margot Feist became the youngest member of Parliament at the ripe age of twenty-two. The pair crossed paths and began an affair despite the fact that he was fifteen years her elder and already married. After Margot gave birth to their daughter Sonja in 1952, Walter Ulbricht strongly encouraged Honecker to get a divorce and marry Margot. Being a dutiful German, Honecker followed orders.

Margot Honecker became Minister of National Education in 1963 while Erich replaced Ulbricht as East German leader in 1971. And while Honecker and his regime dominated the adult citizens in the German Democratic Republic, it was Margot's role to come for the children. This earned her the German nickname of *die Hexe*: the Witch. Undeniably beautiful and often smiling, Margot was a bit of a fashionista in a time and a place where wearing conspicuous clothing was more than a bit suspect. At one point she took things a step further and began to dye her graying hair an unnatural shade of lilac, whereupon *die Hexe* became known as the Purple Witch. Rumors circulated that she flew to Paris every month to get her hair done.[431]

Margot's job was to make sure that East German children grew up to be loyal, obedient citizens—or else. Part of her plan was to make sure that the kids had reliable homes to grow up in. Her definition of reliability was, of course, the degree to which parents were in line with the reigning communist ideology. It only took applying for a visa to leave

East Germany, even for just a trip, to mark someone as unreliable or downright hostile to the GDR, for example. One couldn't very well have such types working in an office environment where they could corrupt others. It made sense to fire them.

Having the mark of getting fired on one's record would lead to the virtual impossibility of a new job. The official position of the German Democratic Republic was that unemployment did not exist there. People weren't unemployed, they were "looking for work." Therefore, if someone was never able to find a job in the fully-employed country, logically speaking it must be due to that antisocial individual's stubborn refusal to work. Antisocial individuals have no business raising children, and the definition of "antisocial" ranged from being out of work to some other sense of not fitting in with the greater East German society.

The GDR took thousands of kids from "unreliable" parents and give them to good communists to raise as their own. Any further contact between parents and their children was impossible, for they had no idea where their kids went. Sometimes the government wouldn't bother to wait a week before taking newborn infants away. Even the mothers in the Gulag, decades prior, had better opportunities with their babies. If any parent was a threat to the Honecker regime in any way, their children could also be "saved" from their clutches by being imprisoned by the government. It was a devious way to ensure that parents were obedient. Every single East German child was effectively a hostage of the government at all times, an extreme measure even by communist standards.

Some parents spent decades trying to track down what happened to their offspring, with varying degrees of success. Sometimes they learned their adult children were no longer interested in seeing them for whatever reason. Others met and stared at one another, two strangers who only had their biology in common. The crucial bonds made when a child is very young are almost impossible to reestablish at a later date.

Yet these forced adoptions weren't Margot's most horrific technique. Nor was it her ideologically driven curricula meant to raise generations of perfect communist East German children. The most notorious of her tools for control was in Torgau. A two-hour drive south from Berlin, Torgau is a town in Saxony that stands on the banks of the river Elbe. It was there, on April 25, 1945, where the United States and USSR anti-Nazi forces came together from West and East respectively, shaking hands for the first time. In this sense, the town of Torgau can be seen as a symbol of dawn, of knowing that the worst is over and that victory lies ahead.

It was at Torgau that Margot ran the worst of the *jugendwerkhof* in East Germany. Though the word means "youth workshop," the reality was that Torgau was a prison for children. One can argue whether the conditions at Torgau were worse than a standard prison or merely the same. What is indisputable is that twelve year olds are not very compatible with being held in solitary confinement—and not for murder or terrorism or the other extreme crimes people tend to associate with solitary confinement. One teenage survivor described being locked up after her stepfather molested her, driving her to attempt suicide. She was nevertheless imprisoned like all the others. Children who are suicidal in the United States are institutionalized just as they were in East Germany, but the East German version of institutionalization is enormously different from the American.

The children at Torgau were locked in with no possibility of escape, without any contact with their families, with no hope of someone letting them out of their 65-square-foot room no matter what they did. They knew that if they panicked or acted out or screamed for help that would only make conditions worse. And if they didn't know, they learned that fact very, very quickly. Margot's staff was there to make sure of that.

When they first arrived at Torgau the children would be kept in holding cells. They would have to wait several days for the director to bother seeing them. While they waited they weren't allowed to sing or whistle or to make any noise at all. Nor were they allowed to even look out the window. That was a whole other world, one that no longer concerned them. The goal was not to save the imprisoned children but to break them, because deviation from the crowd in any sense put them on the radar screen of the authorities.

While it takes quite a bit to lock up an American young person against his or her will—especially if their parents are opposed as well—in the GDR it took relatively little. And just as with any other environment, the predators knew to go where the prey was—and the more helpless the prey, the easier it was for the predators. Not only could the Torgau caretakers assault the children who were ostensibly under their care, they were permitted to take the children home with them on weekends to use however they wanted in the privacy of their own homes.

As German newsweekly *Der Spiegel* reported:

> Not everyone could endure the conditions. A 17-year-old who ran away from Torgau while being transported was so desperate that he jumped into the Elbe River and drowned. Young people used shirts to hang themselves, drank industrial grease and swallowed needles. One boy locked himself in his room, poured floor wax all over his body and set himself on fire.
>
> [Another] teenager tried to sacrifice himself so that others could run away. He told his fellow inmates to kill him and hang his body from the bars on the window of the dormitory to lure the guards into the room. The boy was strangled with a sheet to the point of unconsciousness, but he survived. The attempted escape failed.[432]

In a sense Torgau could be taken as an extreme metaphor for all the people on the far side of the Berlin Wall—or even on the far side of the Iron Curtain. These populations were trapped both literally and figuratively, with no hope of escape, living in countries where human life was nothing, less than nothing—and they knew it. Indeed, what possible argument for hope could there be?

There had been opportunities for escape as the years passed, but they had all failed. The time after Stalin's death was one such example. Imre Nagy was the prime minister of Hungary from 1953 to 1955. When Stalin passed away, Nagy attempted to soften his government's authoritarianism. This displeased the Kremlin and he was pulled from his position.

Then came Khrushchev's secret speech in early 1956, which led to widespread Hungarian unrest. Nagy was returned to power in an attempt to mollify the population, but it did little to ease the tensions. For thirteen days Hungary stood in full revolt against being a Soviet satellite. Nagy announced that his country would be withdrawing from the Warsaw Pact—and that was a bridge too far for Khrushchev. Criticism of Stalin was permitted if not downright encouraged throughout the communist nations, but defiance of Soviet power was still forbidden. On November 4, 1956, the Soviets launched a full invasion of Hungary. Nagy was arrested alongside many others who took part in the uprising, and a new administration in lockstep with Moscow was installed in his place. He was then imprisoned and tortured for almost two years, before eventually being hanged in 1958.

Nor was that the only example. January 5, 1968 witnessed Alexander Dubcek assuming the leadership role in communist Czechoslovakia. As the months went on, Dubcek implemented a series of reforms in an attempt to bring about "socialism with a human face." His guiding principle was the idea of making socialism function as it had been promised, trying to build a thriving nation that abandoned as many elements of authoritarianism as possible.

For months Dubcek rolled out reforms, including attempts to allow greater freedom of expression while decreasing the government's reliance on the secret police in order to maintain political control. Freeing political prisoners became a topic of discussion, and the Slovakian half of the country was given more autonomy. At a certain point it even looked as if Dubcek would be introducing some democratic measures, creating the possibility that the Communist Party would lose its monopoly on power. This period of hopeful reform became known as the Prague Spring, a renaissance of civil society blooming throughout every aspect of the central European country.

As spring turned to summer, word came down from Moscow that Dubcek was moving too quickly. The final straw came when Dubcek started to distance himself from the Warsaw Pact, which was much too reminiscent of Imre Nagy's actions a decade prior. On July 16, 1968, Dubcek was given a written warning by the other members of the Pact that he was playing a dangerous game. Pointing out that the "peoples of our countries won a victory over Hitlerite fascism at the price of immense sacrifices," what became known as the Warsaw Letter went on to state that:

> The strength and solidity of our ties depend on the internal strength of the socialist system of each of our fraternal countries, as well on the Marxist-Leninist policy of our parties, which are playing a leading role in the political and social life of their peoples and states. Policies that undermine the leading role of the communist party will lead to the destruction of socialist democracy and of the socialist system. Thus, the foundations of our ties and the security of the community of our countries will be placed in danger.[433]

Here was born the Brezhnev doctrine, named after the Soviet leader who had succeeded Nikita Khrushchev in 1964. Brezhnev's policy was that the socialist nations—and the USSR especially—had an obligation to defend the gains that socialism had made. If a given nation were to turn against socialism in a counter-revolutionary manner, the other socialist nations had a duty to intervene in order to prevent that—by force, if necessary. It was not only Russian citizens who could not escape the USSR: neither could those countries aligned with the Soviet Union.

One month after the Warsaw Letter, forces from Bulgaria, Poland, Hungary and the Soviet Union invaded Czechoslovakia with East German support. Prague citizens witnessed firsthand whether it was true that the city's cobblestoned streets were easier ones for Russian tanks to navigate. Dubcek was arrested but was spared Nagy's fate, getting expelled from the Party and shuffled off to an obscure forestry job in Slovakia. His successor Gustav Husak slowly but surely undid virtually everything that Dubcek had accomplished. President Lyndon Johnson, his secretary of state, and the American ambassador to the UN all refused to do or say anything.[434]

So where would someone trapped behind the Iron Curtain look for hope? What possible reason would they have to think that totalitarians would ever give up on their absolutist ideology? Why would their rulers ever voluntarily renounce their power—and who could possibly stop them militarily? The Korean War had been a draw. The Vietnam War was a disaster for the West. The Soviet Union clearly wasn't going anywhere.

Marginally intelligent people love importing words from other languages because they signal multilingualism and internationalism—both supposed indicators of brainpower and sophistication. The keyword of this era was *détente*. The approximate English translation of "relaxation" sounds a lot less impressive because the subtext was "stalemate."

Begun under Richard Nixon and heavily associated with his advisor Henry Kissinger, détente codified into a semi-official policy of being "realistic" and acknowledging that the world would be divided into a communist East and a liberal-democratic West for decades to come. People needed to accept things as they were, not simply how they wished or imagined them to be. Pretending otherwise was both utopian and naïve, and dangerous to boot. We would just have to figure out a way to live with one another. As such, it was important for both superpowers to acknowledge this state of affairs and to figure out ways of lessening tensions and increasing communications with one another whenever possible.

Dovetailing with the idea of détente was the concept of MAD, Mutual Assured Destruction. Both the United States and the Soviet Union had enough nuclear weapons at this point to blow up one another dozens of times over, almost certainly destroying life on earth in the process. As such, it was crucial to take steps to avoid the Cold War escalating into open warfare as had happened several times over the past decades. The bipartisan American foreign policy consensus was tethered to the view that—like it or not—the Soviet Union was here to stay. The experts agreed that only a lunatic playing a dangerous game with nuclear war would think any differently. As one infamous 1964 campaign ad stated, "We must either love each other, or we must die."

It took the pairing of a woman and a man to throw this consensus into the trash. Her view was that "consensus seems to be the process of abandoning all beliefs, principles, values and policies. So it is something in which no one believes and to which no one objects." As for him: "My idea of American policy toward the Soviet Union is simple, and some would say simplistic," he said in 1977. "It is this: we win and they lose."[435]

Chapter 11

LESS THAN NOTHING

What has gone down in history as one of the all-time great political romances might be better viewed as a Hollywood buddy comedy. Though their worldviews were highly compatible and often identical, the relationship between President Ronald Reagan and Prime Minister Margaret Thatcher epitomized the cliché that politics makes for strange bedfellows. He was a smooth operator, always with a joke on hand, relying on anecdotes instead of data to put across his point of view. She was strident and serious to the point of being a scold, someone who did not hesitate to lecture whomever happened to be in earshot. Neither took a traditional path towards heading the governments of their respective countries.

The woman who became the second Mrs. Denis Thatcher was born in 1925 above her father's grocery store in suburban Grantham, the incarnation of the petit-bourgeoisie that Lenin so despised for their small-minded provincialism. Always a daddy's girl, Margaret Roberts' interest in politics was sparked at an early age by her father Alfred's local career. He served on the Grantham town council starting in 1927 before becoming alderman in 1943 and mayor in 1945. He was voted out when Labour took over the council—a quiet trauma that the young Margaret witnessed firsthand.

When she was still in her twenties a fortune teller supposedly told Margaret that she would be as "great as Churchill." It is of some interest to consider how that story got out, for it would be a very clever way for Margaret to boast without having to make the claim herself. Growing up it wasn't obvious that she was destined to any sort of greatness at all. She ended up getting a chemistry degree at Oxford, where her classmates universally agreed that she was fairly unexceptional and possessed little of the charisma or popularity that one would expect from a future politician. Admittedly well-spoken, young Margaret made three attempts for Parliament between 1950 and 1954—and lost all three. Her 1951 marriage to the wealthy Denis Thatcher gave her the financial freedom to study law and pass the bar, as well as the resources to balance focusing on her political career while raising their pair of twins. In 1959 Thatcher was given the nomination for the safe Conservative seat of Finchley, and was elected to Parliament five days before her thirty-fourth birthday.

Reagan's path was quite a different one. Born in 1911 under President William Howard Taft, the rural Illinois native grew up to become a successful lifeguard and a graduate of Eureka College—not quite as impressive as Thatcher's Oxford degree. The tall, handsome Reagan then went on to become a radio sportscaster. There he developed the skill of talking for an extended period of time without actually saying anything—a very useful skill for a future politician to have. "Between pitches and innings, there was usually a lot of dead time that I had to fill with anecdotes and descriptions of the players, the field, and the weather," he recalled. "I wish I could count the number of ways I managed to describe how the rays of the afternoon sun looked as they fell across the rim of Wrigley Field."

Reagan also figured out how to make things seem fine to the public when in fact things were anything but, simply by making things up. After the wire went dead during one of the games he was announcing, he tried to stall in order to keep fans from turning the knob to a competitor's station:

> I decided to let Jurges foul off the pitch, figuring Western Union would soon fix the problem. To fill in some time, I

> described a couple of kids in the stands fighting over the foul ball. […] I had Jurges foul off another ball; I slowed Dean down, had him pick up the resin bag and take a sign, shake it off, get another sign, and let him pitch; I said he'd fouled off another one, but this time he'd just missed a home run by only a few inches. […] Jurges hit a foul ball, and then another…and another. A red-headed kid in the stands retrieved one of the fouls and held up the ball to show off his trophy. […] I continued to let Jurges foul Dean's pitches, and his string of foul balls went on for almost seven minutes. I don't know how many foul balls there were, but I'm told someone reported the foul-slugging spree as a record to "Ripley's Believe It Or Not" column.[436]

A fortuitous trip to Hollywood earned Reagan a contract as an actor, and by eventually getting elected as president of the Screen Actors Guild Reagan was thereby the first union leader to become president of the United States. When he once gave a speech to a citizens' group denouncing fascism Reagan added a line condemning communism as well. The dead silence from the audience made him realize just how prevalent Stalinist infiltration of American culture had become. Reagan eventually testified in front of the House Un-American Activities Committee as a friendly witness three days after Ayn Rand had.

The media claim was that investigating Communist Party activity was all a witch hunt. But as playwright Molly Day Thatcher put it:

> Those witches did not exist. Communists do. Here, and everywhere in the world. It's a false parallel. Witch hunt! The phrase would indicate that there are no Communists in the government, none in the big trade unions, none in the press, none in the arts, none sending money from Hollywood to Twelfth Street. No one who was in the Party and left uses that phrase. They know better.[437]

Arthur Miller's 1953 play *The Crucible* was a transparent metaphor for the search for Communists in Hollywood and Washington. Yet in later years he did not mince words about how naïve he and many of his fellow influencers had been:

> Given the depth of our alienation from the failing capitalism of the time, it would have been intolerable to see the clear parallels between the social institutions of the fascist and Nazi regimes and those of the Soviet Union. Captive trade unions, mass youth organizations, secret police, informers in the workplace and the home, masses of political prisoners, and at the center of it all idolatry of the state and its leader—all of these had originated in the Soviet system. Fascism and Nazism were imitations of Soviet forms, with manic nationalism and racism replacing international proletarian solidarity as their central "spiritual" content. The generic enmity between the two systems turned out to be no deeper than the enmity of England for France at certain times in history, or of Germany for England.[438]

Reagan's relatively brief marriage and divorce to fellow actor Jane Wyman led to him going on a date with a young starlet named Nancy Davis. Davis had reached out to him as a SAG official because she shared the same name as an actress who had been identified as a Communist. The two were inseparable ever since, an odd pairing that sometimes puzzled even their children. Whereas Reagan regarded every stranger as a friend he hadn't met, the ambitious Nancy developed a reputation for being cold and more than a bit of a social climber.

By the 1960s Reagan's acting career began to dry up. He started to spend time criss-crossing America under the auspices of General Electric, speaking about issues from a conservative perspective. Then and always a huge FDR fan, Reagan remained a Democrat despite his political views. Although "I was still saying the same things that I'd said for six years during the Eisenhower administration," he remembered, "I was suddenly being called a 'right-wing extremist.'"[439] It was when he was campaigning for Richard Nixon during the former vice president's 1962 run for California governor that a registrar in the audience stood up and challenged Reagan as to his party of choice. He changed his party affiliation to Republican on the spot before continuing on with his speech.

By then Nixon was already regarded with particular animosity by Democrats and more than a few Republicans. In 1946 Republicans had recaptured the House of Representatives and the Senate for the first time since FDR's New Deal. A whopping 55 new Republican congressmen won seats that year—including the new representative from California's 12th District, Richard Nixon. At the time, many in the media viewed the claims of longtime Democratic State Department apparatchik Alger Hiss being a Soviet spy were basically a widely-discredited conspiracy theory, a right-wing fantasy designed to smear one of our nation's most patriotic public servants. Was there no depth to which the Republicans wouldn't sink? Have you no decency, sir?

There was one little problem: Hiss *was* a spy, and Nixon was key to demonstrating his guilt of working for Stalin. Central to this was testimony from Whittaker Chambers, who had been a fellow traveler with Hiss in Communist Party circles. Hiss was eventually convicted of perjury and spent several years in jail. But the press never forgave Nixon for exposing their malfeasance and never let him forget it.

Springboarding off his anti-communist cred, in 1950 Nixon decided to go for a job promotion and run for the United States Senate. His opponent was Congresswoman Helen Gahagan Douglas, and Nixon successfully painted the "Pink Lady" (not fully a communist Red) as being soft on the Soviet Union. Nixon won by almost twenty points, 59%-40%, an utter massacre. This quickly led to him becoming Eisenhower's running mate in 1952. In six years, Richard Nixon went from being a layman to a representative, a senator, and then one heartbeat away from the presidency. There was no stopping this Dick.

In 1960 Nixon became the Republican candidate for president—and wound up losing the closest election in United States history to John F. Kennedy. There was, in fact, some stopping of this Dick. No matter, he thought. He would run for governor of California and use that to seek the White House again, either in 1964 or 1968. After all, he was still only forty-seven years old. The sitting Democratic governor of California had other ideas. Pat Brown had been elected in 1958 by a margin similar to Nixon's in 1950, 60%-40% over sitting Senator William Knowland. Nixon would have his work cut out for him to make up that margin.

The 1962 campaign for California governor, as with all of Nixon's campaigns, was bitter and divisive. When the results came in Brown was reelected by a five-point margin, 52%-47%. Pat Brown had slain the biggest dragon in the Republican party, the former vice president who had almost been elected president just two years prior. Nixon, humiliated and disgraced, gave his notorious press conference where he lambasted the media. "But as I leave you," he told the reporters, "I want you to know: just think how much you're going to be missing. You don't have Nixon to kick around anymore."

On the national stage things were about to get even worse for the Republicans. Prompted by activists such as Phyllis Schlafly and her self-published *A Choice, Not an Echo*, the argument was made that the Republicans had been having their asses handed to them since Hoover because they had simply nominated "Me Too" candidates for the White House. No one genuinely prefers the store brand, the generic substitute, but they might prefer a different brand altogether. If the American people had the option of a strong conservative nominee that could provide a contrast to the left, then that candidate would win. The 1964 nomination of Arizona Senator Barry Goldwater was easily the Republicans' most conservative pick since the days of Calvin Coolidge, and the party establishment did pretty much everything in their power to Stop Goldwater.

It was very clear that Goldwater had virtually no shot—especially given President Kennedy's assassination the year before—and incumbent Democrat President Lyndon Johnson barely even bothered to campaign. One of the few celebrities to hitch their wagons to the Goldwater campaign was Ronald Reagan. A week before the election he delivered a nationally televised speech making the case for Goldwater's version of conservatism and his personal vision of what America meant, referencing Cuba's relatively recent communist takeover:

> Not too long ago, two friends of mine were talking to a Cuban refugee, a businessman who had escaped from Castro, and in the midst of his story one of my friends turned to the other and said, "We don't know how lucky we are." And the Cuban stopped and said, "How lucky you are? I had someplace to escape to." And in that sentence he told us the entire story. If we lose freedom here, there's no place to escape to. This is the last stand on earth.[440]

Despite Reagan's best efforts, LBJ won reelection with 61%—the highest percentage of the popular vote since James Monroe had been reelected without opposition in 1820. Further—and despite having twenty-six seats up for election to the Republicans' nine—the Democrats still managed to pick up two more Senate seats for a 68-32 majority. The House results were even worse for the GOP, as Democrats picked up 37 seats to cement a 295-140 lead that they had not seen since FDR's heyday. The Republican Party was effectively powerless in Washington, and Goldwaterism was dead and buried. The corporate press, the Democrats, the establishment Republicans: all were ready to proclaim Goldwaterism to be a juvenile, brain-dead philosophy from a bygone era that had now been put before the public and thoroughly repudiated. It's 1964! How are we still having this conversation?

Yet Reagan's speech was very well received, and did more for his political career than it did for Goldwater's. Though she had advised the Goldwater campaign, Ayn Rand grew dissatisfied with what she perceived to be the candidate's increasing anti-intellectualism. She was not alone in looking at the outcome of the election and proclaiming that it "is too late for the 'conservatives.' There is nothing left to 'conserve.'" Nor was she alone in singling out Reagan as the Republican winner of 1964, arguing that the best of the Goldwater campaign "was a speech by Ronald Reagan. [...] All of the candidate's speeches should have been on a level equal to Mr. Reagan's."[441]

With the wind behind him—and at the strong urging of Nancy—Reagan set his sights on the California governor's mansion. In 1965 he released his first autobiography, with the wacky title *Where's the Rest of Me?* being a reference to a movie scene where his character wakes up in a panic to discover that his legs had been amputated. The reaction to Reagan's announcement was as expected: the idea of a "Governor Ronald Reagan" could have been considered a joke if it were actually funny. The washed-up has-been actor should have been slipping on a banana peel in some Vaudeville routine. But the governor's mansion? Oh, please! Didn't he have another movie to make about being friends with a chimpanzee?

Pat Brown thought he had it in the bag when he was running for reelection, especially since LBJ had carried California 59%-41%. When Goldwater advocates claimed that "In Your Heart, You Know He's Right," the reply was "In Your Guts, You Know He's Nuts." And now one of these Goldwater nuts was going to run for governor against the man who had just driven near-president Richard Nixon out of politics forever?

The election ended up being a bloodbath. After Governor Brown fended off a primary challenge from Los Angeles Mayor Sam Yorty, he never quite gained the momentum that he needed. Whereas Reagan promised to "clean up the mess at Berkeley"—an early bit of the future warfare between conservatives and hard-left universities—Brown ran a widely-condemned ad comparing him to Lincoln assassin John Wilkes Booth, using the dubious reasoning that both men had been actors. When Reagan was criticized for having no experience, he had a quick retort: "The man who has the job has more experience than anybody. That's why I'm running."[442] Though a Reagan election victory seemed probable, his margin of victory was a surprise: he trounced the incumbent governor 58%-42%, winning fifty-five out of California's fifty-eight counties (including Los Angeles, and by double digits).

Reagan's ascension to the governor's mansion was paralleled by Thatcher climbing the ladder in Parliament. Under the British system, the opposition party has a shadow cabinet consisting of MPs who serve as parallels to the current members of her majesty's government. When Labour is in power, for example, the Conservatives have a Shadow Health Secretary and so forth. In 1967 loyal Tory Margaret Thatcher was recommended to Leader of the Opposition Ted Heath for just such an assignment, as Heath was looking for women to appoint but had few female Conservatives to choose from. "Yes, Willie agrees that she's much the most able," Heath said, referring to the Tory Whip. "But, he says, once she's there we'll never be able to get rid of her."[443]

Thatcher thus became Shadow Secretary of State for Education and Science in 1967. "I did not make a particularly important contribution to Shadow Cabinet," she later admitted. "Nor was I asked to do so. [...] I was principally there as the statutory woman whose main task was to explain what 'women'—[...]our uniform, undifferentiated sex—were likely to think and want on troublesome issues."[444] After the Conservatives took control of Parliament in 1970, Education Secretary Margaret Thatcher proposed cutting a WWII-era program to subsidize free milk for schoolchildren by limiting it to those under seven years of age. The press savaged her as "Margaret Thatcher, milk snatcher" and she was driven to display the empty contents of her pantry. Thatcher managed to survive, but she gained a lifelong reputation for being cold and indifferent to the poor.

The milk scandal nevertheless taught Thatcher a valuable political lesson. She was far more of a strategic politician than her image of a tough straight talker let on, and her personal analysis of the milk issue showed just how much:

> I had incurred the maximum of political odium for the minimum of political benefit. I and my colleagues were caught up in battles with local authorities for months, during which we suffered constant sniping in the media, all for a saving of £9 million which could have been cut from the capital budget with scarcely a ripple. I resolved not to make the same mistake again. In future if I were to be hanged, it would be for a sheep, not a lamb, still less a cow.[445]

For his part—despite major conflict between the state government and students in Berkeley that left one dead and dozens injured—Reagan was reelected governor in 1970 over Speaker of the California Assembly

Jesse Unruh (also known as "Big Daddy.") Two years after that, Richard Nixon was reelected as president over Democrat George McGovern by margins similar to the LBJ/Goldwater contest, 61% to 38%. The American electorate was enormously volatile in that era, both on the state and national level, as huge percentages of voters switched between the parties during every election. This was partly due to a growing ideological realignment, as conservatives increasingly tended to drift toward the GOP while progressives joined the Democrats.

In 1973 Nixon's running mate Spiro Agnew became the second vice president to resign from office, avoiding jail time on corruption charges by pleading no contest. Writing in 1980, Agnew maintained that he had done so because he felt his life had been threatened:

> I was close enough to the presidency to know that the office could exert tremendous power. I had attended secret sessions of the National Security Council and knew something about the functioning of the intelligence community. [...] Since the revelations have come out about the C.I.A.'s attempts to assassinate Fidel Castro and other foreign leaders, I realize even more than before that I might have been in great danger.
>
> I feared for my life. If a decision had been made to eliminate me—through an automobile accident, a fake suicide, or whatever—the order would not have been traced back to the White House any more than the "get Castro" orders were ever traced to their source.[446]

Agnew's replacement as vice president was House Republican leader Gerald Ford. Ford was well-liked in Washington, and the former football player from Michigan had a reputation for being squeaky-clean—qualities that got him confirmed by large bipartisan Congressional majorities. By 1974 the Watergate investigation—and subsequent revelations of secret White House tape recordings—were making it increasingly difficult for Richard Nixon to remain as president.

Nixon wasn't the only one in danger. The head of the Watergate hotel burglary, G. Gordon Liddy, had similar concerns to Agnew regarding what the Federal government was capable of. He had been party to White House discussions about the feasibility of drugging Pentagon Papers leaker Daniel Ellsberg and of assassinating reporter Jack Anderson. Liddy recounted his concerns about being killed during a conversation with White House Counsel John Dean:

> It would be reasonable; the stakes—the sure loss of the Presidency—were immensely higher and, after all, it was my fault. That raised another problem. So far as I knew, I was the only one readily available to the White House for a domestic sanctioned killing. [...] What was left to them?
>
> What was left would be some well-motivated amateur who didn't know the rules. I didn't mind being killed, if that was thought necessary, but I didn't want some scared-to-death nonprofessional to try it at my home or anywhere else where my family could be endangered. I had visions of shotgun blasts through the kitchen window on a Sunday morning while we were all at breakfast. [...] "I said I was the captain of the ship when she hit the reef and I'm prepared to go down with it. If someone wants to shoot me"—Dean's head snapped up and he stared at me—"just tell me what comer to stand on and I'll be there, O.K.?"
>
> Dean searched my face to see whether I was joking. I wasn't, and he could see that. "Well, uh," he stammered, "I don't think we've gotten there yet, Gordon."[447]

The senator who finally got tasked with telling Nixon that he no longer had enough Senate Republican support to avoid being removed from office was none other than Barry Goldwater. On August 9, 1974, Gerald Ford—who had never run on a national or even statewide ticket—became president of the United States. Less than one month later, on September 8th, Ford used his newfound presidential powers to pardon Nixon. It reeked of a quid pro quo, more corruption from the most corrupt administration in United States history.

The national outrage was apocalyptic. Even partisan Republicans were dumbfounded. As Goldwater later wrote:

> Ford called me just after granting the pardon but before announcing it. It was 4 a.m. when the phone rang at Newport Beach, California, where [my wife] Peggy and I were on vacation. I said, "Mr. President, you have no right and no power to do that. Nixon has never been charged or convicted of anything. So what are you pardoning him of? It doesn't make sense."
>
> Ford said, "The public has the right to know that, in the eyes of the President, Nixon is clear."
>
> I was stunned by Ford's words. This was the same man who had openly admitted that Nixon had deceived the Congress. That was most likely a criminal act—obstruction of justice. I replied, "He may be clear in your eyes, but he's not clear in mine."[448]

The volatile American political situation was paralleled in the UK as energy costs began to go through the roof under the reigning Conservatives. Starting on New Year's Day, 1974, commercial usage of electricity was limited to three days per week and working overtime was prohibited (though essential services were exempt from this rule). Television companies were ordered to stop broadcasting after 10:30 p.m. Under Queen Victoria it had truthfully been said that "the sun never sets on the British Empire" because it stretched across the globe. By the time of Queen Elizabeth II, however, the British couldn't even keep the lights on at home.

In the aftermath of the introduction of the three-day week, Prime Minister Ed Heath called an election for February 1974. Though his government fell, the result was effectively a draw: 301 Labour seats to 297 for Heath's Tories, the balance being held by various minor parties. The new Labour government immediately increased miners' wages by 35% upon assuming office. While this sounds extreme, UK inflation hit 16% in 1974 and would almost reach 27% the following year.

Not being able to govern with such a small margin, now it was Labour Prime Minister Harold Wilson who called an election for that October. A majority of 318 seats is needed in Parliament—and Wilson received 319. With both parties in close ideological alignment, it became almost impossible to persuade swing voters to choose anyone other than those whom they had chosen at the last election. And with both parties in close ideological alignment, it became clear that neither one had the ability to take on the problems that Great Britain was facing. Some began to regard it as karma for imperialism, that a nation that had pillaged so many others didn't deserve to thrive on its own.

One person who did not hold to this POV was Tory MP Airey Neave, who had successfully escaped from a Nazi POW camp only to later be given the honor of reading the indictments to the defendants at Nuremberg. Neave told Heath that he needed to stand down as leader for the sake of the Tories, but Heath refused. What Heath did eventually agree to was a change in the rules to allow a sitting leader to be challenged. Neave then asked three other men to stand against Heath, offering to be their campaign manager, but all three refused. Then Neave asked a woman: Margaret Thatcher. Her vision was of a Tory party that stood for right-wing principles clearly distinct from Labour's, with the voters allowed to have a choice, not an echo. Unlike the British political consensus at the time, Thatcher was an advocate of privatization, deregulation, lowering taxes, and reigning in government spending. "Consensus doesn't really give you any direction in life," she later said.

In January 1975, Heath put himself up for a vote in order to reaffirm his leadership of the Conservatives. In politics it's not unusual for a "stalking horse" candidate to emerge in these sorts of situations. Such a candidate isn't taken seriously themselves, but the level of their support is intended to measure the strength of the sitting leader. If the leader won, then that is that. But if they were shown to be vulnerable, then other, more legitimate candidates could emerge from hiding to challenge them.

Thatcher's challenge to Heath was regarded as a bit of a stalking horse campaign but also as a bit of a joke. Her shtick was that she was the frugal conservative housewife, and she was regarded as more of a nag than a leader. Under the new rules, Heath needed two things to happen to avoid a second-round runoff and win outright: the support of a majority of the 276 Conservative MPs, and a lead of 15% of the vote over Thatcher and a minor third candidate. He ended up getting neither.

When the votes were cast, Heath received 119 votes to Thatcher's 130 in the first round. He withdrew before the second ballot, and Thatcher handily defeated the three new men who thereupon decided to try becoming leader of the Conservative party. For the first time in history, a major Western political party would be headed by a woman—and not just a woman, but *that* woman (or as she became known behind closed doors "TBW": That Bloody Woman.) It was *Red Star*, a Soviet Army newspaper, that then gave her the nickname that stuck with Thatcher throughout her life: the Iron Lady.

Soon after her election as Tory leader, the US Embassy in London sent Secretary of State Henry Kissinger (architect of détente) a classified diplomatic cable assessing Thatcher's prospects. It was a startlingly accurate and downright prescient look at her strengths and weaknesses, down to how annoying many voters found her (literal) voice to be:

> Margaret Thatcher has blazed into national prominence almost literally from out of nowhere. When she first indicated that she intended to stand against Ted Heath for leadership of the Conservative party, few took her challenge seriously and fewer still believed it would succeed. She had never been a member of the inner circle of tory power brokers, and no politician in modern times has come to the

leadership of either major party with such a narrow range of prior experience. […]

There is general agreement among friends and critics alike that she is an effective and forceful parliamentary performer. She has a quick, if not profound, mind, and works hard to master the most complicated brief. She fights her corner with skill and toughness, but can be flexible when pressed. In dealing with the media or with subordinates, she tends to be crisp and a trifle patronizing. With colleagues, she is honest and straightforward, if not excessively considerate of their vanities. Civil servants at the Ministry of Education found her autocratic. She has the courage of her convictions, and once she has reached a decision to act, is unlikely to be deflected by any but the most persuasive arguments. Self-confident and self-disciplined, she gives every promise of being a strong leader.

Even before her great leap upward, Mrs. Thatcher had been the personification of a British middle class dream come true. Born the daughter of a grocer, she had by dint of her own abilities and application won through, securing scholarships to good schools, making a success of her chosen career, and marrying advantageously. It is not surprising then that she espouses the middle class values of thrift, hard work, and law and order, that she believes in individual choice, maximum freedom for market forces, and minimal power for the state. Hers is the genuine voice of a beleaguered bourgeoise, anxious about its eroding economic power and determined to arrest society's seemingly inexorable trend towards collectivism. Somewhat unchivalrously, [Labour's Chancellor of the Exchequer] Denis Healey has dubbed her "La Pasionaria of middle class privilege." […]

> Unfortunately for her prospects of becoming a national, as distinct from a party, leader, she has over the years acquired a distinctively upper middle class personal image. Her immaculate grooming, her imperious manner, her conventional and somewhat forced charm, and above all her plummy voice stamp her as the quintessential suburban matron, and frightfully English to boot. None of this goes down well with the working class of England (one-third of which used to vote Conservative), to say nothing of all classes in the Celtic fringes of this island.[449]

What was good for the goose was good for the gander. If the moderate Ed Heath could be knocked from his party leadership by a right-winger, then maybe just maybe so could President Ford. There was no question that Ford was on shaky ground, even independently of his pardon of Richard Nixon. Unemployment hit 8.8% under his presidency, with inflation reaching over 12% in 1974 alone. Just as with the British politicians, Ford seemed excruciatingly incompetent when it came to meeting this challenge. His campaign to Whip Inflation Now—complete with WIN buttons—seemed both clueless and pointless. The premise may have been a sound one: a rejection of Nixon's wage and price controls in favor of private citizens doing their part to stem inflation. Suggestions like "having more Americans plant vegetable gardens, turn down their thermostats and carpool as a way of cutting down on energy use and helping to restrain prices" do not even pretend to address the root causes of inflation or even to identify them. The rising prices and falling buying power of the dollar were a function of things like the money supply, costs of production, and prices set by business—none of which the average citizen had much control over.

But was taking down a sitting president too much even for the always-underestimated Ronald Reagan? The last time an incumbent had been denied his party's nomination had been an ailing Chester A. Arthur in 1884—and akin to Ford, Arthur had been a vice president who only succeeded to the Oval Office when James Garfield was assassinated. Yet there was still some more recent precedent. A few years after LBJ's historic landslide win against Barry Goldwater, Senator Eugene McCarthy's upstart 1968 campaign caused the president to declare that he would not be seeking reelection.

In 1976, for the first time in history, every state would have a primary or caucus to determine their delegates to the Republican convention instead of having party bosses control some of the votes. For Reagan this was a golden opportunity, due to his enormous appeal to the party faithful that disproportionately make up primary voters. But though unelected, Gerald Ford still had the power of the presidency at his disposal. It was much more impressive to get a phone call from the White House than from Ronald Reagan's campaign bus, and Ford knew how to leverage the power of the Oval Office to get the support he needed.

One of the biggest issues separating the Republican candidates was America's attitude toward the Soviet Union. Under the principles of détente, any acts that could be perceived as hostile would preferably be avoided—and of course, Soviet leaders had no qualms about attacking anything they disliked as a "provocation." Yet cracks were nevertheless beginning to appear in Russian society for one big reason: technology.

The ability to spread information was becoming cheaper and easier. The Soviet bloc witnessed the rise of *samizdata*, blurry photocopies of forbidden texts secretly passed around by the citizens. Aleksandr Solzhenitsyn's *The Gulag Archipelago* revealed the practices of the Soviet prison camp system to the world, and was banned in the USSR. Now it began to be read, and citizens in communist countries understood that the work—unlike what was in *Pravda* that day—was truthful in all its essentials. Solzhenitsyn avoided execution and was merely arrested and expelled from the USSR. Yet President Gerald Ford publicly refused to meet with him for fear of offending the Russians.

By the time of the Republican convention in 1976 no one had any idea what the outcome would be. President Ford entered having won twenty-six states to Reagan's twenty-four. Both candidates claimed to have enough delegates to win. Neither were correct, and both men were experienced enough to understand that a delegate's pledge was worth only as much as it could benefit them or their state. Reagan was also sixty-five years old, older than Eisenhower had been when he was first elected and older than anyone elected president since James Buchanan in 1856—universally regarded as one of the worst presidents. Ford was merely two years younger, but he was the sitting president at the time. It was supposedly now or never for Reagan, whereas this was Ford's opportunity to prove that his presidency was something that he had earned and not some mere historic fluke.

Reagan made an enormous blunder before the convention started. In the early days of the United States, where North and South had such different cultures, "geographic balance" was the name of the game for presidential tickets. One candidate from the Northeast would pair with one from the South to assure that there wouldn't be dominance of one part of the country over another. Over time this somewhat gave way to ideological balance, with centrists choosing more hardcore partisans (or vice versa) as their running mates to gin up the party's base. In 1952, for example, Richard Nixon was seen as being firmly on the right, and the largely non-ideological Dwight Eisenhower selected him as VP as a sop to the Republican base. Goldwater was a notable exception to this rule, choosing unknown New York Congressman Bill Miller for VP on the grounds that he "drives Johnson nuts."

Historically a candidate only announced their running mate once their nomination had been secured. In 1976 traditionalist Reagan decided to break with precedent and in July, a month before the convention, he announced that his choice for VP would be moderate (read: liberal) Pennsylvania Senator Richard Schweiker. Reagan's supporters were aghast. For years they had witnessed establishment Republicans sing their tune during the elections—and then promptly govern like Democrats the second that they landed in Washington. Reagan was supposed to be different. Yet before he had even been nominated—let alone elected—he had picked as his #2 a senator who had been endorsed by the AFL-CIO over a Democratic opponent. Ford won the nomination and, despite mounting an impressive campaign, lost to Georgia Governor Jimmy Carter in the fall.

While President Carter's inauguration did little to change American economic woes, things in the United Kingdom got worse and worse under Jim Callaghan's Labour government. Late 1978 saw the Winter of Discontent, Britain's largest labor stoppage since 1926. First came a strike by Ford Motors employees, one that was soon supported by the

Transport and General Workers Union. Then came the lorry drivers, the UK's equivalent of the teamsters. Gas stations closed down, and distribution channels within the country were crippled. Then the railwaymen had their turn.

On January 22, 1979, there was a widescale "Day of Action" as over 1.5 million workers went on strike. Schools shut down, and airports were closed. After that the ambulance drivers struck, though still responding to emergency calls in many—but not all—areas. The 1,100 National Health Service hospitals under Britain's socialized system were reduced to only treating emergencies. For a couple of weeks even the gravediggers went on strike. The sick were not getting help, and the dead were not getting buried. When the trash collectors went on strike the rubbish in London's famed Leicester Square soon stood taller than the people. The United Kingdom was fast becoming a dystopian novel.

On March 28, 1979, Leader of the Opposition Margaret Thatcher stood on the floor of the House of Commons and said, "Mr. Speaker, I beg to move, 'That this House has no confidence in Her Majesty's Government.'" Labour only needed a majority of the vote to avoid having to call an election, and there were plenty of seats from minor parties that Prime Minister Callaghan could cut deals with to maintain his hold on office. When the results came in Labour had a total of 310 votes—but 311 members of Parliament had expressed no confidence in the government. It had been the first time a British government had been forced to stand down in over fifty years—and for the first time ever, a woman would be leading the Tories into a general election.

Two days after the vote of no confidence, Airey Neave was murdered when a bomb exploded under his car that was parked mere feet away from the House of Commons. The Irish National Liberation Army, a splinter group from the Irish Republican Army, gloated over their deed:

> In March, retired terrorist and supporter of capital punishment, Airey Neave, got a taste of his own medicine when an INLA unit pulled off the operation of the decade and blew him to bits inside the 'impregnable' Palace of Westminster. The nauseous Margaret Thatcher snivelled on

> television that he was an 'incalculable loss'—and so he was—to the British ruling class.

The man who had been instrumental in Thatcher's rise would not be there to guide her through the general election. She knew this would be her sole opportunity to become prime minister. "There's only one chance for women," she confessed. "'Tis the law of life."

In their own ways both Reagan and Thatcher presented themselves as honest, tough speakers who stated their points of view and let the chips fall where they may. Yet both were acutely aware of the power of image—something no successful actor or politician can ignore. To avoid wearing glasses in public, Reagan had been one of the first Americans to get contact lenses at a time when they were still experimental. "They were big, rigid, and fit over the whites of your eyes like a pair of football helmets and weren't much fun to wear," he wrote in his autobiography. "Each lens had a little bubble over your cornea that you had to keep filled with a saline solution, and every couple of hours, the solution would turn gray and you'd find yourself blinded until you replaced the fluid."[450]

Similarly, even after leaving public office at age 79, Reagan was still insisting that his jet-black hair was all natural. "The rumor about dyeing my hair, incidentally, started when I was governor," he claimed. "My barber told me that after I left his shop people sometimes came in and asked if they could pick up a strand or two of my hair to see if the roots were gray. I'm the first person I know of who was actually happy when gray hair started growing on his head."[451]

As for Thatcher, she got a complete image makeover to the point of secretly taking lessons to lower the tone of her speaking voice. In the lead up to the 1979 election she was exposed for this by a BBC reporter, marking one of the extremely few cases where she found herself at a loss for words. "It's said that Gordon Reese gave you humming lessons to improve the way you spoke," he said to her.

"*Humming lessons?*" she replied, desperately looking away from the reporter. "I'm not a very good hummer." Hence, perhaps, the need for the lessons.

"Your voice is much lower than it used to be."

"Um, yes. I'm not quite sure why, whether it is that one is using it more?"[452]

Her makeover was merely part of a broader, remarkably modern campaign by the Conservatives. Their slogan had consisted of three simple words: Labour Isn't Working. "I can't bear Britain in decline," Thatcher insisted. "I just can't. We who either defeated or rescued half Europe, who kept half Europe free, when otherwise it would be in chains. And look at us now." 44% of the voters agreed with her, enough to give the Conservatives 339 seats to Labour's 269. Margaret Thatcher was going to be the United Kingdom's first female prime minister.

Approximately two months later, President Jimmy Carter gave what came to be known as his "malaise" speech. He spoke about a crisis of confidence in America, particularly with regards to rising energy costs and decreasing gasoline availability. His solution was to raise taxes on energy producers and to limit gasoline imports, as well as to encourage people to use less electricity. He asked citizens to "take no unnecessary trips, to use carpools or public transportation whenever you can, to park your car one extra day per week, to obey the speed limit, and to set your thermostats to save fuel." Living a colder life, literally so, would be a way to turn shortages into a surplus. "Every act of energy conservation like this is more than just common sense," he insisted. "I tell you it is an act of patriotism." Asking the public to solve an energy shortage by using less energy was akin to solving food shortages by eating less. It made sense on one level but missed the broader point entirely.

The GOP now saw a golden opportunity to recapture the White House, but many in the party establishment were terrified that Reagan would be a disaster of a candidate. The 1964 Goldwater catastrophe was fresh in Republican minds. If Goldwater could only carry six states, Reagan didn't seem to be able to do much better. He was too extreme, and now even older than he had been when he was already too old in 1976. Polling in January of 1980 had Reagan losing to Carter 33% to 62%, an even bigger landslide than Goldwater's final result.[453]

Iowa was the first state for Republican voters to weigh in on their choice for the party's nominee, and the relatively obscure George H. W. Bush managed to pull ahead of Reagan to take the win. Bush had most recently served as Director of the CIA for a year, previously having been head of the RNC, Ambassador to the UN, and a two-term member of Congress—none of which were great stepping stones to the White House. This was a Stop Reagan campaign, pure and simple, and Bush was quick to position himself as the frontrunner after taking Iowa: "Now they will be after me, howling and yowling at my heels. What we will have is momentum. We will look forward to Big Mo being on our side."

Bush pulling out a win in the New Hampshire primary would put Reagan in major trouble. In an effort to avoid Federal Election Commission guidelines, Reagan's campaign sponsored a debate to be hosted by a local newspaper. He then invited all the other Republican candidates, while Bush was under the impression that the debate would just be between the two of them. An argument erupted on stage, with moderator Jon Breen finally asking the sound man to turn Reagan's mic off. In one of the few moments when Reagan lost his cool, he turned to the man and snapped, "I am paying for this microphone, Mr. Green!" Reagan got the man's name wrong but that mattered little. The other candidates all applauded him from the stage and the audience erupted into enormous cheers at Reagan putting a journalist in his place. From then on it was a straightforward path for Reagan to get the nomination.

Sensing an opportunity, liberal Republican Congressman John Anderson announced that he would be running for president as an independent. His hope was to form a coalition drawing from those who thought Carter was too inept but Reagan too conservative. Less than two months before election day, the organization sponsoring the presidential debates determined that Anderson was polling well enough to invite him to debate both Reagan and Carter. President Carter refused, no doubt calculating that validating Anderson's candidacy would only hurt his own chances on net. Reagan went ahead and debated Anderson regardless, and did well for himself. Reagan eventually acceded to Carter's demands to debate the president one-on-one.

In retrospect President Carter did not seem to know what he was getting himself into. During the debate he came off as peevish and miserable, while Reagan stood there in full Hollywood mode and appeared to handle the questions effortlessly. Rather than coming off as a far-right madman who would get the United States into nuclear war, Reagan seemed reasonable and qualified. His home run moment was when Carter criticized Reagan for having previously been against Medicare. Reagan smiled and calmly said, "There you go again!"—as politely as possible calling the president of the United States a liar to his face in front of a captive national audience. He ended the debate with a very simple question to the voters: "Next Tuesday all of you will go to the polls, will stand there in the polling place and make a decision. I think when you make that decision, it might be well if you would ask yourself, are you better off than you were four years ago?"

When the election results came in, it was Goldwater in 1964 all over again—only this time it was the incumbent president cast as the electoral loser. In addition to Washington DC—and just as Goldwater had—Jimmy Carter only took six states. Ronald Reagan was elected in a landslide, with his coattails ushering in a Republican Senate for the first time since Eisenhower. As 1981 began, what had been considered an absurdity five years prior became a reality in both the United States and the UK: both governments were now under the control of members of the right-wing half of each nation's respective right-wing party. That same year British group Fun Boy Three wrote a hit single expressing the views of many individuals in the halls of power about this unprecedented situation. It was entitled "The Lunatics Have Taken Over the Asylum."

Chapter 12

AND YOU KNOW IT

Starting in 1840, every US president elected in a year divisible by twenty had died in office. It started with William Henry Harrison, elected in 1840 and dead within a month of his inauguration. Abraham Lincoln (1860) was next with the first presidential assassination, followed by the murders of 1880's James A. Garfield and 1900's William McKinley. Both Warren Harding (1920) and FDR (1940) died of natural causes while in office, but JFK (1960) was not so lucky. Reagan (1980) was next in the rotation, and ten weeks after he became president almost continued the pattern.

On March 30, 1981, a gunman named John Hinckley Jr. managed to shoot President Reagan, his press secretary, a Secret Service agent, and a police officer before being apprehended. Hinckley was motivated by a deranged attempt to impress teen actress Jodie Foster, who was completely disturbed when she learned about his actions. The president was quickly shoved into a waiting limousine, and one of his agents immediately covered him as a human shield. Reagan began to spit up blood, leading both him and the agent to think that the president had been shoved so hard that he had broken a rib. The decision was swiftly made to reroute the limo from the White House to a nearby hospital. Reagan insisted on walking into the hospital to demonstrate to

Americans that all was well, but swiftly collapsed once inside. It was when the medical team started examining Reagan that they realized that the president had been shot.

A distraught Nancy arrived as Reagan was being prepped for surgery. "Honey," he told her, "I forgot to duck." His nonstop wisecracking must have been simultaneously reassuring and maddening, scribbling down W.C. Fields' quip to his nurse that "All in all, I'd rather be in Philadelphia." Once in the operating room Reagan took a second to remove his oxygen mask and tell the assembled surgical team that "I hope you're all Republicans!" "We're all Republicans today," replied the Democrat surgeon.

The year 1981 was a difficult one for Margaret Thatcher as well. When she had first entered the Prime Minister's residence at No. 10 Downing Street in 1979, Thatcher said that "I would just like to remember some words of St. Francis of Assisi which I think are really just particularly apt at the moment: 'Where there is discord, may we bring harmony. Where there is error, may we bring truth. Where there is doubt, may we bring faith. And where there is despair, may we bring hope.'" Jim Prior, her Secretary of State for Employment, was having none of it. "Oh, that was the most awful humbug," he insisted. "I mean it was so alien to Margaret's beliefs about things. It was the most unutterable nonsense from that particular person."[454] Malcolm Rifkind, who later became her Secretary of State for Scotland, agreed entirely. As he put it, Thatcher was "contemptuous of pragmatism and any search for consensus."[455]

Under the British system, the prime minister's cabinet is composed of members of Parliament. There were plenty of moderate and liberal Tories, and Thatcher appointed several of them to various positions. She derisively referred to them as the "wets," wet being a British pejorative meaning someone limp and ineffectual. In contrast to this were the Thatcherite "dries" on the right wing of the party. The tensions between the two wings played out within cabinet, and many of the wets constantly tested both her leadership and her patience. Thatcher's cabinet would never have a strong dry majority throughout her entire prime ministership.

The Tories were traditionally the home of titled men born to privilege. Many of them had a sense of noblesse oblige but few principles other than some vague idea of managing the government effectively and efficiently for the sake of the people. Implicit in this was the premise that they should be the ones managing it, as they had been born and raised to do. Answering to a grocer's daughter? Such abominations were rarely seen outside of Leviticus. From their perspective, Thatcher's ideological views were simply the wrong path to take.

As Thatcher anticipated, her monetarist approach to the economy caused a short-term worsening of economic conditions as a means of eventually resolving the problems of both rising unemployment and of inflation. "Yes, the medicine is harsh," she acknowledged, "but the patient requires it in order to live...We did not seek election and win in order to manage the decline of a great nation." As she also anticipated, by 1981 the worst economic news was beginning to pass and Thatcher's political hand strengthened.

That September, in a bid to assert her control of the government, Thatcher had a very public reshuffling of her cabinet in what became known as "the purging of the wets." The men who were fired never recovered from their humiliation at the hands of That Bloody Woman. When interviewed about it years later they came off like Disney cartoon villains, in that the thickness of their British accents was in exact proportion to how entitled, embittered, and repulsive they appeared. "There wasn't a phalanx of these allegedly superior snobbish people," insisted Ian Gilmour, Baron Gilmour of Craigmillar. "It's a figment of Mrs. Thatcher's fevered imagination."

Reagan and Thatcher had a largely synonymous vision of those who she called "our people": the hardworking homeowners who would form the basis of a thriving society. The two of them were largely interchangeable on domestic issues and made it a point of publicly saying so as much as possible. "As soon as I met Governor Reagan, I knew that we were of like mind, and manifestly so did he," Thatcher said.[456] Nevertheless, her private opinion of said mind was not always positive. During one meeting in the Oval Office, for example, Reagan and Thatcher were discussing the highly contentious issue of Apartheid.

Reagan explained to Thatcher that "the South Africans are whites and they fought for us during the war. The blacks are black and are Communists." After she left the meeting she turned to her Foreign Secretary, pointed to her head regarding Reagan, and said, "Peter, there's nothing there."[457]

Yet despite their identical philosophy of governance, internationally Thatcher and Reagan often had differing agendas. They both represented two different countries, and the two countries were sometimes rivalrous of one another. It was in 1982 that Thatcher's prime ministership had its ultimate test. The idiosyncratic Ayn Rand had been opposed to a female president due to her views on gender roles. "It is not to a woman's personal interest to rule man," she insisted. "It puts her in a very unhappy position. I don't believe any good woman would want that position." Though her novels were all defined by powerful, self-assured female characters, Rand had one very specific reservation about one in the Oval Office: "A commander-in-chief of the army? A woman? I think it's unspeakable."[458]

In the United Kingdom it is the monarch who is technically commander-in-chief. One can only guess what Rand's reaction would have been when Margaret Thatcher was suddenly thrust into the role of leading the British military less than one month after Rand died. On April 2, 1982, Argentina invaded the nearby Falkland Islands, a loyal British colony for over a century. The Thatcher government had withdrawn HMS *Endurance* from the area a few months prior despite the warnings of former Labour Prime Minister (and former Foreign Secretary) Jim Callaghan. This retreat led the Argentinian junta to believe that Great Britain would be either unwilling or unable to reclaim the islands if they were returned to Argentinian rule after roughly 150 years.[459] It was Thatcher's Foreign Secretary Lord Carrington who took the fall for the crisis, resigning his position for his inability to foresee Argentina's desire to exploit what they perceived as British weakness.

If Thatcher couldn't bear to see Britain in decline, this was her opportunity to demonstrate that there was still life yet in her beloved country. Everything was now on the line, including Thatcher's government and Great Britain's dignity itself. She decided to send a task force to secure the islands. They were so far away that it would take

British forces weeks to get there. In the interim, President Reagan dispatched his feisty Secretary of State Al Haig to No. 10 in hopes of (unofficially!) mediating a diplomatic solution of some sort. Haig suggested a compromise, with the Argentinian forces withdrawing in order to give way to British administration under some to-be-determined international authority. Thatcher was aghast. There could be as much diplomacy as anyone would like, but only once the aggression had been reversed and the status quo returned:

> Interim authority! To do *what*? I beg you to remember that in 1938 Neville Chamberlain sat *at this same table* discussing an arrangement which sounds very much like the one you are asking me to accept; and were I to do so, I would be censured in the House of Commons—and properly so! Britain simply will not reward aggression—that is the lesson of 1938.[460]

Soon a war zone was declared around the Falklands. Despite the enormous difficulties in fighting so far away from the United Kingdom—and so close to Argentina—British troops made strong headway. On April 25th Secretary of Defence John Nott stood alongside Thatcher on Downing Street to announce that they had successfully taken one of the islands after limited Argentinian resistance and with no British casualties. He then read a message from the commander of the operation: "Be pleased to inform Her Majesty that the White Ensign flies alongside the Union Jack in South Georgia. God save the Queen."

When reporters began to shout further questions Thatcher quickly put a stop to it. "Just rejoice at that news and congratulate our forces and the marines," she snapped. "Rejoice!" Journalists proceeded to criticize her for years for what they described as her triumphalism. Thatcher was similarly criticized for deciding to sink Argentina's ship *General Belgrano* a week later, killing over three hundred troops aboard in the process. The ship was technically outside the declared Maritime Exclusion Zone, within which the British had declared any vessels to be fair targets. Thatcher knew that ships were perfectly capable of turning around and—in the view of the Foreign Office—"If it hadn't wanted to be sunk, it shouldn't have been there."[461]

A peaceful resolution to the conflict was veering on impossible. Chilean dictator Augusto Pinochet, as Thatcher later put it, "was this country's staunch, true friend in our time of need when Argentina seized the Falkland Islands," offering the use of his ports as well as crucial intelligence and logistical operations.[462] Thanks in part to his support (earning him Thatcher's loyalty long after everyone else had repudiated him), by the end of May the British were clearly on their way toward accomplishing their goals. Nevertheless Reagan again tried calling to deescalate the situation on May 31st—and Thatcher was again having none of it.

As the president of the United States kept trying to interject with "Margaret…but Margaret," Thatcher tore him a new one. "This is democracy and our island," she insisted, "and the very worst thing for democracy would be if we failed now…I didn't lose some of my finest ships and some of my finest lives to leave quietly under a ceasefire…How would the president feel supposing Alaska were invaded?"[463] Indeed, Al Haig's successor as Secretary of State, George Shultz, later wrote that President Reagan "was getting a little fed up with her imperious attitude on this matter"[464]—the exact term that had been used by the US Embassy in 1975 to describe Thatcher's approach.

Two weeks later, the Argentinian forces surrendered and British control over the Falkland Islands was restored. In 1976 the Sex Pistols had topped the UK charts by insisting that there was no future in England's dreaming. Thatcher demonstrated otherwise, with an unambiguous victory that many Britons hadn't seen in their lifetimes. That, with the combination of an economy in upswing, gave Thatcher an enormous parliamentary victory the following year. The Conservatives gained 58 more seats while Labour was reduced to 209, their worst result since 1935. Thatcher was no longer Heath's token female or a transitional figure, but clearly an established government leader in her own right.

It was only a few months after Thatcher's electoral landslide that Reagan stabbed her in the back, and hard. Grenada is a small island nation off the coast of Venezuela with a population of about 90,000 people. Despite a 1979 communist coup, Grenada nevertheless remained a member of the British commonwealth with Queen Elizabeth II as head of state. Questions arose when American naval vessels were spotted near Grenada in late 1983. On October 24, 1983, Thatcher's right-hand man Geoffrey Howe addressed these concerns on the floor of Parliament. Howe insisted that there was no reason to think there would be any United States intervention in Grenada. He claimed—and believed—that the Reagan and Thatcher administrations were in close contact, and that Thatcher's government would be given fair warning if matters were to turn militarily. What Howe didn't know was that President Reagan had already approved an invasion of Grenada by the United States two days earlier, and that he chose to keep the matter from Thatcher. Worse, he intentionally misled her if not downright lied to her. "I didn't want her to say no," Reagan later admitted.[465]

Thatcher was completely humiliated when the United States subsequently invaded in order to "liberate" the island nation. She had consistently trumpeted the newly rekindled "special relationship" between Great Britain and the United States. Now, it was obvious that she had either been lied to or—at the very least—not bothered to have been consulted or even notified. A photographer caught the exact moment when a startled Reagan was told that Thatcher was on the phone as he was meeting with congressional leaders about the invasion of Grenada. As Reagan went to take the call, the politicians in the other room could hear him desperately trying to get in a word edgewise. "Margaret...But Margaret..." At one point he held the phone away from his ear, grinning the whole time at her feistiness. "Isn't she great?" Reagan said after the call ended. "She'll get over it."

Not long after that Reagan called Thatcher to apologize. "If I were there, Margaret," he said quickly, "I'd throw my hat in the door before I came in." Meaning, to see if the coast was clear in order to enter.

"There's no need to do that," she replied, waiting to hear what he had to say for himself.

The president began spouting nonsense about not telling her because he was concerned there would be a leak (as if a day's notice would have changed things in Grenada very much), telling her in classic political jargon that "we regret very much the embarrassment that's been caused to you." There was little Thatcher could do other than accept his explanation. Her thoughts must have turned to World War II's Yalta conference, when her idol Winston Churchill had to sit impotently by as FDR developed a demented bromance with the man that they both called "Uncle Joe" Stalin.[466]

Unlike in the United States, the British prime minister has to go down to the floor of Parliament and face questions from the opposition—and this time Labour had Thatcher dead to rights. "I must return to this debate in the House," she told Reagan. "It's a bit tricky."

"Well, all right," Reagan replied. "Go get 'em. Eat 'em alive!"

Thatcher now had to answer what she knew, when she knew it, and why on earth Geoffrey Howe had said the exact opposite mere days prior. It wasn't humming lessons that she had needed but tap-dancing lessons, in order to dodge the questions she received. Thatcher did the best she could and the situation eventually boiled over. Reagan was quite right: Thatcher did eventually get over it, but she remained painfully aware of Great Britain's relative powerlessness as compared to the United States. No matter how special the relationship was or seemed, it was the United States that was the superpower and leader of the free world and not her beloved United Kingdom.

A couple of months later, about a week before Christmas of 1983, the IRA successfully planted a car bomb outside London's world-famous Harrods department store. The area failed to get evacuated even though the IRA had called in the threat. Six people were killed and dozens more injured as the bomb damaged five floors of the store, showering Brompton Road in glass and debris. A few days later a defiant Denis Thatcher went shopping there for presents. "It wasn't as crowded as it normally is," he confessed, "but no damned Irishman is going to stop me going there."[467]

The following year Denis almost had to eat his words. In mid-October 1984 Denis was staying with Margaret and many other Tory luminaries at Brighton's Grand Hotel for a Conservative Party conference. By then Thatcher had a well-established reputation for how little sleep she needed. Government apparatchiks who tried to overwhelm her by handing over voluminous documents at the last possible moment invariably found them returned in the morning full of her underlines signifying approval and squiggles for things that needed reworking.

At approximately 3 a.m. on the morning of October 12th—a few minutes after she finished editing her speech—Thatcher heard a loud thud followed by a different sound. She immediately knew it was a bomb, and only learned later that the second noise was that of a falling chimney making its way through several floors. Thatcher was safe in her hotel sitting room but had narrowly escaped serious harm. "The glass had come in," she later recalled, "which would have been very nasty had one been in the bathroom at that time." Five people were killed and a few dozen injured, some very seriously, but none of them were the main targets of the bombing. The following day the Irish Republican Army took credit in a ruthlessly coldblooded statement: "Today we were unlucky, but remember we only have to be lucky once. You will have to be lucky always."

The conference went on as planned.

Nine days later President Reagan took part in his second and final debate against the Democratic nominee, Jimmy Carter's Vice President Walter Mondale. The first debate had gone poorly for Reagan, who nevertheless maintained a massive lead in the polls due to a surging economy and his unflagging optimism. Yet Reagan's age had been a factor in 1976 and 1980, and now his age seemed to have visibly affected his performance.

The moderator addressed this issue head on, giving Reagan an opportunity to respond. He brought up the example of the 1962 Cuban missile crisis, where Khrushchev had placed nuclear missiles pointed at the United States mere miles from Florida. Eventually President Kennedy got the Soviet Union to back down in exchange for quietly disarming America's own nukes in Turkey. Yet for two weeks the world came closer to nuclear war than at any time previously. "You already are the oldest president in history and some of your staff say you were tired after your most recent encounter with Mr. Mondale," said the moderator. "I recall yet that President Kennedy had to go for days on end with very little sleep during the Cuban missile crisis. Is there any doubt in your mind that you would be able to function in such circumstances?"

"Not at all Mr. Trewhitt, and I want you to know that also I will not make age an issue of this campaign," Reagan replied. "I am not going to exploit, for political purposes, my opponent's youth and inexperience." The actor delivered the line exactly as if he were on a sitcom. Reagan calmly took a drink of water, standing there and letting the quip ride. The audience laughed. The moderator laughed. Mondale laughed. "You will see that I was smiling," Mondale later said, "but I think if you come in close, you'll see some tears coming down because I knew he had gotten me there."[468] Reagan went on to win every state with the exception of Mondale's native Minnesota, which he only carried by around 3,800 votes out of two million. The popular vote was 59% to 41%, almost a perfect inversion of LBJ's landslide over Goldwater twenty years prior.

In 1984 relations between the Soviet Union and the United States were quite poor. Both President Ford and President Carter had successfully met with Brezhnev, Khrushchev's successor. After Carter and Brezhnev signed the Strategic Arms Limitation Treaty (Salt II) in 1979 Brezhnev had thanked him with a big kiss on each cheek, to Carter's clear discomfort. Reagan tried his best to meet with Brezhnev as well, but it never seemed to happen. In 1982 Reagan reiterated his invitation to meet in New York City when Brezhnev would be at the United Nations. Brezhnev in turn suggested a summit instead of a meeting, possibly in Finland or Switzerland in the fall.[469] That would never come to be, as Brezhnev suffered a fatal heart attack on November 10, 1982. Nor could Reagan meet with Brezhnev's successor, Yuri Andropov, nor *his* successor, Konstantin Chernenko because, as Reagan pointed out, "they kept dying on me."

Though Thatcher had the well-deserved reputation for being the more strident of the two, Reagan was a touch more hostile toward his rival superpower than she was. Reagan's critics, steeped in the consensus politics of détente, viewed any antagonism toward the Soviet Union as a provocative step closer toward the apocalyptic scenario of a nuclear war. In 1983 Reagan had spoken before an audience of evangelicals and denounced the popular impression that both sides were somewhat to blame for the increase in nuclear arsenals:

> I urge you to beware the temptation of pride–the temptation of blithely declaring yourselves above it all and label both sides equally at fault, to ignore the facts of history and the aggressive impulses of an evil empire, to simply call the arms race a giant misunderstanding and thereby remove yourself from the struggle between right and wrong and good and evil. […]
>
> Yes, let us pray for the salvation of all of those who live in that totalitarian darkness–pray they will discover the joy of knowing God. But until they do, let us be aware that while they preach the supremacy of the State, declare its omnipotence over individual man, and predict its eventual domination of all peoples on the earth, they are the focus of evil in the modern world.

To refer to the Soviet Union both as an "evil empire" and "the focus of evil in the modern world" was not the language of diplomacy, to put it mildly. Reagan's antagonistic approach did much to harden Kremlin attitudes against any sort of summit, which would be seen as rewarding his aggression. Nor was this entirely Reagan's preferred style. His forte was humor. Eyebrows were raised at the Kremlin when audio of Reagan messing around during a soundcheck leaked to the press. "My fellow Americans," he had said, "I'm pleased to tell you today that I've signed legislation that will outlaw Russia forever. We begin bombing in five minutes." It fed into very sincere Russian fears—backed up by the fears of American experts—that Reagan was edging the world closer and closer to nuclear conflict.

Reagan enjoyed recounting humorous stories that undermined conventional narratives and put his point across without being entirely explicit. This was exactly how the Russians had used their *anekdoti* to thumb their nose at their rulers under the guise of not being serious, and Reagan enjoyed repeating some of those to American audiences:

> The commissar in the Soviet Union who went out to one of those state collective farms, grabbed the first worker he came to. He said, "How are the crops?"
> "Oh," he said, "the crops. Never had been better, just wonderful."
> He said, "How about potatoes?"
> "Oh," he said, "comrade commissar, if we could put the potatoes in one pile, they would reach the foot of God."
> And the commissar said, "This is the Soviet Union, there is no God here."
> He said, "That's all right, there are no potatoes."

It was a tactful way for the president of the United States to publicly declare that the Soviet Union was a godless country that couldn't feed her own people.

With American and Soviet relations at an impasse, Thatcher saw an opportunity. Many Hungarians had remained skeptical if not hostile toward the Soviet Union after their failed 1956 revolution. By the 1980s the Hungarian government had begun experimenting with economic liberalism while still claiming ideological fealty to the USSR. Thatcher thus chose the Hungarian capital of Budapest as her first trip to the far side of the Iron Curtain in early 1984. She wanted to both encourage Hungary in its attempts toward freedom while also possibly encouraging a further divide between Hungary and the Soviet Union.

Andropov died a few days after Thatcher returned to the UK. She realized that flying to Moscow for the funeral would be a good strategic move because it "would give me the opportunity to meet the man who to our surprise emerged as the new Soviet leader, Mr. Konstantin Chernenko."[470] She took the opportunity of this personal contact to invite some of the USSR's leaders to visit her in Great Britain. It was in December 1984 that a group of Soviet officials came calling—including one Mikhail Gorbachev. Rumors had already begun to swirl that he was next in line to be the head of the Soviet Union despite—or because of—his explicitly reformist perspective.

On the morning of December 16, 1984, Gorbachev drove down to meet Thatcher for lunch at Chequers, the country estate set aside for the prime minister's use. He barely had a chance to pick up his fork before Thatcher started lecturing him. She lectured him about how central planning doesn't work and how markets do. She lectured him about the Soviets funding the British unions in the midst of another national strike. She lectured him about the USSR refusing to let Jewish citizens emigrate to escape anti-Semitism, while letting others leave the country if that was their desire. Then she lectured him for not having touched his food.[471]

Gorbachev chose his words carefully and replied with the Russian equivalent of dry British wit. "I know you are a person of staunch beliefs," he told her, "someone who adheres to certain principles and values. This commands respect. But please consider that next to you is a person of your own ilk. And I can assure you that I am not under instructions from the Politburo to persuade you to join the Communist Party."[472] She "burst into a hearty laugh," and both then put their notes aside and had a sincere heart-to-heart.

Thus it was Thatcher and not Reagan who first took notice of Gorbachev. "I like Mr. Gorbachev," she famously told the BBC shortly after the visit. "We can do business together."[473] Her foreign policy advisor later quipped that "Mrs. Thatcher came close to claiming that she discovered, even invented, Gorbachev."[474] A politician can hardly be expected not to boast or even inflate their accomplishments—real or otherwise—but investing in a personal relationship with Gorbachev ended up paying extraordinary dividends for Thatcher. It would reach a point that members of the British foreign office pointed out that "the PM seems to go uncharacteristically weak at the knees when she talks to the personable Mr. Gorbachev."[475] Two days after his meeting at Chequers Gorbachev further broke barriers by delivering a speech to Parliament.

Like any politician, Gorbachev had his own agenda with regards to the Thatcher relationship. "I knew that to some degree I was being used as a stalking horse for President Reagan," she freely admitted. "I was also aware that I was dealing with a wily opponent who would ruthlessly exploit any divisions between me and the Americans." One week later Thatcher visited Reagan at the president's retreat, Camp David.[476] She made it a point to tell Reagan what she thought Gorbachev was up to—and a point to proclaim to him how loyal she had been and remained to the "special relationship" between the United States and Great Britain. As the declassified memorandum of their conversation put it:

> Mrs. Thatcher underlined that she had told Gorbachev there is no point in trying to divide Britain from the United States. This ploy will never succeed. Britain is part of the Western Alliance of free nations and the Soviets should drop any illusions about severing Europe or Great Britain from the United States. She also told Gorbachev that she and the President have known each other since before they assumed their current positions and dividing Europe from America is simply "not on."

However, there was one big issue that Gorbachev wanted Thatcher to communicate to Reagan that she was more than happy to share: "Tell your friend President Reagan not to go ahead with space weapons." Specifically, Gorbachev wanted her to try and figure out a way to assist him in stopping Reagan from developing Star Wars.

Chapter 13

THE LAST STAND ON EARTH

Mikhail Gorbachev was born in the Russian village of Privolnoye in 1931. Within a couple of years, three of his father's siblings would succumb to the famine which killed somewhere between a third to a half of the village. The following year his paternal grandfather would be arrested for not meeting the government's sowing plan regardless of the fact that he had never been supplied with the necessary seeds to sow. His maternal grandfather was likewise caught in Stalin's Great Terror, arrested in 1937 for allegedly being part of a Trotskyist organization. As with many other Soviet children, young Gorbachev thereupon became an instant pariah due to being related to a class enemy. His home became viewed, in his words, as a "plague house." "Even the neighbors' kids refused to have anything to do with me," he recalled.[477]

Gorbachev thus witnessed firsthand what Stalinism meant in practice. After his maternal grandfather was eventually released, Gorbachev learned exactly what his captors had done to him: "Trying to get him to confess, the investigator blinded him with a glaring lamp, beat him unmercifully, broke his arms by squeezing them in the door. When these 'standard' tortures proved futile, they invented a new one: they put a wet sheepskin coat on him and sat him on a hot stove." Yet his grandfather, like so many other loyal Communists, kept the faith until the very end.

"He was convinced that Stalin did not know about the misdeeds of the NKVD and he never blamed the Soviet regime for his misfortunes,"[478] Gorbachev wrote, though "misfortunes" is quite the odd word for him to use here.

Despite all this Gorbachev grew up as a firm believer in the Soviet system, and through diligence and hard work rose swiftly through the ranks of the Party after graduating from university. Due to his work he thus became one of the few Russian citizens permitted to go abroad. It was when Gorbachev visited Prague in 1969 that he first understood how the Soviet Union was seen by citizens in other communist countries. It had only been a year since the Russians had sent in the tanks to put down the Prague Spring, and when Gorbachev visited a factory the workers literally turned their backs to him in a blatant show of contempt.[479] The USSR's power was not viewed—as the Soviet papers claimed—as "fraternal help."

Seven weeks after Reagan's second inaugural, on March 11, 1985, Mikhail Gorbachev was appointed as the new General Secretary, the first Soviet leader to be born after the Russian Revolution. In yet another historic first, the Western European leader who had formed the closest bond with him was also the most pro-capitalist one, namely Margaret Thatcher. A relatively youthful fifty-four years old, Gorbachev was strongly interested in furthering the cause of international peace.

As Gorbachev saw it, one of the primary obstacles preventing peace was Reagan's Strategic Defense Initiative program. Both Reagan and Gorbachev viewed a nuclear exchange between the two rival superpowers as effectively bringing about the end of the world. To paraphrase the first female Congresswoman Jeannette Rankin, "You can no more win a [nuclear] war than you can win an earthquake."

Even before he assumed office as president, Reagan took part in a discussion about what would happen if the Soviet Union struck first. One participant in the meeting argued that, should missiles be fired, that the United States should just launch a response before we were hit. "That would be the wrong thing to do," Reagan said. His advisers left the meeting "almost certain that he would not retaliate in the event of an attack".[480]

Gorbachev did Reagan one better. After he assumed leadership of the USSR, Gorbachev was walked through a simulated nuclear strike so that he would know what to do should the unimaginable ever happen. As he sat there being told that missiles were flying toward the Soviet Union, Gorbachev refused to take part in a retaliatory strike. "I will not press the button even for training purposes," he said.[481] The two men with the most powerful nuclear arsenals in the world were thus committed to never using them—though neither could be sure that the other felt the same.

Both men understood that they would not be in office forever. Could the threat of nuclear war be something that could be permanently removed from mankind's consciousness? Thatcher later made the case for this sort of approach:

> The history of warfare, viewed from a technical perspective, is that of an unrelenting competition between offensive and defensive weapons and strategies, with progress in the development of one being countered by corresponding improvements in the other. Thus swords were countered by armour, gunpowder generated new techniques of fortification, tanks were opposed by anti-tank weapons and the bomber—known at the time as "the ultimate weapon"—led to the development of radar systems capable of tracking its flight and the use of anti-aircraft guns and fighter planes to shoot it down. It was, therefore, written into the essential nature of warfare that exclusive reliance on that other "ultimate weapon," the nuclear deterrent, could not last indefinitely: at some point the technology of defensive weapons would catch up.[482]

This was the thinking behind the Strategic Defense Initiative (SDI). The concept was to figure out a way to stop nuclear missiles from hitting their target after they had been fired. How this was to be done was an enormously difficult question, for effectively it would be akin to shooting a bullet with another bullet after the trigger had been pulled. One of the hypothesized solutions would be defensive missiles fired from satellites, which earned the program the nickname "Star Wars."

Critics thought the program unworkable and derided the entire project to be an enormous waste of money. As Thatcher herself told Reagan at their Camp David meeting, "Even if an SDI system proved 95% successful—a significant success rate—over sixty million people would still die from those weapons that got through."[483] But what if it did work? In that event, with the Soviet Union's missiles rendered powerless, the United States would have a de facto nuclear monopoly against the USSR, just as it had in the brief window after World War II before Stalin got the bomb. For Gorbachev this was of course completely unacceptable, as he made plain both publicly and to Thatcher directly.

Reagan understood the Soviets' concern and came up with what he perceived to be the perfect compromise. "Privately," he wrote, "I had made a decision: I was going to offer to share SDI technology with the Soviets. This, I thought, should convince them it would never be a threat to them."[484] Buoyed by Thatcher's budding personal relationship with Gorbachev, Reagan had Vice President Bush and Secretary of State Shultz pass him a handwritten letter when they went to Moscow to attend Chernenko's funeral. Warm correspondence between Reagan and Gorbachev ensued, until a meeting was set for the two men for November 1985 in Geneva.

To help Reagan prepare, that September Thatcher sent the president a letter offering her advice. Despite receiving plenty of input from his own people, "I think you would expect me to give my own views nonetheless!" she began. Five pages later she caught herself: "I certainly don't want you to feel that I am lecturing (perish the thought)!" First and foremost, she recommended, was making plain to Gorbachev "that we in the West are *not* in the business of undermining the Soviet state." She also reminded him that "the West's greatest single asset" was "your sincerity and seriousness of purpose".[485]

Reagan took Thatcher's advice to heart, and when he met the Soviet leader he tried his best—like any good negotiator—to establish common interests and focus on areas of agreement. Journalist Lou Cannon captured exactly what that meant to Reagan:

> In Hollywood [Reagan] became an avid science-fiction fan, absorbed with a favorite theme of the genre: the invasion from outer space that prompts earthlings to put aside nationalistic quarrels and band together against an alien invader. Reagan liked this idea so much that he tried it out on Gorbachev in their first meeting at Geneva in 1985, saying that he was certain the United States and the Soviet Union would cooperate if Earth were threatened by an invasion from outer space. Reagan's idea was not part of the script, and it startled his advisers. It may also have startled Gorbachev, who did not have at his fingertips the Marxist-Leninist position on the propriety of cooperating with the imperialists against an interplanetary invasion. In any event, Gorbachev changed the subject. Reagan thought this meant he had scored a point, and he proudly repeated what he had said to Gorbachev to a group of Maryland high school students after he returned to the United States. He also repeated it to his advisers, to mixed reactions.[486]

After that Colin Powell, then the deputy national security adviser, "struggled diligently to keep interplanetary references out of Reagan's speeches."[487] When the subject came up, Powell would roll his eyes and say to his staff, "Here come the little green men again."[488]

Yet it was clear that Reagan came to agree with Thatcher in regarding Gorbachev as a man that Reagan could do business with. As Shultz observed after Geneva, "the big story was that they had hit it off as human beings."[489] The main sticking point between the two was SDI, but their groundwork was clear: a nuclear war was unwinnable and unthinkable, and the two nations would have to do whatever was in their power to make sure that would never happen. The two agreed to meet again in hopes of having further substantive discussions.

Several weeks later, Gorbachev offered Reagan a proposal: the complete abolition of nuclear weapons by the turn of the century. The only catch was that President Reagan would have to give up on SDI. To apply further pressure, Gorbachev made his offer publicly. Reagan and his advisers had two different reactions. The president wanted to take the Soviet offer at face value and to even go one better. "Why wait until the end of the century for a world without nuclear weapons?" Reagan asked his team.[490]

Thatcher represented the opposing view. Privately she found Reagan's perspective both delusional and naïve, and had no problem quietly making that clear. "It was one of the few times, you know, when I think his aspirations left the reality of human nature," she said.[491] "The fundamental truth here is that the nuclear weapon cannot be disinvented. A world without nuclear weapons is thus quite simply a fantasy world."[492] And despite her warm feelings toward Gorbachev, she still understood how politics worked: "It is inconceivable that the Soviets would turn over their last nuclear weapon. They would cheat. I would cheat."[493]

As the clock ticked toward the next US-USSR meeting, two events made clear how omnipresent the threat of war was—and just how dangerous nuclear arsenals could be. On April 5, 1986, a bomb went off in a West Berlin nightclub popular with US troops, killing two Americans and injuring dozens of others. Reagan placed the blame on Libya and its dictator Muammar Gaddafi, with whom tensions had been increasing for several years. The president decided to order strikes against the north African nation.

For various reasons, the governments of France, Spain and Italy all refused to allow the United States to use their bases or airspace. When Reagan then asked Thatcher to use British air bases, she was more than happy to oblige:

> It had the effect of cementing the Anglo-American alliance. There's another point: What's the good of having bases if when you want to use them you're not allowed to by the home country? It made America realize that Britain was her real and true friend, when they were hard up against it and

> wanted something—and that no one else in Europe was. They're a weak lot, some of them in Europe, you know. Weak. *Feeble*.

Less than two weeks later the Soviet Union experienced the worst nuclear accident that the world had ever seen. On April 26, 1986, Lenin Nuclear Power Station reactor number 4 in Chernobyl, Ukraine, experienced a meltdown. Firefighters failed to put out the blaze, so then helicopters were brought in to dump sand and other materials in order to try and smother the flames. No one from the nearby area was evacuated for over a day as radiation spewed unabated into the atmosphere. Deputy Prime Minister Boris Shcherbina arrived within eighteen hours of the incident and assisted in keeping matters quiet. "Panic is worse than radiation," he claimed.[494]

Shortly thereafter the radiation was detected in Sweden, prompting questions from the Swedish government. Not wanting to accept responsibility and make the USSR look bad, Soviet authorities at first denied there was an issue. They were forced to admit that an accident had occurred when Sweden threatened to file a safety report with the International Atomic Energy Agency. It became clear that this was no minor incident as citizens began to become violently ill and tens of thousands of people finally began to be evacuated. Now the concern was that the molten core would melt down into the earth and contaminate the groundwater with radiation, killing an enormous number of people.

Eventually the solution of a "sarcophagus" to seal the problem was developed and implemented. Many men volunteered to assist, knowing it would cost them their lives. It took months for the disaster to be contained, at an enormous financial and political cost. For Gorbachev this was proof-positive of two things: the dangers of nuclear power, and the backwardness of having a nation run by a faceless, unaccountable bureaucracy. He publicly denounced the Soviet system that caused so much damage that July.

> For thirty years you scientists, specialists and ministers have been telling us that everything was safe. And you think that we will look on you as gods. But now we have ended up with a fiasco. The ministers and scientific centres have been working outside of any controls. Throughout the entire system there has reigned a spirit of servility, fawning, clannishness and persecution of independent thinkers, window dressing, and personal and clan ties between leaders.[495]

It was akin to Khrushchev's secret speech, except instead of denouncing Stalin, Gorbachev was denouncing central planning itself.

That September, eager to get things back on track, Gorbachev wrote to Reagan suggesting a "quick one-on-one meeting [...] to prepare the ground for a Washington summit." This was going to be the meeting before the big meeting, "possibly with only our foreign ministers present."[496] Gorbachev proposed either Iceland (halfway between the two nations) or Thatcher's home turf of London as the two possible locations for the get together. Reagan agreed to meet in Iceland.

The two men picked the date and the location—and only then bothered to let the Icelandic government know that, within two weeks, Reykjavik would be hosting an event of historic proportions. Finding lodging for the political teams (Reagan and Gorbachev both decided, in the end, to bring an entourage) would be difficult; finding lodging for the international media outlets on the small island nation would prove close to impossible. Reykjavik's city administrator offered the best welcome he could to the horde of journalists flying in to his city. "We are the descendants of the most boring people in Europe, the Norwegians," he explained, "and the drinkingest, the Irish."[497]

Author Suzanne Massie taught President Reagan the Russian rhyme *doverai no proverai*, which means "trust, but verify." It was one of two slogans that guided his thinking in negotiations with the USSR: the two countries would have a basis of trust in their discussions and agreements, but this needed to be supplemented by some mechanism to ensure that each party was holding to its commitments. Alongside this was the concept of "peace through strength," akin to Teddy Roosevelt's "speak softly and carry a big stick." It was a lot easier to fight for peace when one is prepared for the opposite. In Reagan's view, it wasn't his famous charm that was crucial to getting the Russians to negotiate but the US military spending which had more than doubled since he had assumed office. As Reagan sarcastically put it: "Trust and understanding, it is said, will lead to arms control. Hearing people say that is like meeting grown-ups who still believe in the tooth fairy."[498]

Gorbachev could not commit to an escalating arms race even if he had wanted one. Yet another one of Reagan's jokes illustrated the problem that Gorbachev was facing, as the president discussed the plight of the consumer in the Soviet Union:

> You have to wait ten years there for delivery after you order an automobile. And so a fellow had finally gotten the money together and was going to buy an automobile—only about one out of seven families have them in that country—and he went through all the paperwork and everything and finally signed the last paper, laid down his money. And then the man behind the counter said, "Come back in ten years and get your automobile." And the man said, "Morning or afternoon?'" And the fellow behind the counter says, "Well, what difference does it make ten years from now?" And he said, "Well, the plumber is coming in the morning."

The Marxist argument was that without capitalists appropriating the workers' surplus value for themselves in the form of profit, a socialist command economy could produce enough for everyone at a fraction of the workload. Almost seventy years after Lenin seized power, few continued to make that claim. American experts had argued whether the USSR was spending 9-11% of their GDP on the military or if it was closer to 11-13%. The actual figure was somewhere between 30-40%. To provide perspective, the United States was spending 35% of its GDP on the military for a brief period during the height of World War II. The

Soviets were spending around that much every single year—a clearly unsustainable cost that would be almost impossible to increase.[499] Gorbachev would admit as much to Reagan: "The US has money and can do things that the Soviets cannot do."[500]

As the two world leaders sat down in Reykjavik to discuss matters, a couple of things quickly became obvious. First, both were excited about the possibility of making progress toward a nuclear-free world and a better relationship with one another. Second, Reykjavik wasn't just some precursor to a later, major summit as they had originally planned. This was possibly a once-in-a-lifetime meeting for both men and they were both determined to make the most of it.

Reagan's proposal at Reykjavik was a fairly straightforward one. As he recalled:

> I proposed that in the first phase of our plan to eliminate our nuclear weapons each of us would scrap fifty percent of our missiles while continuing research on a missile defense system. If and when the SDI reached the point at which it could be tested, the United States would permit Soviet observers at the tests, and if the tests demonstrated that the system was effective, and once we had scrapped fifty percent of our missiles, each of us would destroy the balance of our missiles and both countries would share all SDI technology. At the ten-year point, when all ballistic missiles were eliminated, each of us would deploy the SDI system simultaneously.[501]

As Reagan's deputy director of the CIA put it, "there appeared to be only two people on the planet who actually thought SDI would work: Reagan and Gorbachev."[502] Nevertheless, it remained a sticking point throughout their entire negotiations in Iceland. Gorbachev found it absolutely unbelievable that Reagan would share SDI technology with the USSR. Indeed, as Reagan's Director of the US Arms Control and

Disarmament Agency Ken Adelman admitted, "there was no way he ever would."[503]

Reagan kept insisting on the need for SDI by using a metaphor, pointing out that "when the use of chemical weapons was prohibited after World War I, the world did not reject gas masks. They were the guarantee of our protection against such a weapon in case someone decided to use it."[504] Over and over Gorbachev brought up reasons why SDI was unacceptable to the Russians and—Reagan being Reagan—over and over the president brought up his gas masks metaphor. "That's the tenth time you talked about gas masks!" Gorbachev eventually snapped, only exaggerating slightly.[505]

Reagan was a smooth politician when he wanted to be. But Gorbachev was a Russian, and he had no shortage of cunning at his disposal. He agreed with Reagan about reducing and possibly eliminating not only nuclear missiles but nuclear weapons. He agreed with Reagan about the need for transparency and mutual verification. When Reagan pointed out he couldn't withdraw nukes from Europe and leave them vulnerable to invasion, Gorbachev volunteered to massively reduce conventional forces. "I couldn't believe what was happening," Reagan thought. "We were getting amazing agreements…I thought we were in complete agreement and were going to achieve something remarkable."

Gorbachev sat there and gave Reagan everything he wanted. They ignored the scheduled noon deadline and kept working. It was then, after hours of breakthroughs in the negotiations, that Gorbachev reminded Reagan of just who he was dealing with. He leaned forward, smiled at the president, and said, "This all depends, of course, on you giving up SDI."[506]

What was supposed to be a frank discussion between the president and Gorbachev has come to acquire an almost mythical status within conservative circles. "Reagan at Reykjavik" is shorthand for holding fast to one's principles when everything is on the line politically. Early in his administration, Reagan had famously worked together with Democrat Speaker of the House Tip O'Neill and conservative Democrats to reform the tax code. When he came in to office the top marginal rate was 70%, meaning the Federal government alone took 70% of any money an individual earned over $108,300 (in addition to the rest of a person's earnings being taxed at lower rates). Reagan left office with close to a flat tax, with no Federal taxes for individual income up to $17,850 and 28% taken out of any income after that.

But Reagan never had a Republican House majority, and by the sixth year of his presidency there was little appetite among congressional Democrats for Reagan's conservative proposals. If he was going to have a win in his second term it would have to take place in terms of foreign relations. All he had to do was give up his silly SDI program, which at best was many years from being technologically feasible. He just had to compromise.

Reagan refused.

As expected, the Democrats savaged the president, with Senator Al Gore speaking for many in calling the summit "a major fiasco."[507] Nor was the reaction from his allies much better. In many ways Reykjavik became for Reagan what the Falklands were for Thatcher—and just as with the Falklands, Thatcher and Reagan once again did not see eye-to-eye. "My own reaction when I heard how far the Americans had been prepared to go was as if there had been an earthquake beneath my feet," wrote Thatcher. "The whole system of nuclear deterrence which had kept the peace for forty years was close to being abandoned."[508] Behind closed doors Thatcher even began to say that "the Americans were crazy."[509]

Gorbachev had it a little easier. As Reagan once pointed out to him, there was a large asymmetry between the Russian and the American systems:

> A Russian and American were arguing about our two countries. The American said, "Look, I can walk into the Oval Office. I can pound the President's desk, and I can say, 'Mr. President, I don't like the way you are running our country.'" And the Russian said, "I can do that.'" The American said, "You can?" He said, "Yes, I can go into the Kremlin to the General Secretary's office, pound his desk, and say, 'Mr. General Secretary, I don't like the way President Reagan is running his country.'"

Gorbachev didn't have to deal with being publicly denigrated by his media. Right after the summit ended he savaged Reagan to the Politburo, attacking the president's "extreme primitivism," "caveman cast of mind" and "intellectual feebleness."[510] Though he didn't have to deal with media critics, Gorbachev still had to deal with his problems at hand. Namely, what was going to be done about the threat of nuclear war and the Cold War more broadly?

Maybe SDI didn't have to be such a sticking point? On the one hand, if SDI didn't work as planned, the large amount of money the United States committed to research—including some for UK companies to encourage support from Thatcher—could surely result in some strong discoveries that would benefit Americans (quite possibly in defiance of agreements like the ABM treaty). On the other hand, the Russians soon realized that a working SDI could be outmaneuvered at a fraction of the cost. All they would have to do was to fire a huge number of dummy missiles, making it functionally impossible to shoot them all down. But this was an escalation toward a nuclear exchange—the exact opposite direction from where Gorbachev wanted to go.

It is almost impossible to convey to a free people what it is like to live in a totalitarian dictatorship. But Gorbachev had seen it firsthand. He saw it and lived it his entire life—and he saw the alternative. He saw that he could do business with the president of the United States and with the prime minister of Great Britain, and the advantages that a more liberal society could bestow on its citizens. Indeed, early in his career he already had more firsthand experience with Western democracies than most of the Soviet leadership at the time, having visited Italy, Belgium, the Netherlands, France, and West Germany in the early 1970s as a member of Soviet delegations. As he put it, "my previous belief in the superiority of socialist democracy over the bourgeois system was shaken as I observed the functioning of civic society and the different political systems. [...] [P]eople there lived in better conditions and were better off than in our country."[511]

Gorbachev had also spent a week in Canada in 1983 as part of the Central Committee's Secretariat for Agriculture, studying farming techniques from a nation with a similar climate. He had learned a great deal due to frank discussions with Soviet Ambassador to Canada Alexander Yakovlev, who had lived there for a decade and developed a good understanding of Western political economies. All these lessons taught Gorbachev that liberalization was key for the well-being of the citizens of the USSR

Earlier in 1986 Gorbachev had given a speech to the Communist Party Congress, announcing a policy of *perestroika*—rebuilding—in conjunction with the concept of *glasnost*, or openness. He saw that honest conversations with Reagan and Thatcher, where all parties involved made plain their concerns and goals, allowed for—if not mutual agreement—at the very least mutual trust and respect. Gorbachev did not regard the Soviet Union as it currently stood to be either desirable or sustainable, and the man who occupied Stalin's chair was in a position to do something about it.

Naturally this new liberalization of information met with no small measure of hostility from entrenched bureaucrats and Party officials. As Gorbachev realized

> the removal of the curtain of secrecy was tantamount to a death sentence for some organizations—their uselessness would be exposed. And the ideologists, who stood watch over the system, assumed, and rightly so, that truth would undermine faith in our system. Not just the emperor but the entire 'court' would be found to have no clothes.[512]

But once the floodgates were open, little could stop them. Revelations about Soviet labor camps and Stalin's collusion with Hitler became topics of public discourse, eventually culminating in the serialization of *The Gulag Archipelago* in the major Russian periodical *Novy Mir.* Even Vladimir Nabokov's extremely controversial novel *Lolita* was cleared for publication by a Russian court. As historian Michael Dobbs pointed out, "The rewriting of Soviet history became so extensive that Soviet secondary schools were obliged to cancel all history exams, pending the release of new textbooks."[513]

Certain Western shows began to appear on Soviet television. While airing pro-Western propaganda was not first on the agenda, in a sense everything foreign in the Soviet Union could be seen as a form of propaganda. Capitalist propaganda is anything which gives a good impression of capitalism as a way of life. Anything that sells people the idea that life in America is good and that people are free and happy would, in a way, be capitalist propaganda.

Programs like the drama masterpiece *Dallas* and its lobotomized ripoff *Dynasty* were almost entirely apolitical. If taken literally, the storylines about the lives of the most wealthy capitalist elites and their amoral behavior could be considered as anti-capitalist propaganda. Yet in a country where politics pervaded quite literally everything, the shows did more to influence Russian opinion than any American newscast ever could.

Because such programs were very clearly not designed to have a political message, that implied that their content was somewhat true to life. Viewers saw for themselves what life was like abroad—and not just for the wealthy, but for their staffs. It was by watching the maids of the rich that those behind the Iron Curtain could see how the working poor lived overseas. They saw that they owned automobiles, and they did not have to worry about their phones being tapped. They did not live in terror of their employers. They did not have to worry about cold weather—not in their fur coats!—or about food. They were never shown waiting in line for food or even being hungry.

Marx's worldview was heavily informed as a 19th century reaction to the Industrial Revolution. Dobbs explained the consequences of decades of the Soviet focus on industrialization at the expense of raising people's quality of life:

> By the early eighties the Soviet Union led the world in such basic economic indices as the production of iron, coal, timber, and cement. It boasted the world's biggest hydroelectric dam, largest steel factory, heaviest tractors, most powerful rockets. At the same time, industry was

> unable to produce a decent razor blade or meet the demand for toilet paper.[514]

As Gorbachev admitted, "the arguments of our ideologists regarding the 'creation of the basis of socialism,' its 'complete and final victory' and, finally, 'the construction of a developed socialist society,' which were purely apologetic and scholastic, could no longer satisfy anyone."[515]

Much of the Russian population was living under a system of public lies and private truths, wherein they smiled and nodded in public spaces about the gloriousness of the Soviet system before coming home and dropping the whole façade. Gorbachev's reforms also allowed for increased contact with relatives abroad. A woman could contact her cousin living in America, saying that her "neighbor" was thinking of visiting in the fall—only to be told that the following spring would make for much better weather. The American understood that there was no neighbor and that the woman was asking about herself—and the government agent listening in on the phone understood it too. Everyone knew the coded language, but increasingly no one cared enough to do anything about it.

A few months after Reykjavik Gorbachev invited Thatcher to visit Moscow in March of 1987. On February 27, 1987, she held a seminar with the UK's greatest experts on the Soviet Union to prepare. The experts informed her that there was "no sign of adoption of market principles in the Soviet economy" and "no likelihood that Soviet ideology would change fundamentally." If anything there would be "only limited change which fully preserved the powers and guiding role of the Party."[516] The Foreign Office—which Thatcher had a lifelong disdain for—gave her two silver-handed hairbrushes as her official gift to Gorbachev, even though she pointed out the obvious fact that he was completely bald.[517]

Thatcher and Gorbachev got along very well when she got to Moscow, arguing for hours but in an atmosphere of mutual admiration rather than mutual distrust. She walked with him in Red Square, waving to the Russians who had been told for decades that they would never be allowed to leave their country. And now, a few meters away from where

Lenin's preserved corpse remained on display, the woman who was the incarnation of petit-bourgeois values was being chaperoned by the General Secretary of the Communist Party. Further, he was clearly signaling to the population that she was not someone to hate but rather a friend to appreciate.

For a woman who was excruciatingly proper, Margaret Thatcher still knew very well how to be seductive. In 1977, a couple of years before becoming prime minister, journalist Christopher Hitchens conceded an argument that he was having with her:

> I gave her the point and made a slight bow of acknowledgment. She pierced me with a glance. "Bow lower," she commanded. [...] "No, no—much lower!" [...] Having arranged matters to her entire satisfaction, she produced from behind her back a rolled-up Parliamentary order-paper and struck—no, she thwacked—me on the behind.[518]

Similarly, longtime French President François Mitterand is often quoted as saying that Thatcher possessed "the eyes of Caligula and the mouth of Marilyn Monroe." But Mitterand's aide Jacques Attali insisted that this was a misquote: Mitterand had actually said her eyes were those of Stalin.[519]

It was that mouth and those eyes that were now trained on the Soviet people. In a move without precedent, Thatcher was interviewed for an hour on Soviet television by three Russian journalists. It was then aired, unedited, that same evening. Over 120 million people ended up watching the Iron Lady (although, to be fair, it's not like there was much else on). When she had been Leader of the Opposition, the US Embassy described Margaret Thatcher as "frightfully English." Yet the imagery of a strong, forthright woman secure in her opinions, able to put men in their place with her words and a glare, was something that the Russian people were all too familiar with.

It was Thatcher at her best, and her message was crystal clear. Over and over she stuck to her point. "We both want above all peace," she insisted. "I value peace, with freedom and justice, above everything else, and because at the moment I believe that the nuclear deterrent stops anyone from starting a major war, I believe in keeping it." Acknowledging the enormous price the Soviet Union paid against Hitler—and reminding the audience that for a time "Britain had to stand alone" against the Nazi dictator—she pointed out how nuclear weapons kept Europe largely free of warfare for decades because the costs of a nuclear exchange would be incalculable.[520]

Thatcher also let the Russians know that it was the Soviet Union's deployment of intermediate-range ballistic missiles that had caused missiles to be stationed in Western Europe, and that the USSR "has a very good anti-ballistic missile defence system around Moscow"—meaning SDI was neither a provocation nor without precedent.[521] Neither of those things were known to the Soviet public before, and it was painfully obvious to the audience that Thatcher was being more honest about Soviet weaponry with them than their own leadership had been. When she flipped the script and asked one of the interviewers, "What do you think are the advantages of a socialist society?" they simply ignored her and moved on. To have this question go unanswered on Soviet television would have been impossible a few years prior.

A few months after Thatcher's visit, Reagan planned a trip to West Berlin in order to deliver a speech for the city's 750th anniversary celebration. Drafts of his speech had gone back and forth between Reagan and his team, with one specific sentence causing major problems. "I really think that line [...] is going to be an affront to Mr. Gorbachev," commented Secretary of State George Shultz.[522] They were still going at it up to the morning of the speech. "I'm the president, right?" Reagan pointed out. "Then it stays in."[523] Still, Reagan knew he was taking a risk.

On June 12, 1987, as Reagan drove in the presidential limo to Berlin's famous Brandenburg Gate, he turned to his Chief of Staff Ken Duberstein and reiterated his decision. "The boys at State are going to kill me," he said, "but it's the right thing to do." Directly behind the Brandenburg Gate lurked the Berlin Wall and all that it symbolized. Reagan stood in front of an enormous crowd—and an array of television cameras from all over the world—and issued his challenge. "General Secretary Gorbachev," he said, "if you seek peace, if you seek prosperity for the Soviet Union and Eastern Europe, if you seek liberalization, come here to this gate. Mr. Gorbachev, open this gate. Mr. Gorbachev, *tear down this wall*."

The audience erupted into hysterics. The East German authorities were livid, and the Soviet ones not much better. What was seen in the West as a call of defiance was taken in Moscow as a challenge to Gorbachev personally and to the USSR specifically. Savvy minds on the far side of the Iron Curtain understood that if the Berlin Wall were torn down then the entire communist system would likely be torn down with it. Because Reagan and Thatcher were both on the right wings of their respective nations' right-wing parties, there was no one to outflank them and accuse them of being doves who were soft against Soviet aggression. This allowed them a certain amount of freedom to do just that, focusing more on diplomacy than on hostility and bluster.

Yet old habits have a way of dying hard. Though Gorbachev had far more institutional power than either the president or the prime minister, he still had to manage a gigantic decades-old bureaucracy quite averse to change. He had to move craftily, assuring the old guard that the moves he was making would strengthen the Soviet Union. This, despite his publicly stating that "the guilt of Stalin is enormous and unforgivable"—and during the seventieth anniversary of the Russian Revolution, no less.

The following year it would be Reagan's turn to walk Red Square with Gorbachev. Politicians being politicians, at one point the Soviet leader took a little boy from his mother's arms and pointed him at the American president. "Shake hands with grandpa!" Gorbachev told the kid. When Gorbachev had been the boy's age, contact with a foreigner would have been a one-way ticket to the Gulag. Now, to some extent it was something to celebrate, not to fear. A clever reporter soon asked Reagan if he still regarded the USSR as an evil empire. "No," he confessed, "I was talking about another time, another era."[524]

Reagan was speaking the truth. One month later, Gorbachev took to the stage at the 19th All-Union Conference of the Communist Party of the Soviet Union and delivered his opening speech, pointing out that

> the imposition of a social system, way of life, or policies from outside by any means, let alone military, are dangerous trappings of the past period. Sovereignty and independence, equal rights and non-interference are becoming universally recognized rules of international relations, which is in itself a major achievement of the 20th century. To oppose freedom of choice is to come out against the objective tide of history itself. That is why power politics in all their forms and manifestations are historically obsolete.[525]

No one—not even Gorbachev himself—realized that in uttering those words, he had committed himself to freeing half the world. The rest was just application.

Chapter 14

BECAUSE YOU ARE FREE

It started with Poland.

White smoke rose from the Sistine Chapel's chimney on October 16, 1978 to signify that Karol Wojtyla, Archbishop of Krakow, had been selected as the new pope. The man who chose the regnal name of Pope John Paul II would be the first non-Italian pope since the Dutch Adrian VI held the papacy from 1522-3. As Polish historian Pawel Skibinski put it, "It came as a shock to Communists that it was possible to elect someone from the area they controlled without asking them for permission. The Western world, in turn, was shocked at the election of a person from behind the Iron Curtain as it was generally known that a great majority of the region's inhabitants were controlled by communist authorities."[526]

Pope Paul VI had very much wanted to visit Poland in 1966, in order to mark the 1,000 year anniversary of Christianity coming to Poland—but he had been refused. This was the Polish People's Republic; there was no God here. Brezhnev tried to pass on a similar message to the new pope in 1979. "We know that Wojtyla is such a wise man," he said to Polish ruler Edward Gierek. "Tell him he must announce that he is sick. It will be better for him not to come to Poland."[527]

Pope John Paul made a pilgrimage to his homeland regardless, and in perfectly good health. He delivered a series of several outdoor masses, with over ten million Poles coming out over the course of his trip to join him in worship. On June 2, 1979, he stood in Victory Square, the largest city square in Warsaw, in front of a crowd of almost 300,000 citizens. The pope offered a prayer for his home country and her people, concluding with a desperate plea: "I cry out from the depths of this millennium—let your Spirit descend and renew the face of the earth. The face of this land." The huge crowds who came out to see him over the course of his trip demonstrated to the Polish people that—despite years of communist occupation and propaganda—it was the faithful who were the true believers, who had the numbers, and not those who preached the doctrine of communism.

The following July saw a round of labor strikes throughout Poland, as workers protested a hike in prices without a corresponding increase in their wages. The state media did its best to suppress the news in hopes that each city would be left unaware of conditions elsewhere. But this was 1980, not 1940. It was far more difficult to suppress the flow of information, and far easier to create underground newspapers and radio broadcasts. In this case, the strikers won.

The Gdansk Agreement of August 1980 reaffirmed the people's constitutional rights to freedom of speech and of the press. As importantly, it allowed for the establishment of a trade union not under the control of the ruling Polish United Workers' Party and guaranteed workers the right to strike. Partly inspired by the pope's admonition to do what is right and to fight for the future of Poland, the newfound labor organization christened itself as Solidarity.

As the nationwide movement continued to advocate for the workers, the Polish authorities began to more openly discuss the possibility of cracking down on dissent. By December of 1981 Solidarity was threatening a crippling general strike if any such measures were taken—and the Polish authorities called their bluff. They had little choice. They had been informed by Moscow in no uncertain terms that if they allowed the situation to spin out of control, then the Soviets would send in the tanks just as they had done in Hungary in 1956 and in Czechoslovakia in 1968—and in Poland in 1939. Backing up the Soviet position was Erich

Honecker, who prepared East German troops just in case. Poland was at the mercy of both Russian and German forces. It was World War II all over again.[528]

At 6 a.m. on December 13, 1981, the Polish government declared martial law and abandoned even the pretense of a country where law had any meaning. Hundreds of telecommunication exchanges were raided and telephone lines cut in order to prevent what they called "misinformation" from spreading. A nationwide curfew was imposed as huge swathes of industry were placed under military control. Airports were shut down, the borders sealed, and travel to and from major cities was heavily controlled.

When coal miners in Wujek went on strike in protest the government fired at them, killing eight men. Other protests throughout Poland were met with similarly deadly consequences. The persecution worked: the protests died down, allowing martial law to finally be suspended a year later. Solidarity's leaders were given relatively short prison sentences, but the organization was officially banned. What had been a nationwide labor movement now became a heavily weakened underground resistance force.

Thatcher visited Poland in November 1988, meeting with the same General Wojciech Jaruzelski who had imposed martial law seven years prior. In the years since, however, the Polish leader had gradually toned down the authoritarianism and let Thatcher know that he wanted to open dialogue with Solidarity. Happy to act as an intermediary, she then went to visit their leader Lech Walesa. She felt comfortable that she could help him get Jaruzelski to not just permit Solidarity to exist, but to grant it legal recognition. She urged Walesa to meet with Jaruzelski and exchange views, to make sure the authorities heard what he was telling her. Walesa pointed at the ceiling. "No problem," he told her. "Our meetings are bugged anyway."[529]

The following month Mikhail Gorbachev delivered a major speech at the United Nations. Reagan and especially Thatcher had consistently told the Soviet leader that a major reason why nuclear missiles were stationed in Western Europe was to serve as a counterweight to the USSR's enormous strength in conventional forces. Gorbachev could have used his troops as a bargaining chip, but instead he decided on another course to build trust with his rival powers and with the world at large.

Within two years the Soviet military would be reduced by half a million personnel, he announced. Rather than sending in the tanks Gorbachev would be withdrawing them—from East Germany, Czechoslovakia and Hungary, in addition to withdrawing tens of thousands of Soviet troops. He would also be cutting ten thousand tanks and hundreds of aircraft.[530] It was a massive move toward a more peaceful world, and a massive signal to the communist nations as to what kind of leader Gorbachev intended to be.

Polish government officials were thus free to negotiate with Solidarity without the barrel of a Soviet gun to their backs. Even though still technically illegal, by this point Solidarity's support had grown very strong, with huge strikes causing massive disruption against a backdrop of a calamitous Polish economy. Jaruzelski knew that he needed to win over Solidarity or perhaps coopt their ideas in order to maintain power.

The Party was not having it, yet they didn't have many options. "We do not have a choice but to start these talks," Jaruzelski told them, pointing out that even martial law had not destroyed the Solidarity movement. Poland's Prime Minister Mieczyslaw Rakowski backed up the First Secretary. "We are not dreaming about giving up power," he insisted. "We are talking here about arranging to retain power."[531] The Polish system being less centralized in the executive than the Soviet system was, it remained unclear whether the Party votes for such a move were there.

Jaruzelski decided to gamble it all, threatening to resign if he didn't get his way. The Prime Minister, Interior Minister and Defence Minister all joined the First Secretary in his threat. The government was already losing its sense of legitimacy with the population, and a new leadership team after close to a decade would have an extraordinarily difficult time solving the crisis. Jaruzelski asked for—and won—a vote of confidence from the Party in his leadership. The very next day he announced that he would be engaging in official talks with Solidarity.

For two months the government met with Solidarity leaders and discussed every issue on hand. Ninety-two total sessions of these Round Table Talks ended up taking place, so called due to the circular negotiation tables used to ensure that no one could be seen as sitting in a position of dominance at the head of the table. Shockingly, Solidarity was also given official access to the airwaves, where they could explain to the Polish people what was currently being negotiated that very day. It was instantly obvious that Solidarity's leaders were far more similar to the average Polish citizen than whatever caricature government propaganda had made of them during the preceding decade.

In March of 1989 another nation followed Poland's lead. Thatcher had been correct in seeing Hungary as the most liberal of the communist nations. Now Hungarian Prime Minister Miklós Németh paid a personal visit to Gorbachev in Moscow to let him know of a major decision—and, tacitly, to ask him for permission. Three hundred kilometers of barbed wire and electrified fencing separated Hungary from democratic Austria. Németh wanted to tear it all down, telling Gorbachev that it had outlived its usefulness. Hungary was not isolated from the outside world. Hungarians had been permitted to travel abroad, and the Hungarian capital of Budapest had become a tourist destination. The fence was not cheap and did little good, with fewer than a dozen Hungarians trying to annually cross it anyway.

Gorbachev didn't bat an eye at this news. Nor was he particularly upset at the Hungarian government's decision to open talks with oppositional forces just as Poland had done. It seemed as if Gorbachev was tacitly disavowing the Brezhnev doctrine. To be completely sure that he had permission to proceed, Németh reminded the Soviet leader that the USSR still had eighty thousand troops stationed in Hungary. He didn't want a repeat of 1956. While Gorbachev said that he didn't agree with a multi-party system, either in principle or in Hungary specifically, "you can be certain that there would be no instruction or order from us to crush it."[532] He himself was allowing for very limited elections in the USSR for the Congress of People's Deputies. Though the system was rigged to guarantee a Communist Party victory, it still permitted the seating of several critical voices.

That same day Gorbachev met with Károly Grósz, General Secretary of the Hungarian Socialist Workers' Party. The USSR had secretly had nuclear weapons in Hungary for years, and Grósz wanted them gone. Gorbachev agreed. Grósz decided to push his advantage. In order to "distance us from the memories of 1956, I put it to you that all Soviet troops should leave Hungary." Gorbachev agreed as well, but had wanted to hold off to see if he could use the troop withdrawal as a bargaining chip to get NATO forces reduced in Europe as well. As a sign of good faith, hundreds of tanks and five thousand Soviet troops were withdrawn from Hungary in short order. Grósz was dumbfounded—and so was the East German leadership.

Any border is only as strong as its weakest point. Removing the physical barrier between Hungary and the liberal democracy of Austria was a major breach in the Iron Curtain. Worse, none of the other Warsaw Pact members had been consulted about this decision. To add insult to injury, the Soviet leadership was fine both with the idea and with how it had been decided. The East Germans phoned the Hungarian leadership and were assured that East Germans would not be permitted to use Hungary as a pit stop to fleeing to the West. Days later massive demonstrations took place in Budapest. One dissident leader stood in front of the parliament building and proclaimed to the crowd that "History has pronounced its death sentence on the system called socialism."[533] Instead of incarceration his only consequence was massive applause from the people.

Nor was Hungary alone. On March 26, 1989 another nation followed Poland's lead: the Soviet Union itself. Understanding that the Soviet bureaucracy could often serve as an impediment to his perestroika agenda, Gorbachev invoked Lenin's slogan of "All power to the Soviets!" and called for a limited election to replace the Supreme Soviet with a more pluralistic Communist legislature. Getting one's name on the ballot was an extraordinarily difficult process, but for those who persevered the results paralleled Poland's. As Dobbs wrote:

> When the election returns came in, the apparatchiks received a huge shock. In most places where there was a clear choice, the party-approved candidate was defeated. The list of the vanquished read like a who's who of Soviet public life: Politburo members, generals, cosmonauts, government ministers, and the mayors or party bosses of

> Moscow, Leningrad, Kiev, Minsk, and many other big cities.[534]

The final details of Poland's Round Table Talks were agreed to two weeks after that. Solidarity would be legalized and given official recognition. One third of the seats in the lower house of Congress and all one hundred seats in the Senate would now be democratically contested. The Polish government saw this not as a loss of power but as a way of integrating the opposition into the state and validating its authority. It was regarded as a "ten- to fifteen-year process"[535] toward a stable power-sharing arrangement.

But these hopeful trends were not the same throughout the Warsaw Pact. Romania especially veered in a different direction. Communism in practice often resulted in the elevation of the mediocre to the highest levels of power, and there are few better examples of this than Romanian leader Nicolae Ceausescu. One glance at the man whose bottom lip always stuck out called to mind those unfortunate people that can be seen wandering around at airports, who cannot help the fact that they were born fucked up. In a free country Ceausescu would have been a mailroom clerk baffled if a written address was mismatched between 757 Legion Street and 757 Legion Avenue. The Czechs had just such an *anekdot* about one of their Communist rulers:

> President Antonin Novotny released his fury on a maintenance man who was taking a long time to repair an ordinary door lock; he told the worker that he could have done it himself in no time. The maintenance man's response could not have been any truer for the time: "Well yes, Mister President, because you are a locksmith, but I'm a university professor."[536]

One of Ceausescu's youthful comrades described him as "completely uninteresting" and "always pretending to be more important than he really was". He recalled that the young Ceausescu was "afflicted with a risible stammer, which was so bad that people avoided him—they didn't want to laugh in his face. His stammering spasms were sometimes so violent that his leg would twitch uncontrollably to the rhythm of the stammer, and this got on people's nerves." He was "a youngster whom everyone despised."[537]

As Ceausescu grew older his biggest skill was knowing how to work the system, which made him the right man at the right time to replace Romanian leader Gheorghe Gheorghiu-Dej when he died of cancer in 1965. No one particularly liked Ceausescu but no one particularly hated him either. He was the perfectly acceptable compromise candidate.

When Ceausescu took over Romania he did so as an unorthodox communist leader. In 1968, for example, he very publicly denounced the Soviet Union's invasion of Czechoslovakia, and he often did not follow Moscow's lead in other matters. On the other hand Ceausescu implemented Decree 770 in 1967, which was aimed at increasing Romania's population by 50%. Proclaiming that the fetus "is the property of the entire society,"[538] both abortion and contraception were made illegal for women under the age of forty or with fewer than four children. Childlessness was taxed and the marriage age lowered to fifteen. Romanian women of childbearing age were given mandatory gynecological exams every month under the supervision of the so-called "menstrual police." A miscarriage would result in questioning by the authorities, where the traumatized woman would be forced to prove that she had in fact lost her baby organically.

Ceausescu visited both China and north Korea in 1971 and became heavily inspired by the Stalinist personality cults developed there by Chairman Mao and the Great Leader Kim Il Sung, respectively. Soon Romanians were constantly told about his unparalleled brilliance and leadership skills. Part of the ensuing propaganda was expanded to include his wife Elena, whose utterly nonexistent beauty was praised in unfettered terms just as highly as her utterly nonexistent intelligence was. As historian Edward Behr pointed out, "as conditions inside Romania worsened, Romanians not only had to endure new privations but also had to praise those responsible for inflicting them in increasingly fulsome terms."[539]

After dropping out of school at age fourteen, Elena had been expelled from the Bucharest Municipal Adult Education Institute night-school courses for cheating on a test.[540] Nevertheless, as First Lady of Romania she received a fraudulent PhD in Chemistry in 1967. Her scientific ignorance was painfully clear to her subordinates when she was appointed director of Bucharest's Institute of Chemistry. Funding requests for "ethyl alcohol" would be denied by her out of concerns that the researchers wanted to, in her words, make their own "home brew." The researchers then simply asked for C_2H_6O funding—the chemical formula for ethyl alcohol—which was thereupon granted.[541] Ghostwritten scientific papers were presented as having been written by the barely-educated woman, and the Romanian government lobbied international publications and organizations to publish "her" work and grant her honorary degrees. The state media could then reasonably speak of Elena as being a world-renowned scientist.[542] Despite all this, Elena never treated her subordinates with any sense of gratitude for the work that they did on her behalf. On the contrary, Romanian health minister Eugen Proca regarded her as "very vain and almost illiterate" as well as "unadulterated evil."[543]

Ceausescu sought to triangulate Romania between the USSR and the West in order to receive favors from both, and his efforts met with a great amount of success. As the 1970s proceeded, Romania's economy became industrialized via heavy loans from Western governments. Despite turning Romania into the most authoritarian of the Soviet bloc nations, Ceausescu's posturing against the USSR allowed him entrée into Western circles that were eager to exploit differences within the communist Second World.

Nicolae and Elena waved from the White House balcony as the guests of both Presidents Nixon and Carter, and danced with President Ford in the streets of Bucharest. The Ceausescus' antics naturally continued abroad. On one official visit to the United States, for example, for some reason Elena insisted that all their menus be written out in French despite the fact that neither of them spoke it.[544] In 1978 Queen Elizabeth II gave Nicolae the royal welcome in London by making him a Knight Grand Cross of the Order of the Bath, her highest award for a foreign leader.[545] On the other hand, as Gorbachev later wrote, Ceausescu "was not particularly welcome in Moscow. He was not forgiven for his ambitions and his demonstrative flirtations with the West."[546]

As leader Ceausescu undertook a plan he called "systemization," which sought to abolish the line between urban life and rural life by a massive process of destruction and reconstruction:

> In the countryside, village householders were given short notice to evacuate their homes, which were then bulldozed. They were rehoused in concrete boxes, often with communal kitchens, toilets, and washing facilities. Some five hundred villages were razed in this way, and thousands more were due for demolition. The aim was to do away with "archaic" village life and get rid of the difference between factory and agricultural workers. Needless to say, cooped up in apartment blocks, people were far easier to keep under surveillance than had they continued living in individual houses. As a result of production bottlenecks, cheap materials, inadequate budgets, and corruption, the new "village suburbs" were abysmally built, often with no plumbing or running water. In these new Ceausescu complexes, it was impossible to keep rabbits, chickens, ducks, or geese, which had been a small mainstay for many Romanians as the food situation steadily deteriorated.[547]

As the 1980s rolled around those international loans to Romania came due. Just as Stalin had done during his assault on the kulaks, Ceausescu focused on exports at the expense of his population. For the Romanian citizenry the prices for goods and services increased dramatically as cuts were made in government spending on housing, health care and education. Food was strictly rationed. Television broadcasting was limited to three hours a day, with many neighborhoods not having enough electricity for even that. Behr noted the consequences of "the sudden power cuts that forced coal miners to climb up ladders in the dark at the end of their shifts or compelled surgeons to abort surgical operations at the last moment." This was in addition to "infants whose life-support machines were suddenly disconnected" or "the patients whose iron lungs suddenly stopped".[548]

The combination of Romania's poverty with the forced increase in birthrate resulted in disastrous consequences. Mortality rates among pregnant women and infants set European records. An entire generation was raised by government "orphanages" dedicated to children whose parents simply could not afford to feed them and who were encouraged to abandon them to the superior wisdom of state experts. The Romanian government could not afford to raise them well either, resulting in years of room upon room of infants chained to their cribs, in puddles of their own waste, to little or no caretaker response. Malnutrition which resulted in stunted growth and mental disabilities was the norm, with both physical and sexual assault against the children not uncommon. AIDS spread among the orphan population due to tainted (and often medically unnecessary) blood transfusions.[549]

British journalist Bob Graham was an eyewitness to the rooms in which the children were raised. In addition to the pervasive stink of urine, it was the silence that he found most disturbing:

> Usually when you enter a room packed with cots filled with children, the expectation is of noise, chatter or crying, sometimes even a whimper. There was none, even though the children were awake. They lay in their cots, sometimes two to each cot, sometime three, their eyes staring. Silently. It was eerie, almost sinister. [...] They were inhuman. Stalls where children, babies, were treated like farm animals. No, I am wrong—at least the animals felt brave enough to make a noise.[550]

In 1984 Ceausescu personally laid the cornerstone for the People's House, a gargantuan edifice meant to have approximately five times the square footage of Versailles. It was to become the heaviest building on earth, and though it was supposedly built for the Romanian people it would serve the Ceausescus as the largest palace that had ever been constructed. Both the military and ordinary citizens were drafted to assist in its construction while hundreds of citizens literally froze to death every year in the Romanian winter. Many others died from asphyxiation due to turning on their stoves to provide heat, having the gas go out, and then having it come back on unlit. Eventually construction costs for the People's House were roughly the same as Romania's entire welfare budget.[551]

Ceausescu's holier-than-thou attitude increased over time as he began to believe all the nonsensical propaganda fed to the Romanian people about his greatness. Gorbachev observed that "anyone with the slightest political experience could see his delusions of grandeur as well as his psychological instability." The Soviet leader was not alone in his impressions of the man that the Romanian media referred to by such titles as "the Living Fire," "the Treasure of Wisdom and Charisma," or even "the New Morning Star."[552] As Gorbachev put it:

> I have encountered many ambitious people in my life. Indeed it is hard to imagine a major politician without his share of vanity and self-confidence. In this sense, though, Ceausescu was in a class of his own. An absolute ruler for decades, he always wore an arrogant smirk, treating others with apparent contempt, everyone from retainers to equal partners.[553]

Ceausescu did his best to keep Romanians unaware of the changes that Gorbachev was implementing in the Soviet Union. When Gorbachev visited Bucharest in 1987 he attempted to get Ceausescu to open his country to the outside world. Ceausescu thought this would be disastrous, both for communism and himself. Their arguments degenerated into shouting. Doors and windows were shut to make sure that no one could hear what was transpiring between the two leaders.[554]

Ceausescu insisted on doubling down even when there was reason to relax his oppressive measures. In April 1989, about a week after the announcement of Poland's Round Table Agreement, Ceausescu had a major announcement of his own. On the one hand, he proclaimed, Romania's foreign debt had now been paid off, and months ahead of schedule. On the other hand, the crippling rationing and lack of electricity would nevertheless continue. But now that the Soviet Union had a much better relationship with the West, there was virtually no reason for Western countries to court Ceausescu as an antagonistic force against the USSR. The situation for the Romanian people seemed to be completely hopeless.

The month after Ceausescu's announcement saw elections being held in East Germany. Though it was certain that the Communist Party would win everything, there was still a mechanism for courageous citizens to register their defiance. All they had to do was take their ballot and—instead of placing it in the ballot box by the entrance—walk across the room in front of the police into a secret booth. Their names would be of course taken down and the Stasi would naturally follow up with such dissidents. The number who chose to undertake this quiet act of defiance never amounted to more than a small percentage of the population.

In 1989, however, things were a bit different. Several priests and a few activists who were tolerated by the government insisted on their constitutional right to watch the votes being cast. The authorities agreed, knowing that there was absolutely no possibility of them losing the election. Indeed, when the results came in the Communists announced that they had been returned to office with 98.6% of the vote. The poll watchers, however, announced that that number was a fraud, that the number of protest votes was somewhere between 9-10%. This still would have resulted in a 90% vote for the Communists. They were lying even when it was unnecessary, and the West Germans made big news about this information. Worse, the East German authorities could do little to prevent their citizens from watching those newscasts—or coming to realize just how many of their countrymen were displeased with the government.

This was the backdrop to the Polish elections on June 4, 1989. The Communists had insisted on a swift vote after their agreement with Solidarity, hoping that this would reestablish their role as Poland's natural leaders and relegate the labor movement to an impotent parliamentary opposition force. The Polish voting process was counterintuitive, with voters having to cross out the names of candidates they did not want rather than merely choose the ones that they did. An enormous percentage of the population reveled in finally having the opportunity to cross out the names of those Communist officials that they despised.

The final result in Poland was almost a perfect inversion of the East German vote. There were thirty-five seats up for election in the lower house of Parliament; Solidarity won thirty-three of them in the first round of voting. In the Senate all one hundred seats were up for election. Solidarity won ninety-nine of them. The Prime Minister, Interior Minister and Defence Minister who had threatened to resign if the Party did not support General Jaruzelski now had no choice but to leave, since all three were voted out of office. But would the Polish United Workers' Party honor the results and seat the opposition? As amazing as it sounds, the unprecedented election where a nation democratically voted out their Communist Party wasn't even the biggest worldwide news that day. That was because June 4, 1989 is remembered for a far more ominous event: the Tiananmen Square massacre.

For weeks protests against the government had spread throughout China, largely fueled by students and other young people. A huge number of protestors occupied Beijing's Tiananmen Square, site of Mao's mausoleum where—much like Lenin in Moscow—the Communist leader lay embalmed on display for visitors to come pay their respects. The dissidents constructed a thirty-three-foot high statue of the Goddess of Democracy out of foam and papier-mâché to symbolize their aspirations for a free, democratic China. Those aspirations would soon be quashed. On the night of June 3rd and into the morning of June 4th, Chinese officials had had enough. They sent in the tanks.

The Chinese government managed to do a good job of keeping international observers from getting footage of the massacre itself. It remains unclear how many were slaughtered by the government. Hundreds? Thousands? Yet the most enduring image of the Tiananmen Square massacre was that of the individual who came to be dubbed Tank Man. A lone man, whose name and fate remain unknown, stood in the middle of Changan Avenue the day after the Chinese government killed its protesting citizens. Holding a shopping bag in his hand, he forced the tanks leaving Tiananmen Square to halt before he was eventually whisked away by God knows who to God knows where. He remains a worldwide symbol of the power—or even the duty—of the average individual to defy the forces of authoritarianism.

Internationally the reaction to Tiananmen Square was largely that of horror and sadness. In Poland specifically there was great concern that Jaruzelski would once again declare martial law. Senior Solidarity figure Bronislaw Geremek expressed the concerns of many, for "we knew we had won" but "we also knew they had all the guns."[555] Yet this was Poland, not China. Communications between Warsaw and Moscow demonstrated to the Polish government that there was no appetite in the Soviet leadership for using force against the voters. Journalist Timothy Garton Ash was eyewitness to the events, and as he described it: "Three things happened at once: the communists lost an election; Solidarity won; the communists acknowledged that Solidarity won. That might sound like a syllogism. Yet until almost the day before, anyone who had predicted these events would have been universally considered not a logician but a lunatic."[556] The Polish authorities decided to put their faith in the electorate again, to try and win the presidency when the Polish parliament convened in a few weeks' time.

The East German government had a different take on the Chinese massacre, with news programs repeatedly playing their authorities' congratulations to the Chinese government "for its prompt action in dealing with disturbances in Beijing that were instigated by Western imperialist agents."[557] East German citizens got the message all too well. As a result of this, many East Germans who were taking vacations in Hungary decided against going back. One after another they also began driving their Trabi automobiles to Budapest. The plan was to somehow eventually make their way via Austria to West German soil, where as Germans they would gain citizenship automatically. In the same way that citizens had vanished in the old Soviet Union, now the East Germans couldn't help but notice how many people were quietly disappearing one by one.

The East German authorities asked the Hungarians to return their citizens to them. Despite their earlier assurances when they had torn down the border between Austria and Hungary, now the Hungarian authorities explicitly refused to repatriate those East Germans within their borders. Rather than looking at them as predominantly citizens of the German Democratic Republic, Hungary now regarded them as refugees—and by this point there were a lot of them, around 85,000.[558] Honecker was apoplectic, and even more so when the Russians refused to get involved. He was told that he would somehow have to settle matters with the Hungarians by himself.

This was not Honecker's only problem. Matters in neighboring Poland were also proceeding rapidly. In Lech Walesa's view, electing Jaruzelski as president would grant the Polish transition international legitimacy and would allow both the United States and the Soviet Union to endorse the new government. Many members of Solidarity were aghast at his plan, and refused to endorse the man who had cracked down and imprisoned them. The Soviets still had thousands of troops in Poland, and it was very easy to envision a European Tiananmen Square. Eventually a compromise was reached. Jaruzelski was elected president, with some support from Solidarity. Conversely, Solidarity was permitted to form a government, with some support from the Communists.

Hungary swiftly followed suit. The previous year, activists had tried to commemorate the anniversary of Imre Nagy's murder before being violently suppressed by the police. A year later, Gorbachev had personally assured both the Hungarian Prime Minister and the General Secretary of the Hungarian Socialist Workers' Party that the Soviet Union was no longer in favor of using force to impose its will on Hungary. Something else had happened: a promise from the Hungarian government to allow the exhumation, identification and reburial of Nagy's remains, which had been long hidden in order to keep his grave from becoming a shrine. The government's official position on the events of 1956 changed as well. It was no longer referred to as a "counter-revolution" but instead as a "popular uprising."[559]

So it was that on June 16, 1989, Nagy and his four closest associates finally got an official funeral—with a sixth coffin alongside theirs to represent the Unknown Insurgent, all the other Hungarians, many anonymous, who gave their lives in a failed effort to liberate their country from Soviet rule. Audio of one of Nagy's speeches was blasted over the loudspeakers at Heroes' Square in Budapest. Roughly 200,000 Hungarians came out to pay their respects, laying flowers on top of the coffins of those who had given all.

The day's star was Viktor Orban, spokesman of the Alliance of Young Democrats (better known as Fidesz). Orban felt safe enough to say what would had been unspeakable mere months prior: "If we can trust our souls and strength, we can put an end to the communist dictatorship; if we are determined enough we can force the Party to submit itself to free elections; and if we do not lose sight of the ideals of 1956, then we will be able to elect a government that will start immediate negotiations for the swift withdrawal of Russian troops."[560] Orban was correct. Ten days after Nagy's funeral, Grosz ceded power to a presidium of himself and three other men. The dam broke swiftly and decisively for the most liberal of the Warsaw Pact nations.

Honecker and Ceausescu were beside themselves, demanding that Gorbachev intervene in both Poland and Hungary. Gorbachev's answer was unambiguous, telling them that "those who are afraid had better hold on because perestroika has only just begun." He particularly didn't care about the Romanian leader's concerns, dismissively telling his aides that "Ceausescu is just worried for his own skin."[561]

Honecker could do nothing, for his own life was in the balance. He was in Romania on July 8, 1989 for the annual Warsaw Pact leadership summit. After he gave a predictable speech about the dangers facing communism, he grabbed his side and collapsed in extreme pain. The Bucharest hospital's preliminary diagnosis of gallstones was reevaluated by Berlin doctors when Honecker returned home; he had gallbladder cancer. The ultracentralized East German government was effectively silenced as Honecker recuperated, and GDR officials sat on their hands as matters escalated out of their control. No one wanted to assume responsibility, which would be seen as undermining Honecker's leadership in a country where the official line was—as it always was—that everything is fine.

Hungary then went full-throttle on liberalization in other ways. Hungary's reformist Minister of State Imre Pozsgay teamed up with Franz Joseph Otto Robert Maria Anton Karl Max Heinrich Sixtus Xaver

Felix Renatus Ludwig Gaetan Pius Ignatius von Habsburg-Lorraine, better known as Otto van Habsburg, last crown prince of Austria-Hungary, to promote a "Pan-European Picnic." The border between Austria and Hungary would be temporarily opened on the afternoon of August 19, 1989 near the town of Sopron, exactly where the electrified fencing between the two nations had been taken down. A ceremonial gate would be constructed and its doors opened, with delegations from both countries then crossing the border in a demonstration of support for freedom of movement.

Word got out to the refugee community to make their way to Sopron, and both the Austrian Red Cross and the Austrian authorities made preparations to receive an influx of East Germans.[562] Behind the scenes, the Hungarian authorities quietly told their border guards to stand down should any refugee attempt to cross over into Austria on that day. The head of the border guard explicitly told his officers to simply order refugees to turn back—but to do absolutely nothing to prevent them from doing so. Around two thousand refugees crossed from Hungary into Austria that day, in disbelief that this wasn't all some big trick.

The East Germans remaining in Budapest began to mob the West German consulate in order to get West German passports. Refugee centers were set up throughout Hungary to service the needs of those East Germans making their way west. The GDR demanded to send planes and trains to repatriate their refugees, but their requests were immediately dismissed by Hungarian officials. They compromised on allowing diplomatic observers from East Germany to monitor the situation—all of whom turned out to be Stasi. When a Stasi officer demanded to know the names of everyone going in and out of one of the centers he was refused. Then the Stasi stationed a van outside one center and instead began to photograph everyone who came and went. A Hungarian mob gathered and began to stone the van. The next night it was vandalized—and the night after that it was gone.

After a certain point the East German authorities could no longer ignore the number of missing people, not entirely. The refugees were then publicly denounced as either political illiterates or criminals—but no one listened. The contrary news reports about the refugees from the West were incessant, and word about their fate swiftly spread though the

GDR. By and large, what mattered to the East Germans was how their former countrymen were being treated—and whether they themselves should risk everything in what came to be known as the Exodus. East German Foreign Minister Oskar Fischer met with Soviet Foreign Minister—and firm Gorbachev ally—Eduard Shevardnadze. Now, instead of the USSR remaining non-committal, Shevardnadze sided with the refugees explicitly. He encouraged the GDR to allow for emigration, telling Fischer that "it will not be bad" and "will ease your economic burdens."[563]

Matters in Poland reached their culmination that same month. Though 65% of the parliamentary seats had been allocated to the Communists, that number included a significant amount of seats set aside for the rural United People's Party and the Alliance of Democrats, which were both Communist satellite parties. As in several other nations, historically such parties were impotent and existed at the discretion of the main Communist Party in order to grant the appearance of an air of opposition.

Now, however, the two parties that had been oppositional on paper became oppositional in reality. No longer under the thumb of the Polish United Workers' Party, Walesa persuaded them to switch their allegiances to side with Solidarity. In one fell swoop, President Jaruzelski lost his majority even on paper. It remained Jaruzelski's role to choose the new prime minister from a list of three candidates suggested by Walesa and Solidarity. He was comfortable with the choice of Solidarity leader Tadeusz Mazowiecki, who assumed office on August 24, 1989.

Within less than a year the Communists went from controlling every aspect of Polish society, having all the parliamentary seats and all the guns, to nonexistence, with the Polish United Workers' Party officially dissolving itself in January of 1990. By the end of 1990 Jaruzelski resigned from the presidency and officially handed the office over to Lech Walesa. The Communists never again regained a foothold on power in Poland.

Hungary's version of the Round Table Talks were held around a triangular table, but the results were even more dramatic than what had happened in Poland. The Hungarian agreements resulted in free elections open to all parties with no set-asides for the Communists, as well as massive political liberalization. The ruling Hungarian Socialist Workers' Party rebranded itself as the Hungarian Socialist Party, eventually becoming the main center-left party in Hungarian politics. By 1998 Orban would be elected prime minister at the age of thirty-five. After leaving office upon the completion of his first term, he would return to lead his Fidesz party to four more parliamentary victories from 2010 through 2022.

To paraphrase Ernest Hemingway, the Poles and the Hungarians were thus liberated in two ways: gradually, then suddenly. But they were not the only ones.

Chapter 15

DIE HARD

Domino theory was used to justify the United States entering what became the Vietnam War. The idea was that if one country became communist, then communist forces would overrun neighboring countries like a series of falling dominoes. It didn't seem to enter the heads of American experts that the reverse could occur as well.

On August 25, 1989, the day after Tadeusz Mazowiecki became Poland's prime minister, Hungarian Prime Minister Miklos Nemeth secretly flew to the West German capital of Bonn to meet with West German Chancellor Helmut Kohl. Nemeth did not waste time with pleasantries. "'We have decided to allow the GDR citizens to leave freely, mainly on humanitarian grounds," he informed Kohl. "It seems you may have to deal with 100,000 or even 150,000 new citizens arriving very quickly."

The West Germans were skeptical. They were happy to keep the matter quiet from the East Germans. The propaganda appeal could not be overstated. Here was absolute proof that, given the choice, the people of Germany preferred the liberal West to the communist East—to the point of leaving behind all of their belongings and risking their lives. That left the elephant in the room: the Soviet Union. Did the Russians know? How would they react? Though Kohl had been the first to know, Nemeth assured him that Gorbachev would not interfere. And if Honecker refused to allow the East Germans to head west—as he most certainly would—then Nemeth was prepared to suspend Hungary's travel agreement with the GDR.

Kohl wasn't taking any chances. He had been drafted by the Nazis at the age of 15 right as World War II was drawing to a close. Though he had avoided combat he still remembered the devastation that the Russian forces had inflicted on Germany. Kohl phoned Gorbachev to be sure that there would be no escalation of tensions between the two nations. According to Kohl, all Gorbachev told him was that the "Hungarians are good people."[564] It was the Soviet leader's tacit endorsement of everything that was going on.

Now they just had to let the East Germans know.

While Honecker recuperated, the Hungarians told Fischer that they intended to let all the refugees who wanted to leave for the West. "That's treachery," Fischer said. "This will have grave consequences for you." He insisted that if the refugees returned to the GDR that they would not be punished, but the Hungarians did not believe this. Nor, more importantly, did the refugees.

The East Germans were livid. They wrote to Budapest and they wrote to Moscow. They tried to rally all the Warsaw Pact leaders to descend on Hungary and force the government to submit, but the Poles said no and the Russians were uninterested. "Hungary is betraying socialism," fumed the head of the Stasi, not entirely incorrectly—but there was nothing he could do about it.[565] On September 10, 1989, all border controls were lifted in Hungary. Within three days over 18,000 East Germans made their way west, assisted by buses helpfully provided by the West German government.

Things did not go unnoticed in East Germany. It was immediately clear that a crack had formed in the totalitarian power of the GDR's regime, and the East German population intended to make the most of it. On September 11th, the day after Hungary opened its border, an organization called New Forum was founded in the GDR in hopes of achieving dialogue with the government. It was instantly found to be illegal, but that didn't matter: a few days later over 150,000 East Germans did the unprecedented and publicly signed their names to a petition calling for talks with the state.

That same month demonstrations began to loosely coalesce in Leipzig, East Germany's second-largest city. The community had been succumbing to filth and pollution as factories spewed smoke into the atmosphere as the populace gradually fled to seek refuge elsewhere. Meeting at the 800-year-old St. Nicholas Church, protestors lit candles every Monday evening and began to march. Soon thousands joined, if only because there was so little else for them to do. Claiming that the "Chinese comrades must be lauded" because they "were able to smother the protest before the situation got out of hand," Stasi leader Erich Mielke insisted on East Germany having its own Tiananmen Square massacre. "The situation here now is comparable and must be countered with all means and methods," he told his subordinates. But the East German leadership was still torn to the point of paralysis. By September 18, 1989 the Leipzig protestors numbered 15,000 marchers. The Stasi arrested a hundred of them, running over others as they sped away. But that did little to stop the masses, and did much to further alienate the population from the regime.

In between East Germany and Hungary, both geographically and politically, stood Czechoslovakia. Czechoslovakian leader Milos Jakes had temporarily closed his border with the GDR to make it more difficult for East Germans to use his country as a throughway to Hungary and then to the West. Now he had a problem with all the East Germans left remaining in Prague. They were overwhelming the West German Embassy and something had to give.

An ailing Honecker came up with a solution so bizarre and out-of-touch that only a government bureaucrat could have conceived of it. He cut a deal with the Czechoslovakian authorities and the West Germans to allow the East German refugees to emigrate. The one condition was that they had to return to the GDR in order to travel west, handing in their ID cards and losing their East German citizenship in the process. The migrants were confused. Surely this was a trap. And if not a trap, what was the catch? Giving up East German citizenship for West German citizenship—and passports—at the price of being called a traitor to Honecker's regime? It took the West Germans some effort to persuade the refugees to trust them. Soon, in an almost perfect inversion of World War II, train-cars packed full of refugees began to be deported from East Germany—except in this case they were making their way west, and to freedom.

After that, thousands more began to drive their East German cars to Czechoslovakia. The timing could not have been worse for Honecker. October 7, 1989 was the date of a massive nationwide event to commemorate the fortieth anniversary of the founding of the German Democratic Republic. Part of the event featured a visit from Gorbachev, and the Soviet leader did not mince words in his speech. When he insisted that "Life punishes those who fall behind," it was clearly a passive-aggressive slap at Honecker, who could only sit there and bite his tongue at the humiliation in front of his colleagues. When the torchlit procession passed the dais where all the leaders sat, the chants from the marchers—East Germany's most politically reliable citizens—were clearly heard by all. "Gorby, help us," they pleaded. "Help us!"

Gorbachev's German was poor, but he understood what they were saying. He also understood even better than Honecker himself how quickly the political geography was changing in East Germany. There were still almost 400,000 Soviet troops stationed in the GDR. The evening after Gorbachev left, their commander received a phone call with orders from the Soviet ambassador: "Do not interfere in any way with internal GDR developments. Let them take their course."[566] Double-checking with Moscow resulted in confirmation of the orders. Regardless of what was to happen in East Germany, the Russians would be on the side of peace.

That same evening demonstrations erupted throughout the GDR by citizens who had realized that Gorbachev was on their side and not Honecker's, and that their authorities' strength was decreasing. Over a thousand people were arrested throughout the following day in Berlin alone, many beaten by the Stasi both publicly and behind closed doors. But what was a thousand people in a nation of over sixteen million?

Matters reached a peak the following night, on October 9, 1989. There were eight thousand people at St. Nicholas Church alone, far too many to fit inside. The Stasi were ready for them—and so were members of the military. Bloodshed was not just a possibility but a promise. "We will fight these enemies of our country, if necessary with arms," read an editorial in the Leipzig Communist Party newspaper.[567]

The army was stationed on the route of the demonstration, and the men were handed pistols and plenty of ammunition. Many of the young soldiers burst into tears because they knew that their wives or parents or siblings were planning on marching that night, some with their children—and they knew what their guns could do to them. Some did their best to warn their families, but to what end? If it wasn't their own mother it would be someone else's. They had enlisted to protect their country and now were being asked to murder families for walking down the street.

By five o' clock there were over seventy thousand protestors outside the church. Local Party officials called Berlin repeatedly, hoping for a peaceful resolution. It was Helmut Hackenburg, second secretary of the Party district leadership, who finally made the call, both figuratively and literally. He decided that there would be no force used. He eventually connected with Honecker's second-in-command Egon Krenz on the phone and got him to agree. All the government forces in Leipzig were told "to take no active action against persons if there were no anti-state activities and attacks against security forces, objects and facilities."[568]

And so the Leipzigers lit their candles and marched. They held up signs insisting that they wanted peaceful change. The Stasi had spent decades infiltrating protest groups, but the East Germans had also spent decades learning their tricks. When Stasi officers in plainclothes broke their cover and tried to pull people's banners away, they were swiftly surrounded by the crowd. The chant was steady and the same: "We are the people. No violence." It was the largest protest East Germany had ever seen. Footage of the march was aired on West German television, and swiftly all of the GDR was aware of what was going on—and how nothing was being done to stop it. Leipzig earned the nickname of *heldenstadt*: hero city.

Now the politicians began to speak up. Leipzig's mayor asked for dialogue, as did the mayor of Dresden (which sat just by the border with Czechoslovakia). Many in the Party leadership knew that a change was necessary. Things could have swiftly gotten out of control in myriad ways. Another Tiananmen Square was right around the corner as long as

Honecker remained in charge. A quiet revolt was organized behind the cancerous man's back.

On the following Monday, October 16th, over 120,000 people came out to protest. The ones who had understandably been afraid had now seen for themselves that no one had been harmed the previous week, neither by the Stasi nor by the military. The GDR's top officials watched the live footage for themselves that evening—broadcast from West Germany, of course. They heard the same chants: "We are the people. No violence." But now they also heard a new chant: "Down with the Wall." Honecker sat there with his men and repeated the same thing over and over. "Now, surely something has to be done," he insisted.

Among the men in the room was Colonel-General Fritz Streletz, Chief of Staff of the army. Streletz was no weakling and no dove, to put it mildly. As a member of the Nazi Wehrmacht, he had spent over three years as a Soviet prisoner after World War II. He was and remained a committed Communist. But Streletz looked at Honecker and—as tactfully as possible—told the East German ruler to go fuck himself. "We can't do anything," Streletz said. "We will let the whole thing take its course peacefully."

The next morning the East German Communist Party leadership had a meeting. Just as had been planned, Prime Minister Willi Stoph interjected as soon as everyone was called to order. "I suggest a new first item be placed on the agenda," he said. "It is the release of Erich Honecker from his duties as General Secretary, and the election of Egon Krenz in his place."[569]

Honecker did not react. There was no precedent for this and it caught him entirely by surprise. Sensing the mood in the room, knowing that he couldn't simply ignore Stoph's request, he turned to those he had regarded as his most loyal allies—but Honecker had no allies left. One by one, as they had planned, all the men took turns using their words to denounce the leader, stabbing him not in the back but in the front. The vote was unanimous because Honecker, being a good communist, accepted the decision of the collective and voted against himself as well. After he left Party headquarters he phoned the Soviet ambassador to let him know the news. Then he called Margot to tell her as well. She herself would be sacked as education minister a few weeks later.

The GDR elite thought that, by sacrificing the despised Honecker to the masses, they would have a honeymoon period under Krenz's leadership. In this they were as out of touch as Honecker himself had grown. It was Krenz who had been shown repeatedly on East German television shaking hands with the Chinese leadership after Tienanman Square. The week after Honecker's ouster over one million East Germans took to the streets in continuing protests.

On November 1st, Krenz flew to Moscow to meet with Gorbachev, who viewed him as another Honecker. The new East German leader had two big items to discuss. First, he had learned that the GDR's finances were completely disastrous. A majority of the machines being used industrially were write-offs, meaning that the cost to repair them outweighed any benefit.[570] Worse, East Germany was days away from defaulting on interest payments on foreign loans. Once that happened, getting further credit would be close to impossible and economic collapse virtually certain.

Austerity measures akin to Romania's rationing were not a viable solution, not when one million East Germans (out of a nation of almost 17 million) were already taking to the streets. Would the Soviet Union help bail them out please? "After all," Krenz said, "the GDR is in a sense the child of the Soviet Union and one must acknowledge paternity of one's children."[571] Gorbachev refused, and instead argued for more reforms in the vein of what he had introduced into the Soviet Union. Above all he urged Krenz to embrace glasnost, openness, and level with the East German people about the financial situation instead of continuing with the decades of lies.

Now Krenz used the obfuscatory language of a bureaucrat to hold his citizens hostage. If what was happening in Leipzig hit Berlin, then it was quite possible the Berliners might storm the Wall itself. "That would be awful," Krenz pointed out, "because then the police would have to intervene and certain elements of a state of emergency would have to be introduced."[572] In other words, he was threatening Gorbachev with unleashing the power of the East German state against his own people. Disgusted, Gorbachev sent Krenz back to East Berlin empty-handed. Then Gorbachev sent a memo to the heads of the Soviet forces stationed in the GDR, reminding them to do absolutely nothing to intervene if matters took a turn for the worse there.

That same day, the East German government reopened its border with Czechoslovakia in an attempt to demonstrate that things had changed from the Honecker era. Prague, on the other hand, had followed Hungary's lead and simply opened their own border to West Germany in order to get all the refugees off their hands. Within three days over fifty thousand East Germans drove their way to the West via Czechoslovakia. It was like a dam had been breached and now a second hole had burst open.

Three days later Krenz's prediction to Gorbachev came true. Over 700,000 Berliners took to the streets once again under the slogan of "We are the people." Some political figures tried to coopt the energy but the masses were not having it. Even dialogue with the Communist government following the Polish model would no longer satisfy the people. Propaganda chief Gunter Schabowski took to the platform in a show of support for the crowds, but was booed off the stage. The audience did not appreciate that they were booing the man who would soon be their liberator.

On November 8th, Helmut Kohl met with Lech Walesa in Poland to discuss the ongoing situation throughout Central Europe. Walesa had seen how quickly Poland transitioned from a totalitarian state into the beginnings of a liberal parliamentary democracy. "You know," Walesa said, "the Wall will come down soon. I don't know when, but I really think very soon, maybe weeks."

Kohl laughed in his face. "You're young and don't understand some things," he told Walesa, who was forty-six. "There are long historical processes going on and this will take many years."

Both men were wrong.

The imagery of thousands of citizens camped out as refugees had been enormously humiliating to the GDR's international prestige. The new East German government attempted a novel approach to try and control the massive number of citizens that were fleeing the country. Having no really good options, it was decided that they would be allowed to emigrate if they asked for permission while on East German soil. Then at least the authorities would still have some measure of control over the whole mess, and could possibly be able to hide the extent of the situation from the outside world.

Another attempt by the new government to provide the appearance of fundamental reform was by fielding open questions from reporters. On November 9th Schabowski accordingly held his daily press conference. After an hour of talking with the press he said that he had time for one more question. Word had gotten around that there were new travel regulations under consideration and the media wanted to know more. Schabowski was prepared for this, having spoken to Krenz about the issue immediately beforehand. Krenz had even given him a copy of the decree to look over.

Schabowski explained that "we find it unacceptable that this movement is taking place across the territory of an allied state, which is not an easy burden for that country to bear. Therefore we have decided today to implement a regulation that allows every citizen of the German Democratic Republic to leave the GDR through any of the border crossings." Then he read from the draft text that Krenz had handed him:

> Applications for travel abroad by private individuals can now be made without the previously existing requirements (of demonstrating a need to travel or proving familial relationships). The travel authorizations will be issued within a short time. Grounds for denial will only be applied in particular exceptional cases. The responsible departments of passport and registration control in the People's Police district offices in the GDR are instructed to issue visas for permanent exit without delays and without presentation of the existing requirements for permanent exit. [...]
>
> Permanent exit is possible via all GDR border crossings to the FRG. These changes replace the temporary practice of issuing authorizations through GDR consulates and permanent exit with a GDR personal identity card via third countries.[573]

When asked when this new policy was to take effect, a nervous Schabowski shuffled through his documents. He didn't notice the sentence on the back of one paper embargoing the information until the following morning. "That comes into effect," he replied, "according to my information, immediately, without delay."

"Does this also apply for West Berlin?" one journalist asked.

Schabowski shrugged and then, frowning, looked back at his papers. He reread the key passage: "Permanent exit can take place via all border crossings from the GDR to the FRG and West Berlin, respectively." In other words, the propaganda chief of East Germany announced live on camera that East Berliners were free to leave to West Berlin without any fear of repercussions. Not only did he announce it, but he had repeated it for good measure.

The Berlin Wall was effectively now just a concrete structure.

The East German broadcast of the press conference began at 7:30 p.m.—and the East Berliners began to storm the Wall immediately thereafter.[574] The guards had heard different rumors themselves and were left unsure of what to do. "Open the gate!" chanted the people. "The Wall must go!" For the first time in their lives, the citizens felt comfortable arguing with soldiers and Stasi officers—and they were safe to do so. The armed men argued back but there was no move on their part to escalate matters to violence.[575] It was a little after 9 p.m. when word came down from the bureaucracy: the more aggressive citizens were to be let through, but they should not expect to be allowed to return back. They were effectively not emigrating but being deported. To the East Berliners, those terms were acceptable.

By this point all six East Berlin border checkpoints were mobbed, with twenty thousand people at the Bornholmer Strasse checkpoint alone. Harald Jager, the border guard commander stationed there, made a professional assessment of the situation. "All I was thinking about now was to avoid bloodshed," he later explained. "There were so many people and they didn't have space to move. If a panic started, people would have been crushed. We had pistols. I had given instructions not to use them, but what if one of the men had lost his nerve?"

Jager made an executive decision: he ordered his men to open the gate. One hour later, unaware of what had happened at Bornholmer Strasse, border guard commander Gunter Moll independently made the same decision at the notorious Checkpoint Charlie crossing. As a deluge of his countrymen ran past him to West Berlin, abandoning their cars behind them, he stood there wondering why the hell the crossing had ever been closed to begin with. The video footage of the young border guards stepping aside as hundreds of East Berliners ran past them is particularly notable for one big reason: for once the guards were smiling.

The citizens of the GDR were greeted in West Berlin with flowers and champagne by their fellow Germans. By midnight all six checkpoints were wide open, with all 12,000 border guards sent back to their barracks. Soon the entire world was watching in shock as residents of a united Berlin were literally dancing atop the Berlin Wall. There were, still, some half-hearted attempts to get them down. The East German police at one point tried to blast them off with a hose—only to be defeated by an umbrella.[576] Helmut Kohl—who wasn't young but nevertheless still didn't understand some things—cut his trip to Poland short. "I'm at the wrong party," he said.[577]

Nobody thought to phone Moscow until 5 a.m., and even then no one bothered to call Gorbachev. He only learned what had happened when he woke up the following morning to scenes that seemed unimaginable. He called Krenz to give his consent after the fact. "You made the right decision because how could you shoot Germans who walk across the border to meet other Germans?" he said. Gorbachev still didn't quite realize that it hadn't really been Krenz's decision so much as a historic accident on Schabowski's part.[578]

Stuck in between Hungary and East Germany was Czechoslovakia, but Communist Party leader Milos Jakes intended to stay the course. "As long as the economy holds up here," he had told his colleagues, "we'll be all right."[579] Just to be sure nothing went wrong, he increased patrols in areas used for popular gatherings—or uprisings. But there was one popular gathering that the Czech authorities could not quash: the fiftieth anniversary of the murder of Jan Opletal. Opletal was a twenty-four-year-old medical student shot by the Nazis for protesting against their occupation of Czechoslovakia. It was the Czech Communists themselves who had propagandized him as a martyr in the decades following World War II.

The anniversary march proceeded as planned on Friday, November 17, 1989, eight days after the Berlin Wall was opened. The crowds held banners denouncing communism and commemorating the Prague uprising of 1968—but the police did nothing. When the march ended most of the crowd dispersed, except for a group of mostly students who then made their way to Prague's historic Wenceslas Square. As they approached the Square they found their way blocked by both riot police and anti-terrorist squads, batons at the ready.

The protestors gave the police their candles and they gave the police their flowers. They sat down in the street, chanting "We have no weapons" and singing songs. Then another group of riot police came up behind them. They were trapped on the street for two hours, singing songs in the freezing cold. When they asked if they could go home the police said nothing. It was at 9 p.m. when a riot squad van arrived and began ramming into them. That's when the police began their beatings. Over five hundred people were injured—men, women and children alike—and the 120 who were arrested were thereupon beaten again.[580] Supposedly there was one casualty—but the lesson of Jan Opletal was that the life of one student can make a powerful difference.[581]

Rumors in communist nations were often far more truthful than any official media source, and soon a story got out that the police had murdered a student by the name of Martin Smid. Foreign media outlets such as the BBC and Voice of America reported the unverified story as fact. There were, in reality, *two* students by the name of Martin Smid studying at Prague's Charles University at that time, and the government swiftly produced them both to demonstrate that they were perfectly safe and unharmed. After over four decades of communist rule, the authorities actually were telling the truth—and after over four decades of communist rule, the people did not believe them.

Now that the authorities had chosen violence, everything was on the table. That weekend saw demonstrations that hadn't been seen in Prague since 1968, with the spot where the police had beaten the protestors taking on the form of a secular shrine. Students were now joined by every type of citizen, and all that the government could think to do in response was to arrest the activist who had spread the claim that Smid had been killed.

The Czech analogue to Lech Walesa was Vaclav Havel, their version of the dissident figurehead who fought the authorities for decades while getting arrested and subsequently released. A prominent playwright, Havel's career was destroyed due to his support of the Prague Spring. His works were banned in Czechoslovakia while he himself was forbidden from leaving the country. Havel had suspected that the end of the Berlin Wall meant that things would change swiftly in Czechoslovakia as well, and he returned to Prague from the countryside to take part in the escalating drama.

Havel began to organize at a theater with the fortuitous name of the Magic Lantern. The protestors called themselves the Civic Forum and presented themselves as spokesmen for the people. They issued four demands:

1) the resignation of the leaders who had crushed the Prague Spring;
2) the resignation of the ministers who had ordered the attacks on the students;
3) an independent inquiry into the recent events;
4) the immediate release of all political prisoners

The protests grew and continued over the following days. The energy was felt in every segment of the country. Actors went on strike, and so did the football players. The Monday alone after the police violence saw 300,000 protestors. A new symbol of defiance arose: holding up keys and shaking them in the air, telling the Communists to pack their crap and leave. The Magic Lantern became a beacon to a wide swath of ideologies which had one agenda in common: freeing Czechoslovakia from Communist Party rule. This was to be a revolution, but a soft and peaceful one. It became known as the Velvet Revolution for just that reason.

The authorities considered sending in the tanks—not the Russian ones this time, but their own. That was the position of Defence Minister Jaroslav Vaclavik. Jakes agreed. "Force has to be met by force," he said.[582] He saw what had happened in Berlin just days prior. All the government apparatchiks saw. Finally, on Wednesday, November 22nd, they decided to call out the People's Militia. They were about to prove Bakunin right, that the people are not much happier when they are beaten by "the People's Militia." There was just one problem: the People's Militia refused to take up arms against their countrymen, especially the students. That was enough for Vaclavik. He went on television that very evening and let the citizenry know that the army would not fight them.[583]

Havel had joked that it was time for another Russian invasion, since he expected that this time the Russians would be on the side of the people. He was not entirely incorrect. Gorbachev dispatched the head of the Party's international department to Prague to see firsthand what was going on. The man went directly to the Magic Lantern and personally met with the Civic Forum himself. The Soviet embassy also received a delegation from the Civic Forum. These were unmistakable signals that the Russians regarded the organization as a legitimate, respectable political force in Czechoslovakia.[584]

The Czechoslovakian government tried to censor the imagery of the protests from the television news, but there was too much foreign coverage to keep the information from the public. Nor was it possible to sweep the story under the rug, not when hundreds of thousands of people were demonstrating in freezing weather. Word of mouth alone would have been enough to inform the entire population, in the cities at the very least.

Friday evening—a week after it all started—Alexander Dubcek, leader of the Prague Spring, appeared alongside Havel on a balcony at the Melantrich Building and spoke to the audience of half a million who had gathered in Wenceslas Square. For the audience below it was like being visited by a character from a history book, as if Martin Luther King, Jr. had reappeared in Washington, DC and began to sing "We shall overcome!" to the crowd. The spirit of 1968 was alive and well in Prague.

One hour later both men held a press conference at the Magic Lantern. As they disagreed with one another about the future—Dubcek still regarded communism as salvageable in his sense of "socialism with a human face"—the news broke across the entire country: the Communist Party leaders were all resigning. Garton Ash had joked to Havel, "In Poland it took ten years, in Hungary ten months, in East Germany ten weeks: perhaps in Czechoslovakia it will take ten days!"[585]

Ten days was a ridiculously optimistic estimate—and, it turned out, an overly conservative one. Instead of ten days it had taken seven.

As a test, the Civic Forum called a nationwide general strike for Monday the 27th. The strike was to last two hours, but would clearly demonstrate who was on which side—and whether the caretaker government would or even could do anything to stop them. It was instantly clear—as it had been in that crucial vote in Poland—that virtually all the workers were on the side of the protestors and against the Communists. The television anchor who delivered news of the strike simultaneously announced that he was joining it.[586] The Communist Party officially abandoned power the very next day.

Instead of sending in the tanks, now the leaders were concerned for their own safety. Prime Minister Ladislav Adamec secretly met with Havel to try and secure guarantees that there would be no repercussions for him and his cabal for the decades of oppression that they had imposed upon the people of Czechoslovakia. They were effectively and understandably acknowledging that in a week the man had gone from a pariah to the de facto leader of the country. It is the one example where the Czechoslovakian Communists were prescient and in touch with the masses.

By the end of 1989, Havel would be officially sworn in as president of Czechoslovakia while Dubcek became chairman of the parliament. They did not seek vengeance for the former Communist leaders. Additionally, all five of the Warsaw Pact nations who had taken part in the 1968 invasion of Czechoslovakia now officially renounced and condemned their past actions. The Velvet Revolution ended in forgiveness and peace.

By 1992 the Czech and Slovak peoples would come to realize that they would prefer to peacefully go their own separate ways, and the Velvet Revolution would give way to the Velvet Divorce. After some intense negotiations, the country of Czechoslovakia was dissolved as of the end of 1992 and birthed the nations of Slovakia and the Czech Republic.

In 2001 the Museum of Communism opened up in Prague a few blocks from Wenceslas Square. Visitors can tour exhibits dedicated to showing how "Collectivization is one symbol of the depravity of the

Communist regime" and "Just as today cigarette packs warn us that smoking causes serious damage to our health, back then spending time in a Communist country could also seriously damage your health."

The Czech Communist Party was one of the few communist parties that did not try to rebrand, continuing to compete for parliamentary representation. Never again in government, they reached a high point of forty-one out of two hundred seats in 2002 before eventually falling below the 5% minimum threshold and losing all parliamentary representation in 2021.

But as Czechoslovakia chose to separate, the two Germanies sought to reunify. The Berlin Wall was also a sort of political dam, and when it fell the fortunes of the East German Communist Party fell with it. Egon Krenz only managed to last forty-six days in office, as decades of hatred for the East German government spilled out into the open without fear of repercussions. By the end Stasi chief Erich Mielke was reduced to being openly booed in parliament, an 81-year-old dinosaur blubbering "I love you all!" and "I love all human beings!"[587] The Stasi went from absolute power to absolute impotence:

> In a bizarre reversal of authority, the protestors took the Stasi building on December 4, 1989. The guards asked to see their papers as they entered the building. The protestors dutifully complied—before seizing and occupying it, sitting nervously in the hallways of the agency that had spied on them all.[588]

Desperate to maintain some semblance of power, East German Party members proceeded to do everything possible to blame their predecessors for the oppression that they had visited upon the citizenry. The party's official name was changed from the Socialist Unity Party to the Party of Democratic Socialism. Mielke was stripped of his Party card, as were Krenz, Schabowski, and Honecker. Parliamentary elections in East Germany resulted in the former Communists placing a respectable third place, setting the stage for German reunification on October 3, 1990.

Krenz was eventually arrested and imprisoned for a few years for his crimes. Schabowski only served one year before receiving a pardon due to his consistent public recantation of his past actions. Mielke became Germany's oldest prisoner before being released after several years due to his senile dementia. He ended his days in a nursing home, having imaginary conversations with Stasi officers on a telephone that wasn't even plugged in. Honecker spent his few remaining years in a constant battle against both cancer and prosecution before passing away in 1994. As for Margot, she got on her proverbial broom and escaped to Chile. There she survived, unapologetic and unrepentant, until the age of 89, before returning to hell in 2016.

Of all the Warsaw Pact countries, it was Romania that was most determined to stay on its unique path while the nations surrounding it overthrew their communist governments one after another. News of the international unrest had breached even Ceausescu's firmly-guarded borders, but Nicolae and Elena weren't going anywhere if they had their way. Yet by the time reporter Kenneth Auchincloss had interviewed him in late 1989, he said that Ceausescu "had no presence at all, no aura, no eloquence. The impression you had was of a pathetic figure, completely cut off from the realities of Romania, living in the past, in a dreamworld."[589]

The troubles in Romania started with a pastor named Laszlo Tokes. Unlike many other clergymen in Romania, Tokes was not in collusion with the authorities. His sermons took subtle digs at Ceausescu, and at one point he even publicly joined in on criticism of Ceausescu's systemization policy. For this Tokes was arrested, and soon church leaders—all highly subservient to the government—tried to have him evicted from his Timisoara home. As his battle in court proceeded, a group of four men broke into his house and beat him in front of his three-year-old son and pregnant wife. When she yelled at the police stationed outside for help—Tokes was of course under surveillance—they did nothing. The four men were clearly not home invaders but officers from Romania's version of the KGB, the Securitate, who were just following orders.[590]

Having lost his legal appeals, Tokes was due to be evicted on December 15, 1989. At first his congregation gathered together in a sign of protest. Very quickly a larger crowd formed, as protesting Tokes' eviction became a mechanism for protesting the Ceausescu government itself. The protests continued to the next day, and now Ceausescu ordered arrests. It was too little, too late. The demonstrators took over Communist Party headquarters and ransacked the building. Tokes and his family were taken into custody and he was once again beaten. The officers threatened to beat his pregnant wife as well unless he signed a blank piece of paper, which was meant to later be used to show that he had accepted the verdict against him.[591]

Unsatisfied, Nicolae and Elena demanded blood. "Fidel Castro is right," he said. "You do not quiet your enemy by talking to him like a priest, but by burning him…They've got to kill the hooligans, not beat them." He then fired the Defence Minister, Minister of the Interior and chief of the Securitate troops on the spot. "Do you know what I'm going to do with you?" he asked them. "Send you to the firing squad."

"We've got to take radical measures," agreed Elena. "We can't be indulgent."[592]

Having put the fear of the bullet into his officials, Ceausescu then reinstated them. They knew what he wanted to be done. That evening the Romanian army took control of Timisoara and opened fire on the crowds. Rumors swept through Romania that thousands had been killed—and since the official media said nothing, that only made the most outlandish numbers seem that much more truthful. The actual deaths were fewer than one hundred, but it didn't matter much. Ceausescu was clearly prepared to shed large amounts of blood to maintain his power, and the people knew it.

Ceausescu held a rally in Bucharest on December 21, 1989. His goons packed the audience with the most reliable Romanians they could find. The televised speech would reassure the country that Ceausescu remained in control and was as popular as ever. Boos from the crowd began just a few minutes after he began to speak. Then came the chants of "Timisoara!" and "We are the People!". The moment where Ceausescu realized the crowd had turned against him, the second he paused and looked confused at the impossible becoming real, was broadcast live throughout Romania.

Then the screen went blank.[593]

Eventually the television stations resumed broadcasting—and they showed the crowds and the chaos. Ceausescu huddled in the building with his most loyal henchmen and Elena for an entire day as rioting broke out. Used to following orders from the dictator, the Romanian army waited in their barracks as the unrest spread. The next day Ceausescu tried to pin the blame on the unrest on Defence Minister Vasile Milea and fired the man, who then shot himself.

It was almost exactly twenty-four hours after his rally that the Ceausescus fled to the roof of the building, where a helicopter had just landed for them. They knew that there were several countries to which they could escape, and they had hundreds of millions of dollars stashed away in Swiss bank accounts. But Ceausescu wasn't about to give up power so easily. Into the helicopter stepped the Ceausescus, their two bodyguards, and both the prime minister and deputy prime minister. It was a great deal of weight for the copter but it made it into the air. Ceausescu ordered the pilot to take them to their palace in the town of Snagov. Attempts to contact the Securitate in the Oltenia region failed. Unbeknownst to the passengers, everyone at the Securitate communications center had fled.

Claims that Milea was responsible for the unrest fell on deaf ears. For decades the Romanian people had been told, constantly told, that it was Ceausescu who was responsible for their country and what happened in it. Accusing a scapegoat was an absurdity. If anything, Milea was seen as yet another Ceausescu victim. Hearing what happened to him made the armed forces take sides with the people. The soldiers made it a point of showing that their guns were unloaded. Others stood up from their tanks and waved to the crowd.[594]

Once at Snagov Palace Ceausescu worked the phones, trying to figure out which parts of the country remained under his control. The helicopter pilot, eager to get out of the situation, insisted that the copter couldn't hold that many people again. The group now took off without the prime minister and deputy prime minister, making their way to the town of Pitesti. Knowing that copters had been grounded all over the country, the pilot flew high to make sure that he'd be visible. "We've been spotted by radar," he told Ceausescu. "We could be shot down at any moment."[595]

Panicked, Ceausescu told the pilot to land in the field beneath them, close by to the road. There the pilot abandoned the Ceausescus with their bodyguards. One of the bodyguards flagged down a car, and the three of them squeezed in. The other bodyguard flagged down another car and followed, until the driver lied and said he was running out of gas. That bodyguard got out by the side of the road as the relieved driver made his way to safety.

The Ceausescus made their way to the village of Vacaresti, switching to a better car that they had spotted. A few days prior, Nicolae Ceausescu could have done virtually anything in Romania. Now he was trying to be anonymous in a country where his image was everywhere, where the entire population was told about his exploits from sunrise to sunset, seven days a week. He told the new driver to take them to one of his prized steel factories, but when they arrived they discovered that—like every other Romanian factory—it was on strike. Instead of being welcomed in, the car was greeted with rocks being thrown by the workers. They drove instead to Tirgoviste, leaving their last bodyguard behind for reasons that are unclear. They were finally welcomed at the Plant Protection Center, an establishment used to showcase Ceausescu's supposed accomplishments.

The Center's director called the militia to pick up the Ceausescus and drive them to safety. A militia car picked them up but could only take them around in circles as Tirgoviste was in full-fledged rebellion. The Tirgoviste army commander understood by this point that both the Romanian people and the military had turned against the Ceausescus. His barracks was only five hundred yards away from the militia building, and he decided to occupy it. The Ceausescus were instantly taken into custody when they arrived there, four hours after leaving the Center.

"Well, what's the situation?" barked Ceausescu. "Give me your report." He thought he was still commander-in-chief, but eventually came to understand that he was not the military men's leader but their prisoner.[596] Nor was Ceausescu an easy prisoner to accommodate. For almost two days he and Elena harangued their captors about everything from the food—"Don't give me that crap"—to the bathroom accommodations—they had to bring her a chamber pot—to the clothing that they were given. Ceausescu demanded to be allowed to open a window so he could address the people outside who were chanting for his blood while oblivious to his proximity. The military men understandably refused. Elena's most reasonable fit came when the diabetic Nicolae was given tea with sugar. She demanded insulin for her husband but wouldn't give it to him when she finally received it, possibly due to a worry that it had been poisoned.

Shortly before midnight on the 24th, the militia building came under fire from Securitate troops. The prisoners were taken to an armored car, hiding on the floor for five hours while gunfire was exchanged. Eventually the secret police were beaten back. Now it was clear to the soldiers that time was of the essence, and that they would not be able to imprison the Ceausescus indefinitely. If anything, they were putting their own lives at risk by holding them captive.

Already a group called the National Salvation Front was trying to establish itself as government of Romania. General Victor Stanculescu arrived in Tirgoviste to bring the case of the Ceausescus to a close. It was decided to put the couple on trial, then and there. When he was fifteen, young Nicolae told his brother-in-law that he was going to be "Romania's Stalin."[597] Now he and Elena were going to be the defendants in a trial so absurd that even Stalin would have blushed.

A classroom in a nearby school was hastily set up to serve as the court. The defense attorney was given ten minutes to confer with his clients. The best he could come up with was to plead insanity, which Elena especially found to be unconscionable. "I do not recognize this court," Ceausescu insisted, not unreasonably. "I refuse to answer those who have fomented this coup d'etat. I am not the accused. I am the president of the republic, I am your commander in chief. We have been working for the people since the age of fourteen."[598]

The prosecutors charged the couple with genocide, organizing armed action against the people and the state, the destruction of public assets and buildings, sabotage of the national economy, and attempting to flee the country with funds of more than US$1billion deposited in foreign banks.[599] At one point the prosecutor even stopped to ask Elena if she was "mentally defective."[600] "Let's get this over with," barked Ceausescu.

The trial took less than an hour, and after a five-minute recess the judges returned to the courtroom and delivered a verdict of death. As both of the Ceausescus got their hands bound with rope, Nicolae insisted that "Romania will live and learn of your treachery." Under Romanian law, a death sentence could only be carried out ten days after a verdict had been delivered. For a brief period the couple still felt somewhat secure.

There is often a question as to whether rulers like the Ceausescus believe their own bullshit. In Elena's case, at least, that definitely seems to have been her view. "I brought you up like a mother!" she shrieked at the soldiers.

"Lady," one of them replied, "you're in real trouble."

Her reply was either "You keep away from me, you motherfucker"[601] or "'Go fuck your mother"[602]—a very unfortunate choice of words given what the seventy-three-year-old woman had said to them moments prior. It was only when the Ceausescus were taken outside to the school courtyard—and not to some helicopter waiting to return them to Bucharest—that the two of them realized what was about to happen. "Look," Elena said, "they're going to shoot us like dogs." The couple were placed up against the wall, and then the waiting soldiers proved the bitch correct. There were over one hundred bullets shot in total by the time they stopped firing their AK-47s at the Ceausescus.

As usual it was bitterly cold in Romania that winter day, with the temperature not even reaching 45°F in the capital city of Bucharest. And though no snow fell, it didn't seem to make much of a difference. That day—December 25, 1989—was still the best Christmas that the Romanian people had ever had.

Chapter 16

THE WHITE PILL

Part of Gorbachev's reordering of the Soviet Union's political structure allowed for other, alternate voices to emerge. The Stalinist insistence on complete orthodoxy gave way to a far more disparate process of discussing issues and looking for solutions. This not only allowed but pretty much guaranteed that other personalities would emerge to achieve prominence in the USSR. The best example of this was Boris Yeltsin.

At the end of 1985, Yeltsin was appointed First Secretary of Moscow's City Committee (a position roughly akin to mayor) despite his reputation for having a fondness for the bottle. This wasn't entirely uncommon in the Soviet Union, which in many ways was less puritanical than the United States. Gorbachev started his memoirs recounting a scene where he was summoned to Chernenko's office while he was himself inebriated: "It should be pointed out that in those days it was customary to drink liquor quite frequently on various occasions," he wrote, somewhat defensively. "However, having never had a propensity for alcohol, I was in a fairly normal state when I arrived".[603]

From the very beginning Yeltsin exploited his position to further his personal ambition. As Gorbachev recounted:

> It seems to me that Yeltsin happened to be in the eye of the storm, since it was in the capital that the interests of the city, republic and central institutions of the old system were most closely entwined. He tried to rally Moscow Party organizations and the Muscovites themselves against these structures, and in my opinion he was right in this attempt. However, from the very beginning he used populist methods to achieve his goal. He would suddenly appear at a factory, take the manager and lead him to the workers' cafeteria to give him a public dressing-down, acting as if he were the protector of the people and the manager a monster of cruelty. Sometimes he would get on a bus or a tram, or drop into a shop or hospital, and the next day all of Moscow would be filled with rumours of this. To the enraptured applause of Muscovites he promised that problems of housing, medical care and services would be resolved in record time. He displayed colourful drawings of meat processing plants and dairies being built around the capital to do away with the eternal shortage of sausage and buttermilk. All of this was trumpeted in the Moscow press, radio and television. His search for new forms of Party work was also meant mostly for effect. For example, meetings of the Moscow city committee began to be held at eleven or twelve at night.[604]

Tensions between Yeltsin and Gorbachev as well as Yeltsin and the Communist Party eventually spilled out into the public. In late 1987 Yeltsin made a speech that called out Gorbachev, the Communist Party, and perestroika itself for good measure. Not only that, but he quit the Politburo in the guise of giving all the leaders of the Soviet Union an ultimatum. It was the most head-on assault on the power of the General Secretary since Trotsky. Yeltsin's speech was seen less as an act of integrity and more a dishonest act of pride and ambition, throwing people under the bus in order to further his personal standing.

Things reached a low shortly thereafter on the morning of November 9, 1987, when Yeltsin was found covered in blood. Gorbachev recounted how Yeltsin would later claim he had been mugged and fought off his attackers and "of course, he had 'tossed them about like kittens', but still he had received a knife wound. Needless to say, this tale sounded much more heroic. By then, I had already discovered Yeltsin's talent for fiction."[605] In reality the wound was clearly self-inflicted, possibly a suicide attempt. Gorbachev explained how the doctors said that "the wound was not critical at all; the scissors, by slipping over his ribs, had left a bloody but superficial wound."[606]

In Yeltsin's defense, all this could have occurred during one of his drunken stupors. Years later it would be Bill Clinton's turn to deal with Yeltsin's hijinks. Clinton confidentially discussed the matter with author Taylor Branch:

> Clinton had received notice of a major predawn security alarm when Secret Service agents discovered Yeltsin alone on Pennsylvania Avenue, dead drunk, clad in his underwear, yelling for a taxi. Yeltsin slurred his words in a loud argument with the baffled agents. He did not want to go back into Blair House, where he was staying. He wanted a taxi to go out for pizza. I asked what became of the standoff. "Well," the president said, shrugging, "he got his pizza."[607]

Gorbachev phoned Yeltsin in the hospital to demand that he discuss his speech with the Moscow city committee. "I can't," Yeltsin said. "The doctors won't even let me get up."

"That's OK," Gorbachev replied sarcastically, "the doctors will help you." They pumped Yeltsin full of sedatives and an antispasm agent and sent him on to meet his fate. Yuri Plekhanov—the KGB head tasked with protecting Soviet leaders—was at the hospital and even he thought this was too sadistic. But Yeltsin had ruffled too many feathers, and publicly so. For four hours he was berated by two dozen speakers before admitting his guilt and accepting his dismissal.[608] While he lost his political position, he nevertheless became a symbol of people's distaste with the Soviet system—the very system Gorbachev was trying to reform and salvage.

Indeed, it was only under the old system where Yeltsin could have been kept out of office. When Gorbachev led the way to introduce the Congress of People's Deputies of the Soviet Union in 1989, Yeltsin was elected as a delegate with 92% of the vote. He quickly became an oppositional leader in the newfound parliamentary body. It was in that capacity that he visited the United States later that year.

After touring the Johnson Space Center on September 16, 1989, Yeltsin took an unscheduled visit to a Randall's supermarket in Houston, Texas. Photos exist of him being awed by the boxes of Kool-Aid popsicles and the overflowing bins of onions. He was told that the store stocked thirty thousand items, while the typical Soviet store ostensibly carried fewer than a hundred but in practice often had bare shelves. It would have seemed like ridiculous pro-American propaganda but for the fact that Yeltsin was witnessing it all with his own eyes. Average Americans could buy things out of reach of the wealthiest Soviet citizens. The conquest of bread had been won by the West.

As Yeltsin flew on to Miami he clutched his head in his hands, his brain rewiring itself from decades of being told things that were simply not true. He also understood that those saying such things couldn't have been just "misinformed," not to this extent. They were knowingly, brazenly lying, or at the very least completely indifferent to the facts. "They had to fool the people," he realized. "It is now clear why they made it so difficult for the average Soviet citizen to go abroad. They were afraid that people's eyes would open."[609]

Not only was Gorbachev losing standing as the sole leader in the USSR as Yeltsin emerged, but the Soviet government itself began to lose power as the sole decision-making body. The USSR's Republic of Lithuania held elections in February 1990. The vote led to a Supreme Council issuing what was called the Act on Re-establishment of the State of Lithuania, a declaration that Lithuania was a sovereign nation free of Soviet rule. Gorbachev immediately declared the Act null and void and implemented an economic blockade against the small Baltic nation.

Lithuania was not East Germany or Hungary. It was still part of the USSR, and as such was under his purview. From his perspective, there was a process for secession, and that process would have necessarily involved a Lithuanian referendum.

The economic consequences grew dire for the Lithuanian people, with inflation hitting 100%. Nevertheless, the Lithuanian authorities persisted. And despite Gorbachev's misgivings, in May 1990 Yeltsin was elected chairman of Russia's parliament. In doing so he now represented the republic that contained half of the USSR's population, 76% of its land and 90% of Soviet oil production. The issue with democracy is that sometimes the votes don't go the way a person would like them to.

After all that had happened in the previous couple of years, the Russians finally chose to send in the tanks to Lithuania. On January 11, 1991, Russian troops fired in a crowd of protestors, killing over a dozen and wounding many more. When the Soviets later claimed that the protestors shot first, their story was instantly debunked by foreign reporters who were eyewitnesses to the whole affair. Soviet troops stormed the TV tower in the capital city of Vilnius, as well as the National Radio and Television building in an attempt to take control of the narrative of information. All this had the opposite result from what the Soviets wanted. Thousands of unarmed Lithuanians then took to surrounding their parliament building around the clock to protect their government against further Soviet aggression. They kept themselves warm by building huge bonfires out of Soviet propaganda. Gorbachev claims all this was done without his permission or even knowledge, and that he later tried to figure out who gave the order to use force when he heard the news. In either case, he was either complicit or appeared powerless to stop it.

Other nations condemned the USSR in no uncertain terms, and three weeks after the attacks Iceland officially recognized the Republic of Lithuania. Five days after that the Lithuanian government held their national referendum, with over 90% of the votes being cast in favor of Lithuania staying independent. Uncomfortable with the blood that had already been spilled, Gorbachev was against further escalating the situation. Instead, however, the idea of secession was quickly spreading to other Soviet republics.

Alongside Russia, Ukraine and Byelorussia, Transcaucasia had been one of the four founding members of the USSR in 1922. In 1936 it was split into its three constituent parts of Armenia, Azerbaijan and Georgia. On March 31, 1991, Georgia too held a referendum on independence, and 99.5% of the voters chose to leave the Soviet Union. Yeltsin got another promotion in June, overwhelmingly becoming elected president of Russia with almost 59% of the vote. His closest rival—Gorbachev's choice of Nikolai Ryzhkov—received only 16%. There was now a president of Russia, Yeltsin, and a president of the Soviet Union, Gorbachev. Who was in charge of whom was an increasingly difficult question to answer.

Men like KGB head Vladimir Kryuchkov had the most to lose if the Soviet Union fell apart. As one republic after another tested the waters of independence and national sovereignty, Gorbachev tried to hold the country together under the idea of a Union of Sovereign States. Yeltsin specifically told Gorbachev that dismissing Kryuchkov would be necessary if people were to believe in this newly reformulated Union of Sovereign States. But despite having this discussion with Gorbachev on a balcony in an attempt to avoid eavesdropping, the hidden KGB microphones picked up their conversation anyway.[610] The Union of Soviet Socialist Republics was falling apart—and those in power weren't going down without a fight. The forces of authoritarianism were not ever going to give up.

Kryuchkov spent weeks getting his allies prepared. When Gorbachev left Moscow for his Crimean dacha on August 4, 1991, the plotters began to get their plan in order. On August 18th, Gorbachev was informed that a group of comrades was there to see him. Not expecting anyone, he was livid that his security team let a party get this close. His personal bodyguard explained that they had come with Yuri Plekhanov—the same KGB official who had been in the hospital with Yeltsin.

Still miffed, Gorbachev gave instructions to have them wait. He picked up a phone to make a call, only to find the line was dead—as was the second phone, and the third, and the fourth. Finally he lifted the cover for the red phone to be used in the event of a nuclear attack on the USSR, a phone so important that no one was permitted to touch it even just for dusting. It too was dead. Now Gorbachev understood that a coup was underway. He went outside to discuss the matter with his wife Raisa. Highly educated, she understood how dangerous of a situation the two of them were in.

Gorbachev returned to his study to be greeted by five elite Soviet officials, Plekhanov among them. The men were clearly nervous, and Gorbachev was still enraged. He began interrogating them about what was going on. They explained to him that they came as representatives of the "Emergency Committee" and rattled off a list of its members, men that owed their positions to Gorbachev and that he had considered trustworthy. They claimed that Yeltsin was on the verge of arrest as well. They gave Gorbachev two options: to either declare a state of emergency, or to transfer his power to Vice President Yanayev, who had joined his name to the coup.

"To hell with you," Gorbachev told them.

"Mikhail Sergeyevich," his chief of staff said, "you don't understand what the situation in the country is."

"Shut up, you prick. How dare you give me lectures about the situation in the country!"[611]

The men flew back to Moscow a bit rattled by the meeting. The following day the media issued the plotters' declaration: due to Gorbachev's "state of health," Vice President Gennady Yanayev was now assuming the responsibilities of the president in accordance with the Constitution of the USSR. Boris Yeltsin was awakened to news of the coup by his youngest daughter, and like many other Russians was completely baffled by what the proclamation meant. He tried to call Yanayev but Yanayev refused to speak with him, and when Yeltsin tried to call Gorbachev the call could not get put through.

For all of his escapades, Boris Yeltsin was no dummy. A few weeks prior, he had bonded with high-ranking General Pavel Grachev over bottles of vodka. "If our lawfully elected government in Russia were ever threatened—a terrorist act, a coup, efforts to arrest the leaders—could the military be relied upon?" Yeltsin had asked him. "Could *you* be relied upon?"

"Yes," Grachev replied.

Knowing he had to scramble as fast as possible, Yeltsin called Grachev to remind him of their conversation. Though Yeltsin did not realize it, Grachev's fingerprints were all over the coup. He stammered about needing to obey his superiors before decency got the better of him. "I'll send you a security detachment," he promised Yeltsin.[612]

As recently as 1989, copy machines in the Soviet Union were locked up by law. But this was 1991, and the members of the coup were acting as if they could still somehow control the flow of information despite all the technological advances that had been made since the Stalin era. Yeltsin issued a statement denouncing the coup in no uncertain words, and his faxed declaration was then disseminated around the world.[613] Donning a bulletproof vest, Yeltsin got into his limo and began the ride to his office in Moscow's White House. On his way to the government building he passed hundreds of armored vehicles.

When Yeltsin got to the White House he was greeted by a crowd of journalists, who were themselves heavily outnumbered by the citizenry. "At least fifty tanks are on their way to this building," Yeltsin announced. "Anybody who wants to save himself can do so."[614] He then made his way up to his office on the fifth floor. When the tanks eventually arrived Yeltsin went back down to greet them. In a public display of fearlessness, Yeltsin approached one tank and posed for pictures while shaking the hands of its commander. "Apparently they are not going to shoot the president of Russia just yet," he quipped.[615] In the Soviet Union, dark humor was like food: not everyone got it. In this case, they all got it, and so did everyone watching the scenes unfold on televisions around the world.

Back at Gorbachev's dacha, Raisa was a bit more fearful than Yeltsin appeared to be. The Gorbachevs could only receive information from outside the compound via Mikhail's transistor radio, and they were unable to send messages to the outside world. When Raisa heard the announcement that Gorbachev was being deposed due to his health, she understood that this might not be a lie so much as a threat. She hid food so that the family would have something to eat and refused to serve anything that hadn't already come prepackaged. Her husband wouldn't back down no matter what was done to him—but their grandchildren were at the dacha with them. "We all knew our history," she later said.[616]

That history taught Raisa how persuasive threats to one's family could be—and how often those threats were actually carried out in the Soviet

Union. Desperate to get his message out, Gorbachev recorded a speech discussing what had happened and demonstrating that he remained in good health. He repeated his speech four times and then cut the tape into four sections. He gave one section each to his personal secretary, his doctor and an aide while keeping the fourth for himself.[617] This was his insurance that the truth would be heard if the worst came to pass.

Yeltsin was in a far better position than Gorbachev to fight the plot, and he did so with every tool at his disposal. He did not acknowledge the coup's legal authority and proceeded to govern accordingly. He issued warrants for the arrests of the plotters, declared himself commander-in-chief of Soviet troops on Russian soil, called an emergency session of Russian parliament, and suspended Russia's Communist Party.[618] As for the plotters, they sat down to plan for a storming of the White House. Operation Thunder was set to begin at 3 a.m. on Wednesday, August 21st. It seemed inevitable that things were going to turn very violent very quickly.

Grachev kept true to his promise and quietly got word to the Russian leaders in the White House that the building was going to be attacked. He suggested getting a crowd of average citizens to surround the building, believing that military forces would be extremely unlikely to shoot civilians. Soon the streets around the White House were filled by tens of thousands of locals—just as Tiananmen Square had been, a little over two years prior. That Tuesday night, Yeltsin took to the airwaves, asking for the people's support. "Law and constitutional order will triumph," he promised. "Despite everything, Russia will be free!"[619] At 11 p.m. thousands of citizens remained, defying the curfew decreed by the plotters and staying in the streets.

The Alpha Group tasked with storming the White House had that name with good reason. They were the best that the KGB had to offer. But after some reconnaissance, deputy commander Mikhail Golovatov had some second thoughts about their task at hand. Thousands of the civilians were themselves armed, and extracting Yeltsin and the others without heavy losses would be impossible. Golovatov was no coward, and he was no novice. He had personally led the Soviet assault on the Lithuanian facilities. He decided to ask his men what they thought.

"We will not go to the White House to kill people," a member of his team told him.

"And we will not lead you there," Golovatov agreed.[620]

Grachev had a quick discussion with the head of the air force, and came to the same conclusion as the Alpha Group. "Let's just sit by our phones," Grachev decided, "and try to avert any stupidities."[621] Thousands of lives were potentially saved because strong men with guns defied their orders, choosing peace over force. Nevertheless, a few lives were still lost. One drunk young man climbed atop an armored personnel carrier and engaged with the gunner, losing his life when he fell headfirst off the vehicle. Another APC gunner fired into the air when he was being besieged, and a ricocheting bullet killed a second man. A third man died when he began to throw rocks at an APC and was shot in response. Yeltsin could hear the fighting outside and hid in a bomb shelter under the White House for the night, hoping for the best.

For hours, Kryuchkov was befuddled as to why Grachev's men weren't clearing the way for the Alpha Group to storm the White House. At 2 a.m. he got the call: the army was not going to do anything. He was on his own. Voices were raised and fingers were pointed, but in the end there was little else that the plotters could do. Soviet citizens woke up to hear the news that Kryuchkov was sending a delegation to visit Gorbachev and check up on his health. Raisa thought this was it, and began wracking her brain as to where her husband could hide. In her panic she suffered a minor stroke, leaving her mute and partially paralyzed for several hours.

When the plotters arrived a furious Gorbachev refused to speak with them, demanding that his phones be restored before he would see them. The message came back that this would take a great deal of time. "I am not in a hurry to go anywhere," he snapped.[622] It took almost two hours, and Gorbachev's first priority was making calls to officials at home and abroad about what had transpired. At 8 p.m. a delegation from the Russian government also arrived at the dacha, and Gorbachev met with them immediately. It was a joyous reunion, as all the men realized how close they had come to calamity—if not personal destruction as well. After tears and some arguing, they agreed on the next steps.

Late that night, the bulk of the plotters were separated from Kryuchkov and flown back to Moscow on their own. Deprived of his security, Kryuchkov was seated in the back of the Russians' plane alongside General Sterligov, an aide to the Russian vice president. After Gorbachev, his family, and the Russian officials got off the flight, Kryuchkov moved to follow them.

"Wait a little bit," Sterligov told him. When Kryuchkov tried to get up again a few minutes later, Sterligov again told him to remain seated.

"I think I understand what is happening," Kryuchkov said.

"You have understood correctly."

Vladimir Kryuchkov, the last functional member of the KGB, was thereupon arrested and, alongside his accomplices, charged with high treason. His KGB successor, Vadim Bakatin, didn't even last one hundred days before dissolving the organization. "The traditions of chekism must be eradicated," Bakatin declared.[623]

Gorbachev returned to work the following day. In the past forty-eight hours, sensing the chaos in the USSR and fearing a resurgence of Soviet aggression, Latvia and Estonia had both taken the opportunity to affirm their sovereignty as independent nations just as their sister Baltic state of Lithuania had done previously. But Gorbachev had a more pressing concern on his desk, far closer to home. He was informed that documents were being destroyed at an intensive rate at the Communist Party's Central Committee building as a mob besieged the structure. Gorbachev immediately signed an order suspending any activity in the building. The good Communists, obedient to authority, dutifully stopped what they were doing and peacefully evacuated the building. It was, indeed, a smart move to protect themselves as well. The mob had unsuccessfully tried to tear down the statue of secret police founder Feliks Dzerzhinsky the night before, so the Russian authorities had removed it via a crane to prevent bedlam from breaking out.

Gorbachev and Yeltsin soon appeared together at the White House, and announced a decree suspending the Communist Party. "At the time of its demise it had fifteen million members," wrote Dobbs. "Not a single one of them put up any resistance."[624] He broke it down even further:

> For seven decades after the 1917 Revolution the Communist Party had deliberately cultivated a sense of mystery as a key to maintaining its own power. Separated from the people they ruled by a wall of ritual, party leaders acquired an aura of omniscience and aloofness. Scarcely anything was known about their private lives or personal political views. No ordinary mortal was allowed to know how these bureaucratic supermen acquired their fine clothes, what kinds of books and films they enjoyed, or how they made a seemingly miraculous appearance on top of Lenin's tomb in Red Square on public holidays. Everything was hidden behind the veiled curtains of the Central Committee building and the limousines that swept through the silent city. As the mysteries were gradually explained, the party's grip over society was automatically undermined. Now the final curtain was ripped away, to reveal a group of frightened and rather unremarkable people, more intent on saving themselves than the regime they served.[625]

A few days later Belarus declared its independence from the Soviet Union, with Azerbaijan following shortly thereafter. One week later, on September 6, 1991, the Soviet Union officially acknowledged Lithuania's independence. Two weeks after that Armenia declared its independence as well. Then, on December 1st, Ukraine held a referendum of its own on the question of national sovereignty: 92% of Ukrainian voters chose to secede from the Soviet Union.

As president of Russia, Yeltsin then worked quietly behind the scenes with the leaders of Ukraine and Belarus as to next steps. Between them the men represented three of the four founding Soviet republics, only missing Armenia, Azerbaijan and Georgia who had then made up the Republic of Transcaucasia. On December 8, 1991, the three men issued the Belovezh Accords which decreed that "the Union of Soviet Socialist Republics is ceasing its existence as a subject of international law and a geopolitical reality." Both Russia and Ukraine, the two most populous Soviet Republics by far, were officially seceding from the USSR.

It was only hours later that Stanislav Shushkevich, president of Belarus, got on the phone with Gorbachev. In response to Gorbachev's questions, he confessed to two things. First, the men had called President George H. W. Bush way before they had called him, and second, the Belovezh Accords were already signed and binding. Mikhail Gorbachev had been the youngest leader of the Soviet Union since Stalin when he assumed office in 1985. By 1991 he was already an old man from another time.

On Christmas Day, 1991, Mikhail Gorbachev resigned his position as president of the Soviet Union. At 7:35 p.m., the hammer and sickle flag of the USSR was permanently lowered from the Kremlin. The following day, the Union of Soviet Socialist Republics—now a government without a country—officially voted itself out of existence.

Cynics like to lie and call themselves realists. Hoping for positive outcomes—and they happen often—can thus be dismissed as being "naïve" or "utopian." In 1981 the overwhelming expert consensus was one of détente, the premise that the world would be split between a communist USSR and a democratic USA for decades to come. Realpolitik—yet another foreign word imported to signal sophistication—included the premise that the corrupt and decaying USSR wasn't going anywhere. Few of the experts ever admitted that they were wrong, and had been wrong the entire time, that they were the ones who had been unrealistically naïve and dystopian. As historian Archie Brown observed, "Politicians and analysts were finding a variety of reasons why the previously impossible [...] had either been inevitable all along or had needed only additional American military and economic pressure on Moscow to make it happen."[626]

In politics, the argument is that power never cedes power without massive war and bloodshed—except in those cases when it does, in which case those in power never had a choice and the whole thing was inevitable the whole time. But those in power always have some kind of choice. That is the definition of power, having the ability to make choices.

Within ten years, the Soviet Union went from being a perpetual world-dominating superpower to literal nonexistence, and is now becoming a forgotten chapter of world history, more of a kitschy joke than a cautionary tale. But Ayn Rand was right: this was no laughing matter. Millions of people were trapped for decades in countries where human life was nothing, less than nothing, and they knew it. They lived in constant terror from morning til night—and at night they were waiting for the doorbell to ring, in countries where there was no law or any rights of any kind, where basic necessities like food and housing were a constant struggle for everyone, and that they were absolutely forbidden to leave. Did they all live happily ever after when the Soviet Union dissolved? Of course not. Utopias don't exist—but progress does, and so do victories by good over evil. They happen all the time, both personally and politically.

The foes of liberty are many and they are powerful—but they are not particularly impressive. They will do everything within their ability to convince others that their might is eternal, that battle against them is pointless and doomed to fail. This is just another one of their many lies. It is said that they will never give up. Yet does wanting power over others mean that they will necessarily get it, and get it easily? Does the fact that they supposedly will never give up somehow imply that their opponents should—or does it imply the opposite? Evil people surrender all the time. At a certain point the costs—in every sense of the term—simply become too high. They are not all-knowing—far from it. They are often not even particularly bright. They are not all-powerful. They are men and women, far closer to snakes than they are to gods. They can, will, and have been defeated many, many times.

It is possible that those of us who fight for the dignity of mankind will lose our fight. It is not possible that we must lose our fight.

That is the white pill.

Notes

[1] Barbara Branden, *The Passion of Ayn Rand* (New York: Doubleday, 1986), p. 43
[2] Ayn Rand, *Letters of Ayn Rand* (New York: Dutton, 1995), p. 637
[3] Ayn Rand, *The Return of the Primitive* (New York: Meridian, 1999), p. 125
[4] https://www.youtube.com/watch?v=UwyMdteppoA
[5] http://www.theatlasphere.com/metablog/869.php
[6] Branden, *The Passion of Ayn Rand*, p. 81
[7] https://www.audible.com/pd/We-the-Living-Audiobook/B002V1CN3S
[8] https://letters.aynrandarchives.org/document/42006
[9] Granville Hicks, *Part of the Truth* (New York: Harcourt, Brace & World, 1965), p. 3
[10] Hicks, *Part of the Truth*, p. 258
[11] Their parallel paths culminated when he denounced her 1957 masterwork *Atlas Shrugged* in the *New York Times,* claiming "it seems clear that the book is written out of hate."
[12] https://en.wikipedia.org/wiki/Anthem_(novella)
[13] http://aynrandlexicon.com/ayn-rand-works/the-fountainhead.html
[14] Ayn Rand, *The Fountainhead* (New York: Bobbs-Merrill, 1943), p. 691
[15] Rand, *Letters of Ayn Rand*, p. 75
[16] Branden, *The Passion of Ayn Rand*, p. 184
[17] https://archive.lib.msu.edu/DMC/AmRad/screenguideamericans.pdf
[18] Ayn Rand, *Journals of Ayn Rand* (New York: Dutton, 1997), p. 382
[19] ibid
[20] Robert Mayhew, *Ayn Rand and* Song of Russia (Lanham: Scarecrow Press, 2005), p. 97
[21] William Wright, *Lillian Hellman* (New York: Simon & Schuster, 1986), p. 213
[22] Mayhew, *Ayn Rand and* Song of Russia, p. 33
[23] Mayhew, *Ayn Rand and* Song of Russia, p. 34
[24] Mayhew, *Ayn Rand and* Song of Russia, p. 27
[25] http://www.enterstageright.com/archive/articles/0997huac.htm
[26] https://www.mcgill.ca/oss/article/history/how-dynamite-spawned-nobel-prizes
[27] https://archive.org/stream/al_Johann_Most_Action_as_Propaganda_a4/

Johann_Most__Action_as_Propaganda_a4_djvu.txt
[28] Charles Robert Plunkett, "Dynamite!,"*Mother Earth*, July 1914, p. 164
[29] Philip S. Foner, *The Autobiographies of the Haymarket Martyrs* (New York: Monad, 1977), p. 53
[30] Michael J. Schaack, *Anarchy and Anarchists* (Chicago: Schulte, 1889), p. 273
[31] Schaack, *Anarchy and Anarchists*, p. 631
[32] ibid
[33] Schaack, *Anarchy and Anarchists*, p. 634
[34] Emma Goldman, *Living My Life* (New York: Knopf, 1931), p. 9
[35] *Mother Earth*, May 1907
[36] Goldman, *Living My Life*, p. 42
[37] Goldman, *Living My Life*, p. 86
[38] https://www.britannica.com/event/Homestead-Strike
[39] https://www.history.com/topics/industrial-revolution/homestead-strike
[40] https://www.pbs.org/wgbh/americanexperience/features/carnegie-strike-homestead-mill/
[41] *New York Times*, July 25, 1892, p. 4
[42] Paul Avrich, *Sasha and Emma* (Cambridge: Belknap, 2012), p. 87
[43] Goldman, *Living My Life*, p.105
[44] Solon Lauer, *Mark Hanna: A Sketch from Life and Other Essays* (Cleveland: Nike, 1901), p. v
[45] *Leavenworth Times*, September 11, 1901, p. 8
[46] *Goodland Republic*, September 13, 1901, p. 4
[47] *Morning Press*, September 11, 1901, p. 1
[48] ibid
[49] Alexander Berkman, *Prison Memoirs of an Anarchist* (New York: Mother Earth, 1912), p. 417
[50] https://www.presidency.ucsb.edu/documents/first-annual-message-16
[51] Arthur Herman, *1917* (New York: HarperCollins, 2017), p. 145
[52] Victor Sebestyen, *Lenin* (New York: Pantheon, 2017), p. 84
[53] https://www.theatlantic.com/magazine/archive/1954/10/when-lenin-returned/303867/
[54] https://www.smithsonianmag.com/travel/vladimir-lenin-return-journey-russia-changed-world-forever-180962127/
[55] Alexander Berkman, *The "Anti-Climax"* (Berlin: Berkman, 1925), p. 9
[56] Wendy Z. Goldman, *Women, the State & Revolution* (New York: Cambridge, 1993), p.1
[57] Goldman, *Women, the State & Revolution*, p. 9
[58] Goldman, *Women, the State & Revolution*, p. 10
[59] Goldman, *Women, the State & Revolution*, p. 231
[60] George S. N. Luckyj, *Literary Politics in the Soviet Ukraine* (Durham: Duke, 1990), p. 49
[61] Gregory Maximoff, *The Guillotine at Work* (Chicago: Berkman Fund, 1940), p. 5
[62] Maximoff, *The Guillotine at Work*, p. 36
[63] https://alphahistory.com/russianrevolution/cheka/
[64] *Novaya Zhizn*, July 14, 1918
[65] Louis Rapoport, *Stalin's War Against the Jews* (New York: Free Press, 1990), p. 31
[66] Sebestyen, *Lenin*, p. 37

[67] Sebestyen, *Lenin*, p. 379
[68] Maximoff, *The Guillotine at Work*, p.42
[69] Simon Sebag Montefiore, *Stalin: The Court of the Red Tsar* (London: Weidenfeld & Nicolson, 2003), p. 85
[70] Stephane Courtois, *The Black Book of Communism* (Cambridge: Harvard, 1999), p. 70
[71] *Krasnaya Gazeta*, September 1, 1918
[72] Maximoff, *The Guillotine at Work*, p. 75
[73] Maximoff, *The Guillotine at Work*, p. 76
[74] Maximoff, *The Guillotine at Work*, p. 78
[75] Maximoff, *The Guillotine at Work*, p. 56
[76] https://g.co/arts/tBSSbwvd1RV95cLr7
[77] Alexander Berkman, *The Bolshevik Myth* (New York: Boni & Liveright, 1925), p. 28
[78] Berkman, *The "Anti-Climax"*, p. 9
[79] Paul Avrich, *The Russian Anarchists* (Princeton: Princeton, 1967), p. 189
[80] Berkman, *The Bolshevik Myth*, p. 90
[81] Emme Goldman, *My Disillusionment in Russia* (New York: Doubleday, 1923), p. 50
[82] Emma Goldman, *My Further Disillusionment in Russia* (New York: Doubleday, 1924), p. 8
[83] Goldman, *My Further Disillusionment in Russia*, p. 9
[84] Maximoff, *The Guillotine at Work*, p. 122
[85] *Pravda*, September 20, 1918
[86] Berkman, *The Bolshevik Myth*, p. 148
[87] Berkman, *The Bolshevik Myth*, p. 121
[88] Berkman, *The Bolshevik Myth*, p. 172
[89] Berkman, *The "Anti-Climax"*, p. 13
[90] https://www.imdb.com/title/tt0028012/
[91] https://alphahistory.com/russianrevolution/kronstadt-sailors-15-point-manifesto-1921/
[92] Avrich, *Kronstadt 1921*, p. 146
[93] Paul Avrich, *Kronstadt 1921* (Princeton: Princeton, 1970), p. 211
[94] Avrich, *Kronstadt 1921*, p. 296
[95] Berkman, *The Bolshevik Myth*, p. 302
[96] Micheline R. Ishay, *The Human Rights Reader* (New York: Routledge, 2012), p. 248
[97] Berkman, *The Bolshevik Myth*, p. 303
[98] Avrich, *Kronstadt 1921*, p. 215
[99] Avrich, *Kronstadt 1921*, p. 227
[100] Maximoff, *The Guillotine at Work*, p. 42
[101] Maximoff, *The Guillotine at Work*, p. 188
[102] Avrich, *Kronstadt 1921*, p. 226
[103] Goldman, *My Disillusionment in Russia*, p. xv
[104] Goldman, *My Disillusionment in Russia*, p. xvii
[105] Goldman, *My Disillusionment in Russia*, p. xviii
[106] Goldman, *My Further Disillusionment in Russia*, p. 172
[107] Goldman, *My Disillusionment in Russia*, p. xvi
[108] Goldman, *My Disillusionment in Russia*, p. xiv
[109] Maximoff, *The Guillotine at Work*, p. 222
[110] ibid
[111] Goldman, *Living My Life*, p. 964

[112] Avrich, *Sasha and Emma*, p. 326
[113] Maximoff, *The Guillotine at Work*, p. 204
[114] Maximoff, *The Guillotine at Work*, p. 282
[115] https://hoover.blogs.archives.gov/2020/04/08/hoover-and-20th-century-presidents-franklin-roosevelt/
[116] https://en.wikipedia.org/wiki/Russian_famine_of_1891—1892
[117] Sebestyen, *Lenin*, p. 472
[118] Sebestyen, *Lenin*, p. 469
[119] Sebestyen, *Lenin*, p. 471
[120] Sebestyen, *Lenin*, p. 489
[121] Roy Medvedev, *Let History Judge* (New York: Columbia, 1989), p. 31
[122] Sheila Fitzpatrick, *Everyday Stalinism* (New York: Oxford, 1999), p. 47
[123] Fitzpatrick, *Everyday Stalinism*, p. 208
[124] Fitzpatrick, *Everyday Stalinism*, p. 122
[125] https://en.wikipedia.org/wiki/Soviet_famine_of_1930–1933
[126] Anne Applebaum, *Red Famine* (New York: Doubleday, 2017), p. 216
[127] Fitzpatrick, *Everyday Stalinism*, p. 120
[128] S.J. Taylor, *Stalin's Apologist* (New York: Oxford, 1990), p. 211
[129] Applebaum, *Red Famine*, p. 267
[130] Applebaum, *Red Famine*, p. 270
[131] Applebaum, *Red Famine*, p. 293
[132] Robert Conquest, *Reflections on a Ravaged Century* (New York: Norton, 2000), p. 94
[133] Robert Conquest, *The Harvest of Sorrow* (New York: Oxford, 1986), p. 231
[134] Anna Reid, *Borderland* (Boulder: Westview, 1999), p. 123
[135] Fitzpatrick, *Everyday Stalinism*, p. 45
[136] Eugene Lyons, *Assignment in Utopia* (New York: Harcourt Brace, 1937), p. 636
[137] Walter Duranty, *Duranty Reports Russia* (New York: Viking, 1934), p. 90
[138] Duranty, *Duranty Reports Russia*, p. 101
[139] Duranty, *Duranty Reports Russia*, p. 102
[140] Duranty, *Duranty Reports Russia*, p. 118
[141] Duranty, *Duranty Reports Russia*, p. 120
[142] Duranty, *Duranty Reports Russia*, p. 225
[143] Laurel Leff, *Buried by the Times* (New York: Cambridge, 2012)
[144] Duranty, *Duranty Reports Russia*, p. 275
[145] Duranty, *Duranty Reports Russia*, p. 288
[146] Duranty, *Duranty Reports Russia*, p. 308
[147] Duranty, *Duranty Reports Russia*, p. 318
[148] Duranty, *Duranty Reports Russia*, p. 339
[149] Duranty, *Duranty Reports Russia*, p. 336
[150] Duranty, *Duranty Reports Russia*, p. 284
[151] Applebaum, *Red Famine*, p. 374
[152] https://www.nytimes.com/1933/03/31/archives/russians-hungry-but-not-starving-deaths-from-diseases-due-to.html
[153] Applebaum, *Red Famine*, p. 358
[154] Applebaum, *Red Famine*, p. 360
[155] Taylor, *Stalin's Apologist*, p. 205
[156] Taylor, *Stalin's Apologist*, p. 206
[157] Taylor, *Stalin's Apologist*, p. 353

[158] https://www.census.gov/library/publications/1958/demo/p60-030.html
[159] Medvedev, *Let History Judge*, p. 866
[160] Upton Sinclair, *Terror in Russia?* (New York: Rand School, 1938), p. 41
[161] Eugene Lyons, *Moscow Carrousel* (New York: Knopf, 1935), p. 178
[162] https://goaravetisyan.ru/en/stalinskaya-teoriya-narastaniya-klassovoi-borby-klyuchevoi/
[163] Alexander Orlov, *The Secret History of Stalin's Crimes* (London: Jarrolds, 1954), p. 67
[164] John Dewey, *Not Guilty* (New York: Harper, 1938), p. 286
[165] Orlov, *The Secret History of Stalin's Crimes*, p. 193
[166] Orlov, *The Secret History of Stalin's Crimes*, p. 194
[167] Orlov, *The Secret History of Stalin's Crimes*, p. 110
[168] Lyons, *The Red Decade*, p. 236
[169] Fitzpatrick, *Everyday Stalinism*, p. 19
[170] Montefiore, *Stalin: The Court of the Red Tsar*, p. 249
[171] Conquest, *The Great Terror*, p. 297
[172] Maximoff, *The Guillotine at Work*, p. 304
[173] Conquest, *The Great Terror*, p. 295
[174] Rosemary Sullivan, *Stalin's Daughter* (New York: HarperCollins, 2015), p. 161
[175] Fitzpatrick, *Everyday Stalinism*, p. 208
[176] Montefiore, *Stalin: The Court of the Red Tsar*, p. 125
[177] Dewey, *Not Guilty*, p. 283
[178] Stuart Kahan, *The Wolf of the Kremlin* (New York: Morrow, 1987), p. 294
[179] Fitzpatrick, *Everyday Stalinism*, p. 119
[180] Dewey, *Not Guilty*, p. 281
[181] https://www.thedailybeast.com/when-stalin-met-lady-macbeth
[182] Elinor Lipper, *Eleven Years in Soviet Prison Camps* (Chicago: Regnery, 1951), p. 19
[183] Orlov, *The Secret History of Stalin's Crimes*, p. 220
[184] Lipper, *Eleven Years in Soviet Prison Camps*, p. 37
[185] Anne Applebaum, *Gulag* (New York: Doubleday, 2003), p. 96
[186] Orlov, *The Secret History of Stalin's Crimes*, p. 239
[187] https://tarnmoor.com/2012/11/18/the-general-who-came-back-from-the-dead/amp/
[188] Lipper, *Eleven Years in Soviet Prison Camps*, p. 48
[189] Rapoport, *Stalin's War Against the Jews*, p. 77
[190] Rapoport, *Stalin's War Against the Jews*, p. 76
[191] Applebaum, *Gulag*, p. 138
[192] Robert Gellately, *The Specter of Genocide* (New York: Cambridge, 2003), p. 232
[193] Applebaum, *Gulag*, p. 128
[194] Rapoport, *Stalin's War Against the Jews*, p. 54
[195] Applebaum, *Gulag*, p. 123
[196] Conquest, *The Great Terror*, p. 83
[197] Applebaum, *Gulag*, p. 124
[198] Rapoport, *Stalin's War Against the Jews*, p. 46
[199] James W. Ford, *The Negroes in a Soviet America* (New York: Workers Library, 1935), p. 5
[200] Ford, *The Negroes in a Soviet America*, p. 12
[201] Ford, *The Negroes in a Soviet America*, p. 28
[202] Applebaum, *Gulag*, p. 123

[203] Fitzpatrick, *Everyday Stalinism*, p. 193
[204] https://www.marxists.org/archive/khrushchev/1956/02/24.htm
[205] Hannah Arendt, *The Origins of Totalitarianism* (New York: Meridian, 1958), p. 323
[206] Montefiore, *Stalin: The Court of the Red Tsar*, p. 222
[207] Fitzpatrick, *Everyday Stalinism*, p. 206
[208] Lipper, *Eleven Years in Soviet Prison Camps*, p. 49
[209] Lipper, *Eleven Years in Soviet Prison Camps*, p. 34
[210] Applebaum, *Gulag*, p. 127
[211] Lipper, *Eleven Years in Soviet Prison Camps*, p. 8
[212] The First Circle, p. 545
[213] Lipper, *Eleven Years in Soviet Prison Camps*, p. 18
[214] Sullivan, *Stalin's Daughter*, p. 198
[215] Applebaum, *Gulag*, p. 150
[216] ibid
[217] Orlov, *The Secret History of Stalin's Crimes*, p. 87
[218] Dewey, *Not Guilty*, p. 363
[219] Conquest, *The Great Terror*, p. 402
[220] Applebaum, *Gulag*, p. 137
[221] Montefiore, *Stalin: The Court of the Red Tsar*, p. 252
[222] Dewey, *Not Guilty*, p. 247
[223] Orlov, *The Secret History of Stalin's Crimes*, p. 267
[224] Rapoport, *Stalin's War Against the Jews*, p. 52
[225] Orlov, *The Secret History of Stalin's Crimes*, p. 269
[226] https://apnews.com/article/7358d0af4048ba6df87f10bdb9782dac
[227] https://peashooter85.tumblr.com/post/122468070432/general-rokossovskys-steel-teeth-one-of-the
[228] Lipper, *Eleven Years in Soviet Prison Camps*, p. 23
[229] Orlov, *The Secret History of Stalin's Crimes*, p. 157
[230] Orlando Figes, *The Whisperers* (New York: Metropolitan, 2007), p. 248
[231] Conquest, *The Great Terror*, p. 127
[232] Orlov, *The Secret History of Stalin's Crimes*, p. 54
[233] https://pbs.twimg.com/media/ERtzOhQW4AEK-1n?format=jpg
[234] Maximoff, *The Guillotine at Work*, p. 306
[235] Gustav Herling, *A World Apart* (New York: Arbor House, 1986), p. 65
[236] Lipper, *Eleven Years in Soviet Prison Camps*, p. 40
[237] Medvedev, *Let History Judge*, p. 490
[238] Montefiore, *Stalin: The Court of the Red Tsar*, p. 252
[239] Maximoff, *The Guillotine at Work*, p. 245
[240] Medvedev, *Let History Judge*, p. 490
[241] https://www.nytimes.com/2017/08/12/opinion/why-women-had-better-sex-under-socialism.html
[242] Hicks, *Part of the Truth,* p. 145
[243] https://www.adamsmith.org/blog/orwell-and-the-left
[244] https://dorothyparker.com/2021/08/1966-radio-interview.html
[245] https://www.commentary.org/articles/lionel-trilling/young-in-the-thirties/
[246] Eugene Lyons, *The Red Decade* (New York: Bobbs-Merrill, 1941), p. 242
[247] Lyons, *The Red Decade*, p. 245

[248] https://www.newstatesman.com/culture/books/2021/12/hg-wells-claire-tomalin-review
[249] Conquest, *Reflections on a Ravaged Century*, p. 136
[250] Conquest, *Reflections on a Ravaged Century*, p. 126
[251] Rand, *Journals of Ayn Rand*, p. 113
[252] Robert Conquest, *The Great Terror* (New York: Oxford, 1990), p. 474
[253] Lyons, *The Red Decade*, p. 242
[254] Lyons, *The Red Decade*, p. 243
[255] Rapoport, *Stalin's War Against the Jews*, p. 112
[256] Sullivan, *Stalin's Daughter*, p. 84
[257] Conquest, *The Great Terror*, p. 274
[258] Conquest, *Reflections on a Ravaged Century*, p. 100
[259] S. S. Masloff, *Russia After Four Years of Revolution* (London: P. S. King, 1923), p. 80
[260] Lipper, *Eleven Years in Soviet Prison Camps*, p. 71
[261] Orlov, *The Secret History of Stalin's Crimes*, p. 226
[262] Orlov, *The Secret History of Stalin's Crimes*, p. 227
[263] Herling, *A World Apart*, p. 4
[264] Lyons, *Moscow Carrousel*, p. 86
[265] Fitzpatrick, *Everyday Stalinism*, p. 204
[266] https://www.marxists.org/archive/marx/works/1843/critique-hpr/intro.htm
[267] Fitzpatrick, *Everyday Stalinism*, p. 128
[268] https://slate.com/news-and-politics/2008/10/how-fdr-saved-captialism-in-eight-days.html
[269] Upton Sinclair, *I, Candidate for Governor* (Los Angeles: End Poverty League, 1935), p. 6
[270] Sinclair, *I, Candidate for Governor*, p. 125
[271] Greg Mitchell, *The Campaign of the Century* (New York: Random House, 1992), p. 98
[272] Mitchell, *The Campaign of the Century*, p. 121
[273] Mitchell, *The Campaign of the Century*, p. 419
[274] Sinclair, *I, Candidate for Governor*, p. 200
[275] Sinclair, *I, Candidate for Governor*, p. 58
[276] Sinclair, *Terror in Russia?*, p. 23
[277] Sinclair, *Terror in Russia?*, p. 10
[278] Sinclair, *Terror in Russia?*, p. 56
[279] Sinclair, *Terror in Russia?*, p. 11
[280] Sinclair, *Terror in Russia?*, p. 13
[281] Sinclair, *Terror in Russia?*, p. 20
[282] Sinclair, *Terror in Russia?*, p. 21
[283] Sinclair, *Terror in Russia?*, p. 53
[284] Sinclair, *Terror in Russia?*, p. 57
[285] Sinclair, *Terror in Russia?*, p. 60
[286] Conquest, *The Great Terror*, p. 486
[287] Eugene D. Genovese, "The Question," *Dissent* magazine, Summer 1994, p. 371
[288] Sinclair, *Terror in Russia?*, p. 62
[289] Sinclair, *Terror in Russia?*, p. 56
[290] Sinclair, *Terror in Russia?*, p. 63
[291] Dewey, *Not Guilty*, p. 361
[292] Arendt, *The Origins of Totalitarianism*, p. 367

[293] Kenneth Lloyd Billingsley, *Hollywood Party* (Rocklin: Forum, 1998), p. 74
[294] https://www.thebalance.com/unemployment-rate-by-year-3305506
[295] Richard Moe, *Roosevelt's Second Act* (New York: Oxford, 2013), p. 199
[296] Moe, *Roosevelt's Second Act*, p. 230
[297] http://content.time.com/time/subscriber/article/0,33009,829748,00.html
[298] https://time.com/5937507/roald-dahl-anti-semitism/
[299] https://www.atlassociety.org/post/howard-roark
[300] Patricia Neal, *As I Am* (New York: Simon and Schuster, 1988), p. 286
[301] John C. Culver, *American Dreamer* (New York: Norton, 2000), p. 343
[302] https://constitutioncenter.org/interactive-constitution/blog/looking-back-at-the-day-fdr-died
[303] Lyons, *Moscow Carrousel*, p. 229
[304] Applebaum, *Gulag*, p. xix
[305] John P. Diggins, *Up From Communism* (New York: Harper & Row, 1975), p. 435
[306] Henry Wallace, *Soviet Asia Mission* (New York: Reynal & Hitchcock, 1946), p. 20
[307] Wallace, *Soviet Asia Mission*, p. 34
[308] Wallace, *Soviet Asia Mission*, p. 72
[309] Wallace, *Soviet Asia Mission*, p. 84
[310] Wallace, *Soviet Asia Mission*, p. 117
[311] https://tengrinews.kz/kazakhstan_news/56-rasstrelyannyih-pensioner-povedal-strashnoy-nahodke-403400/
[312] Wallace, *Soviet Asia Mission*, p. 36
[313] https://www.wilsoncenter.org/publication/three-days-auschwitz-without-gas-chambers-henry-wallaces-visit-to-magadan-1944
[314] https://www.wilsoncenter.org/publication/three-days-auschwitz-without-gas-chambers-henry-wallaces-visit-to-magadan-1944
[315] Wallace, *Soviet Asia Mission*, p. 92
[316] Wallace, *Soviet Asia Mission*, p. 137
[317] Wallace, *Soviet Asia Mission*, p. 142
[318] Wallace, *Soviet Asia Mission*, p. 212
[319] Wallace, *Soviet Asia Mission*, p. 240
[320] Wallace, *Soviet Asia Mission*, p. 205
[321] Conquest, *Reflections on a Ravaged Century*, p. 136
[322] Wallace, *Soviet Asia Mission*, p. 210
[323] Wallace, *Soviet Asia Mission*, p. 93
[324] https://www.rbth.com/history/327846-henry-wallace-magadan-kolyma-collusion
[325] Applebaum, *Gulag*, p. xvii
[326] Applebaum, *Gulag*, p. xvi
[327] Applebaum, *Gulag*, p. 20
[328] Applebaum, *Gulag*, p. 22
[329] Applebaum, *Gulag*, p. 24
[330] Applebaum, *Gulag*, p. 161
[331] Applebaum, *Gulag*, p. 164
[332] Applebaum, *Gulag*, p. 166
[333] Applebaum, *Gulag*, p. 169
[334] Applebaum, *Gulag*, p. 170
[335] Lipper, *Eleven Years in Soviet Prison Camps*, p. 148
[336] Applebaum, *Gulag*, p. 171

[337] Lipper, *Eleven Years in Soviet Prison Camps*, p. 95
[338] https://www.wilsoncenter.org/publication/three-days-auschwitz-without-gas-chambers-henry-wallaces-visit-to-magadan-1944#_ftn11
[339] Applebaum, *Gulag*, p. 36
[340] Applebaum, *Gulag*, p. 94
[341] Conquest, *The Great Terror*, p. 326
[342] Conquest, *The Great Terror*, p. 327
[343] Conquest, *The Great Terror*, p. 320
[344] Applebaum, *Gulag*, p. 237
[345] Applebaum, *Gulag*, p. 238
[346] Applebaum, *Gulag*, p. 239
[347] Applebaum, *Gulag*, p. 241
[348] Applebaum, *Gulag*, p. 209
[349] Applebaum, *Gulag*, p. 305
[350] Applebaum, *Gulag*, p. 306
[351] Applebaum, *Gulag*, p. 214
[352] Lipper, *Eleven Years in Soviet Prison Camps*, p. 90
[353] Conquest, *The Great Terror*, p. 316
[354] Lev Razgon, *True Stories* (London: Souvenir, 1998), p. 186
[355] Lipper, *Eleven Years in Soviet Prison Camps*, p. 278
[356] Applebaum, *Gulag*, p. 97
[357] Applebaum, *Gulag*, p. 304
[358] Herling, *A World Apart*, p. 129
[359] Lipper, *Eleven Years in Soviet Prison Camps*, p. 259
[360] Applebaum, *Gulag*, p. 217
[361] Lipper, *Eleven Years in Soviet Prison Camps*, p. 108
[362] Applebaum, *Gulag*, p. 251
[363] https://philnel.com/2011/07/30/cjrk_b/
[364] https://prospect.org/civil-rights/albert-einstein-racist/
[365] Peter Biskind, *My Lunches with Orson* (New York: Metropolitan, 2013), p. 66
[366] https://www.wilsoncenter.org/publication/three-days-auschwitz-without-gas-chambers-henry-wallaces-visit-to-magadan-1944#_ftn37
[367] Lipper, *Eleven Years in Soviet Prison Camps*, p. 267
[368] Lipper, *Eleven Years in Soviet Prison Camps*, p. 112
[369] https://delong.typepad.com/sdj/2013/02/henry-a-wallace-1952-on-the-ruthless-nature-of-communism-cold-war-era-god-that-failed-weblogging.html
[370] Michael Dobbs, *Down with Big Brother* (New York: Knopf, 1997), p. 8
[371] https://www.nationalchurchillmuseum.org/sinews-of-peace-iron-curtain-speech.html
[372] Montefiore, *Stalin: The Court of the Red Tsar*, p. 245
[373] https://www.washingtonpost.com/wp-dyn/content/article/2005/12/17/AR2005121700018.html
[374] https://digitalarchive.wilsoncenter.org/document/111309
[375] Montefiore, *Stalin: The Court of the Red Tsar*, p. 40
[376] Montefiore, *Stalin: The Court of the Red Tsar*, p. 67
[377] Rapoport, *Stalin's War Against the Jews*, p. 56
[378] Montefiore, *Stalin: The Court of the Red Tsar*, p. 518
[379] Montefiore, *Stalin: The Court of the Red Tsar*, p. 517

[380] Montefiore, *Stalin: The Court of the Red Tsar*, p. 519
[381] Michael Jones, *After Hitler* (London: John Murray, 2015), p. 45
[382] Sullivan, *Stalin's Daughter*, p. 93
[383] Charles E. Bohlen, *Witness to History 1929-1969* (New York: Norton, 1973), p. 203
[384] Rapoport, *Stalin's War Against the Jews*, p. 58
[385] Rapoport, *Stalin's War Against the Jews*, p. 58
[386] Rapoport, *Stalin's War Against the Jews*, p. 60
[387] Rapoport, *Stalin's War Against the Jews*, p. 208
[388] Sullivan, *Stalin's Daughter*, p. 121
[389] Rapoport, *Stalin's War Against the Jews*, p. 64
[390] Rapoport, *Stalin's War Against the Jews*, p. 160
[391] Rapoport, *Stalin's War Against the Jews*, p. 104
[392] Rapoport, *Stalin's War Against the Jews*, p. 105
[393] https://jwa.org/encyclopedia/article/stern-shtern-lina-solomonova
[394] Rapoport, *Stalin's War Against the Jews*, p. 112
[395] Rapoport, *Stalin's War Against the Jews*, p. 102
[396] Rapoport, *Stalin's War Against the Jews*, p. 148
[397] Gareth Jones, *Experiences in Russia—1931* (Pittsburgh: Alton, 1932), p. 28
[398] Vaksberg, *Toxic Politics*, p. 77
[399] Arkadi Vaksberg, *Toxic Politics* (Santa Barbara: Praeger, 2011), p. 80
[400] Rapoport, *Stalin's War Against the Jews*, p. 149
[401] Rapoport, *Stalin's War Against the Jews*, p. 152
[402] Rapoport, *Stalin's War Against the Jews*, p. 162
[403] Rapoport, *Stalin's War Against the Jews*, p. 170
[404] Rapoport, *Stalin's War Against the Jews*, p. 178
[405] Rapoport, *Stalin's War Against the Jews*, p. 185
[406] Rapoport, *Stalin's War Against the Jews*, p. 186
[407] Rapoport, *Stalin's War Against the Jews*, p. 213
[408] Sullivan, *Stalin's Daughter*, p. 184
[409] Sullivan, *Stalin's Daughter*, p. 186
[410] Sullivan, *Stalin's Daughter*, p. 194
[411] Rapoport, *Stalin's War Against the Jews*, p. 218
[412] Rapoport, *Stalin's War Against the Jews*, p. 219
[413] James Burnham, *The Struggle for the World* (New York: John Day, 1947), p. 71
[414] https://www.nytimes.com/1992/09/24/world/germans-find-mass-graves-at-an-ex-soviet-camp.html
[415] Frederick Taylor, *The Berlin Wall* (New York: HarperCollins, 2007), p. 162
[416] Taylor, *The Berlin Wall*, p. 262
[417] Taylor, *The Berlin Wall*, p. 356
[418] Dobbs, *Down with Big Brother*, p. 281
[419] Dobbs, *Down with Big Brother*, p. 280
[420] *Stasiland*, p. 22
[421] Taylor, *The Berlin Wall*, p. 198
[422] https://archive.nytimes.com/www.nytimes.com/books/first/k/koehler-stasi.html?_r=2
[423] Anna Funder, *Stasiland* (London: Granta, 2003), p. 201
[424] Funder, *Stasiland*, p. 200
[425] Timothy Garton Ash, *The File* (New York: Vintage, 1998), p. 21

[426] Garton Ash, *The File*, p. 222
[427] Funder, *Stasiland*, p. 191
[428] https://www.washingtonpost.com/archive/politics/1993/02/28/e-germany-ran-antisemitic-campaign-in-west-in-60s/418db6f8-fc45-4504-94c0-95184f8f11a6/
[429] https://hubertus-knabe.de/der-blick-nach-rechts/
[430] Funder, *Stasiland*, p. 169
[431] Timothy Garton Ash, *We the People* (London: Granta, 1990), p. 70
[432] https://www.spiegel.de/international/germany/second-class-victims-east-german-children-s-home-prisoners-ignored-a-747216.html
[433] Jaromir Navratil, *The Prague Spring 1968* (Budapest: CEU, 1998), p. 234
[434] Daniel Kelly, James Burnham and the Struggle for the World (Wilmington:ISI, 2002), p. 306
[435] https://web.archive.org/web/20110501052925/
http://www.hoover.org/publications/hoover-digest/article/7398
[436] Ronald Reagan, *An American Life* (New York: Simon & Schuster, 1992), p. 72
[437] Billingsley, *Hollywood Party,* p. 242
[438] Arthur Miller, *Timebends* (New York: Penguin, 1995), p. 86
[439] Reagan, *An American Life*, p. 137
[440] https://www.americanrhetoric.com/speeches/ronaldreaganatimeforchoosing.htm
[441] Ayn Rand, "Check Your Premises," *The Objectivist Newsletter*, Dec. 1964
[442] Archie Brown, *The Human Factor* (New York: Oxford, 2020), p. 66
[443] Richard Aldous, *Reagan and Thatcher* (New York: Norton, 2012), p. 22
[444] Margaret Thatcher, *The Path to Power* (New York: HarperCollins, 1995), p. 144
[445] Thatcher, *The Path to Power*, p. 182
[446] Spiro Agnew, *Go Quietly…Or Else* (New York: Morrow, 1980), p. 189
[447] G. Gordon Liddy, *Will* (New York: St. Martin's, 1991), p. 353
[448] Barry Goldwater, *Goldwater* (New York: Doubleday, 1988), p. 280
[449] https://wikileaks.org/plusd/cables/1975LONDON02415_b.html
#efmAB5ACiAhZAlkAnDBGUBHbBWABfpBq7BsCB06
[450] Reagan, *An American Life*, p. 88
[451] Reagan, *An American Life*, p. 207
[452] https://www.margaretthatcher.org/document/103864
[453] https://web.archive.org/web/20170630070844/
http://www.gallup.com/poll/110548/gallup-presidential-election-trialheat-trends-19362004.aspx#4
[454] https://www.youtube.com/watch?v=a6L6kelnvwg
[455] Malcolm Rifkind, *Power and Pragmatism* (London: Biteback, 2016), p. xii
[456] https://www.usatoday.com/story/news/world/2013/04/08/thatcher-reagan-political-soulmates/2063671/
[457] Charles Moore, *Margaret Thatcher: The Authorized Biography, Vol. 1* (New York: Knopf, 2013), p. 547
[458] https://libertarianreality.wordpress.com/2014/12/23/ayn-rand-on-the-phil-donahue-show-1979-transcript/
[459] Brown, *The Human Factor*, p. 103
[460] Aldous, *Reagan and Thatcher*, p. 84
[461] Moore, *Margaret Thatcher: The Authorized Biography, Vol. 1*, p. 713
[462] https://www.margaretthatcher.org/document/108383
[463] Moore, *Margaret Thatcher: The Authorized Biography, Vol. 1*, p. 737

[464] George Shultz, *Turmoil and Triumph* (New York: Scribner's, 1993), p. 152
[465] Aldous, *Reagan and Thatcher*, p. 159
[466] Brown, *The Human Factor*, p. 11
[467] https://news.google.com/newspapers?nid=1946&dat=19831221&id=-T0lAAAAIBAJ&sjid=jaUFAAAAIBAJ&pg=1079,37495
[468] https://www.pbs.org/newshour/spc/debatingourdestiny/interviews/mondale.html
[469] https://www.nytimes.com/1982/04/21/world/reagan-again-asks-to-meet-brezhnev.html
[470] Margaret Thatcher, *The Downing Street Years* (New York: HarperCollins, 1993), p. 458
[471] Brown, *The Human Factor*, p. 51
[472] Mikhail Gorbachev, *Memoirs* (New York: Doubleday, 1996), p. 160
[473] https://www.margaretthatcher.org/document/105592
[474] Brown, *The Human Factor*, p. 3
[475] Geoffrey Howe, *Conflict of Loyalty* (London: Macmillan, 1994), p. 430
[476] https://www.margaretthatcher.org/document/109185
[477] Dobbs, *Down with Big Brother*, p. 121
[478] Gorbachev, *Memoirs*, p. 26
[479] Brown, *The Human Factor*, p. 42
[480] Paul Lettow, *Ronald Reagan and His Quest to Abolish Nuclear Weapons* (New York: Random House, 2005), p. 35
[481] https://bostonreview.net/forum_response/vladislav-m-zubok-gorbachevs-nuclear-learning/
[482] Margaret Thatcher, *Statecraft* (New York: HarperCollins, 2002), p. 54
[483] https://www.margaretthatcher.org/document/109185
[484] Reagan, *An American Life*, p. 631
[485] https://www.margaretthatcher.org/document/143042
[486] Lou Cannon, *President Reagan* (New York: Simon & Schuster, 1991), p. 61
[487] ibid
[488] Cannon, *President Reagan*, p. 63
[489] Shultz, *Turmoil and Triumph*, p. 602
[490] Shultz, *Turmoil and Triumph*, p. 700
[491] Charles Moore, *Margaret Thatcher: The Authorized Biography, Vol. 2* (New York: Knopf, 2016), p. 588
[492] Thatcher, *Statecraft*, p. 50
[493] Moore, *Margaret Thatcher: The Authorized Biography, Vol. 2*, p. 588
[494] Dobbs, *Down with Big Brother*, p. 160
[495] Gorbachev, *Memoirs*, p. 191
[496] Brown, *The Human Factor*, p. 173
[497] Ken Adelman, *Reagan at Reykjavik* (New York: HarperCollins, 2014), p. 50
[498] Brown, *The Human Factor*, p. 170
[499] Adelman, *Reagan at Reykjavik*, p. 315
[500] Adelman, *Reagan at Reykjavik*, p. 105
[501] Reagan, *An American Life*, p. 676
[502] Robert M. Gates, *Duty* (New York: Knopf, 2014), p. 159
[503] Adelman, *Reagan at Reykjavik*, p. 160
[504] Adelman, *Reagan at Reykjavik*, p. 89

[505] Adelman, *Reagan at Reykjavik*, p. 153
[506] Reagan, *An American Life*, p. 676
[507] https://www.chicagotribune.com/news/ct-xpm-1986-10-15-8603170599-story.html
[508] Thatcher, *The Downing Street Years*, p. 471
[509] Moore, *Margaret Thatcher: The Authorized Biography, Vol. 2*, p. 598
[510] Brown, *The Human Factor*, p. 182
[511] Gorbachev, *Memoirs*, p. 102
[512] Gorbachev, *Memoirs*, p. 204
[513] Dobbs, *Down with Big Brother*, p. 208
[514] Dobbs, *Down with Big Brother*, p. 89
[515] Gorbachev, *Memoirs*, p. 249
[516] Brown, *The Human Factor*, p. 192
[517] Brown, *The Human Factor*, p. 195
[518] https://www.lrb.co.uk/the-paper/v16/n20/christopher-hitchens/on-spanking
[519] https://www.theglobeandmail.com/community/inside-the-globe/thatcher-caligula-monroewait-did-i-hear-that-right-the-dangers-of-misquoting/article4101423/
[520] https://www.margaretthatcher.org/document/106604
[521] Brown, *The Human Factor*, p. 198
[522] https://www.archives.gov/publications/prologue/2007/summer/berlin.html
[523] Steven F. Hayward, *The Age of Reagan* (New York: Three Rivers, 2009), p. 2
[524] Brown, *The Human Factor*, p. 232
[525] Mikhail Gorbachev, *19th All-Union Conference of the CPSU Documents and Materials* (Moscow: Novosit, 1988), p. 34
[526] https://poland.pl/history/historical-figures/pope-changed-poland/
[527] https://www.youtube.com/watch?v=vQyfju4byCg
[528] Dobbs, *Down with Big Brother*, p. 44
[529] Thatcher, *The Downing Street Years*, p. 781
[530] Brown, *The Human Factor*, p. 241
[531] Victor Sebestyen, *Revolution 1989* (New York: Pantheon, 2009), p. 246
[532] Sebestyen, *Revolution 1989*, p. 259
[533] Sebestyen, *Revolution 1989*, p. 262
[534] Dobbs, *Down with Big Brother*, p. 231
[535] Sebestyen, *Revolution 1989*, p. 270
[536] Museum of Communism (Prague) display
[537] Edward Behr, *Kiss the Hand You Cannot Bite* (New York: Villard, 1991), p. 57
[538] https://borgenproject.org/tag/romanian-decree-770/
[539] Behr, *Kiss the Hand You Cannot Bite*, p. 173
[540] https://paperpile.com/blog/elena-ceausescu-scientist-fraud/
[541] Behr, *Kiss the Hand You Cannot Bite*, p. 141
[542] https://www.theguardian.com/world/2021/dec/22/a-moral-issue-to-correct-the-long-tail-of-elena-ceausescus-fraudulent-scientific-work
[543] Behr, *Kiss the Hand You Cannot Bite*, p. 182
[544] Behr, *Kiss the Hand You Cannot Bite*, p. 162
[545] Dobbs, *Down with Big Brother*, p. 300
[546] Gorbachev, *Memoirs*, p. 473
[547] Behr, *Kiss the Hand You Cannot Bite*, p. 221
[548] Behr, *Kiss the Hand You Cannot Bite*, p. 203

[549] https://www.abc.net.au/radionational/programs/allinthemind/inside-the-iron-curtain's-orphanages/5543388
[550] https://theworld.org/stories/2015-12-28/half-million-kids-survived-romanias-slaughterhouses-souls-now-they-want-justice
[551] Sebestyen, *Revolution 1989*, p. 275
[552] Sebestyen, *Revolution 1989*, p. 161
[553] Gorbachev, *Memoirs*, p. 474
[554] Sebestyen, *Revolution 1989*, p. 274
[555] Sebestyen, *Revolution 1989*, p. 290
[556] Garton Ash, *We the People*, p. 29
[557] Sebestyen, *Revolution 1989*, p. 298
[558] Sebestyen, *Revolution 1989*, p. 311
[559] Garton Ash, *We the People*, p. 47
[560] Garton Ash, *We the People*, p. 51
[561] Sebestyen, *Revolution 1989*, p. 309
[562] Sebestyen, *Revolution 1989*, p. 312
[563] Sebestyen, *Revolution 1989*, p. 317
[564] Hannes Adomeit, *Imperial Overstretch* (Baden-Baden: Nomos, 2016), p. 475
[565] Sebestyen, *Revolution 1989*, p. 324
[566] ibid
[567] Sebestyen, *Revolution 1989*, p. 337
[568] https://de.wikipedia.org/wiki/Helmut_Hackenberg
[569] Sebestyen, *Revolution 1989*, p. 340
[570] Taylor, *The Berlin Wall*, p. 415
[571] Sebestyen, *Revolution 1989*, p. 345
[572] Sebestyen, *Revolution 1989*, p. 346
[573] https://digitalarchive.wilsoncenter.org/document/113049.pdf
[574] Dobbs, *Down with Big Brother*, p. 283
[575] Sebestyen, *Revolution 1989*, p. 354
[576] Sebestyen, *Revolution 1989*, p. 356
[577] Sebestyen, *Revolution 1989*, p. 360
[578] Sebestyen, *Revolution 1989*, p. 358
[579] Sebestyen, *Revolution 1989*, p. 368
[580] Garton Ash, *We the People*, p. 80
[581] Sebestyen, *Revolution 1989*, p. 369
[582] Sebestyen, *Revolution 1989*, p. 375
[583] Sebestyen, *Revolution 1989*, p. 376
[584] Garton Ash, *We the People*, p. 92
[585] Garton Ash, *We the People*, p. 78
[586] Garton Ash, *We the People*, p. 106
[587] Taylor, *The Berlin Wall*, p. 432
[588] Funder, *Stasiland*, p. 6
[589] Behr, *Kiss the Hand You Cannot Bite*, p. 270
[590] Sebestyen, *Revolution 1989*, p. 382
[591] Sebestyen, *Revolution 1989*, p. 383
[592] Sebestyen, *Revolution 1989*, p. 385
[593] Sebestyen, *Revolution 1989*, p. 387
[594] Sebestyen, *Revolution 1989*, p. 389

[595] Behr, *Kiss the Hand You Cannot Bite*, p. 12
[596] Behr, *Kiss the Hand You Cannot Bite*, p. 16
[597] Behr, *Kiss the Hand You Cannot Bite*, p. 57
[598] Behr, *Kiss the Hand You Cannot Bite*, p. 22
[599] Sebestyen, *Revolution 1989*, p. 3
[600] Behr, *Kiss the Hand You Cannot Bite*, p. 24
[601] Behr, *Kiss the Hand You Cannot Bite*, p. 26
[602] Sebestyen, *Revolution 1989*, p. 5
[603] Gorbachev, *Memoirs*, p. 4
[604] Gorbachev, *Memoirs*, p. 244
[605] Gorbachev, *Memoirs*, p. 247
[606] Moscow, December 25, 1991, p. 53
[607] Taylor Branch, *The Clinton Tapes* (New York: Simon & Schuster, 2009), p. 198
[608] Conor O'Clery, *Moscow, December 25, 1991* (New York: PublicAffairs, 2011), p. 53
[609] Dobbs, *Down with Big Brother*, p. 318
[610] Dobbs, *Down with Big Brother*, p. 372
[611] Dobbs, *Down with Big Brother*, p. 379
[612] Dobbs, *Down with Big Brother*, p. 386
[613] Dobbs, *Down with Big Brother*, p. 387
[614] Dobbs, *Down with Big Brother*, p. 388
[615] Dobbs, *Down with Big Brother*, p. 389
[616] Dobbs, *Down with Big Brother*, p. 377
[617] https://www.tampabay.com/archive/1991/08/26/gorbachev-made-secret-video-during-period-of-house-arrest/
[618] Dobbs, *Down with Big Brother*, p. 396
[619] Dobbs, *Down with Big Brother*, p. 402
[620] ibid
[621] Dobbs, *Down with Big Brother*, p. 403
[622] Dobbs, *Down with Big Brother*, p. 408
[623] J. Michael Waller, *Secret Empire* (Boulder: Westview, 1994), p. 59
[624] Dobbs, *Down with Big Brother*, p. 421
[625] Dobbs, *Down with Big Brother*, p. 416
[626] Brown, *The Human Factor*, p. 288

Made in the USA
Columbia, SC
31 January 2025

a7e09914-ed41-4764-8c4c-0c93c09266c1R01